..............on AB
T5N 3H6

May 06

'THE HOLY FOX'

Andrew Roberts took a First in Modern History at
Gonville and Caius College, Cambridge. This is his first
book. He also writes reviews for the *Sunday Telegraph* and
the *Literary Review*. He lives in London.

'THE HOLY FOX'

A LIFE OF
LORD HALIFAX

ANDREW ROBERTS

M

PAPERMAC

To
SIMON AND KATIE ROBERTS

Copyright © Andrew Roberts 1991

All rights reserved. No reproduction, copy or transmission
of this publication may be made without written permission.
No paragraph of this publication may be reproduced, copied
or transmitted save with written permission or in accordance
with the provisions of the copyright Act 1956 (as amended).
Any person who does any unauthorised act in relation to this
publication may be liable to criminal prosecution and civil
claims for damages.

The right of Andrew Roberts to be identified as author of
this work has been asserted by him in accordance with the
Copyright, Designs and Patents Act 1988.

First published in Great Britain 1991
by George Weidenfeld and Nicolson Ltd
This edition published in paperback 1992 by
PAPERMAC
a division of Pan Macmillan Publishers Limited
Cavaye Place London SW10 9PG
and Basingstoke

Associated companies in Auckland, Budapest, Dublin,
Gaborone, Harare, Hong Kong, Kampala, Kuala Lumpur,
Lagos, Madras, Manzini, Melbourne, Mexico City, Nairobi,
New York, Singapore, Sydney, Tokyo and Windhoek

ISBN 0-333-57529-6

A CIP catalogue record for this book is available from the
British Library

Printed in Hong Kong

Contents

CONTENTS

Illustrations

Chamberlain leaves for Berchtesgaden, seen off by Sir Alexander Cadogan, Sir Horace Wilson, Lord Halifax and R. A. Butler

Oliver Harvey and Anthony Eden walking in St James's Park (*The Hulton-Deutsch Collection*)

Benito Mussolini, Count Ciano and Neville Chamberlain in Rome, January 1939 (*by courtesy of Lord Holderness*)

Taking the salute in Rome (*by courtesy of Lord Holderness*)

The Cabinet, September 1939

Relaxing with their grandchildren at Garrowby on leave from Washington, 1942 (*by courtesy of Lady Alexandra Metcalfe*)

'Exchange of notes with Winston C...', Cabinet, 6 May 1940

Chancellor of Oxford University, with his son Peter as train-bearer

Franklin Delano Roosevelt

The problem: hunting with the Plunket Stewarts in Philadelphia, March 1941

The solution: 'De-icing Edward', a photo opportunity out west

With the Hon. Angus McDonnell

Halifax and Churchill on the steps of the British Embassy in Washington, August 1941

Unless otherwise stated, the photographs are from the Earl of Halifax's private collection and are reproduced with his kind permission.

Acknowledgements

I should like to acknowledge with thanks the gracious permission of Her Majesty The Queen to research in and quote from the Royal Archives at Windsor. I should also like to thank Her Majesty Queen Elizabeth The Queen Mother for her reminiscences of Lord Halifax.

It cannot be altogether without some misgivings that the family of the subject of a biography view the prospect of an outsider commenting on their loved one. All the more so when, as in this case, the book is clearly not going to be as uncritical as the earlier ones have been. Nevertheless, although they have been most helpful with papers, reminiscences, photographs and comment, Lord Halifax's family have never once attempted to influence me in what I have written. It has been a great relief not having to worry whether, like Ramsay MacDonald, I would 'succumb to the aristocratic embrace'. For that and other kindnesses I should like to thank the Earl and Countess of Halifax, Anne, Countess of Feversham and the late Ruth, dowager Countess of Halifax.

In my subject's son and daughter-in-law, Lord and Lady Holderness, I have found unfailing help, understanding and generosity, for which I will always be deeply grateful. Lord Holderness's comments on my proofs were forthright, painstaking and often hilarious, and my association with him has been one of the great pleasures of writing this book. He has also very kindly allowed me to quote from his unpublished memoir of his mother.

I should also like in particular to thank Lady Alexandra Metcalfe, who as a close friend of the Halifaxes since the 1920s, has kindly put up with incessant visits from me and has allowed me to quote from her wartime letters and diaries and to reproduce photographs from her albums. Lady Juliet Townsend kindly lent me the extensive interview notes taken by her father, the Earl of Birkenhead, for his official biography of Lord Halifax, which was published in 1965. These were meticulously taken and have proved invaluable. For their kind permission to quote from private and unpublished papers I should also like to thank: Rt Hon. Julian Amery, Viscount Astor, Mr David Benson, Sir Edward Cazalet, Mr Somerset de Chair, Mr Clarence Hellewell, Sir Ian Jacob, Mr Valentine Lawford, Hon.

Hector McDonnell, Major-General Viscount Monckton, Mr Victor Montagu, Lady Peake, Mr Kenneth Rose, Mrs Patricia Smyly, Mr Max Taylor, Mr Charles Wenden and Hon. Mrs Reginald Winn.

At the outset of writing this book I decided to try to meet as many of Lord Halifax's friends and colleagues as possible, as well as other historians and commentators on this period. I was not prepared for the extraordinary hospitality and helpfulness with which I was greeted. For their great kindness I would like to thank: Hon. David Astor, Mrs Joan Astley, Lady Balfour, Lord Beloff, Sir Isaiah Berlin, Mr Michael Bloch, Hon. Mrs Dinah Bridge, Mr Ivor Bulmer-Thomas, the late Lord Caccia, Professor Donald Cameron Watt, Mr Alan Campbell Johnson, Mr Robert Cecil, Dr John Charmley, Lord and Lady Charteris, Mr Nirad Chaudhuri, Hon. Mrs Julian Chetwynd, Lord Colyton, Lord Cudlipp, Mr Nicholas Cull, Mr Piers Dixon, the late Mr Dudley Danby, Sir William Deakin, Mr Kenneth de Courcy, Professor David Dilks, Lady Elliot of Harwood, Mr Douglas Fairbanks Jr, Rt Hon. Michael Foot, Sir Berkeley Gage, Mr Martin Gilbert, Sir Martin Gilliat, Lord Gladwyn, Major John Gordon Duff, Mr Jeffrey Hamm, Sir William and Lady Hayter, Lord Home of the Hirsel, the late Lord Inchyra, the late Major Thomas Ingram, Mr David Irving, Sir Ian Jacob, Lord Jay, Mr Frank Johnson, Lord Keyes, the late Colonel Francis Lane Fox, Dr Sheila Lawlor, Mr Adrian Liddell Hart, Mr Kenneth Lindsay, the Earl of Listowel, the Earl of Longford, Mr Thomas Martin, Mr Philip Mason, Mrs K. M. Maxwell, Mr Leonard Miall, Sir George Middleton, Sir Guy Millard, Mr Victor Montagu, Sir Godfrey Nicholson, the Earl of Onslow, Pamela, Countess of Onslow, His Grace the late Duke of Portland, Count Edward Raczynski, Dr David Reynolds, Mr Robert Rhodes James MP, Sir Denis Rickett, Sir Frank Roberts, the late Mr Jasper Rootham, Baron Robert Rothschild, Sir Algernon Rumbold, Lord Sherfield, Mrs Sheila Sokolov Grant, Herr Reinhard Spitzy, the late Mr Albert Sylvester, the late Sir Charles Taylor and Lord Tranmire.

For their letters containing reminiscences about Lord Halifax I should like to thank the following correspondents: the late Sir George Abell, Sir Richard Acland, Lord Abinger, Lord Aldington, Colonel Gordon Alexander, Mr Alistair Cooke, Sir John Cotton, Sir Geoffrey Cox, Senator Hamilton Fish, Sir Richard Fry, Senator J. William Fulbright, Lady Hambleden, Mr Alger Hiss, the late Lady Leonora Howard, Herr Dr Otto John, Professor R. V. Jones, the late Sir Ivo Mallet, Sir John Peck, Viscount Margesson, the late Mr H. Montgomery Hyde, Hon. Lady Mosley, Lord Muirshiel, Sir Edward Playfair, Sir Patrick Reilly, Mr A. L. Rowse, M. Maurice Schumann, Sir Peter Tennant, Mrs Laurence Thompson, the late Mr Guy Vansittart, Mr S. J. Willis and the late Group Captain Frederick Winterbotham.

ACKNOWLEDGEMENTS

Lord Halifax's papers are housed at the Borthwick Institute, the archives of the University of York. I should like to thank the staff there for their unfailing friendliness and efficiency. So also should I like to thank Mrs Bennett at the Churchill Archives in Churchill College, Cambridge; the Institute of Historical Research, University of London; the Public Record Office at Kew; Mr Michael Bott at the Archives of the University of Reading; the British Library; the National Sound Archives; the Cambridge University Library; the Archives of Trinity College, Cambridge; the House of Lords Record Office; Dr Benedict Benedikz at the University of Birmingham; the Bodleian Library, Oxford; the National Film Archives; the Colindale Newspaper Library; Lady de Bellaigue at the Royal Archives at Windsor; the India Office Library and Records; the National Library of Scotland; the Scottish Record Office; the Bank of England Record Office; and the Liddell Hart Centre for Military Studies, King's College, London. The publication of this book has been assisted by a grant from the Twenty-Seven Foundation.

For reading my manuscript and for their many invaluable suggestions and corrections I am enormously indebted to Mr Michael Bloch, Dr John Charmley, Mr Martin Gilbert, Mr Dean Godson, Lord Holderness, Mr Kenneth Rose, Miss Lindsay White and Mr Peter Wyllie. Mrs Ruth Godson kindly translated various documents for me. I should also like to thank Messrs Nigel Morgan and Andrew West for their splendid hospitality during the writing of this book. I am deeply indebted to Linda Osband for her advice and superb editing skills. I must also thank my literary agent and publisher, Mr Andrew Lownie and Mr David Roberts, for giving me the opportunity of spending these last three years doing something I have so thoroughly enjoyed.

Finally I must thank my parents, to whom this book is dedicated, without whose generosity and support it would not have been written, and without whose love and devotion it would not have been worth writing.

ANDREW ROBERTS
London

Introduction

Judgement

Only a matter of hours before Hitler unleashed his *Blitzkrieg* on the West, four men met in the Cabinet Room at No. 10, Downing Street, to decide who should be Britain's war leader. Virulent and mounting personal opposition in the House of Commons had forced Neville Chamberlain to realize that he could not continue as Prime Minister. He and David Margesson, the Government Chief Whip, therefore convened a meeting for 4.30 p.m. on Thursday, 9 May 1940, to decide upon a successor.

The two contenders, Edward, Lord Halifax and Winston Churchill, could not have been more different. Halifax, the Foreign Secretary, was a calm, rational man of immense personal prestige and *gravitas*, his career an uninterrupted tale of achievement and promotion. He had also for some time seemed to be Chamberlain's heir apparent. Across the Cabinet table sat Churchill, the romantic and excitable adventurer, whose life was a *Boys' Own* story of cavalry charges, prison escapes and the thirst for action.

Often portrayed as a set-piece contest between curriculum vitae and genius, this was actually nothing of the sort. For all his oratorical abilities, Churchill was universally regarded as lacking that essential quality for a Prime Minister: Judgement. Baldwin had put it best when he said:

> When Winston was born lots of fairies swooped down on his cradle with gifts – imagination, eloquence, industry, ability – and then came a fairy who said, 'No one person has a right to so many gifts,' and picked him up and gave him such a shake and a twist that with all these gifts he was denied judgement and wisdom. And that is why while we delight to listen to him in the House we do not take his advice.[1]

The ill-fated action Churchill had taken over Gallipoli, the Sidney Street siege, the Russian Civil War, the Gold Standard, Indian policy, the Abdication, Palestine and a host of other issues had led to deep distrust of his political acumen. The Tories could not forgive his decade-long attack on the government from their own back-benches nor forget that he had twice crossed the floor of the House. Labour regarded his zeal at Tonypandy, at the General Strike and over India as the mark of the blackest reactionary.

Finally, it had been Churchill who, as First Lord of the Admiralty, had been most closely responsible for the greatest débâcle of the war so far, the very setback which had precipitated the present crisis: the defeat of the expeditionary force to Norway.

Halifax, however, was regarded by many as a perfect foil for Churchill's impetuosity. His Viceroyalty of India had been seen as a triumph of patience and reform. His efforts to stiffen resistance after Munich made him the acceptable face of Chamberlainism. His ceaseless campaign to bring all parties into the Government was appreciated by the Opposition leaders, with whom he kept on good personal terms. His calm resolution, Olympian manner and, above all, his respectability and reputation for sound judgement led many to think of him as the ideal national leader, who could oversee Churchill's day-to-day running of the war.

Both Chamberlain and King George VI wanted Halifax. The Government wanted Halifax. The great majority of Conservative MPs wanted Halifax. *The Times*, the City, the House of Lords and Whitehall all wanted Halifax. Opposition leaders had indicated that they would prefer him and even Churchill himself told friends that he too would serve under him.

Neither would Halifax's peerage block his accession, although naturally he did use that afterwards as the reason to explain his decision. The King wanted to put his peerage 'into abeyance' and Chamberlain, a few months earlier, had taken secret soundings which ascertained that under certain circumstances a peer could sit and speak in the Commons. Anyhow in this crisis it is inconceivable that a Britain willing that month to suspend habeas corpus would have allowed such esoteric constitutional niceties to dictate her choice of leader.

It is also untrue to say that Halifax never wanted the job. His nonchalant air of ambivalence towards high office was a stock feature of the make-up of any grand Tory politician of that period. In different circumstances he would, especially if it had been presented to him by friends as being his patriotic duty, undoubtedly have accepted the Premiership. The supreme prize of British politics was there for the taking and he had merely to nod for it to be his. But he knew in his heart that he was not of the calibre required for a wartime premier, and that Winston Churchill was.

Proposing Churchill in his stead was a supreme act of self-abnegation, one for which history has afforded him scant credit. It was perhaps Halifax's greatest service to his country. There were many more. Not least of these was his success in shadowing and restraining Churchill during 1940, when he fulfilled the unspoken role allotted to him after Chamberlain's fall of preventing Churchill's commendable exuberance from landing Britain in any more Gallipolis.

Churchill used to say that only History could relate the full story, and that he would be writing it.[2] Certainly History, written for the most part if not by Churchill then by Churchillians, has awarded Halifax abuse rather than plaudits.

His piety has been castigated as hypocrisy, his loyalty as unctuousness, his reserve as aloofness and his best efforts to save peace as having brought eternal shame on his country. He has been indicted on charges of which he was innocent, yet not brought to trial for some acts of which he was guilty. He has been accused of gullibility, slavishness, lack of patriotism, ignorance, naïveté and even pro-fascism and incipient treachery.

He was, in fact, a shrewd, patriotic and tough politician, ever alive to the swings of public opinion and expert at the art of getting his way. He was certainly not above deft use of the political knife when occasion demanded. His part first in championing and then in dismantling the policy of appeasement is a case study in statesmanship. It is the tale of how a decent man can come to the realization that the policy associated with his name is wrong and yet, without a rift with his colleagues or a word in the press, can by political will and guile succeed in turning it back to front.

So much attention has focused on the 'anti-appeasers' who were in the wilderness during this period that little tribute has been paid to those politicians who stayed in Government and, in the face of stiff opposition from Chamberlain, succeeded in reversing appeasement during the year between Munich and the outbreak of war. Yet it was they who had by far the greater influence on public policy. The foremost of them was Lord Halifax.

The Churchill family's nickname for him played on his fondness for High Church services and fox-hunting, while making a rather weak pun on his title. But it became popular in Westminster and Whitehall because it also pointed to something deeper: that for all his pious and patrician reputation, Halifax was as wily and quick-witted as any of his opponents. These were no bad faculties to possess in facing the dictators of the 1930s and, although intended pejoratively, Halifax should have rejoiced in his nickname. This is the story of 'The Holy Fox'.

Birth, Boyhood, Bereavement

Edward Wood was born on 16 April 1881 in Devon, a fact which many years later he inadvertently vouchsafed to King George VI on a train journey there. He soon regretted it when the King, displaying all his heavy Hanoverian drollness, pointed to every shack and cow-shed along the way, asking, 'Is that where you were born, Edward?', until the butt of his constantly reiterated joke found it hard to continue his courtly laughter.

The Woods of Hickleton were a fortunate family. For centuries they had been respectable York merchants, providing justices of the peace, aldermen and the occasional distinguished soldier or sailor. They were worthy but not of national eminence. Just before the start of the Industrial Revolution, they were wealthy enough to buy an estate near Doncaster and to settle as moderately landed squires. Some short time later, they discovered themselves to be sitting on several hundred acres of Britain's deepest and finest coal seam, the great Barnsley field. It was seventy yards deep in places and all of the highest quality. This left them wealthy enough to do whatever they pleased.

Charles Wood, born in 1800, went into politics. He married the daughter of Earl Grey, the Whig Prime Minister, and rose to become Chancellor of the Exchequer and Secretary of State for India. His Whiggery was a tough creed, combining a belief in minimal reform at home and pugnacious optimism abroad. He was awarded a viscountcy in 1866 and was one of those ministers considered close enough to Queen Victoria to be awarded the task of attempting to bring her out of her seclusion years after the death of Prince Albert.

The first Viscount Halifax displayed a number of characteristics that were to reappear in his grandson. He was never a party-minded politician. He contracted a sparkling marriage to the daughter of an earl, which, once his son and grandson had followed suit, gave

4

the family more social standing than their 218th in the precedence of peerage might otherwise imply. He devoted a large part of his life to reform in India, especially in the field of education, holding office there both before and after the Mutiny. Finally, his friendship with the Queen started a tradition of confidentiality and intimacy with the Royal Family that was to prove invaluable to his grandson seventy years later.

In Charles, the second Viscount Halifax, there existed a curious paradox between unquestioning faith in God, which dominated every hour of his ninety-four years, and a fascination for other-worldly phenomena. He was also one of Victorian England's most splendid eccentrics. He saw himself as the last of the Cavaliers, sported a Vandyke beard and devoted his life to contesting the 'singularly deserted battlefields' of theology.[1] For half a century the senior lay figure on the 'High' side of the Anglican Church, he had been at Oxford during the second phase of the Oxford Movement. His love of ritual, extreme partisan High Anglicanism and all but Catholic beliefs set him at loggerheads with most of his Church for much of his life. He was never happier than when indulging in theological – and preferably also legal – controversy. His Presidency of the English Church Union from 1866 to 1920 saw him champion the High Anglican wing of the Church of England in ecclesiastical disputes virtually incomprehensible today even to aficionados of the genre. He threw himself into the most obscure (and expensive) legal battles over the Public Worship Regulation Act of 1874 to the point that he had to resign as Groom to the Prince of Wales's Bedchamber for advocating the breaking of the law.

He passed on to his son Edward acceptance of Transubstantiation and all the standard Catholic doctrines, barring Papal Infallibility and the Immaculate Conception. When in London, he and Edward worshipped at St Mary's, Bourne Street, the Church of England's 'highest' and most baroque church. If there was a criticism of Edward Wood's religion as imparted to him by his father it was, as his friend Fr Ted Talbot wrote in 1949, that 'In a sense his religion, admirable in its loyalty and diligence, has not one feels had to encounter the sharp north-east wind of deep questioning.'[2] Nevertheless, there was a strong sense of realism in the High Anglicanism of both father and son which was to come out in the latter's politics.

Realism was distinctly lacking in much of the rest of the second Viscount's life. His strange streak of mysticism and eccentricity led him to edit an excellent book of ghost stories, to be utterly feudal in his politics, to have priest-holes and secret passages built into his house, and to keep yaks, emus and kangaroos in the park at Hickleton. In September 1870, only a year married and father of a six-week-old baby, he went over to France to help fight disease amongst prisoners captured in the Franco-Prussian War. In response to his letters about pulling Zouave corpses out of water butts, his mother felt that he 'had no right to leave Agnes for the shells, smallpox and cholera of another country's war'.[3] Lady Agnes, Edward's mother, was a kind, loving and long-suffering soul, who gave him the stability it was not in his father's power to bestow. The second Viscount did, however, impart to him a deep affection for the East Riding of Yorkshire, which was to dominate his son's view of the world throughout his life.

Edward was born without a left hand. He does not seem to have been adversely affected by this at all, though it may have added to a tendency to be slightly sensitive. He was certainly highly successful at putting it into the background. He had a false hand in the form of a clenched fist with a thumb on a spring, which he became so adept at manipulating that when out hunting he had no trouble in opening a gate while holding his reins and horn. Many years later, when crossing the Atlantic in a battleship, his Private Secretary, Charles Peake, 'could not but admire the beautiful judgement and economy of movement with which he went up a vertical ladder using only his right hand without haste or hesitation'.[4] He was also born with a slight lisp, which, far from conveying the sense of weakness it sometimes can, made his sonorous voice more interesting to listen to.

Far more than any of this, Edward's character was moulded by a series of tragedies which befell his family between his fifth and tenth birthdays. His three elder brothers died, each within two years of one another and each of classic Victorian child-killing diseases. Henry died of lung congestion in 1886 aged seven, Francis of the same in 1888 aged fifteen, and Charles of pleurisy after a long illness in 1890 at the age of twenty. Those last two years, 1888 to 1890, saw the deaths of a bewildering succession of family and friends, leaving the second Viscount with only Edward on whom to concentrate his boundless ambitions and devotion. From being the sixth of six, and very much physically the runt of the litter, the nine year old was catapulted into being the sole focus of his father's almost fanatical love.

The second Viscount never spoke down to his sons and always wrote to them as equals, but the pressure he exerted on Edward would horrify a modern child psychologist. At the age of eleven the boy received weekly letters at prep-school telling him 'You are to get a first class at History at Oxford and do all sorts of grand things.' An only mildly critical Maths report would bring the admonition, 'I want for my darling to do everything perfectly' because, as he never tired of pointing out, 'I long for you to do your best ... that you may turn out the pride and happiness of our life – we have all had so much sorrow in the past that now everything seems to centre on you.' If Edward became old before his time, and became rather serious, sensitive but ambitious, it was due to emotionally blackmailing letters such as that received on his twelfth birthday: 'You do not know how precious you are in my eyes my own dearest child – my only little son left now that God has taken my other three to himself – all my hopes and joy are bound up in you ... what should I do without you?'[5]

Edward Wood had a blameless Eton, where he concentrated on those sports which his disability allowed him, such as tennis, fives and bicycling. He also kept up a lively theological correspondence with his father. But it was at Christ Church, Oxford, that he blossomed and where he could indulge his appetite for country sports and High Church services. He joined the dining clubs Loder's and the Bullingdon, got into slight debt, went beagling and generally did all the other things expected of wealthy and well-born undergraduates. Already, though, there were signs of wisdom beyond his years; an Oxford contemporary, Lord William Percy, remembered how, 'On Mafeking night, each member of Loder's drank a bottle of port to celebrate. Everyone got completely drunk, but Halifax immediately went out and tickled his throat to make himself sick, thus avoiding the worst effects. This was typical.'[6] Through impressive management of his time combined with a capacity for hard work which never left him, Wood took a first in History and then won a Fellowship to All Souls. These merely whetted his father's ambitions: 'I am quite determined that you are to be Prime Minister and reunite England to the Holy See.'[7]

On going down from Oxford, Wood found himself wealthy. Dispersed for a generation amongst uncles and aunts, the family wealth tended to percolate back down to him. In 1904, an aunt left him both No. 88, Eaton Square, and Temple Newsam, the Jacobean palace outside Leeds known with good reason as 'the Hampton Court of the North'. The year before, his father had also offered him Garrowby, the largest of the family estates. Wood decided to go on a Grand Tour of the Empire, secure in the knowledge that he had a fortune to return to in England.

He stayed with Lord Curzon at Calcutta, visited Benares, Agra, Ceylon and New Zealand, saw the Act of Federation in effect in Australia and met members of Milner's 'Kindergarten' in South Africa. Finally, in 1907, he visited Canada, scene of the reforms of his Whig great-uncle, Lord Durham. On his return he took the most sensible course open to a man of conservative political instincts at that time and stayed well out of politics. The Liberals had won a landslide victory in 1906 and so Wood instead took up his Fellowship at All Souls. This putting off of the start of his parliamentary career showed a talent for felicitous political timing that was not to leave him. It was in the civilized and intellectually gifted atmosphere of All Souls that he wrote a life of his father's hero, John Keble. Because of his desire to be objective, this turned out to be a well-researched and closely argued but excruciatingly dull book.

The political climate had sufficiently improved by the time *John Keble* was published in 1909 for Wood to decide to follow his grandfather into politics. The Whig Party was long since dead, its traditions ignored by the Liberal Party which had ingested it. Wood therefore, more for lack of an alternative than for any positive reason, decided to stand for the Conservatives. His ideological commitment to Conservatism was never strong, although he did inherit from his father a slightly whimsical belief in oligarchy.

Only two more ingredients were necessary for the career of a bright and successful young Tory politician: Wood required a wife and a safe seat, both of which came within four months of one another. In the eighty or so interviews I have conducted with her husband's colleagues, friends, relations and servants, one constant rejoinder has been made: all agree that Lady Dorothy Onslow was in charm, friendliness, sympathy and kindness a paragon amongst women. She was the perfect wife and they proceeded to live that most infuriating thing for a modern biographer – model lives together. Her tremendous personality and wisdom proved invaluable to him. Although a constant source of strength, she never had, nor sought, any influence over policy. None of his great offices – the Viceroyalty of India, Foreign Secretaryship or the Ambassadorship to Washington – could have been accepted unless Lady Dorothy had been up to them. Capable men were regularly turned down for such posts because of an unsuitable wife. Lady Dorothy fulfilled a vital role in complementing her husband's image of a sound family man who could always be trusted to do the decent thing.

Neither was she merely the political wife who stares adoringly up at her husband during interminable speeches and belaboured jokes. Her giant Garrowby housekeeping account books, kept between 1911 and 1939 and listing to the last farthing how much was paid to the poulterer, confectioner, fishmonger and so on, show her to be more than just a hostess. Her engagement diaries, detailing exactly which white lie she had told to whom to excuse herself from which social occasion, stand testament to her common sense. On other matters she could be remarkably candid: she openly admitted that her mother was born illegitimate, despite *Burke's Peerage* generously attesting to the contrary. She had lived in New Zealand for a time when her father was Governor-General and had all the independent spirit of his family. Her sister-in-law used to get her way by feigning paralysis or throwing inkpots and once walked into a crowded diplomatic party stark naked. Her nephew kept a parrot in his bedroom and never went on a train without his pet snake.[8] The family had provided three Speakers of the House of Commons and Dorothy inherited from her father a deep sense of noblesse oblige.

She had to show her mettle very soon after her wedding on 21 September 1909. The honeymoon was cut short so that her husband could take part in the general election campaign. As the heir of a local grandee, Wood had found no trouble in those more deferential times being selected as the Conservative candidate for the nearby seat of Ripon. Lady Dorothy's friend, Blanche Lascelles (who later married George Lloyd), recorded in her diary how, when out canvassing in the biting cold of January 1910, they took it in turns to buy blue silk for the rosettes and chilblain-cream for their feet.[9] Wood was elected with a 1,244 majority in a poll of 11,000, which, although it was reduced eleven months later to 874, was considered strong enough to dissuade anyone from standing against him again. A political career spanning half a century was thus based on only two contested elections.

This immensely tall, rather sad-eyed twenty-nine-year-old on the verge of his political career had had an early life rich with influences. The loss of his brothers, combined with a profound sense of Original Sin, had produced a tolerant, practical, slightly diffident man. Although intensely private, he cannot be described as shy. Truly shy people do not go into politics and Wood did not find speaking to large crowds more than normally harrowing. Anyhow, there was too much Yorkshire and his father in him for shyness. It is doubtful, however, whether he had much of a sense of humour. One biographer has detected 'a lugubrious sense of irony'.[10] His set-piece jokes were laborious and, although he enjoyed teasing and gossiping amongst close friends, he appears to have been responsible for virtually no bons mots or witty remarks. He tended to speak in an Establishment tongue which colleagues had no difficulty in understanding, despite his circumlocution. He once started a sentence, 'I should have thought that one might say that it could be reasonably held that ...'. For foreigners it was different. The Soviet Foreign Minister, Andrei Gromyko, complained that 'he would express his thoughts in so ornate a way that few could understand him'.[11]

There is also the fact of his legendary stinginess. He had somehow contracted 'a deep-seated abhorrence of everyday expenditure', which stayed with him for the rest of his life.[12] This was more than merely a case of being 'Yorkshire tight' and cannot exclusively be explained by his father's prodigious expenditure on ecclesiastical campaigns and the building of secret passages at Garrowby. R. A. Butler recorded how at the Foreign Office, 'one day a messenger brought in four biscuits and two cups of tea. Halifax pushed away two biscuits and said, "Mr Butler does not want these. Nor do I. Do not charge me." '[13] There are many such examples of this sort of parsimonious behaviour. But these must be set against the great generosity he showed in 1925 when he sold Temple Newsam to the City of Leeds for less than he could have realized on the open market, and again in 1948 when he gave 164 paintings to the museum the City had opened there.

Wood had a genuine modesty and found it hard to lose his temper. His life until then had been a conventional and faultless progression along a well-trodden aristocratic career path. Hon. Edward Wood MP was, in January 1910, a patient, dispassionate and reserved man who was keen to find reason and logic in the world. He was about to enter the worst possible place for someone of that temperament – the pre-First World War House of Commons.

2

'Blameless Rather Than Brilliant'

In the four years between the death of King Edward VII and the outbreak of the Great War, any observer would be forgiven for thinking that British society was on the verge of collapse. Violent industrial unrest disrupted economic life; Lloyd George's budgets read like class hatred erected into a system of government; civil war loomed in Ireland; far-reaching constitutional reform was forced through Parliament by one House blackmailing and intimidating the other; suffragette agitation split households; and all the time Germany was building a High Seas Fleet which threatened to challenge the naval supremacy on which the very security of the British Empire depended. Nowhere was the breakdown in social consensus more apparent than in the House of Commons, where intransigence and incitement so took over from reasoned debate that it engendered in Wood a lifelong distrust for the House of Commons as a contemplative body.

His own debut on the parliamentary scene could hardly have been less auspicious. After a six-week bout of appendicitis, his maiden speech was delivered to an almost empty House on a topic of which he knew nothing, after being given virtually no warning by the Whips. He was used solely as a stop-gap before the Party leader, A. J. Balfour, returned from dinner. The result was every young MP's nightmare. He spoke near-gibberish about white racial superiority in Egypt for a quarter of an hour. The only thing notable about the occasion was that his argument was cut to shreds by the notorious fraudster Trebitsch Lincoln. After this undistinguished start Wood sat back and, except for some desultory interventions on obscure topics such as Welsh Disestablishment, said nothing until called upon to cheer for the announcement of war with Germany. He dithered over the Parliament Bill whilst his father characteristically proclaimed himself a 'Last Ditcher'. Eschewing the uncongenial passions of Parliament, Wood concentrated instead on family life, a daughter, Anne, being born to him in July 1910 and a son, Charles, in October 1912.

The manoeuvres over Wood's candidacy for membership of Brooks's brought his name into brief prominence among clubland cognoscenti in early 1914, when a rump of elderly members planned to blackball him on the grounds of his being a Conservative and a member of the Carlton. Rumours of this sent the second Viscount into paroxysms of intrigue. Halifax asked Lord Henry Cavendish to withdraw from seconding his son and persuaded Lord Lansdowne to get Sir Edward Grey, whose Whig credentials were impeccable, to second him instead. If Grey's nominee were blackballed, the Foreign Secretary himself would have found himself obliged to resign from the Club. Halifax also let it be known that the blackballing of his son would lead to the reciprocal blackballing of Viscount Althorp, whose ancestor, Earl Spencer, had been one of the early members of the Club in 1764. At the tense election meeting in February 1914, 'it really was just like the Montagues and the Capulets,' wrote Halifax to his son, with his supporters having 'threatened war to the knife if you don't get in'.[1] Common sense prevailed, both sides came back from the brink and no blood was shed in St James's.

In Europe things were different. Writing to his wife on 3 August 1914, Wood described the scene in the Commons the night before:

> The House was packed from floor to roof. Chairs in the middle. I was surprised by the absence of any considerable body of opposition to the Government policy.... Grey made it plain I think how cynically the Germans had behaved.... Cheered in all quarters – many members visibly moved – myself among them.[2]

Wood had long been a Territorial and, despite his disability, took a commission in the Queens' Own Yorkshire Dragoons. He spent the first three years of the war in Flanders, fulfilling those unedifying tasks the cavalry were allotted after the establishment of trench warfare: capturing deserters, repairing roads, providing escorts and burying the dead.

His wife, meanwhile, turned Temple Newsam into a hospital for Belgian refugees, where she worked hard throughout the war. So popular was she with the Belgians that she was still exchanging Christmas cards with some of them sixty years later.

On his leaves, Wood made speeches calling for compulsory national service, a smaller War Cabinet and more vigorous prosecution of the war – even if it meant a Labour Government. On 2 May 1916, he attacked the Asquith Government for being 'hopelessly out of touch with the mass of the people of the country'.[3] His frustration in being of the war but not in it, recorded in his daily letters to his wife, was made all the worse by seeing swathes of school and university friends cut down. A second son, Peter, was born in October 1916. In September 1917, he took up the post of Deputy Director of Labour Supply in the Ministry of National Service. The only notable contribution he made to this job (which was as dull as its name) was a speech in December 1917 in which he declared: 'I dislike the genuine conscientious objector as much as anybody. . . . I am told that in the United States they do not waste time about passing special laws and legislation as to conscientious objectors, but that if they are quite sure they have the right people they compel them to wear scarlet uniforms and walk the streets.'[4] He went on to support their disenfranchisement for the duration.

If all this sounds like the talk of a rising hope of the stern and unbending Tories, his attitude towards Lord Lansdowne's November 1917 proposal for peace with Germany was very different. It is clear from his correspondence with his father that he was not as unreceptive to the proposals as has hitherto been supposed. Indeed, his immediate impression was that, 'Except for the phrasing, [I] don't quarrel with the substance, but think its moment of promulgation singularly ill-judged.' He also thought 'the House of Commons is too stupid an assembly' to discuss the idea rationally.[5]

This briefest of flirtations apart, Wood was numbered amongst those Tory hardliners who demanded a Carthaginian peace against Germany. At the end of the war he wrote to his father:

> I am dreadfully afraid of events turning out in a way to let the Germans off and it goes against the grain not to burn some of their towns, etc. . . . But the great thing – in spite of [Woodrow] Wilson – is to humiliate the German powers that be, beyond the possibility of [mis]understanding.

To that end he joined 202 other Conservative MPs in signing the Lowther Petition, a telegram sent to Lloyd George to pressurize him into concluding a harsher peace.

Despite oft-repeated fears that his constituents had forgotten him, the 1918 general election went well both for Wood and his Party. It produced a majority of 250 for the Coalition, of which the Conservatives were by far the largest component. The problem for the bright young men on the Coalition's back-benches, therefore, was how to get noticed. With no chance of parliamentary defeat, the authority of the Whips was consequently greatly diminished. So a group of about a dozen of the cleverer, wealthier, younger and more liberal Conservative MPs decided to adopt the age-old parliamentary tactic of joining together to rebel just enough to be noticed and promoted. Happy to distance themselves from the harsh, new-monied and more right-wing intake of Tory MPs, they embraced a number of progressive views such as subsidies for housing and agriculture, voting equality for women, support for the League of Nations and regional devolution. Wood went further and wrote a 100-page political manifesto in conjunction with Sir George Lloyd, which they entitled *The Great Opportunity*.

Despite being very much the junior partner in the enterprise, it is not difficult to spot which parts were Wood's. It is almost inconceivable to modern ears that the worthy banalities the pamphlet contained – on the force of religion, the importance of national unity, the traditions of public service, and so on – could have had the influence it did. It is packed with lightweight remarks about 'responsible trade unionism' and of turning 'unnecessary public houses' into centres for 'healthy social recreation'. But the book sold well and added to Wood's reputation for intellect. The doctrine of controlled and constructive criticism paid off handsomely. Of the dozen 'rebels' – Wood, Lord Wolmer, Samuel Hoare, Walter Guinness, William Ormsby-Gore, Philip Lloyd-Greame, Walter Elliot, J.C.C.Davidson, George Lane Fox, Lord Winterton and Sir John Hills – all but one were to achieve ministerial rank.

For Wood this came in April 1921, when he was appointed Under-Secretary at the Colonial Office. The Secretary of State there, Winston Churchill, had wanted someone else and put off even meeting Wood for a fortnight. Finally, Wood marched into Churchill's office and demanded to see him. 'Mr Churchill,' he told his astonished superior, 'I have no desire to be your Under-Secretary, nor to have any other office. I am prepared to resign and leave this office tomorrow, but, so long as I remain here, I expected to be treated like a gentleman.'[6] Churchill asked him to sit down, offered him a drink, and was all charm and smiles. This forthright policy was the one Wood adopted with Churchill throughout his life and it always served him well. Years later he advised Cabinet colleagues always to stand up to Churchill, who, he said, despised yes-men.

Despite being only seven years Wood's senior, Churchill was already a household name. He had seen action in India, Cuba, Egypt and South Africa and had held office as Home Secretary, First Lord of the Admiralty and Minister of Munitions. In the brief period Wood had to work under this dynamo, they developed the feelings they were to have towards one another for the rest of their lives. Wood found Churchill fascinating, unpredictable and tiring to work with. Churchill found Wood dependable but distant, unsympathetic and largely impervious to his charm.

During the winter of 1921–2, Wood toured the British West Indies to report on political and social conditions there. A close reading of his report, which was published in June 1922 and sold well, shows the considerable development his thinking had undergone since the white supremacy days of his maiden speech. Had they bothered to read it, 'The West Indies Report' would also have given a warning to those die-hard imperialists who welcomed his later appointment to the Viceroyalty of India. 'Movements towards elective representation must be met,' he wrote, as 'even in India diarchy is admitted to be mainly of value as a temporary device for training the elective element in the task of administrative responsibility, a device which is to be gradually superseded when experience is gained.' Elsewhere in the report he enunciated a central tenet of his political faith, that, 'We shall be wise if ... we ... avoid the mistake of endeavouring to uphold a concession ultimately inevitable until it has been robbed by delay of most of its usefulness and all of its grace.'[7]

Through the summer and autumn of 1922, Wood slowly came round to the opinion that the Coalition Government of which he was a very junior member was moving in a direction in which he had no desire to go. The Prime Minister, David Lloyd George, was precisely the sort of politician Wood most despised. He had been wary of 'the Welsh Wizard' ever since he had been rumoured to be coming to Ripon to canvass for the Liberal candidate in the 1910 election. He increasingly felt that this lecherous adventurer was guilty of debasing the standards of public life. The sale of honours infuriated him as much as the man's sexual antics disgusted him. (Once asked whether he would be taking his wife to the Paris Peace Conference, Lloyd George replied: 'Would you take sandwiches to a banquet?') The brinkmanship diplomacy conducted over the Foreign Secretary Lord Curzon's head worried Wood, especially when it looked like involving Britain in an unnecessary clash with Turkey. Different factors led others of Wood's colleagues of sub-Cabinet rank to see Lloyd George as an electoral liability rather than an asset. A memorandum written by Leo Amery, a junior minister at the Admiralty, entitled 'Thoughts on Some of the Present Discontents of the Conservative Party', listed no fewer than fourteen criticisms, from 'distrust of the Prime Minister' to the high price of beer.[8] Many Tory MPs were unimpressed by the way in which the Government almost casually gave away twenty-six Irish counties after a few late-night meetings at No. 10. Others looked askance at the unemployment figures and by-election losses. All were furious with the lack of security precautions which had allowed the Great War commander, Field Marshal Sir Henry Wilson, to be gunned down by the IRA on the steps of his London home.

Resentment might smoulder amongst junior ministers and on the backbenches, but to rebel against the Prime Minister was nevertheless a brave act. It was, after all, the war-winning Coalition, and it commanded the combined and undeniable genii of Lloyd George, Austen Chamberlain, Lord Birkenhead, Lord Curzon, Winston Churchill and Arthur Balfour. For a group of Under-Secretaries to attempt to bring down this galaxy of talent meant running the risk of at best decapitating the Conservative Party and at worst letting the socialists in. Failure could mean the end of political careers almost before they had begun. Nevertheless, by September 1922 Wood was willing to take the risk. Walking back to their homes in Eaton Square on 20 September he told Amery that 'he was definitely of the opinion that the Government had much better break up'.[9] This meant the Conservatives withdrawing from the Coalition and governing on their own without Lloyd George, Churchill and the other Coalition Liberals.

The conspiracy gathered momentum as Lloyd George's pugnacious foreign policy threw up a serious crisis over Turkey. It was feared that hot-heads in Lloyd George's Cabinet were planning British military intervention against Kemal Atatürk's sabre-rattling in the Near East. At a luncheon held on 16 October 1922, the Government's Under-Secretaries unanimously agreed to the Party going it alone should they be returned as the largest party after the next election. The following evening Wood was delegated with two other colleagues to put this case to Austen Chamberlain, the Conservative Party Leader and heir apparent to Lloyd George. Chamberlain, hoping to keep the Coalition together and badly underestimating the extent of the discontent, decided to bluff the junior ministers out.

Some of the junior ministers came up with a compromise. The Party could fight the election as a Coalition and only afterwards decide on its future. It was a superficially attractive arrangement, but Wood considered it impossible to go to the electorate split over the vital question of who was to be Prime Minister. Amery's diary for the next day records how, 'Presently Edward Wood picked me up and we walked as far as Victoria discussing our position and both concluded that if the compromise were accepted we were still personally bound to resign.' It was during these tense deliberations that Wood came to know and grew greatly to respect the President of the Board of Trade and chief anti-Coalition conspirator, Stanley Baldwin.[10]

In order to quell the revolt, Chamberlain called a meeting of all Conservative MPs at the Carlton Club for Thursday 19 October. The evening before, Baldwin secured the agreement of the former Party Leader, Andrew Bonar Law, to speak against the continuation of the Coalition. The voting slips on which each MP recorded 'Aye' or 'No' to the motion that the Party should contest the next election as an independent force show Major the Hon. Edward Wood's bold 'Aye' above a confident 'E.W.' The motion was carried by 185 to 88. This immediately caused a haemorrhaging of the Coalition as Lloyd George resigned, taking Chamberlain, Balfour, Churchill (who had appendicitis) and Birkenhead with him. For those joining Bonar Law's Government, such as Wood and Amery, it meant Cabinet rank years before their time.

The Coalitionists never forgave those who brought them down. Years later, walking in his orchard, Lloyd George pointed out a tree to a friend. 'Observe its rich foliage,' he remarked, 'see how magnificently it casts its shadow, but it bears no fruit. I call this tree Halifax.'[11] Ten years later, Churchill recalled how, 'In the twinkling of an eye I found myself without an office, without a seat, without a party, and without an appendix.'[12] Yet for all the Coalitionists' sneers at 'the Government of the Second Eleven', Baldwin and his colleagues were to stay at the crease for far longer than had the Coalition first team.

Knowledge of, or even interest in, one's subject was not considered a necessary prerequisite for a Cabinet post in the 1920s. Certainly Wood had evinced no interest in educational matters before being appointed President of the Board of Education two days after the blood-letting at the

Carlton Club. H.A.L. Fisher's Education Act of 1918 had settled education policy for a generation, so all Wood was left with was the unpleasant
task of implementing spending cuts. The entire department employed less
than a thousand people, and Wood found time to go hunting twice a week.

The Middleton had hunted some forty miles of the East Riding since
1764. Wood was joint Master for many years and, after 1938, continued in a
more or less honorary capacity until his death. When he found it difficult to
get up to Yorkshire, he would go out with the local hounds wherever he
happened to be staying. Hunting was a constant love, the metaphors of the
chase peppered his conversation and it afforded him a therapeutic and
wholly satisfying form of relaxation. It also added to his public image as a
solid figure in society. The work at Education bored him and he never let it
intrude upon the active social life that his wife mapped out for him. A
glance at their engagement diary of the period shows them spending most
weekends at the house parties of the nation's most distinguished families.

This closeness to the upper reaches of British aristocracy proved to be
invaluable to the man who had become his new close friend and political
mentor, Stanley Baldwin, when in November 1923 the Duke of Devonshire
and the Marquess of Salisbury decided to oppose the calling of a snap
election. Baldwin, who had succeeded Bonar Law as Prime Minister in the
May of that year, was committed to honouring his predecessor's promise
not to introduce Protection without first seeking the support of the
electorate. It soon became clear to Wood that Devonshire, Salisbury, Lord
Novar and Lord Robert Cecil, as well as others outside the Cabinet, were
contemplating resignation on the issue. Indeed, he himself had considered
resigning but dismissed it as too self-indulgent.

Wood was no economist and viewed the Free Trade/Protection debate in
purely practical terms, rather than the semi-mystical and moralistic way
some others did. It was his good offices that put Salisbury and Baldwin
together after an Empire dinner on 14 November, where they hammered
out an agreement on the back of the menu card. The rebels won various
assurances, but had to back down on the central issue. Baldwin had his
election that December and lost it. As one of the three men engaged to sit on
the post-mortem committee, Wood dutifully found that Labour's 'Dear
Food' slogan and the Conservative's slack constituency work, rather than
Baldwin's volte-face over tariffs, were to blame for the defeat.

Wood used his eleven-month spell in Opposition to change emphasis
from education to agricultural issues, putting down a marker for the
Agriculture portfolio when the Conservatives next returned to power. He
followed his father out to Malines in Belgium to take part in the Conversations that Halifax was conducting with the Belgian Cardinal Mercier there.
The intended outcome of these Conversations was nothing less than the
eventual union of the Anglican church with the Roman. Unlike his father,
Wood was far too much of a realist ever to invest much emotional capital in

this, the ultimate will-o'-the-wisp. The Conversations none the less provided Wood with an intellectually stimulating holiday as he prepared for his next period in government.

There was nothing auspicious about Wood's time at Agriculture. He was subject to the same financial restraints as he had experienced at Education. In the short spell he spent in the Ministry, he did display some of the hallmarks of his later career. He tried unsuccessfully to set up a conference of all interested parties in agriculture, seeing his job as primarily one of 'striking balances'. He was opposed by Churchill, this time over the question of smallholdings and occupier ownership. He also found plenty of time to hunt. There is an illuminating interview with him published in a book called *The Conservative Mind* in 1924. Written by the intriguingly named 'Gentleman with a Feather Duster', it gives a good insight into Wood's political views on the eve of his Viceroyalty.

His imperialism at that stage was still of the messianic variety. He was 'convinced that the Empire promises better social conditions at home, a greater and healthier race of English-speaking people for the future and also by far the most powerful influence for world peace' and 'the influence of a powerful British Empire, in friendly relations with the United States of America, may at least keep war at bay until the democracies of the world are on higher spiritual ground'.[13] On domestic and social issues Wood put his faith in government intervention: 'We shall never get value for the money we spend ... until the people live in better houses and are assured of regular employment. The whole atmosphere of their lives must be changed.'[14]

The whole atmosphere of his life changed when, in October 1925, Baldwin offered him the Viceroyalty of India. This hybrid task comprised the duties of King-Emperor and Prime Minister, ruling over a subcontinent larger than Europe of 320 millions. There were numerous languages, five major religions and eighty-six semi-independent principalities. Wood was forty-four, virtually unknown in Britain and completely unknown in India; furthermore, he had no great achievement to his name. He was appointed solely because his character commended itself to King George V and Baldwin, albeit after a number of other better-qualified men such as Earl Haig had been turned down. As the King's Private Secretary explained to the Secretary of State for India: 'His personality is unquestionable and he has a charming wife.'[15] It is hard not to sympathize with Birkenhead's petulant and somewhat self-congratulatory remark on hearing that Wood had been chosen for the post which he himself so coveted: 'How much better in life and how much more paying it is to be blameless rather than brilliant.'[16]

The great show of reluctance with which Wood accepted the offer of the Viceroyalty, even taking into account the fact that he had a father of eighty-seven whom he was unlikely therefore to see again, strains our

17

credulity. Initially he even seemed to refuse it, with the coy proviso that if Baldwin and his friends 'thought that a situation had arisen in which from their point of view it was my plain duty to say yes, then *that* would compel me to reconsider'. Reconsider he soon did, and, after being raised to the barony of Irwin of Kirby Underdale, he and his wife left for India from Victoria Station on 17 March 1926.

3

India

Neither British nor Indians appear to have had any idea what to expect from the Irwins. *The Times* called it an 'unexpected but peculiarly interesting appointment' and explained that 'Edward Wood is one of those rare characters in the public life of the country that no great post falls vacant without the suggestion that he is admirably qualified to fill it.'[1] But even that newspaper, edited by his old friend and fellow Yorkshireman Geoffrey Dawson, which was to accord him unswerving support throughout his life, was bound to add, 'Mr Wood has no experience whatever of Oriental problems and administration.... He has never, so far as the public is aware, displayed any special interest in Indian affairs.' In January 1926, the Commander-in-Chief in India, Field Marshal Sir William Birdwood, wrote to the King's Assistant Private Secretary, Sir Clive Wigram, how the appointment was 'a great surprise to all of us out here, as no one seems to have heard his name mentioned'.[2] But, as Birdwood continued, 'From many letters I have had from home, he seems to be a really first-class English gentleman, and, as such, seems to be exactly what we want.'[3]

The central question facing the British in India was much the same as that which Thucydides posed in the fifth century BC: how can a democracy rule an empire? How can a government whose legitimacy relies on consent rule over a subject people who have little or no say? Irwin's answer was a good deal more honest than those of a number of his predecessors and critics. They spoke airily of a sacred trust which would be redeemed when the natives were ready for self-government, whilst mentally reserving no specific date whatsoever for that eventuality. Irwin suspected Birkenhead had a rough timescale of 600 years in mind. He himself believed eventual Indian self-government to be inevitable and, with proper safeguards, that Britain should carefully guide India to that end in the short to medium term. These were fairly radical views for a Conservative of the mid-1920s and they were shortly to fling him up against the strong and articulate imperialist wing of his own Party.

Before coming to any conclusions about future constitutional developments for India, Irwin spent three years studying the sub-continent. He soon learnt that part of the secret of the miracle of British India was that the Empire rested upon the Indian's sense of awe towards the Raj and thus 'the whole position is essentially psychological'. With Indians outnumbering the 160,000 Britons by two thousand to one, it could hardly have been otherwise. In 1925, British troops numbered a mere 57,000 throughout the entire sub-continent. He found the ancient problems of poverty, illiteracy and Hindu–Muslim communal strife jostling with the relatively new one of the growing demands for self-government. Irwin found himself reaping the whirlwind, the seeds of which were sown by his grandfather's educational reforms of the 1850s which had educated the tiny Indian middle class into a nascent sense of political and national consciousness.

Set against these problems was his power, which was immense. He virtually had his own foreign policy to conduct. In Persia, Arabia and China, it was Delhi which counted as much as Whitehall. Despite some power devolved to the nine provincial governors, and an ambiguous relationship with the Indian princes and independently minded officials, the Viceroy's powers were pre-eminent. The Legislative Council had advisory powers which Irwin frequently ignored. The Montagu–Chelmsford Reforms of 1919 had instituted diarchy, a limited system of power-sharing in which Indians entered provincial government in the less sensitive departments and were groomed for greater responsibilities.

For the first three years of his Viceroyalty it was not in India but London that Irwin's greatest problems lay. The Secretary of State for India, the man who had to answer for India in Parliament and therefore theoretically Irwin's superior, was Lord Birkenhead. Churchill's best friend, his views on imperialism were of the unreconstructed Diamond Jubilee variety and he had been the only member of the Coalition Cabinet to oppose the Montagu–Chelmsford Reforms. 'F.E.', as he was universally known, had been a victim of the Carlton Club revolt, although his self-evident and self-proclaimed genius soon won him a place in Baldwin's Cabinet. Irwin knew that so long as Birkenhead stayed at the India Office, little progress could be made towards greater self-determination for the sub-continent.

He was instead condemned to make continual but unheeded calls for an end to the Hindu–Muslim communal strife. This had seen a recrudescence on Irwin's arrival, with a riot in Calcutta which lasted a fortnight at the cost of 100 lives. In 1926, there were thirty-five Hindu–Muslim clashes classed as 'serious', often sparked by the proselytizing of one faith amongst the poorer communities of the other. Irwin denied that this ancestral antagonism was both a justification for and a mainstay of the continued British presence in India and made constant calls for All-India patriotism and tolerance. His well-intentioned pleas have often been seen as naïve, and he has often been cast in the role of an *ingénu* who thought that ancestral vendettas could be quelled by a few high-sounding phrases in an after-dinner speech to the Chelmsford Club. In fact, Irwin was under no illusions as to the effect his words would have, but, with Birkenhead at the India Office, he had little more to offer. He also considered them worth saying, if nothing else for the propaganda value they had abroad.

For this latter reason, he also refused to ban the crude anti-Hindu book *Mother India*, written by an American author called Katherine Mayo, which was published in August 1927. This book, which criticized Hindu customs and especially sexual mores, was likely to cause more disturbance of the peace than many of the other politically seditious books which were banned. However, it is clear from his letters to family and friends that Irwin actually considered the book likely to be 'beneficial', in that it might help reconcile American opinion to British rule in India.

At the outset of Irwin's Viceroyalty the Independence movement was a weak and demoralized affair. Mahatma Gandhi had led a Civil Dis-obedience movement in 1920, which had fizzled out and was formally suspended in December 1924, after which he left active politics for his village loom. For all its extravagant claims, the Congress Party was over-whelmingly a middle-class movement, led almost entirely by lawyers, with little appeal amongst the Indian masses. Irwin soon learnt that the Indian politician was primarily 'concerned to try & save his face ... their real mind is only partially represented by their public utterances'.[4] Despite its pretensions to political leadership for the whole country, the Congress Party had failed to secure any significant support amongst the Muslims.

The Muslim League, under Mohammed Ali Jinnah, took an un-ashamedly communalist stance, demanding separate electorates and fed-eral safeguards. It was also enthusiastic about a British withdrawal, but wished to see the British replaced by a central government weak enough to allow Muslim control over those provinces where they predominated – the Punjab, Bengal and the North-West Frontier. The distinguished historian of India, Sir Penderel Moon, has described the mid-1920s as 'the beginning of a general scramble for power' by many racial, religious or social groups conscious that Britain would not be directing the affairs of India forever. Thus the rising Sikh nationalism in the Punjab, the agitation of the 'De-pressed Classes' for special voting rights and the formation of the Hindu Mahasabha – a militant orthodox organization – were all differing elements of the same phenomenon.

There were, however, plenty of moderate Indian politicians who were content to co-operate with Britain and move at a more leisurely pace towards a greater degree of self-government. Sir Tej Bahadur Sapru's Liberals held office in the provincial legislatures under diarchy, but gradu-ally found the ground cut from under them as Congress tended to radicalize

Indian politics. The leaders of the Independence movement – Motilal Nehru and his hot-headed son Jawaharlal, the Patel brothers Vithalbhai and Vallabhai, and the idol of Calcutta, Subhas Chandra Bose – were always on the look-out for passing bandwagons. Ironically, the best bandwagon of them all was driven by Irwin himself in September 1927 when he made the gravest error of his Viceroyalty.

A central provision of the Montagu Act of 1919 was that within ten years a parliamentary commission had to be appointed to look into the working of the Reforms and make further recommendations for progress towards greater self-government. Birkenhead, fearful of a Labour victory at the polls and thus a socialist commission which might propose far-reaching reforms, decided to appoint the commission two years early. He and Irwin then made a blunder so fundamental that it was to wreck any hopes of tranquillity for the rest of the Viceroyalty. For a series of in themselves very good reasons, Irwin advised Birkenhead, who had long been of the same opinion, not to have any Indians on the commission at all. This totally underestimated the sense of outrage which the prospect of an all-white commission reporting on India's future engendered right across the Indian political spectrum. Irwin had made the error of ignoring his own dictum about India and had relied too much on logic and not enough on psychology.

Irwin's reasoning was sound as far as it went: he feared that the Indians on the commission would join the Labour members to outvote the Conservatives; he predicted that the Muslims and the Hindus on the commission would clash; he could not see which Indians could be appointed without antagonizing others; and he argued that as it was a British parliamentary commission, it was not unreasonable that it should consist of British parliamentarians. Finally, as he wrote to his friend Viscount Cecil of Chelwood of his brother-in-law George Lane Fox, who had been recently appointed to the commission, 'I do honestly believe that seven Lane Foxes will advise Parliament better about this than Indians however able they may be.'[5] He failed to appreciate the extent to which the decision would give the opposition a grievance, strengthening the hands of extremists against moderates and angering many Indians not normally interested in politics at all.

Furthermore, Gandhi saw his chance to return to politics. The calls for a boycott of the commission managed the hitherto impossible feat of uniting the Muslim League, the Hindu Mahasabha and the Liberals in support. But Congress outbid all three by adopting Jawaharlal Nehru's call for complete independence from Britain.

The Times called the commission 'a terribly weak team' and, although he had some knowledge of India, the choice of the Liberal politician Sir John Simon to head it was unfortunate. Cold, legalistic and humourless, Simon had none of the personal qualities needed to beat the boycott. In a letter to

Neville Chamberlain, Irwin described Simon's horrible practice of 'keeping all his personality within locked doors while inviting other people to disclose theirs'.[6] When the commission, consisting of four Conservatives, two Labour (one of whom was Clement Attlee) and Simon himself landed in Bombay on 3 February 1928, they were greeted by vast 'Black Flag' demonstrations. These were staged wherever they went around the country. In one, the venerable and elderly Hindu writer, Lajpat Rai, received two lathi blows from a British policeman and died a fortnight later. This served to embitter relations for some considerable time. It is important not to concentrate overmuch on these occasional outbreaks of trouble; for almost throughout the period India was one of the world's most tranquil places. Even at the height of the agitation, Britons lived in no great personal danger either from mob violence or terrorist attacks, except perhaps for a very short period in certain parts of Bengal.

The Irwins were a welcome change from the stiff and pompous Readings and they let it be known that a new informality could be expected in the etiquette of the Viceregal Court. This was all relative; for example, the number of curtseys expected from ladies in the course of an evening was reduced from seven to three and some dinners at which white tie and decorations were worn were relegated to the almost informal black tie.

The Irwins used to allow their numerous dogs to scamper around their feet as they went along the huge receiving lines. Their children, who by then also included Richard, who had been born in October 1920, lent the Court a relaxed family atmosphere. 'The Irwins had a happy knack', remembered one of their aides-de-camp, John Gordon Duff, 'of being able to switch from formality to informality without loss of dignity'.[7] Entertaining was done on a huge scale. There were three dinner parties a fortnight of between seventy-five and 120 people, garden parties, dances and huge state balls. Lady Irwin calculated that in 1930 in the cold weather they never sat down to any meal with less than forty-two. All this was made possible by two private secretaries, a comptroller, six aides-de-camp and over a thousand indoor servants.

The year was split between winters in Delhi and summers spent at the Viceregal Camp in Simla, 7,000 feet up in the Himalayas. In 1925, the young Lord Knebworth described life in Simla to a friend: 'The Governmental idea of camp life and roughing it is rather exceptional. You have 50 servants, a laundry, a horse each, two hot baths a day, a bungalow to live in, 190 coolies, exquisite food, bridge and a private post office.' He was equally impressed by his father's Governor's House in Darjeeling, where,

> At meals there is one huge man in a turban and red and gold behind each chair ... buttonholes just happen on your dressing-table, cocktails appear; at tennis there is one head man and fourteen boys to pick

up the balls! There are horses to ride simply by saying the word ...
and the country is more beautiful than anything you ever imagined.[8]

On the journey from Delhi to Simla, and during the July rainy season, a
special train would take the Viceregal party on tours of the provinces and
visits to the self-governing Indian states. These often occasioned monumental extravagance from the princes. It was during Irwin's Viceroyalty,
however, that British India outdid them all and planned, financed and built
the twentieth-century's supreme expression of imperial self-confidence and
grandeur – the Viceroy's House in New Delhi. Its architect, Sir Edwin
Lutyens, stayed with the Irwins for Christmas 1926 and immediately established a rapport with Lady Irwin, whom he found businesslike and imaginative. The Irwins finally moved into the house in 1930. It is a hugely imposing
edifice and expressed in stone a confidence in a continued British power and
presence in India that Irwin was coming to question. Harold Nicolson
voiced one criticism that was to be echoed by Lady Irwin, that,

> superb though it is, [it] was designed with slight consideration for the
> needs of Vicereines. ... Lutyens, who was himself indifferent to com-
> fort, seldom seems to realize that great works of architecture were
> sometimes places in which men and women and servants were ex-
> pected to live.[9]

The photograph album of Colonel Francis Lane Fox, another of Irwin's
aides-de-camp, conveys the relaxed yet magnificent life of the Viceregal
party. Tiny black-and-white snapshots record the stereotypical pageant:
state elephants parading in the Udaipur palace; moustachioed officers
lounging in wicker chairs wearing jodhpurs and reading the *Daily Telegraph*
with their dalmatians at their feet; Lady Irwin presenting the prizes at the
Delhi Horse Show; majestic and endless Himalayan peaks; sacred mon-
keys on immaculate lawns; a biplane on the North-West Frontier; young
ladies in flapper hats and long strings of pearls; chukkers of bicycle polo;
and everywhere dutiful liveried servants smiling from behind their vast
whiskers.

Apart from a brief bout of malaria in December 1928, Irwin enjoyed
good health and made a point of travelling as much as possible, going
through the Khyber Pass and up the Irrawaddy River. He was a highly
popular Viceroy amongst the British in India and inspired great loyalty.
When the editor of the *Pioneer* newspaper called Irwin a 'Bolshie' in June
1928, a senior army officer asked Sir William Birdwood's permission to go to
Allahabad and 'quite unofficially' horsewhip him.[10] It was refused.

Throughout his time in India, friends and allies kept Irwin minutely
informed as to political developments back at home. Diligent correspondence with Baldwin, Neville Chamberlain, Samuel Hoare, J.C.C.
Davidson and many others proved invaluable in helping him keep abreast
of the momentous events taking place in Britain.

Part of the explanation for his improbable popularity in the Labour Party can simply be put down to his good fortune in not having been in Britain during the General Strike and the Great Depression. His family having by then sold their coal interests, Irwin could afford to take a detached view of the dispute. His attitude was not much different from that of his friend Lord Cecil, who wrote to Irwin, 'How I hate these employers,' despite being a member of Baldwin's Cabinet.[11] The best evidence of Irwin's attitude was a letter he wrote to Philip Cunliffe-Lister in October 1926 urging magnanimity in victory: 'Do not please let the Government drift into a settlement that will take advantage of the men's exhaustion.'[12]

Reacting to jibes that it offered no credible alternative policy, Congress presented its own manifesto, Motilal Nehru's 'Report'. This called for 'full responsible government' and immediate Dominion Status – the constitutional state which would put India on a par with the white colonies of the Empire. The document served merely to antagonize the Muslims by refusing their claim for reserved seats in any future central legislature. It also angered the young radicals in Congress, led by Motilal's son Jawaharlal, who did not want India to retain any political association with Britain whatsoever.

At Congress's annual conference in Calcutta at the end of December 1928, a compromise was reached between those moderates, such as Gandhi and Motilal Nehru, who supported the Nehru report, and the more extreme elements led by Jawaharlal Nehru and Subhas Chandra Bose, who thought that it did not go far enough. They announced that should the Government of India not accept the report by the last day of 1929 – something they knew Britain could not do – the non-co-operation campaign would be resuscitated with the aim of forcing the British to quit India.

The editor of The Times, Geoffrey Dawson, was a Fellow of All Souls and an old friend whom Irwin had first met on his Grand Tour in South Africa. He stayed with the Irwins for three months in the winter of 1928/9. There they discussed ways in which the burgeoning Indian political consciousness could be reconciled to the continuation of British rule. Irwin despaired of the Simon Commission, boycotted and derided, coming up with any sufficiently imaginative proposals. He paid lip-service to it but no more. Instead, he conceived a plan so bold that it would leapfrog the Commission and defeat the Calcutta Conference threat by detaching liberal Indian opinion and splitting Congress. Often seen as some sort of altruistic gesture, Irwin's plan was, in fact, a shrewd political move calculated to recapture the initiative. Whilst he fully appreciated that it was likely to bring down the full weight of right-wing Tory wrath upon him, Irwin believed from the political intelligence he had been receiving that with the support of Baldwin and The Times the risk was worth taking.

4

The Declaration

Irwin's opportunity came in July 1929, when the Conservatives lost the general election and Labour's William Wedgwood Benn became Secretary of State for India. Irwin welcomed Benn as 'a nice fellow, keen, with lots of ideas and a gentleman.... He was always rather a friend of mine in the Commons.'[1] Irwin's intention was to persuade the new Government to authorize him to announce that the constitutional development that Britain had in mind for India was nothing less than full Dominion Status. Commenting on the 'boycott Simon' movement to the King's Private Secretary, Lord Stamfordham, in April, he estimated that 'the lower orders remain, so far as I can judge, entirely unaffected by this agitation'.[2]

Irwin ignored the tradition by which Viceroys stayed in India during their whole term of office, and returned home in the summer of 1929. The planned announcement, by immediately addressing the problem of India's future, would turn on its head the established process whereby a commission took evidence, reported and had its recommendations debated and eventually passed into legislation. He proposed to leave the venerable Simon Commission high and dry. To each of the interested parties Irwin presented a different aspect of the announcement's appeal. To Labour ministers he spoke of the rights of the native people. To Indian moderates he reflected on the shortly-to-be-expected benefits attendant on Dominion Status. To the King-Emperor he emphasized that the power of the princes would remain largely unaffected. To liberal Conservatives he pointed out the enlightened and well-precedented nature of his proposals; and to right-wing Conservatives he explained how Congress would be split and assured them that the actual attainment of Dominion Status was still some way off.

To none of them did he point out the underlying truth that the very term 'Dominion Status' had completely changed its meaning since it was first used with regard to India in 1917. Then the pull of the mother country on the other white Dominions had been all-powerful and 'Dominion' meant little in terms of self-determination. By 1929, all the white Dominions were only a year and the Statute of Westminster away from independent statehood. Irwin took full advantage of the way in which these terms of nomenclature had changed.

On arriving in London, Irwin found that the new Prime Minister, Ramsay MacDonald, and Wedgwood Benn were both enthusiastic about his suggestions. They were keen to be seen to be responsible but enlightened in their dealings with the Empire, and Irwin's policy had the added attraction of being certain to split the Tories. His proposal that the Indian leaders should attend a conference in London also found favour. He laid the King's fears to rest over the shooting weekend at Sandringham in September. The Liberals were a more difficult obstacle. The formulator of the original 1917 Declaration, Lloyd George, was not interested so much in the proposed reforms as in using the issue as a stick with which simultaneously to beat the Labour Government and the Conservative Opposition. Since 1922 there had been no love lost between him and Irwin and nothing substantial could be agreed. Irwin's predecessor as Viceroy, the Marquess of Reading, was profoundly sceptical, but said he would go along with the proposed announcement as long as Simon was also in favour.

Baldwin, ever alive to the political advantages of seeming constructive, was amenable to Irwin's plan in a conversation they had before he went on holiday to Bourges. It therefore came as no surprise for Baldwin when, on 20 September, he received a Downing Street Private Secretary with a letter from the Prime Minister which read, 'Both Irwin and Wedgwood Benn are greatly concerned if possible to take steps that may have a sedative effect on the Indian situation, which is causing some anxiety,' and which asked him to support both an announcement about Dominion Status and a proposal 'to invite Indians to [a] conference and discussion before the Government has formulated any draft proposals of their own'.[3]

Without a chance to canvass his Shadow Cabinet colleagues, but trusting in Irwin's ability to sell the policy, Baldwin agreed the next day that, 'in the circumstances, I am prepared to concur in what is proposed and you may rely on my doing all that is in my power to secure the unanimous support of my party'.[4] But this was no blank cheque, for Baldwin made the proviso that his support was conditional on Simon's agreement. At first Simon saw no objection either to the announcement or to the conference. But when on 19 September he was asked to approve an 'open' agenda for the conference rather than one determined by his commission's deliberations, he revolted. The commission went into conclave and, on 24 September, Simon told Benn that they were firmly against both the announcement and any conference with an agenda not set by his commission's report. The next day both Simon and Reading came out strongly against Irwin's plans. Reading was concerned lest the Declaration raised Indian expectations and provoked resentment later when it became clear how long it was going to take before Dominion Status was granted. But Irwin vigorously supported the announcement, which he termed the Declaration, and described it as a vital part of his strategy against the coming campaign of non-co-operation and non-payment of taxes.

Baldwin returned home on 25 September and stayed with the Irwins at Garrowby on the 29th. It was later alleged that Baldwin did not know of Simon's opposition to the proposals until the Shadow Cabinet meeting on 23 October and that somehow the Benn–Irwin partnership had kept him in the dark. Irwin certainly knew of Simon's position by the time Baldwin stayed at Garrowby and it is inconceivable that the subject was not mentioned there. A far more likely explanation was that Irwin correctly apprised Baldwin of the position, which was still fairly fluid, but Baldwin underestimated the depth of die-hard Tory opposition and allowed his friend considerable leeway, whilst always reserving for himself the right to make any final decision.

On 8 October, Irwin sent Baldwin a revised Declaration, incorporating some of Reading's suggested amendments, as well as a list of quotations from various statesmen over the previous fifteen years designed to prove that there was not 'anything startlingly new in openly proclaiming Dominion Status ... to which we look through the constitutional developments foreshadowed in 1917'.[5] Two days later, Irwin left for India. On 13 October, a leaked story in the *Sunday Times* forced the issue into the open. Baldwin was quickly made to realize how unpopular the Declaration was likely to be amongst the Conservative Party's rank and file. The crisis came at the Shadow Cabinet meeting he chaired on 23 October, when he was formally informed that Simon had opposed the announcement ever since 24 September. It is inconceivable that a man with Baldwin's acute political antennae, despite his having been on holiday, should have failed to recognize this basic fact for over a month. The Shadow Cabinet was horrified that he had put his name to it at all. Hoare wrote to Irwin, who was by then back in India, that at the meeting, 'Stanley said very little indeed, confining himself to reading your proposed statement and saying that he only approved of it in his personal capacity and not as leader carrying the party with him.'[6] This was a far cry from the answer he had given MacDonald's Private Secretary in Bourges back on 21 September.

In the major internal Tory Party crisis which broke, Baldwin, who had lost two general elections, had to start to fight for his political life. Commentators such as J.C.C.Davidson saw, in the combination of Churchill, Birkenhead, Austen Chamberlain and Lloyd George all attacking Baldwin over India, shades of the old Coalition out for revenge. After the Shadow Cabinet meeting the personification of Tory rectitude, Lord Salisbury, wrote to Baldwin to say:

Of course I realize that you never dreamed that this step was to be taken without Simon's consent. If this last turns out to be true the proposed proceeding would be frankly incredible.... I earnestly hope you will be able to stop it, to convince the Government and convince Edward that the party will be shaken to its centre.[7]

But Baldwin was past being able to 'convince Edward'; Irwin saw his first duty as being to India, rather than to the Conservative Party, and he was determined to go ahead with the Declaration. It was a course of action that took great self-confidence and political bravery. There was no doubt that Simon's role to report 'whether and to what extent it is desirable to establish the principle of responsible government' was completely short-circuited by Irwin. One commentator, who regards Irwin as a 'sagacious and worldly politician', has concluded that, 'it almost appeared as if Benn and Irwin were attempting to rush the announcement through in the confusion. MacDonald was in America, Baldwin on holiday, and the Commission whilst agreeing to one concession had rejected Dominion Status.'[8]

The moment Irwin got back to India he started to leak the gist of the Declaration to moderate Indian politicians with the intention simultaneously of maximizing goodwill and presenting London with a fait accompli. He pointed out to friends that even if he had wanted to go back on the Declaration it would now be impossible without severe loss of face. He also telegraphed Benn and, using a tactic that had always infuriated Birkenhead, claimed that he had received 'private information' to the effect that 'Congress ... will be disposed to accept it and I see a real possibility of the thing coming off as well as the Cabinet had always hoped.' Last-minute pleas were hopeless. The very evening before the Declaration was due to be made, Baldwin telegraphed Irwin personally and begged him to hold it up.[9] Baldwin was his political mentor, father-figure, Party leader, close friend and the man to whom he owed his Viceroyalty. Despite all that, Irwin politely telegraphed back his regrets and went ahead with the Declaration regardless.

His announcement 'that the natural issue of India's constitutional progress ... is Dominion Status' marked the beginning rather than the end of the controversy. On the day of the announcement the leading imperialist popular newspaper, the *Daily Mail*, opined that, 'Lord Irwin had always belonged to a section of the Conservative Party which manifested dangerous leanings towards platonic flirtations with socialism.' What the India Defence League soon dubbed 'Irwinism' became the number-one bogey of the Tory popular press.

It all washed over the man himself, who exhibited a lifelong contempt for all facets of the media, and as the last of the Whigs his regard for reactionary Tory back-benchers was scarcely higher. To the opposition he adopted a studied if slightly contrived attitude of unconcern, as illustrated by his remark to his father on 4 November:

29

My statement ... seems to have precipitated something of a political storm at home. I can't myself conceive the justification for this, as our purpose has always been proclaimed to be that of representative government.... Lloyd George... is, as always, being thoroughly dishonest... die-hards both in England and in India combine to make the task of sensible people as difficult as possible.[10]

The next day he wrote to a friend that, 'what is so important is to make perfectly plain to India that the ultimate purpose for her is not one of perpetual subordination in a white Empire'.[11] As usual it was not so much in India as in London that his Viceroyalty faced its most harrowing test. Here the support of *The Times* was invaluable. The then power of *The Times*, the pre-eminent establishment paper of the day, is comparable to that of the television news channels today. The Commons debate on the Declaration took place on 7 November, by which time Baldwin had recovered his political poise. He was keen to fight the issue not so much on its merits as on the far surer ground of the behaviour of the right-wing press and the character of the Viceroy. The whips had taken very careful soundings and he believed he could count on the support of at least two-thirds of Conservative MPs.

During the debate Baldwin paid tribute to his beleaguered colleague and declared that, 'If ever the day comes when the party which I lead ceases to attract to itself men of the calibre of Edward Wood, then I have finished with my party.'[12] The debate in the Lords the next day saw Birkenhead and Reading on the offensive, but in the week after 7 November the Conservative Party, through instinctive dislike of splits and the lack of any viable alternative leader, rallied to Baldwin. By the 13th, Dawson was able to write to Irwin, 'You have S.B. very largely to thank for stemming the tide.'[13]

The worst was not yet over, but Irwin had survived with his Declaration intact. He felt it had been worthwhile, telling the King on 6 November that it 'has undoubtedly had the effect of rallying moderate opinion'.[14] However, the very virulence of the opposition in Britain had the effect of weakening the force of the Declaration, which had been intended to assure Indians of British good faith. Irwin had short enough time to enjoy the benefits of the Declaration before the onset of renewed agitation and danger, starting with an attempt on his life.

5

Irwinism

The Irwins were returning from a tour of Southern India and as the Vice-regal train approached New Delhi, on the morning of 23 December 1929, a bomb went off underneath it. The terrorists' intention had been to derail the train near a steep embankment, but the explosion was too small and ill-timed; instead the bomb went off harmlessly under the connection between the dining-car and the next coach. Apart from broken windows, some splinters and one slightly injured servant, no real damage was done. The Indian writer, Nirad Chaudhuri, explains: 'It could never have succeeded – we are too incompetent to make good terrorists. They used the wrong type of bomb.'[1] The standard of Hindu terrorism was unimpressive: when Bhagat Singh and a co-conspirator threw two bombs and fired revolvers at the Government benches of the Legislature in April 1929, they failed to kill anyone.

Irwin responded to the assassination attempt with precisely the kind of phlegm expected from a Viceroy. As he wrote to his father:

> I can't pretend that I personally was at any moment greatly disturbed by it. It went off about three coaches in front of me when I was sitting in my saloon reading Challoner. I heard the noise and thought to myself 'that must be a bomb'. . . . I then smelt all the smoke which came down the train and concluded that it was a bomb; but, as nothing happened, I went on reading Challoner till someone came along.[2]

Displaying even more sang-froid he told Lady Harlech that the reason he was not more excited by it all was because he was 'inured to that kind of thing by the Cona Coffee machine which was always blowing up'.[3]

That afternoon he was due to meet the leading Indian politicians – Gandhi, Motilal Nehru, Vithalbhai Patel, Sir Tej Sapru and Jinnah – who, after perfunctory expressions of congratulations on his escape, made demands for immediate Dominion Status and cast doubts on the Government's sincerity in promulgating the Declaration. Instead of expressing satisfaction, the Congress leaders, Gandhi and Nehru, affected to assume that the conference, known as the Round Table Conference, was designed to draft a constitution for an India with Dominion Status. The meeting did not accept Irwin's explanations and broke up without agreement. The moderate Sapru correctly deduced Congress's deliberate misunderstanding to be a ploy to avoid going to London whilst Indian opinion on the merits of constitutional change was still in a state of such flux. Irwin met this setback with his customary combination of patience and regret.

At the Lahore Conference a week later, Congress spurned both the Round Table Conference and the Dominion Status Declaration and instead unfurled the flag of an independent India and proclaimed a new Civil Disobedience campaign. The lukewarm commitment to non-violence by a good number of the delegates was shown by the vote to congratulate Irwin on his escape, which was passed by only 935 votes to 897. The Conference urged members to reject diarchy and to resign their central or provincial government seats. This radical departure represented a victory for the younger Nehru, but Gandhi's sharp political instinct also told him that the time was ripe for Congress to move on to the offensive. The 1920–22 Civil Disobedience campaign had been called off ostensibly because of a few isolated and relatively minor acts of violence. This time Gandhi promised the younger Nehru not to do the same thing. There could be minor infringements of the non-violence rule, but as long as the campaign remained generally peaceful Gandhi promised not to suspend it.

Irwin's policy for dealing with Civil Disobedience had to be formulated by 26 January 1930, the so-called Independence Day on which all Indians were encouraged to demonstrate their opposition to British rule. He recognized that to ban all meetings and demonstrations would provoke violence. He also felt prohibition of their propaganda would be counter-productive. Yet, to take no action at all would merely strengthen Congress's hand against both the Government and those loyal Indian moderates who were content with the gradual route towards Dominion Status. He therefore decided to allow the meetings to go ahead but to arrest the main speakers afterwards and only then if the sedition charges were sure to stick.

The Governor of Bombay, where agitation was often worst, was the First War Chief of the Air Staff, Sir Frederick Sykes. Very much of the old school, he considered Irwin's approach to be 'deplorably weak' and suspected that the policy had been dictated by the socialist Government in London. He was wrong; the decision to take the line of least resistance was solely Irwin's. It was activated partly by the desire to keep the political temperature as low as possible, partly by the knowledge that in the last resort military force could not hold India down anyhow and partly by the desire not to have any major obstacles placed in the way of an eventual settlement. Treason could be professed but incidents were to be avoided. One of Irwin's aides-de-camp, Patrick Bradshaw, remembered how he was 'always reluctant to use military force to quell riots. He thought the use of force was an admission of failure.'[4]

As the unrest spread, moderate Indian politicians were forced to adopt ever more radical postures to avoid being perceived as British stooges. Even Gandhi had to fight a constant battle to retain the movement's leadership. In February 1930, he wrote in *Young India* that British rule was 'a perfect personification of violence', despite its reliance on the rule of law and its minute police and armed forces. Civil Disobedience, the failed weapon of 1920–22, was admitted by Gandhi then to have been a 'Himalayan blunder' when inevitably it turned violent. Participants were, peacefully, to force the Government of India into surrender by their refusal to co-operate in the running of the country. They were to boycott British goods, withdraw their children from government schools, picket shops selling alcohol and foreign cloth, give up public duties, return all their titles and honours, refuse to pay certain taxes, and generally make the hitherto smooth governance of India as difficult as possible.

Gandhi, ever the brilliant propagandist and self-publicist, knew that he needed some eye-catching issue on which to centre his campaign. A list of eleven demands designed to appeal simultaneously to all sections of the public was hastily cobbled together, but proved too contradictory to achieve much. In February 1930, Gandhi at last found his answer – salt. There had been taxes on salt since Moghul times and the present government monopoly had been instituted in 1836. By 1930, the tax was so low, at 2 rupees 8 annas per maund, that it was rarely ever evaded. To pay tax on what was both a necessity and also a natural process had long been a minor source of grievance for Indians and British radicals. Even Ramsay MacDonald had spoken against it in the past. But what made the idea of revolt against the salt tax so potent was the very brazenness of the planned defiance.

Gandhi would spend three weeks walking through dozens of small villages to the sea. There he would ceremonially bend down and scoop up salt from the shore, thereby technically breaking an anachronistic, if only mildly unpopular, law. There was a large element of risk involved: it was of little practical help to the average Indian, did no harm to government revenue and did not force the British to introduce any new or repressive legislation. By its very esoteric nature the gesture lay wide open to ridicule. Certainly Irwin hoped 'this silly salt stunt' would make Gandhi look absurd and he even toyed with the idea of putting Gandhi's entire party in lorries and having them driven direct to the sea.

The march from Ahmedabad on 12 March inaugurated the Civil Disobedience campaign proper and captured the imagination of the world's press, which swiftly turned the salt march into a crusade. The American media took special delight in equating the salt tax with their own unpopular and explosive tea tax of 1776. Irwin was unsure how to deal with the new situation, writing to George Lane Fox in late March, 'Gandhi is filling the stage at present. I learn privately from intercepted letters that they were all greatly bothered with our not arresting him before he started. Incidentally he and his volunteers do not much appreciate not being prevented taking the long walk through the dust.'⁵ Irwin decided not to intervene, so when Gandhi gathered salt at Dandi on 6 April there was not a policeman in sight. Irwin's hunch, that Gandhi courted arrest and that it would be folly to play into his hands, was supported by Benn, who was keen to deny Gandhi 'the halo of martyrdom'. There was also a fear lest Gandhi's high blood pressure and heart condition kill him while in a British gaol. His death at liberty, on the other hand, struck Irwin as 'a very happy solution'.⁶

So Gandhi was left alone despite prima-facie evidence of his law-breaking. His principal lieutenants and other Congress leaders were not so fortunate and Jawaharlal Nehru was arrested on 14 April. Provincial governors were ordered to avoid incarcerating huge swathes of the population but rather to concentrate on taking the ringleaders out of circulation. Even Gandhi was forced to admit that the British were acting with great restraint. The Government of India was encouraged by intelligence reports to believe that Gandhi's continued non-arrest would damage his prestige within the movement. Irwin continually held back those old India hands in his administration who wanted tougher action taken. Sykes advocated outlawing all traitors to the Crown, Field Marshal Birdwood wanted tear-gas used to disperse demonstrations and several provincial governors urged that Gandhi be gaoled forthwith. But for as long as he was able, Irwin overruled them and stuck to his low-key approach, trusting to a combination of selective arrests, relentless pressure and sheer ennui.

That policy was shattered when Civil Disobedience descended into the anarchy and bloodshed long predicted by Sykes and others. It took that ever-present nightmare of all Britons in India – mutiny – to convert Irwin's patient forbearance into tough retribution. On the night of 17/18 April, a party of 100 armed men attacked an army depot in Chittagong in West Bengal killing a British sergeant and stealing large amounts of arms and ammunition. More worrying still were violent riots in Peshawar in the North-West Frontier, which on 23 April surprised police and led to troops killing thirty rioters and wounding thirty-five. Much more serious was the news that two platoons of the Royal Garhwal Rifles, which had been ordered to Peshawar as reinforcements, had refused to obey orders. The situation was quickly remedied when the ever-loyal Gurkhas disarmed and replaced the Garhwalis, but the psychological damage had been done. Since the experiences of 1857, mutinous sepoys had always occupied prime place in the demonology of the British in India.

The Chief Commissioner of Peshawar was forced to withdraw his forces from the city on the evening of 24 April and to abandon it to the mob for ten days. Peshawar was the key to the North-West Frontier and the news that the British had lost control there spread quickly through the province to neighbouring Afghanistan, bringing thousands of Pathan and Afridi tribes-men down from the hills. The Prime Minister enquired whether the situation demanded that he cancel his Lossiemouth holiday and Irwin ordered an immediate press clampdown, explaining to the King, 'The episode is a very uncomfortable one and inevitably sets one thinking.'[7] British and Gurkha troops supported by the RAF eventually retook Peshawar on 4 May, but sporadic fighting continued there until five months of martial law was imposed in mid-August.

After Chittagong and Peshawar, opinion turned decisively towards Sykes's conviction that Gandhi be detained and the initiative regained. Irwin reluctantly concurred and the Bombay authorities quietly arrested the Indian leader on 5 May. The decision soon backfired. The Civil Dis-obedience movement, with all its major leaders behind bars, entered a more aggressive phase and the summer of 1930 was spent in trying to contain escalating violence. At Sholapur in Bombay on 8 May, two lorries full of policemen were attacked by thousands of rioters. The police opened fire on the mob, two policemen were killed and the law courts burnt down. Troops evacuated the Europeans, but three Muslim policemen were captured by the mob, tied together, soaked in petrol and burnt to death. Despite it taking an entire battalion to regain control, a sceptical Irwin held up the imposition of martial law there until 12 May. Overall however, considering the passions aroused and the numbers involved, there was remarkably little violence on either side. As Irwin wrote to the King, the numbers of those who took a real beating from the police 'was nothing compared to those who wished to sustain an honourable contusion or bruise'.[8]

The publication of the Simon Report in June had no impact on events whatsoever. It failed to mention Dominion Status or go into much detail about long-term constitutional aspirations. Irwin told the Legislative Council that any future Round Table Conference 'would have its liberty unimpaired by the Simon Report'.[9] All sides recognized its irrelevance. Irwin continued to pay it lip-service, explaining to Sapru that it 'would only do more harm than good if at this stage they were so to act as to leave the general impression in English political circles that they were throwing the Simon Report in the waste-paper basket'. At exactly the same time, he wrote to Sykes pointing out that it was 'very important to show that neither we nor the Conference are bound by the "littera scripta" of the Simon Report'.

Rumours, inflamed rather than tamed by press restrictions, fed on one another to produce a sense of panic and outrage, often for little reason. This was common to both sides. Nirad Chaudhuri records how the story spread around the British that Bengali revolutionaries were spreading venereal disease by leaving infected handkerchiefs in tramcars where the British sat.[10] In May 1930, at Sykes's insistence, ordinances were published prohibiting intimidation and provincial governments were accorded a freer hand to act against local Congress committees in their own ways. Five provinces were in favour of outlawing Congress altogether, four against. In the end, Congress's Working Committee was banned and Motilal Nehru was arrested.

The Civil Disobedience campaign took to raiding salt depots and breaking forestry laws as well as the usual picketing and boycotting. At each stage of the disturbances Irwin had to be pushed hard by his advisers and provincial governors before he would authorize repressive measures. However discouraging the news, he never lost sight of his eventual goal of a Round Table Conference. A feature of his handling of the situation, which can be seen recurring throughout his life, was his readiness to place responsibility on the man on the spot. Later in his career this brought accusations of laziness, aloofness and lack of executive willpower. Often this was only the obverse side of his desire, if at all possible, to rely on the judgement of local officials, ambassadors and others with specialist knowledge.

By August 1930, the political atmosphere was considered too dangerous for the Duke of Gloucester to be allowed to join his regiment, the Tenth Hussars, which had been posted to India, and Benn told the Cabinet that unless some sort of settlement was reached, at least four provinces, with a total population of almost 100 millions, would have to be put under martial law. Nevertheless, Irwin was loath to introduce new legislation and resolutely opposed calls for an ordinance based on the repressive Defence of the Realm Act. Requests for permission for the closing of local Congress headquarters and the sequestration of their funds were refused by Irwin as they would 'undoubtedly increase the difficulties of an ultimate settlement'. Hopes for this faded when Sapru, whom Irwin had allowed to visit Gandhi, reported that whilst the eleven points were negotiable, a Round Table Conference must concern 'the substance of independence'.[11]

Back in Britain Irwin's soft approach drew impassioned protests from the imperialist wing of the Conservative Party. As early as mid-June, Dawson warned him: 'The tide here is running pretty strongly against your ideas, and you cannot hope to carry them out by depending on the Labour Party alone.' By 24 September, Churchill was confident enough of his position to warn Baldwin not 'to allow your friendship with Irwin to affect your judgement'. It was the support of *The Times* which once again helped pull Irwin through. In December it described Churchill, whose views were becoming ever more outspoken despite his continued membership of the Conservative Business Committee (or Shadow Cabinet), as 'no more representative of the Conservative Party' than 'the assassins of Calcutta' were of India.

If the Simon committee generated vast amounts of paperwork in pursuit of a monumental waste of time, the first Round Table Conference outdid it. This meeting in London of all the major groups in India except Congress lasted from 12 November 1930 until 19 January 1931. Despite the endlessly laborious sessions it achieved nothing. Without Congress participation it was, as Gandhi remarked, like *Hamlet* without the prince. Civil Disobedience, by presenting itself as the most efficacious way of expelling the

36

British, had so cut the ground from under the moderate Indian politicians that they were forced to make up what they had lost by adopting stances almost indistinguishable from those of Congress itself.

The princes, Liberals, Hindu Mahasabha, Muslim League, Sikhs, Depressed Classes, Indian Christians, Anglo-Indians and British business community all sent delegates to meet sixteen Britons from the three political parties. On the day the Conference opened, Irwin published his own constitutional proposals in an attempt to steer the discussions. This comprised a form of diarchy with Indians running everything except the defence, foreign affairs and finance portfolios. It favoured federation, but only as 'still a distant ideal'. All this was a far cry from Irwin's earlier assurance to the King that the Simon Report would 'in fact be the principal basis of discussion in London'; indeed, Simon was not even invited to the Conference.

On the boat over, Sapru persuaded the princes' delegation, led by the Maharajahs of Bikanir and Patiala, to support his call for early federation. This unanimity came as a considerable shock to the British Government, which for its part was pathetically and transparently anxious to reward the Round Table Conference attendees for doing nothing more than simply not supporting Civil Disobedience. The Indians made speeches designed to appeal more to home audiences than to the Conference. This meant the debates soon dissolved, not into bitterness and deadlock, but into vacuity and equivocation. In the end a call for a vague form of federation and responsible government was agreed upon and Ramsay MacDonald closed the Conference with a speech designed to appeal to all sides, particularly through the use of the phrase 'the advance of India to full responsibility for her own government'.

Two days before MacDonald's closing speech, Irwin addressed the Legislative Council to pay tribute to Gandhi's spiritual force and to call for co-operation from Congress. After receiving certain very loose guarantees he then unconditionally released the Congress leaders, including Gandhi, and lifted the ban on the Working Committee. On 17 February, he embarked on a series of eight talks with Gandhi over three weeks in which they discussed every aspect of Civil Disobedience with a view to a deal which could bring it to an end. This was too much for Churchill, who resigned from the Conservative Business Committee and began his long sojourn in the Wilderness.

Irwin's attitude to Churchill's increasingly apocalyptic speeches on India was typical of many politicians of the day. As he wrote to his sister the previous December, 'I cannot help wondering whether he is rather out of heart with politics altogether ... with the result that he is rather maddogging.' Baldwin took Churchill's resignation with characteristic sangfroid and answered Churchill's attack on 'the catalogue of errors and disasters' of Irwin's Viceroyalty with a vigorous defence of the Round Table Conference, speaking for half an hour without recourse to notes.

6

Peace in India

Propagandists on both sides have so coloured perceptions of the Irwin–Gandhi Pact that it is difficult, even at this sixty-year distance, to separate fact from media 'hype'. Journalists and historians have presented the Pact as two 'Great Souls' coming together and finding mutual ground through shared saintly spirituality. The reality, as is quite clear from notes made by Irwin and comments made by Gandhi, was very different. The talks were nothing so much as good-natured but tough political horse-trading. Each had domestic constituencies to satisfy and points on which he was unable to compromise. Both made shrewd calculations as to the strengths, weaknesses, motives and ultimate desiderata of the opponent.

The final agreement consisted of no less than twenty-one substantial clauses. Writing to his sister on 29 November 1930, Irwin said of Gandhi:

> I cannot help thinking that his whole course of action of the last twelve months has been so much dictated by political calculation that it is optimistic to suppose that he could easily have been swept back into a saner current of thought.

And to Benn, just before his first meeting with Gandhi, he said he would play on 'what everybody says is a characteristic, namely vanity of power and personality,' but would in the last resort depend on 'the sincerity that pervaded your doings in London'.[1]

Gandhi, for all his saintly reputation since his assassination in 1948, was a wily lawyer and politician, whose eccentricities were largely part of the image he projected to the outside world. His description of the Government of India as 'satanic' and 'a curse' was largely the natural hyperbole expected of a Hindu politician. His masterly timing in calling off the two Civil Disobedience movements just as they were losing momentum showed his shrewdness and cunning. Irwin was impressed and wrote to the King of 'this strange little man ... rather wizened and emaciated with no front teeth but sharp little eyes and an acutely active mind'.[2] Gandhi attended the meetings in the Viceroy's house wearing his customary loincloth and shawl. As Francis Lane Fox put it, 'He only did it to annoy because he knows it teases. But the boss didn't allow it to tease him.'[3] When someone remarked how tiresome Gandhi was becoming, Irwin answered, 'A lot of people found our Lord tiresome.'[4]

Both of Irwin's long-standing goals, the end of Civil Disobedience and the attendance of Congress at a second Round Table Conference, were agreed. The price was the immediate release of all those arrested, some 19,000, as well as the return of all confiscated property. Irwin undoubtedly won the most from the Pact, partly because his excellent intelligence network let him know how the businessmen who financed Congress were calling for a period of quiet just as volunteers for arrest and imprisonment were becoming harder to find. The issues of salt, picketing, 'police brutality', the boycott, anti-terrorist legislation, remittal of fines, police costs and the publication of news sheets were all at length hacked out to Irwin's satisfaction and advantage.

Irwin told his father how negotiating with 'the inscrutable' Gandhi 'takes a long time because he is long-winded and has a lot to say, and the Indian always has a great desire to settle things, great and small, at once ... it is a wearing business'. But he also called Gandhi 'logical, forceful, courageous, with an odd streak of subtlety'.[5] Stories, mostly apocryphal, abound of incidents in the meetings where walk-outs were avoided by last-minute appeals to spirituality. However, Irwin's notes of the meetings record Gandhi as 'a relentless bargainer, though his firm line was couched in the pleasantest and most informal manner'.[6] Irwin never considered the deal a definitive peace and took pains to warn people not to invest it 'with too high a degree of permanent sanction'.[7]

Although the actual terms of the Pact gave Irwin all he wanted at the cost of nothing more than he could easily afford, the very fact that it had been made at all put Gandhi in an enormously strong position vis-à-vis the Liberals and other Indian political groupings. The wording, 'It has been agreed that', which prefaced the terms was that normally used for peace treaties between nations. Irwin should have taken this increase in Congress's prestige into account. It could not take place in a vacuum, and the man who called India's problems 'ninety per cent psychological' ought to have had, however personally modest, more regard for the Government of India's position. Gandhi had stolen the limelight from the returning Round Table Conference delegates by speaking on equal terms with a Viceroy. The very act of negotiating with a man straight out of gaol had put the relationship between government and governed on a new footing, one which undoubtedly diminished that sense of awe on which British power depended.

The Pact was concluded on 4 March and announced the next day. Benn told Irwin how in the House of Commons there was 'a real storm of cheers ... for the short sentence in which I expressed the thanks of the Government to you. I have often heard cheers in the House of Commons, but none more hearty, and seldom have I heard the second wave of cheering which occurred on this occasion and which marks a real feeling in the heart of Members.'[8] The week before, Churchill had delivered a philippic the eloquence and virulence of which was to set the tone of the debate for the next four years:

> It is alarming and also nauseating to see Mr Gandhi, a seditious Middle Temple lawyer, now posing as a fakir of a type well-known in the East, striding half-naked up the steps of the Viceregal palace, while he is still organizing and conducting a defiant campaign of civil disobedience, to parley on equal terms with the representative of the King-Emperor.[9]

It is easy at this distance to write off the Indian Empire Society and the India Defence League as merely a collection of jingoists, superannuated majors and red-faced blimps. That is certainly how the dirty tricks departments in Conservative Central Office and the India Office attempted to portray them. In fact, Churchill's plea that 'it must be made plain that the British nation has no intention of relinquishing its mission in India' struck a deep chord in perhaps the majority of the rank and file of the Conservative Party.[10]

The Party's India Committee in Parliament became the scene of bitter internecine warfare and Baldwin was very nearly forced to resign the Leadership on 1 March. On 5 March, the day of the announcement of the Pact, Colonel Herbert Spender-Clay informed Irwin: 'Yesterday the lobby opinion was that S.B.'s resignation of the Leadership could not be postponed for more than a few days, but today his position is far stronger.'[11] Irwin must have known that the news of the Pact would come as a much needed fillip for Baldwin's dwindling political fortunes.

The debate on the Pact was brought forward to 12 March by agreement of the front benches of the Government and Opposition, so as to anticipate Churchill's monster anti-Pact rally scheduled for the Albert Hall on the 18th. The night before the debate, Baldwin told his confidant and adviser, T. J. Jones, that he intended to stand by Irwin's policy despite Jones's warning that by so doing 'he might lose his party and his place'.[12] With the sure political touch he always exhibited in such crises, Baldwin focused the next evening's debate away from the Pact and on to the conduct of the Rothermere and Beaverbrook papers and the issue of 'clean politics'. The *Daily Mail* had called Irwin 'a second Kerensky' and Baldwin responded with the speech of his life. He attacked the paper by name, described the Pact as a victory for common sense and begged that India's future should be kept out of party politics. It was a statesmanlike speech, which made

Churchill's contribution sound petulant, anachronistic and parochial by comparison. Five days later, Baldwin delivered the famous address in which he described the press's position of 'power without responsibility' as 'the prerogative of the harlot throughout the ages'. It was said to have lost Baldwin the tart vote, but it won his candidate, Alfred Duff Cooper, the sensational by-election of St George's, Westminster. Irwinism, no less on trial at St George's than Baldwin, was vindicated.

The trouble with die-hards is that they tend to do exactly that. The doomed and increasingly bitter rearguard action they fought against the Government of India Bill lasted until 1935. The controversial methods Churchill and his growing band of allies used, including the Committee of Privileges where he accused the Government of tampering with evidence pushed them on to the peripheries of British politics. Halifax used to enjoy telling the anecdote of the time when before one of the Round Table Conferences he told Churchill that his ideas about India were those of a subaltern of the late 1890s. He offered to introduce him to some of the Indians who were due to attend the Conference. 'I am quite satisfied with my views of India,' replied Churchill. 'I don't want them disturbed by a bloody Indian.'[13]

Churchill's vituperation over this 'betrayal of the Empire' has more than a hint of political opportunism to it. It was, after all, he who had helped negotiate the partition of Ireland in 1921, bowing to Michael Collins's threat of force and allowing the twenty-six counties to leave the Empire. Churchill's Albert Hall warning of 18 April that 'you will never be able to come to terms with Gandhi' actually weakened his case when he came to apply the same language to the threat of Hitler. Perhaps unsurprisingly for one in the Wilderness, Churchill was held to be crying 'wolf'.

Before leaving India Irwin had one more thorny decision to take. Bhagat Singh had been given the death sentence for murdering the policeman, J.P.Saunders, whom he had mistakenly believed to be responsible for the death of Lajpat Rai, and throwing bombs in the Legislative Assembly. Congress appealed for clemency and vast petitions were sent to Irwin pleading that the death penalty on Singh and his three co-conspirators be commuted. Congress's Conference at Karachi, which had been called to ratify the Pact, was about to open and Gandhi visited Irwin to plead for the young man's life, pointing out what a good effect it would have in Karachi should Irwin show mercy. Had he done so he would certainly have left India on a wave of popular goodwill. The decision was his alone and he spent a sleepless night with his conscience. The next morning he refused to commute the sentence and Singh and his co-conspirators were hanged on 23 March. When Muslim traders in Cawnpore refused Hindu demands to close their shops in mourning, three days of communal rioting resulted which left 300 dead. But Irwin's firmness had paid off and on the 30th, after due tributes had been paid to Singh, the Karachi Conference ratified the Pact.

Irwin made a total of 465 speeches while in India. He spoke at banquets, prize-givings, district boards, the Legislative Assembly, statue unveilings, Chambers of Commerce, the Irwin Hospital, Boy Scout jamborees, agricultural conferences, to the Ootacamund Municipal Council and the hill tribes of the Nilgiris. But by far the most revealing was that delivered to the prestigious Anglo-Indian Chelmsford Club shortly before he left. It was a candid reflection of his time in India as well as a warm defence of his policy. It also threw light on his underlying beliefs regarding India's future. On British reactions to his Declaration he complained:

> Instead of saying 'Dominion Status? Of course it's our intention to give India Dominion Status. What other purpose could we have in view as the goal of our growth?' . . . the general note was that anyone who talked about Dominion Status in connection with India must be mentally afflicted. . . . What wonder that Indian feeling was offended, and a real chance of approach thrown away!

He described the die-hard view that Civil Disobedience was the work of only a tiny minority as 'superficial, distorted and wholly divorced from reality'. 'There is a growing intellectual consciousness, or more truly self-consciousness, which is very closely akin to what we generally term nationalism ... it is a real thing and a thing of growing potential force.'

If the solution to Thucydides's problem of how a democracy was to run an empire was through hypocrisy, he wanted none of it: 'No Englishman can, without being false to his own history, and in recent years to his own pledges, take objection to pursuit by others of their own political liberty.' Finally he stated that, 'no one would deny that it was not less an interest and a responsibility of Great Britain, if and when she hands over power, to satisfy herself that in the new dispensation the just rights of minorities will not be imperilled'. The sentiment was an old and worthy one; but it was little short of revolutionary for a Viceroy, in however coded or qualified a way, to talk about handing over power at all. It took someone of Irwin's impeccable social and political credentials to say these things. Had it been tried by, say, the Jewish Lord Reading, British India would have raised all sorts of obstructions. Because the changes were pushed through by a charming, patient and *pukka* aristocrat much of the criticism was diffused.

The divergence between the way Irwin sought to deal with Civil Disobedience and Sir Frederick Sykes's more forthright methods stemmed not so much from operational differences as a profound dichotomy between their imperial philosophies. Sykes believed in Britain's continuing role in India, thought Congress could be beaten by strength and guile, and saw his duty as protecting the ignorant masses from the extremism of unrepresentative middle-class hot-heads. Irwin instead saw himself as fighting a doomed rearguard action against the huge impersonal forces of legitimate nationalism. Irwin's intense distaste at even having to look into ways to crush

Congress stemmed from his suspicion that however much he might tack and turn, in the end Congress had the tide of history running with it. This sense of historical determinism was doubtless the result of his having read too much Whig history whilst at Oxford. Certainly, when friends were later to ask him for reading material on India, he directed them to Macaulay's essays.

His Viceroyalty was characterized by patience, an eye to history, a willingness to grasp opportunities and an overwhelming desire to retain Indian co-operation and goodwill. He also demonstrated, as the Dominion Status controversy, release of Gandhi and hanging of Bhagat Singh all showed, an ability to take tough decisions and stick by them.

The Irwins left India on 18 April 1931. Just before they went, they gave a state ball, described here by the writer and politician Robert Bernays:

> It was a wonderful warm evening, the sort that one dreams might happen for an Oxford Commem Ball and never does. The gardens were illuminated and were infinitely more popular than the ballroom. With the background of Lutyens's fountains, and the lights of Imperial Delhi and the gay uniforms of the men, and the long flowing dresses of the women, and the distant music of the band it seemed as if old Versailles had come to life. It is fun being out here at this time. It is the type of atmosphere that must have pervaded the closing years of the Second Empire. We enjoy the great gala nights of Viceregal hospitality all the more because we wonder uneasily how much longer they will continue.[14]

7

The Rationale of Appeasement

The Irwins landed in England on 3 May 1931 to be deluged with welcomes and honours. He accepted the Order of the Garter and it is believed he was offered an earldom, which he refused so as not to outrank his father. Vast civic receptions were organized for them in Yorkshire; at Garrowby, local schoolchildren were given two days' holiday and sang 'Home, Sweet Home' as Lady Irwin was presented with a bouquet 'with sincere good wishes on your safe return, from the indoor and outdoor staff at Garrowby Hall'. Irwin made a short speech of thanks to the tenantry, after which refreshments were served on the lawn.

It was in this paternal, virtually feudal, state that Irwin was content to stay for over a year before re-entering politics. Historians have tended to take this period at face value, as a rest from India and even a possible retirement from politics altogether. In fact Irwin was resting, but he was also biding his time and waiting for the most opportune moment to return. Just as he had timed his 1910 entry into politics carefully, so was he also content to avoid direct personal involvement in the political turmoil caused by the 1931 financial débâcle. In his autobiography, *Fulness of Days*, he says he was 'no more concerned, any more than any casual pedestrian in Piccadilly,' with the crises that led to the Labour Prime Minister, Ramsay MacDonald, leaving his party to form a National Government and continue in power with Conservative support.[1]

Irwin never really grasped economics and strenuously avoided ever having to come into contact with jobs that demanded a detailed understanding of them. His absence during the bitterness attendant on Ramsay MacDonald's ditching Labour and the debates on balancing the budget and abandoning the Gold Standard was masterly and stood him in good stead in later years. He refused an offer of the Foreign Secretaryship because he was in too bad an odour with the Tory Party right wing, and did not even make his maiden speech in the Lords until December.

He certainly carried himself as a senior member of the Government, even if strictly speaking he wasn't one. It is hard in today's dull political environment, devoid of ex-Viceroys of India, to appreciate where in the political firmament these glorious and peculiar beasts once stood. Their reigns were discussed like those of foreign kings or premiers of earlier centuries and they were invested with unquestioned *gravitas*. This was all the more pronounced if, as in Irwin's case, the recipient was six foot five inches tall. Irwin, either consciously or not, clearly modelled himself on Sir Edward Grey, whose public persona was also that of high intellect, authority and almost unbelievable detachment. For Fallodon and bird-watching Irwin substituted the equally eminent Garrowby and fox-hunting. Also, as with Grey, the lofty demeanour concealed an ability to square circles and effect great efforts of casuistry. In those far more devotional times Irwin's reputation for piety was genuinely respected and his conscience even became a political asset. As Bernays put it, 'Irwin has something more than magnetism. It is a curious spiritual power. His appearance helps him. He has a magnificent head, and his tall figure and Cecilian stoop and sympathetic kindly eyes give more the impression of a Prince of the Church than of a politician.'[2]

His peerage also meant that he posed no threat to anyone else's calculations for the Premiership. This was a considerable advantage when sharks like Samuel Hoare and Sir John Simon swam in the same political waters. His elevated reputation meant that he was asked to undertake various tasks requiring high ethics and disinterestedness, such as chairing the committee which decided ministerial salaries. This very impassiveness gave rise to accusations of pride and aloofness. Even after their marriages he advised his daughters-in-law to call him Lord Halifax. He could unwind with close friends, but they were few, and to everyone else he extended an utterly professional type of charm which he could turn on and off at will. He very rarely lost his temper but would sometimes do so in negotiations for effect. He loved gossip and social tittle-tattle and, although not a snob in the conventional sense, delighted in the company of duchesses and reserved for royalty a special exultation. However, when it seemed likely that their only daughter might become engaged to George, Duke of Kent, Lady Halifax recalled how 'Edward and I were very apprehensive and did not at all like the prospect. It meant that we should lose Anne in a way that we should not do in any other sort of marriage. I felt sure also, knowing the Royals well and their attitude to ordinary life and ordinary people, that Edward and I would always feel very much the poor relatives to the Royal Family.' According to the Earl of Crawford, the Duke went so far as to ask the King's permission. When in the fullness of time 'the matrimonial project ended', it was 'much to the satisfaction of Irwin himself'.[3]

Irwin's public image is best illustrated by Bernays's comment that, 'He is one of those exasperating people who really do debate whether it is a greater honour to be Prime Minister of England or master of the local fox-hounds.'[4] This is unconvincing as there is nothing to suggest that Irwin was any less ambitious than the next politician. He enjoyed and was fascinated by politics; long after retirement he complained after sitting next to the then Prime Minister, Harold Macmillan, that he wanted to talk politics when Macmillan only wanted to talk bishops. Although a sense of public duty was a factor, it was by no means the major one that kept him in Parliament for half a century. The advice he gave to Sir John Reith in 1940 on how to get on in politics is instructive: 'He advocated forbearance, humour, visits to the smoking room and so forth, and contrasted Chamberlain's position ... with that held by Baldwin, who appeared ready to suffer fools gladly in the House of Commons for any length of time.'[5] Halifax was a politician's politician, whose exemption from contesting elections himself never closed his eyes to the realities of doorstep politics for others. 'After all,' he reminded Davidson in February 1930, 'elections are not decided so much by the convinced adherents of either party, as by the middle unattached opinion which does not greatly care about high politics, but forms an impression of men.'[6]

The impression of capability and respectability he ensured men formed of him meant that no post fell vacant after 1931 without his name being canvassed for it. Baldwin was convinced that Irwin's presence in the Government would greatly enhance its standing and persuaded a seemingly reluctant Irwin to join it in June 1932, when he returned to the distinctly unprepossessing post of President of the Board of Education. Although technically a demotion, he would really be largely ignoring Education to concentrate on the India Bill. As he explained to his father, 'one would be wrong to shirk'.

He quickly felt the change. After having had powers of life and death over a sub-continent, he soon found that he could not now get the Ministry of Works to replace the curtains in his office without authorization from above. He was not popular with his civil servants at Education, who often complained that they were treated like the indoor servants at Garrowby. Sir Maurice Holmes, a senior official at the Board of Education, resented the way Irwin used to ask him to ring up the barber at his club to book appointments for him.

The Cabinet in which he found himself in June 1932 was far more congenial company than that which he had left seven years earlier. The landslide victory of October 1931 had won the MacDonald/Baldwin alliance no less than 554 seats against an Opposition tally of only sixty-one. Of the old imperialists of 1925, only Lord Hailsham was left as Birkenhead was dead and Amery, Churchill and Salisbury were out. Helping the Government through its endless battles over the India Bill, Irwin was also often used by ministers as an unofficial conduit of advice, information and warnings to Baldwin.

He was a good listener. The correspondence of the period is littered with people's convictions that they had somehow had an effect on a great issue after coming away from a meeting at which Irwin had promised to 'look into it', 'consider it' or, most non-committal, 'think very carefully on it'. He had the politician's knack of letting people feel their contribution was appreciated, especially when it was not. This interest he showed in people's suggestions gave rise to the erroneous belief that he meekly followed the advice of whoever was last in his room. He had no compunction in using the prestige of his rank to the full. Lord David Cecil remembered how Halifax was 'extremely adroit at avoiding a tiresome or impertinent suggestion without being in the least offensive but at the same time conveying a slight snub'.[7]

The Indian question produced two more Round Table Conferences in 1931 and 1932. Then there were Conservative Party Conferences in 1933 and 1934, which produced a strong rank and file backlash against the Leadership. The struggle came finally to an end with the passing of the Government of India Act in August 1935. *Hansard* records fifteen and a half million words of debate on its 473 clauses, and Churchill's bitter and doomed rearguard action left shadows over future politics which stretched far further than the sub-continent.

Irwin, who became Viscount Halifax on the death of his redoubtable ninety-four-year-old father in January 1934, made the disastrous error of trying to translate his Indian experiences of dealing with Congress into policy for dealing with the problems of Europe. He failed to appreciate the fact that Hitler believed in neither negotiation nor non-violence. Every single view Irwin held in India – that ninety per cent of the problem was psychological; that everything should be done not to slight the Indian *amour-propre*; that much of what their politicians said could be safely discounted; that face-to-face negotiations worked; that short-term humiliations were to be endured in the expectation of a general settlement; and that historical inevitability was ranged against him – worked well in the context of India. When Halifax went on to apply precisely these same criteria to his dealings with Nazi Germany, every one of these assumptions was to prove catastrophic.

Simon's former Private Secretary, Thomas Stopford, wrote to Halifax after a meeting they had had on 20 July 1936 to ask: 'Is there not a certain similarity between characteristics of the chief actors in Germany and India – the same strong inferiority complex, the same idealism, the same belief in the divine mission to lead his people and the same difficulty with unruly lieutenants?' Halifax answered: 'I think, with you, that there is much in common between Germany and India, and part of the trouble during recent years has been that the French have been so anxious to maintain things that evoke Germany's inferiority complex.'[8] A regular visitor to Garrowby recalled how Halifax 'enjoyed describing Hitler. He reminded him of Gandhi in that he had a message to deliver which would be heeded, a prophetic message.... He thought him a very nasty little man, but inspired.'[9] A letter from R.A. Butler to the Governor of Madras, Lord Brabourne, of early May 1935 shows Halifax's faith in the value of talks: 'He is interested in the human side of getting people together and would be very interested in getting together with Hitler and squaring him.'[10]

When Butler, who had spent five years in the India Office, joined the Foreign Office in 1938, he certainly saw similarities between his past and present tasks. 'I cannot help contrasting my period at the India Office with the work I do now,' he wrote to Lord Erskine, the Governor of Madras. 'The major problem seems to me the same one, that of dealing with the "status" of a great people, this time Germany – then India.... The main difference between the two nations is that a mild Hindu is probably less alarming than a vigorous Prussian.'[11]

Most inter-war British policy-makers, including Halifax, profoundly misanalysed the reasons for the outbreak of the Great War. They came to conclusions about the nature of international relations which led directly (given Nazi aggression) towards rather than away from war. For Halifax the process began before the war had even ended. Writing to his father in November 1917 he mused:

> Really it comes, doesn't it, to this. We all profess to be fighting to make future wars impossible, or as impossible as can be. How are we to do this? Not by relying as in the past on Treaties, Frontiers, armaments and Balance of Powers. Rather ... we must have some sort of International coercive 'Pact' machinery. But this can only be effective as, and in so far as, it is inspired by a genuine determination for peace on the part of all human beings who compose the various nations of the world. And this determination depends on the extent to which they have learnt the lesson that has been before them since 1914.

It is now clear that British and French policy-makers drew the erroneous conclusions that it had been the encirclement policy towards Germany of 1904–7, the 'destabilizing' alliance system, the armaments race, faulty communications, secret diplomacy, staff talks and strategic plans which had caused the war.[12] This was the moral espoused by Sir Edward Grey's apologia *Twenty-Five Years*, which was published in 1925 and warned: 'The moral is obvious; it is that great armaments lead inevitably to war.' In fact, the lessons of 1910 to 1914 taught quite a different moral from that unquestioningly imbibed by Halifax. Between 1870 and 1914, French defence spending doubled and British trebled, but the 'vigorous Prussians' increased theirs ten-fold. The British Liberal Government had come to office in 1905 committed to disarmament, but their initiatives to that end in 1907 actually only stimulated the German build-up. Grey's magnanimous 1911 disarmament call was taken by the German Naval Attaché in London as evidence of British weakness, which should be capitalized on by further naval building.

In 1914, Germany was a thrusting, highly nationalistic parvenu power and quite clearly the aggressor, but this unpalatable fact was submerged into theories about the 'inherent instabilities of alliances' and the evils of secret diplomacy. These allowed Halifax and others to avert their eyes from the fact of German delinquency. His dreams of 'a genuine determination for peace on the part of all human beings' was as good as useless without a credible deterrent to would-be aggressors. The breast-beating view that 'we were all to blame' was simply not historically accurate. Britain had nothing to gain from war in 1914, whereas Germany was a hegemonic state keen to assert herself and willing to use war to that end. Halifax, who was an MP all through the pre-war period, should have learnt that simple lesson rather than the complex and erroneous ones which blamed 'systems' and 'modes of thinking'.

It was not only in the field of international relations that the wrong lessons were learnt. The 300 tons of bombs dropped on London in the Great War caused 4,820 casualties, which led the Committee of Imperial Defence to extrapolate 600,000 deaths to be anticipated in the first few months of future bombing. The sense of dread felt about another world war then was analogous with the way we feel about a nuclear war today. Far from the classic bellicose admirals and generals of modern left-wing mythology, the inter-war Chiefs of Staff were highly professional. In 1935, they even advised that the Royal Navy would have trouble in defeating the Italian navy. Halifax's inclination to trust the responsible professional naturally increased the less he knew about the subject and he knew very little about military strategy.

Although today it is considered shameful and craven, the policy of appeasement once occupied almost the whole moral high ground. The word was originally synonymous with idealism, magnanimity of the victor and a willingness to right wrongs. Its greatest practitioner and most eloquent defender, the British Ambassador to Berlin from 1937 to 1939, Sir Nevile Henderson, described appeasement in his book, *Water under the Bridges*, as 'the search for just solutions by negotiation in the light of higher reason instead of by resort to force'.[13] It was further boosted by the feeling that after the Great Depression, the world's economic problems could only be solved through international co-operation. A favourite image for international relations used by Halifax was the inevitably equestrian one in which, 'if you stand sufficiently away from a single horse he can give you a very effective kick; but if you are among a dozen horses in a railway truck they cannot hurt you'.[14]

Sheer abhorrence of war, though undoubtedly the driving force behind the policy, was by no means its sole impetus. It is too simple to suggest that appeasement sprang, fully disarmed, out of the head of Britain's Great War experience. It is an extraordinary fact that in common with the other leading appeasers MacDonald, Baldwin, Chamberlain, Hoare, Simon and Thomas Inskip, Halifax had not himself actually seen any combat in the Great War, whereas such anti-appeasers as Churchill, Anthony Eden, Sir Roger Keyes, Duff Cooper, Louis Spears and Harold Macmillan all had.

Halifax almost personified the moral side of the policy of appeasement, and the opposition had no one to approach him for respectability or general spiritual rectitude. Typical of its genre is the letter which a vicar wrote to Butler after Eden's resignation in February 1938, which read, 'Nobody can say this is a defeat for idealism with Lord Halifax and you in the saddle now.'[15]

His apologists have claimed that the mild-mannered Halifax's Christianity left him somehow incapable of comprehending Hitler's special depravity and he was thus unable to appreciate the threat posed. This, as well as taking Halifax's other-worldliness too much at face value, supposes that his career to date had been simply an extension of his privileged upbringing. In fact, Halifax had seen plenty of evil, not least in the communal strife which culminated in the massacre at Cawnpore. His profound anti-Bolshevism kept him alive to the crimes of Lenin, Trotsky and Stalin. He knew too of the cruelties of Atatürk, Chandra Bose and Sinn Fein. As a historian he was perfectly aware of his country's record against Philip of Spain, Louis XIV, Napoleon and the Kaiser. Nobody who commanded burial details in the Great War needed teaching about the ever-present nature of evil, least of all someone with such deep-rooted a belief in Original Sin. The Permanent Under-Secretary at the Foreign Office, Sir Alexander Cadogan, said he believed 'that Halifax *did* realize what sort of a monster Hitler was. Halifax would give a look of pained surprise at each enormity that Hitler committed, but he fully realized how enormous they were.'[16]

Although one might have expected a stream of sermon-like speeches taking 'Blessed are the Peace-makers' as his text, Halifax's religious convictions played little or no part in his day-to-day politics. On those occasions when church affairs overlapped with politics, when Pastor Niemöller was arrested for example, or when the question arose of an alliance with atheist Russia, Halifax's stance altered not one iota. It would be tempting to portray a kindly monk turning the other cheek to Hitler, but it was simply not so. His great friend and confessor, Fr Ted Talbot, Superior of the Mirfield Community in Yorkshire, wrote to a mutual friend about how

> Edward's view of religion is completely transcendental like Job's. He expects nothing from God, he hopes nothing material, he would not understand 'guidance' or 'being charged' in Dr Buchman's sense. The idea that ... 'I have left it all to God' would ... strike him as

incomprehensible. His religion is one in which the soul is consistently paying tribute to its creator; worship, giving, paying homage, rendering oneself in perfect fullness back to the Divine Life is his philosophy. Whether or not that happens to make you a better man would strike him as quite irrelevant ... he is a little inhuman.[17]

Appeasement has been described as 'a policy pursued towards one nation so as to allow a tougher stance against another'.[18] It was by no means a monolithic phenomenon applied from the 1920s to 1939 towards Germany, Italy and Japan equally. It had endless subtleties, accelerations, reversals and changes of emphasis. After the Great War, the British Empire looked at its most impressive. Its bounds were set wider territorially under George V than they had been even under Queen Victoria. Nevertheless, the great swathes of pink on the schoolroom map concealed the fact of an over-stretched and declining organism, with heavy commitments all over the globe, particularly in Palestine and the Far East, which coincided with a dearth in the financial, commercial, military and human resources necessary to maintain them. Avoidance of a war which would inevitably bring these deficiencies into the open had to be the first duty of the managers of imperial decline.

In domestic politics appeasement was a ruthless policy ruthlessly applied. Critics within the Conservative Party were harried mercilessly by David Margesson and the Whips. Baldwin's successor, Neville Chamberlain, came from the toughest family in British politics and his record of anti-socialism was second to none. His caustic and unrelenting attacks were loathed by Labour. The Chamberlains had built an electoral machine in Birmingham which in 1931 and 1935 had won all the city's twelve seats. The huge popularity the policy enjoyed with the electorate can partly be explained by the way it brought together so many diverse constituencies: anti-communists who saw Germany as a bulwark against Soviet expansionism; League of Nations enthusiasts; imperialists who saw Germany as no threat to the Empire; ex-servicemen who believed that after the last war nobody could possibly want to start another; pacifists of all hues; those who regretted and were embarrassed by the virulence of Great War anti-German propaganda; businessmen who demanded a placid international scene for trade; a very few fascist sympathizers; and the vast numbers of ordinary people to whom magnanimity in victory seemed only decent common sense. Germany was not seen as an ancestral enemy of Britain's in the way that France has been in the past. The British Royal Family came from there, and only a century before had it not been for the Prussians Wellington might have lost Waterloo. Anthony Powell observed in his *Dance to the Music of Time* that to be anti-French and pro-German in the 1920s was considered the height of progressive sophistication and cleverness.

Just as membership of the French Resistance suddenly swelled after VE-Day, so if everyone who professed himself an anti-appeaser in the 1950s actually had been one in the 1930s, the policy could not have lasted a day. Scapegoats were required to show it to have been the work of a small clique rather than the consensus view of both ruling parties for the best part of two decades. Robert Boothby's check-list is quite comprehensive and typical. After castigating Chamberlain's adviser Sir Horace Wilson, Boothby says of appeasement that it had 'Geoffrey Dawson, its Secretary-General; Montagu Norman, its Treasurer; Cliveden which constituted, with All Souls, its GHQ. Between them they conducted us to disaster.'[19]

The reality was more prosaic. Sir Horace Wilson, despite Butler's description of him as 'the uncrowned ruler of England',[20] was really only a highly competent civil servant off whom Chamberlain bounced ideas. Who today criticizes Churchill for surrounding himself with such shadowy and equally unelected figures as Desmond Morton or 'Prof' Lindemann? Just as all Prime Ministers have a Horace Wilson or T.J. Jones, so also do these people inevitably attain bogeyman status. Halifax said he only ever found Wilson most helpful and treated him in much the same way as he had his civil servants at the Board of Education. Roger Makins, who was an acting First Secretary in the Foreign Office in 1939, explained to Halifax's official biographer that 'Halifax tolerated Wilson because he was not concerned with minor characters'.[21] Wilson, who had married beneath himself, was hard to work for and the Private Secretaries at No. 10 adored it when he brought his wife to official receptions and she called jam 'preserves'.[22]

The most cursory glance at the Cliveden visitors' books shows how eclectic was the Astors' taste in house guests. Nancy Astor, herself a Conservative MP, invited socialists such as Wedgwood Benn and Ellen Wilkinson, celebrities like Bernard Shaw and Charlie Chaplin and famous personalities such as T.E. Lawrence and Maxim Litvinov down to her palatial Buckinghamshire weekends. The Royal Family stayed there in April 1938. If there were any recurring names, they were either Americans or old members of the Milner Kindergarten; otherwise the books are merely a *Who's Who* of 1920s' and 1930s' political and social life. The myth of Cliveden being a nest of appeasers, let alone pro-Nazis, is exploded by the regular return to its pages of the signatures of Eden, Macmillan, Duff Cooper and, indeed, Boothby himself. The Halifaxes used to visit Cliveden during Royal Ascot, when Lady Astor took large parties to the races.

After succeeding Grey as Chancellor of Oxford in 1933, Halifax rarely visited All Souls apart from the annual Gaudy and the election of new Fellows on All Saints Day. It is absurd to suggest that the leading All Souls Fellows involved in appeasement – Halifax, Dawson and Simon – were influenced in their thinking to any significant extent by the arguments they heard at the College high table. A Fellow of the day, Sir Patrick Reilly, thinks, 'It would be truer to say, I am sure, that they influenced All Souls than that All Souls influenced them.'[23] As with Cliveden guests, so with All Souls Fellows: their very independent-mindedness should explode the myth of any sense of a 'set' or collective thinking amongst either group. Indeed, at the height of the Munich crisis, the most hawkish advice given to Halifax came from the Warden of All Souls.[24]

Montagu Norman, the Governor of the Bank of England, has long been considered a pillar of appeasement. His papers show him merely to have shared the belief that more and better trade with Germany would humanize Nazism and open it to the civilizing effect of cosmopolitan competition. The suggestion that an unholy alliance of amateurs and non-politicians such as Wilson, All Souls, Cliveden, etc. 'conducted us to disaster' is a fantasy required by a later age to shift blame and excuse itself. Indeed if anything, it is remarkable how little influence bona-fide pressure groups, the press, the Opposition and even the Government's own backbenchers had either on Halifax's opinions or government policy in the years before Munich.

November 1934 saw Churchill warn of the German air menace in the House of Commons. To many parliamentarians this looked like yet another of Churchill's hobby-horses, designed primarily to embarrass the Government. Baldwin, on the other hand, was then at the height of his powers and Halifax was his blue-eyed boy. Countrymen both, they had a deep affinity with the British countryside. 'I often think', Halifax once wrote to a sympathetic Baldwin, 'that the dilatory habits of farmers, that drive the bustling politician and townsman to despair, are due to their instinctive acceptance of the unhurried and unhurrying ways of Nature.'[25] In a note inviting Baldwin to Garrowby, Halifax was moved almost to poetry: 'Let us walk over a Yorkshire wold and smell the East wind and watch the gulls in from the sea following the plough on the bleak tops!'[26] James Stuart, who entered the Commons in 1923 and was one of Baldwin's Whips in 1935, remembered how 'Baldwin relied on Halifax for advice. He was as close to Halifax as anyone in politics, closer in spirit than Neville Chamberlain. He was the *éminence grise* to Baldwin when Neville was the executive.'[27]

In *Fulness of Days* Halifax drew attention to a very different Baldwin from the stolid, pipe-smoking industrialist; one who had a 'romantic, almost mystical streak in his composition'. The extent of his feeling for his master can be seen from the note Halifax sent him on his retirement from the Premiership in May 1937: 'A good deal of the savour of political life so far as I am concerned goes out with you – for the main pleasure of these last years has been the fact that it was being done with you. I think you have taught me more about life than anybody except my father.'[28] Halifax could not have learnt politics from a better practitioner of the art.

In October 1932, Halifax wrote to Simon, then Foreign Secretary, calling for the reduction in the size of British battleships to that allowed to Germany by Versailles, and concluding, 'I am in no doubt that you are on the spot when you judge the disarmament business to be vital to the Government.... A bold move would rally many depressed forces.'[29] July 1934 saw him writing to Baldwin 'for the sake of my own conscience' to say, 'I shd myself hope that in yr Air Statement you might have included words in the sense that (a) we shd continue to hope and strive for disarmament and (b) if our hopes at any time be realized our programme will, of course, be reconsidered.' Baldwin followed his advice almost to the letter. Significantly he was one of the ministers chosen to meet the various deputations organized by Churchill to protest against the state of the nation's defences in July and November 1936 when even the Service ministers were not present.[30]

When Baldwin succeeded MacDonald in June 1935, Halifax gladly exchanged Education for the Army, becoming Secretary of State for War. His five-month spell there was essentially a watching brief until the general election was safely won. It did not need very acute political antennae to tell him that the whisper of a return to 'great armaments' spelt electoral suicide and Baldwin hoped that Halifax's downbeat manner would help to take the steam out of this sensitive area. Lieutenant-General Sir Henry Pownall took a cynical view of the appointment: 'I suppose it is just a stop-gap until they get the Election off their chests. No doubt they will refer to Sub-Committees everything they possibly can over the next few months so as to avoid taking decisions. We shan't get any drive into proceedings with this stale gang.'[31] So it was to prove. Halifax's decisive intervention at the Committee of Imperial Defence was to challenge the Chiefs of Staff assertion that Britain needed an increased pace of rearmament. In December 1935, he asked rhetorically:

> Are we in fact to judge the situation so serious that everything has to give way to military reconditioning of our Defence Forces? Such a conclusion in fact appears to me to rest on premises not only of the inevitability but of a certain degree of certainty as to the early imminence of war, which I am not prepared to accept.

The consensus of the 1920s had been for swingeing reductions in defence expenditure, across all three Services. In 1922, the Coalition fell partly because of its sabre-rattling against a relatively insignificant power like revolutionary Turkey. By 1933, the East Fulham by-election turned a Tory majority of 14,521 into a pro-disarmament Labour majority of 4,820. At the end of the year, defence expenditure fell to £100 million, leaving naval manpower at its lowest for forty years and the RAF only the sixth largest air force in the world. When the time did come to rearm, there was simply not the infrastructure for industry adequately to respond. The years of neglect and nil construction led to an unwillingness to invest in unprofitable areas and a run-down of the specialist armaments industry. Halifax must bear a heavy part of the responsibility for this dangerous state of affairs.

Three weeks after Halifax arrived at the War Office, the League of Nations Union announced the results of their Peace ballot. These were interesting not for the huge majorities in favour of 'Peace' – it could hardly have been otherwise – but the fact that eleven and a half million people took part. For their well-meaning diligence and single-mindedness in a slightly ridiculous pursuit, the League of Nations enthusiasts of the 1930s resemble the modern-day train-spotter. Japan's unprovoked invasion of Manchuria in September 1931 should have tolled the League's knell, but the lip-service politicians continued to pay to it allowed it to continue complicating international relations until the outbreak of war. It was only ever wishful thinking that nations would commit troops for the cause of peace and in 1932 Irwin's father echoed the sentiments of many when he told his son how 'my sympathies are with the Japanese. I think nothing could be more disadvantageous than a quarrel with them and I don't see what business we have to interfere.'[32] His son only ever expressed reservations about the League to close friends like its champion Lord Cecil of Chelwood. In December 1936, he told Cecil frankly that with Great Powers like Germany, America and Japan outside it, he thought that the League was becoming a mockery.[33] It was not a statement he would make publicly, however.

It was Chamberlain who finally blew the gaff by pointing out that the League sanctions on Italy after the invasion of Abyssinia constituted 'the very midsummer of madness'. The desire to be all things to all nations emasculated the League and rendered it a mere talking-shop. On its agenda the week war broke out in 1939 was a discussion on plans for the European standardization of level-crossings. Overall, the League of Nations tended to do Britain more harm than good. Not only did it harm relations with Italy, but it fostered the belief that 'world opinion' mattered. It gave the dictators a forum in which to look strong without giving lustre to the Allies' essential decency.

Baldwin's National Government won another landslide victory in the November 1935 election, which left Labour with a mere 154 seats. Halifax became Lord Privy Seal and Leader of the House of Lords. Free of departmental duties, he could range across the whole gamut of government policy, but he decided to interest himself primarily in foreign affairs. It was in this arena that, within weeks of the election victory, a storm arose which but for Halifax's ruthlessness could well have engulfed the Government.

8

Eminence Grise

The Chiefs of Staff continually reiterated one central message to ministers throughout the 1930s: that the Empire, supported by France but not by America, could not defeat Germany, Italy and Japan simultaneously. At least one of the three had to be detached for as long as it took to fight the others. By 1934, it was clear that Germany was, in the words of the Defence Requirements Committee, 'the ultimate potential enemy'.[1] Although attempts to revive the old Japanese alliance were periodically considered, it was obvious that in the Far East British and Japanese interests were too starkly opposed to permit any lasting entente.

For her geographical position alone Italy cried out for Franco-British wooing. To the north lay Austria, with whom Mussolini liked to believe he had influence and in whose continued independence from Germany of which Italy was understood to be interested. To the west lay a France vulnerable in the south-east should her forces be committed against the Germans in the north. To the south Italy straddled British supply lines to Egypt, India and the Far East. These strategic considerations, combined with a disinclination to take seriously Mussolini's rather theatrical and bombastic version of fascism, led the wooers to make serious advances. It was a considerable triumph when, on 14 April 1935 at Stresa, Italy succumbed and established with them a common front against the nascent Third Reich.

It did not last long. Mussolini's invasion of Abyssinia on 2 October 1935, though criminal and slightly absurd, did not affect any vital British interests, but the public outcry against the unprovoked assault persuaded the Government to join in League sanctions against Italy. These served to alienate Italy from 'the Stresa Front' and draw her closer to Germany, without at the same time significantly affecting her ability to conquer the backward African country. Many high-sounding phrases were trotted out during the November 1935 general election campaign. Of all the subjects

56

mentioned by National Government candidates in their election addresses, support for the League of Nations came out top, appearing in ninety per cent of them. When the news broke that the Foreign Ministers of Britain and France had concluded a Pact which circumvented the League and awarded Italy half of Abyssinia, there was a huge outpouring of righteous indignation. This pragmatic solution was wrecked when the British and French publics indulged in one of their periodic bouts of moral outrage. The deal smacked too much of Machiavellian secret diplomacy and accommodation, and the press in both countries demanded the resignations of Samuel Hoare and Pierre Laval as well as the distancing of themselves by the Governments from the Pact signed on their behalf.

Whilst the British Cabinet had not actually approved the details of the Pact – the negotiations had been conducted by Hoare in Paris – there is little doubt that they would have applauded the outcome had there been no sudden campaign against it. With Halifax due to make an official statement in the Lords the next day, the Cabinet met on the morning of 18 December to decide on a line to follow. Halifax tended to use a ponderous circumlocution in his speeches and Cabinet contributions. His language was usually peppered with qualifying clauses and linguistic double-checks, but at that Cabinet there was no such obfuscation. He waited until the end of the long discussion, during which it became clear that no one was willing to stab Hoare in the back. Unless someone said something Baldwin's own position would be irretrievably weakened. Halifax, who had no desire to face the Lords the next day empty-handed, and whose political debts to his master were legion, therefore announced that he

> had come to the conclusion that while it was possible to make a case against the worst attacks, this could not be done without admitting a mistake. So far as the Government were concerned he would like to make a plain statement of what had happened. . . . But he thought the Foreign Secretary ought to resign. He was affected by another consideration . . . that much more was at stake, namely, the whole moral position of the Government before the world. If the Prime Minister were to lose his personal position, one of our national anchors would have dragged.[2]

This gave the signal for other hitherto silent ministers such as J.H. Thomas, William Ormsby-Gore and Walter Elliot to twist the knife around. However, in the opinion of Hoare's biographer, it was Halifax's contribution which had proved decisive.[3] Yet writing to Chamberlain on Boxing Day, Halifax professed himself 'still puzzled, though, by the condemnation meted out to proposals that were not . . . so *frightfully* different from those put forward by the Committee of Five [of the League]'. Nevertheless, when six months later Hoare returned as First Lord of the Admiralty, Halifax 'criticized Baldwin sharply for yielding to Hoare's importunity'.[4]

On Hoare's resignation, the thirty-eight-year-old Anthony Eden became Foreign Secretary. Eden, another Etonian and North Countryman, was a distant relative of Halifax and the next year his wife's step-brother, the Earl of Feversham, married Halifax's daughter, Anne. Halifax was seconded to Eden at the Foreign Office in an unofficial capacity, partly to take some weight off the Foreign Secretary and partly to keep an eye on him for Baldwin. Eden later wrote that Halifax 'did not have a room, nor a Private Secretary nor any official position, but he eased some of my burden, especially on my brief spells of leave. We had long been friends and I was grateful for an arrangement which never caused me any anxiety, even when we did not agree about the decisions to be taken.'[5]

Ever keeping the Chiefs of Staff's strictures in mind, Halifax tended to provide a *via media* between the *realpolitik* of Baldwin and Chamberlain and the anti-dictator pessimism of Eden. In one such discussion, in May 1936 when the Cabinet was considering dropping oil sanctions against Italy, Halifax proposed 'to keep Signor Mussolini guessing for a time ... avoid any melodramatic action: go as slow as possible, be as unprovocative as possible and conduct most of the business behind the scenes'.[6] This is vintage Halifax from the Cabinet minutes of the period, mixing caution and pragmatism in equal measures whilst all the time attempting to maximize the degree of consensus within the Cabinet.

The Italian dispute was intimately bound up with the next crisis. Mussolini had threatened that should the League make sanctions bite, he would leave it and denounce the 1925 Locarno Treaty, which guaranteed the security of France's and Belgium's borders. Taking this threat as his cue, on 7 March 1936, Hitler ordered his troops to march into the Rhineland, hitherto a demilitarized zone under the provisions of the Versailles and Locarno Treaties. In what was to become standard practice, Hitler craftily accompanied this flagrant violation of treaties with various sops to confuse and weaken his opponents. He offered a twenty-five-year non-aggression pact to France and Belgium, an air pact and the re-entry of Germany to the League, and generally protested his 'unchangeable longing for a real pacification of Europe'. On 9 March, the Cabinet instructed Eden and Halifax to confer with the other Locarno powers in Paris 'to bring about a meeting of the Powers concerned to consider the constructive proposals of the German Government'.[7]

In Paris, Eden and Halifax found a united Franco-Belgian front, which wanted to call Hitler's bluff, believing the Germans would not go to war for the Rhineland. This shocked the Foreign Secretary and his lieutenant, who told the Cabinet on their return two days later that 'our policy of trying for a negotiation was still the right one and the only hope of securing a peaceful outcome',[8] adding that they ought to have 'a reasonable regard for the position into which Germany had got herself'. Eden rejected French Foreign Minister Pierre Flandin's prescient warning that, 'if the German challenge was not taken up now, a much more formidable situation would arise in two years' time'.[9] Halifax's sole contribution to the discussion was to say that any direct approach to Germany should be kept secret from the French. He then travelled to Geneva to attempt to sell the policy to the League.

As MPs returned from their constituencies to Westminster after the weekend, it became clear that the mood against doing anything concrete had stiffened. Baldwin feared war 'would probably only result in Germany going Bolshevik'[10] and there were no discussions in Cabinet about German long-term motives. Resentment instead centred on France, which Baldwin considered 'unfriendly ... to put us in this dilemma'.[11] No one in British politics except Churchill wanted to call Hitler's bluff. The 'anti-appeaser' Secretary for War, Duff Cooper, told the German Ambassador on 8 March that the British public 'did not care "two hoots" about the Germans reoccupying their own territory'.[12] We now know that the German commanders had orders immediately to withdraw if they met any resistance. Hitler's regime may not have survived the humiliation. In his autobiography Halifax blithely commented: 'I have little doubt that if we had then told Hitler bluntly to go back, his powers for future and larger mischief would have been broken.'

Ever the internationalist, Halifax designed a compromise plan under which an international force occupied the zone to a distance of twenty miles either side of the Rhine. Flandin, realizing it was the most he was likely to get out of the British, reluctantly acquiesced. Joachim von Ribbentrop, Hitler's roving envoy, flew out on the afternoon of the 18th to meet Eden and Halifax at 8 p.m. At that meeting he soon established that no military intervention was in the offing – the occupation had taken place a full eleven days previously – so Hitler turned Halifax's plan down.

Halifax's political 'feel' made him realize early on in the crisis that war with Germany over the Rhineland was simply not feasible. The Chiefs of Staff thought war would be 'a disaster for which the Services with their existing commitments in the Mediterranean are totally unprepared'. Labour, the Liberals and the Dominions were against it, South Africa calling instead for 'new appeasement'. Lord Dunglass's report for Baldwin of a meeting of 200–250 National Government MPs on 17 March noted that Hoare's doubts that Britain was even capable of turning Germany out of the zone, and his statement that there was a 'strong pro-German feeling in this country', 'had the support of almost the whole meeting'.[13]

On 1 April, Ribbentrop met Halifax and Eden again, this time to urge them to persuade the French to accept the spurious German 'Peace Plan', which spoke of 'sacred treaties' and 'concrete work to secure European peace'. In fact, the only concrete work being undertaken by Germany was the surreptitious and illegal building of fortifications on the Rhine. That same evening Ribbentrop telegraphed Berlin to report that, 'Both ministers seemed impressed by the plan ... though still murmuring about there being difficulties.'[14] There then began the near-farcical process by which Hitler was sent questionnaires enquiring which of the various treaties Germany had signed he still intended to honour. Despite dozens of meetings and endless debates on the wording of these questionnaires, they came to nothing. Hitler was not to be drawn on his future intentions.

July 1936 saw the outbreak of civil war in Spain and earnest Anglo-French discussions as to how it could either be foreshortened or at least prevented from escalating into a general European conflict. The resulting policy of non-intervention, freely entered into and equally freely disregarded by Russia, Germany and Italy, was agreed upon at a conference in London in September. The Non-Intervention Committee met well over a hundred times and achieved nothing more than the maintenance of the diplomatic fiction that the civil war was solely an internal Spanish affair. Halifax later admitted that he doubted 'whether a single man or gun less reached either side in the war as a result of its activities'.[15] In a meeting of ministers on 8 January 1937, he pronounced that 'the difficulty was that the Powers did not trust each other'.[16] To inform ministers in early 1937 that Germany and Russia did not trust each other was nothing short of platitudinous and it was such comments that gave rise to accusations of gullibility. As the civil war progressed, Britain found herself in more and deeper embarrassments as Nationalist forces attacked and sank merchantmen flying the Red Ensign.

Eden enjoyed considerable autonomy in the realm of foreign affairs partly because they bored Baldwin and partly because from autumn 1936 the Prime Minister was increasingly occupied with the implications of the King's affair with the American divorcee, Mrs Simpson. Halifax's own part in the Abdication crisis seems to have been surprisingly small. As a confidant of the Royal Family, a senior lay figure in the Church of England, a Cabinet minister without portfolio and a close personal as well as political friend of Baldwin, he might be expected to have played some sort of role in it. Yet, beyond his normal duties as a minister, there is no real evidence of any major involvement; indeed, at the first Cabinet in which 'the King's Matter' was officially brought to ministers' attention, he was the only person absent. He had certainly had an early enough warning of the problem; shortly after Edward VIII's succession, the Duchess of Sutherland invited the Halifaxes down to Sutton Place, near Guildford, to a weekend house party. The other guests included the King, Lady Cunard and Mr and Mrs Simpson. When in the evening the Duke of Sutherland showed his magic lantern slide show of his travels to Petra, Lady Halifax overheard the King whisper to Mrs Simpson, 'That is lovely; we must put it down for foreign travel.'[17]

Halifax probably saw the Abdication crisis as a messy and painful business from which little good but a great deal of harm might result, and thus decided to distance himself as far from the public controversies as possible. However, the comment in his memoirs that he saw Baldwin 'regularly through those gloomy days and learnt at close quarters how much King and Country and Commonwealth were indebted to him',[18] as well as two large boxes stuffed full of newspaper cuttings about the crisis amongst his papers, bear witness to the personal interest he took in it. That he did figure fairly early on is testified by a letter from his old friend and Queen Mary's Private Secretary, Sir Gerald Chichester, written two days after the Abdication, which reads: 'Her Majesty remembers with what sympathy you spoke about this unhappy subject at Buckingham Palace a few months ago.'[19] As early as 8 April 1936, Sir John Reith's diary recorded that there was a plan that 'the PM, Speaker and Halifax would visit the King over his "private life" affairs', but nothing came of it.[20]

There can be no doubt about Halifax's stance. His attitude towards divorce was almost that of his father, who had thought that remarriage after divorce was morally indistinguishable from bigamy. The other joint master of the Middleton Hunt, Lord Grimthorpe, was the only divorcé to cross Garrowby's portals until after the Second World War, and only then after some considerable family deliberation on the issue. The second Viscount believed murder to be better than divorce 'as it did less damage to the moral side of the family unit'. When Lord Devon remarried, Halifax père used to refer to the new Lady Devon as 'the woman who considers herself to be in the position of his wife'. Disappointment in the new King's character, horror at the idea of a morganatic marriage and a general disdain for Americans all served to confirm Halifax in the opinion that should the King persevere in his intention to marry Mrs Simpson, he would have to abdicate.

On 30 November, he reported to Baldwin Eden's view that 'action should be taken as soon as possible', adding, 'I am inclined to agree.... I shd have much hoped it might have been possible to get the Cabinet to take a definite decision on Wednesday [2 December]. I am, the more I think of it, afraid of delay.' The very next day, the *Yorkshire Post* reported an address by the Bishop of Bradford in which he said he wished the King would show 'more positive signs of his awareness of God's grace'. This unprecedented public criticism of the King was taken as the signal for Fleet Street to open the flood-gates of public comment and criticism. The Yorkshire connection of Bishop Blunt and Arthur Mann's *Yorkshire Post* led Sir Frederick Leith-Ross to insinuate that Halifax 'planted' Blunt's bombshell.[21] There is nothing whatever to substantiate this, although Mann also 'rather naturally assumed that [Blunt] had been inspired by higher authority to speak as he had done'.[22]

The large demonstrations in Trafalgar Square and Piccadilly were the background to the opinion Halifax later expressed to the Lord Chancellor,

Lord Hailsham: 'I do not believe that we could ever have restored the prestige of the Crown without a change, and I do not feel that any of us would have felt secure against repetition of grave trouble if we had weathered the storm.'[23] The day after seeing the Abdication Bill safely through the Lords, Halifax wrote to Hailsham to say, 'The more I reflect upon it the more cause for thankfulness I feel there is in the matter having turned out as it has.'[24] He was understandably less sanguine in a letter to Queen Mary of the same day: 'Ever since Your Majesty was good enough to speak to me at Buckingham Palace some time ago, I have had the anxiety on my mind ... and with all my heart I wish that it had been possible to prevent things moving as they so unhappily have done.'[25] Halifax played his hand expertly; Lady Halifax became the new Queen's Lady-in-Waiting, and yet during the war the Duke of Windsor stayed with Halifax and confided in him at length, even using him as a conduit for messages to his family.

Nineteen thirty-six did see two happy events for Halifax, however, when his daughter, Anne, married the Yorkshire grandee the Earl of Feversham and his eldest son, Charles, married Ruth Primrose, the grand-daughter of the Earl of Rosebery.

With the crisis over and the new King crowned, Baldwin retired to make way for his long-time heir apparent. At Neville Chamberlain's first Cabinet meeting on 2 June, the two men who had for fourteen years held the Premiership in turns were gone. There was a spirit of optimism and new brooms about the Ministry and a widespread feeling that the wise old Chamberlain and the glamorous Foreign Secretary, who was young enough to be his son, would lead the country to Peace. Halifax moved into MacDonald's place as Lord President of the Council and continued to lead the Lords. He had long been close to Chamberlain politically and greatly admired him – there was much in that vain, calculating old tough to admire – but he was never as personally friendly with the new Premier as he had been with Baldwin, 'the old man'. An MP of the day, Godfrey Nicholson, summed up part of Chamberlain's problem by reference to his father and half-brother: 'Joe was worshipped, Austen was a great gentleman, but poor Neville got the ugly duckling treatment.'[26] Neville was determined that as the only Chamberlain finally to make it to the Premiership, he was going to master foreign affairs better than had the other two.

Under the new regime, Halifax's understudy role at the Foreign Office subtly changed. Chamberlain began to flex his foreign policy muscles in a way Baldwin never had and Halifax instinctively sided with the man who wished simultaneously to rebuild Stresa and appease Germany. At the very first Cabinet of 1937, 'some discussion took place as to the desires of Lord Halifax for improving contacts with Germany'.[27] Later that year, after the cancellation of a visit to Britain by the German Foreign Minister, Baron von Neurath, Halifax suggested writing instead to the Italians to try to effect an entente. On the 27th, a suitably phrased personal letter was sent to Mussolini by Chamberlain. But Eden was not so sure; in early August he wrote to Halifax from the Solent that, 'we should also go slow about Anglo-Italian rapprochement ... the Italians will try and push us into concessions, or the promises of them'. After seeing Eden, Halifax wrote to Chamberlain on the 15th, 'very much for your ears alone', warning him 'entre nous' that in the coming discussions Eden would be inclined to try 'marking time'.[28] He then detailed the areas, such as Spanish shipping, in which Eden was planning to take the offensive. Before too long Halifax became the involuntary catalyst for the eventual break up between Prime Minister and Foreign Secretary.

On 13 October 1937, the Editor-in-Chief of *Field* magazine wrote on behalf of Prince Lowenstein, the President of the German Hunting Association, inviting Halifax, ostensibly in his capacity as MFH, to the International Hunting Exhibition soon to open in Berlin. Chamberlain latched on to this invitation, deciding that it provided a perfect opportunity for the sort of relaxed and informal face-to-face meeting with the Nazi leadership which he believed could achieve much. By late October, he was writing to his sisters that the visit could be the start of nothing less than 'the far-reaching plans I have in mind for the appeasement of Europe and Asia and for the ultimate check to the mad armaments race'.[29]

9

'Counsels of Despair'

The genesis of the idea for a Halifax visit to Hitler can be traced back to conversations Baldwin had with his adviser, Tom Jones, in May 1936. On 2 June, at a lunch at the Carlton Club, Ribbentrop had told Jones that 'if the attempt to secure S.B. failed, the sooner Halifax met the Führer the better'.[1] Halifax had spoken to Butler of his ambition of 'squaring Hitler' back in May 1935, and the fact that he was judged to have done well in the Rhineland negotiations added to his qualifications for the Berlin visit. Any approach from a more senior minister might commit Britain too far, and Eden's well-publicized aversion to dictators made another visit from him inconceivable.

Halifax's reply to the *Field*, which he cleared with Eden on the 14th, was that he would be free on 9 and 10 November 'to see something in the way of German sport'.[2] It was not until late October that Chamberlain had fully formulated his 'far-reaching plans'. After Chamberlain explained them to Sir Nevile Henderson, the Ambassador wrote to Halifax on 29 October to say that

> the way the PM put it to me yesterday your visit takes on a quite different aspect. And in its new light I am infinitely more enthusiastic. ... I hope you will speak as you yourself suggested to me about Nazism in general, quite apart from the political side. I think that very important and a big part of the 'understanding' side of the business.[3]

Concomitant with Henderson's hopes were Eden's doubts. According to his autobiography, Eden told Halifax in late October to 'confine himself to a warning comment about Austria and Czechoslovakia'.[4]

After the war Halifax believed that 'A legend has been established that my going to Berlin was the decision of Chamberlain, bent on appeasement, against the wishes of a robust Anthony Eden.' He therefore wrote to the

Foreign Office ostensibly to 'assist the historian of the future to be accurate',[5] and claimed that on receiving the offer to shoot foxes in Pomerania he
had met Eden and Chamberlain at an official dinner for the Yugoslav
Foreign Minister and 'pooh-poohed the idea, but he (A.E.) stuck to it ... as
a result of their (A.E. and N.C.) joint exhortation to me to take the opportunity,' he agreed to go.[6]

On 6 November, there arrived another message from Berlin asking
whether Halifax could instead come to Hitler's home, the Berghof, high
above the Austrian mountain village of Berchtesgaden. He was invited for
either 14 to 17 November or to Berlin some time after the 25th. It was later
alleged that 'Hitler wished to show his power by dragging Halifax the
length of Germany.'[7] The alternative to travelling to Berchtesgaden was to
wait until after the Exhibition had ended. Eden cabled Henderson on the
8th to say that 'a visit by a leading Cabinet minister to Berlin specifically to
meet Herr Hitler would arouse such publicity and speculation as would
almost certainly defeat its purpose'. The fiction of the Exhibition as the
main reason for the visit had to be adhered to, despite its looking mangier
by the day.

The arguments that had been going on in the Foreign Office ever since it
had dawned on the officials there that Halifax was going to do more in
Berlin than merely admire vast stuffed moose heads, surfaced on the 7th. At
a meeting at Eden's house after office hours, the senior Foreign Office
politicians and civil servants got together to discuss policy towards Germany in general and the Halifax visit in particular. Oliver Harvey, Eden's
Private Secretary, related in his diary how, 'we all favoured approach to
Hitler and offer of a bilateral declaration of our policy, although none of us
like the idea of the Halifax visit ... approach regarding Czechoslovakia
could also be made (i.e. possibility of a German–French–English guarantee if Czechoslovakia gave autonomy to Sudeten)'.[8]

The Sudeten problem is easily summarized: at the Versailles redrawing
of the map of Europe after the Great War an entirely new country, Czechoslovakia, was brought into being which had within its borders roughly
three million German-speaking former citizens of the Austro-Hungarian
Empire. Although these Sudetendeutsche had never been part of Germany,
they increasingly looked towards Berlin rather than Vienna. Hitler, posing
as the protector of the Aryan Sudeten minority against the Slav majority in
Czechoslovakia, made increasingly threatening gestures intended to
encourage the Sudetens to agitate to join his Reich.

The cabal who met in Eden's house on 7 November – Eden himself,
Oliver Harvey, Rex Leeper, Sir Alexander Cadogan, Orme Sargent, William Strang and Lord 'Bobbety' Cranborne – constituted almost the entire
decision-making elite of the Foreign Office. According to Harvey, they were
all in favour of sounding Hitler out, and even of putting pressure on the
Czechs over the Sudetenland. They were wary of Halifax going to Berlin

not only because, as Harvey feared, he would produce 'a plausible and vague account of Hitler which would have a soporific effect on the Cabinet',[9] but also because he was not one of them: he was too close to the Prime Minister and could not be relied upon to put over a Foreign Office rather than a No. 10 line. Nevertheless, on 10 November Henderson conveyed a direct offer of a meeting at Berchtesgaden on 18 and 19 November, which was accepted.

There then followed a row over the wording of the joint Anglo-German communiqué as to which side had initiated the visit. Eden complained incessantly to Harvey, who in turn submitted memoranda urging him to threaten resignation, but Eden 'finally and reluctantly agreed' to the time and place of the visit, whilst reserving the right to sulk. For all his film-star good looks and brilliant reputation, Eden was a highly strung worrier, much inclined to vanity. Harvey condemned the 'precipitancy with which the PM and Halifax have pressed on with this visit ... knowing that A.E. did not favour it, [and which] shows shocking lack of solidarity and even of common decent behaviour'.[10]

On 13 November news of the proposed visit appeared in the Beaverbrook-owned *Evening Standard*, complete with the additional suggestion that,

> The British Government have information from Berlin that Herr Hitler is ready, if he receives the slightest encouragement, to offer to Great Britain a 10 year 'Truce' in the colonial issue.... In return for this agreement Hitler would expect the British Government to leave him a free hand in Central Europe.

This falsehood precipitated a bitter press battle in which the visit was blown up into a major initiative. The Foreign Office denials of any change in policy were ignored. F.A.Voigt of the *Manchester Guardian* believed that the *Evening Standard* story was planted by Vansittart or one of his supporters in the Foreign Office, who had been manoeuvring against the visit. Vansittart had long opposed any appeasement of Germany whatsoever and leaking the news of the visit in such a disobliging manner was clearly an attempt to pull the red carpet from under Halifax's feet. Vansittart only ever made the minimum of effort towards Halifax, once telling a journalist how he 'thinks his morality boring and his subservience to Chamberlain an act of treason'.[11]

The Times dismissed the *Evening Standard* piece as 'insubstantial speculation', the *Daily Telegraph* called it an 'inexcusable indiscretion' and the German press exploded with indignation. Hinting at a postponement of the visit, the official Nazi paper, *Nationalsozialistische Parteikorrespondenz*, called the insinuations – which the *Evening Standard* had provocatively repeated two days later – 'a journalistic swindle', 'inventions from beginning to end' and 'a most shameless piece of journalistic impudence which cannot be sufficiently sharply repelled'. The flood of speculation further angered Eden, who despite suffering from 'flu saw Halifax at 11.30 a.m. on 16 November. He later told Harvey: 'H. was himself much worried at press accounts and felt it made his trip extremely difficult, owing to the great expectations that had been aroused.'[12] Eden then crossed the road to see Chamberlain, where a virtual shouting match ensued, culminating in the Prime Minister dismissively telling his Foreign Secretary to go home and take an aspirin. This encounter marked the beginning of the process which led eventually to Eden's resignation.[13]

The next day *The Week*, a left-wing scandal sheet widely read in Whitehall, purported to tell the facts behind the visit, which it described as 'this extraordinary and somewhat sinister affair', and alleged that 'the plan as a concrete proposal was first got into usable diplomatic shape at the Astors' place at Cliveden on the week-end of October 23rd and 24th'. It went on to assert that Eden had unsuccessfully tried to resign on the 8th, to accuse various Cliveden guests of pro-Nazism and treachery, and to say that the visit was intended primarily for domestic political consumption. The credence given then and even now to these wildly inaccurate pot-shots is astonishing. None of it was true; indeed, it so turns out that the star guest at Cliveden on the weekend in question was none other than Eden himself.

Once the final decision to go ahead with the visit had been taken, battle was joined over what Halifax should say. Eden found Halifax's notes 'very feeble and based on the idea of a Four-Power Pact'.[14] Chamberlain had long dreamt that through a 'General Settlement' he would be able to revise his old enemy Lloyd George's flawed Versailles Treaty, bringing lasting peace to Europe and a glory that would far outlive that of his father and half-brother. The November meeting at Eden's house shows that Foreign Office policy was not as far apart from No. 10's as has since been made out. The fable of a straightforward 'appeasing' No. 10 versus a heroic 'anti-appeasing' Foreign Office is very much a later interpretation and a greatly over-simplified one. The period from February 1938 was one of almost constant crisis and, with such enormous pressures on policy-makers, tensions were bound to appear. The diaries of normally imperturbable people such as Cadogan or Harvey become vociferous in places and return to relative tranquillity as soon as the crises abated. Strains were inevitable and the two institutions can no longer be seen in the stark black and white of the Wheeler-Bennett or Bruce Lockhart school of history.

The visit to Hitler constituted the high-water mark of Halifax's appeasement. Writing to Baldwin of the League of Nations' Commissioner of Danzig Karl Burckhardt's recent conversations with Hitler, he remarked, 'Nationalism and Racialism is a powerful force but I can't feel that it's either unnatural or immoral!', adding on the eve of his departure, 'I cannot myself doubt that these fellows are genuine haters of Communism, etc.! And I daresay if we were in their position we might feel the same!'[15]

For reading matter to brief himself, Halifax specifically asked for and took Henderson's notorious 10 May 1937 Memorandum on the future of Anglo-German relations. On 9 November, before reading it, he agreed with Henderson 'as to the necessity of this country going as far as we possibly can to secure general all-round settlement'.[16] He also referred with approbation to a letter he had received from Henderson in which the Ambassador had argued that 'we should, even if we don't like it, understand and even sympathize with German aspirations for unity'.[17] The 10 May document, which Halifax declared himself 'anxious'[18] to read before leaving for Berlin, is the bible of appeasement. It is worthy of consideration in depth as we know it was read with sympathy by Halifax as he prepared for his meeting with the Führer.

After pointing out the incontrovertible fact that 'Germany herself impinges on no British possession', Henderson sought to revive Joseph Chamberlain's 1899 concept of a German–British–American alliance, adding that 'the whole moral' of Sir Edward Grey's life was 'that he tried to the bitter end to ensure peace by giving [Germany] outlets ... for her pan-Germanic expansionist energies'. In a passage the message of which Halifax was to learn well, Henderson proved that his thinking was not mere philo-Germanic naïveté: 'Though [Grey's] efforts only ended in failure, his reward in 1914 was a united Britain, the support of the British Empire and the goodwill of practically all neutrals.' These three were to be no mean consolation prizes for Halifax in 1939 and would have been completely unrealizable in a 1938 war.

Henderson argued that of the absorption of Austria by Germany (the *Anschluss*), the recovery of the African colonies taken from Germany at Versailles and the drive for living space (*Lebensraum*) in Eastern Europe, 'in themselves none of these aims need injure purely British national interests', but would instead 'restrain both Russian intrigues and ambitions ... as well as Italian aspirations'. He also dutifully trotted out the argument that 'an agreement would increase our influence over Germany and is surely better than none'. With Locarno dead and Versailles badly injured, he argued that Memel and Danzig were bound sooner or later to revert to the Reich. And what if Britain did not 'avoid the insane folly of setting our course for another war'? Then, believed the diplomat, 'Even if we beat Germany again the result, after another period of chaos, would be the same as today.' There had been plenty of 'lost opportunities', which we could not continue to 'go on losing' for ever.

Never far from the surface was the cold language of force: 'We have at least realized ourselves that the League of Nations, collective security and treaty engagements constitute no reliable substitute for a Navy and Air Force. ... Germany is now too powerful to be compelled.' There was also a strong racial element in Henderson's philosophy. 'The German is certainly more civilized than the Slav,' he asserted, and therefore 'it is not [fair] to endeavour to prevent Germany from completing her unity or from being prepared for war against the Slav'. Finally, he looked at the dismal alternatives to his policy, which he saw as 'either to protest vehemently but do nothing if Germany, unfettered by any agreement with us, swallows Austria, annexes the Sudeten-deutsche or rectifies her Silesian frontier; or to revert openly to the bloc system and prepare for war. . . .Both alternatives can only be regarded as counsels of despair.'[19]

This paper infuriated many in the Foreign Office, especially Vansittart, and a number of amendments were attached. Vansittart's central point was that any British intimations 'to Germany of possible acquiescence in territorial changes to Germany's benefit ... might bring the European card-castle tumbling down'.[20] Yet it was precisely such a course that Chamberlain and Halifax intended to take with Hitler at Berchtesgaden.

Hitler took Halifax in, both personally and politically, but as Lord Astor's son, David, points out, 'People make a mistake if they think that those who he misled were all idiots, rather than he was a very subtle and gifted handler of people, although also a monster – it is evidently possible to be both.'[21] Of the other Britons Hitler met – the Marquesses of Londonderry and Lothian, the Duke of Windsor, Lords Allen of Hurtwood and Stamp, Sir John Simon, David Lloyd George, Anthony Eden and Robert Boothby – only the last (who claimed he answered Hitler's 'Heil Hitler!' salute with the cry 'Heil Boothby!') came away untainted with any degree of admiration for the Führer. That great liberal Lloyd George left his 1936 meeting with Hitler likening *Mein Kampf* to the Magna Carta and calling Hitler 'the Resurrection and the Way' for Germany.[22]

By the time of his visit Halifax could have been under no illusions about the nature of Nazi Germany. In the near five years of his Chancellorship, Hitler had suspended civil liberties and press freedoms, suppressed the trade unions, banned all other political parties, purged Ernst Röhm and the SA, harassed the Christian churches, repudiated the Versailles disarmament clauses, outlawed and viciously persecuted the Jews, marched out of the League of Nations and into the Rhineland, instituted two-year compulsory military service, helped Franco, rearmed with a vengeance and, on 6 November 1937, announced the Anti-Comintern Pact, a shrewdly named alliance with Italy and Japan. What Halifax could not know was that, on 5 November, Hitler had called his top admirals and generals together at the Chancellery to what is now known as 'the Hossbach Conference'. There he let them know of his determination to wage a major war for *Lebensraum* within five years and also told them to be ready for a 'lightning attack' on Czechoslovakia some time in 1938. This assault, code-named 'Operation Green', would take place as soon as Hitler was certain that Britain and France would not intervene and create a war on two fronts.[23]

The Hunting Exhibition was a gruesomely Teutonic affair, where the

'Informal Gathering of National Delegates' took place at '5 p.m. (sharp)' and a map showing Germany's 'lost territories' hung alongside huge portraits of Hermann Göring. The German for 'View halloo!' is 'Halali!' so Halifax was nicknamed 'Halalifax', a pun the Berliners found very funny. He got a rousing reception wherever he went, doffing his bowler to the 'Heil Hitler!' salutes. At lunch with the von Neuraths, there was 'some talk about the Führer; of his qualities, artistic, romantic, sensitive'.[24] Those three adjectives were not the first to spring to mind when an Embassy official, Ivone Kirkpatrick, explained at length about the Night of the Long Knives and Nazi persecution of the Christian churches, and took Halifax to the vast Doberitz army camp, informing him that such huge barrack building programmes were being duplicated all across Germany.

Before he left England, friends such as Mrs Arthur Grenfell had written to Halifax with details of the *Kulturkampf* which Joseph Goebbels was pursuing against the churches and begged him to intercede on behalf of various imprisoned pastors. But apart from a passing pro-forma reference to the way in which 'there was much in the Nazi system that offended British opinion (treatment of the Church; to perhaps a lesser extent, the treatment of the Jews; treatment of Trade Unions),'[25] in his conversation with Hitler Halifax did his best to avoid the subject altogether. This was in part so as not to antagonize Hitler, but also because the language and culture of 'human rights', so important to modern diplomacy and international relations, was then in its infancy and the conditions of other countries' internal affairs were not generally considered a wholly valid subject for diplomatic discussion.

The entire initiative was nearly wrecked before it had begun when the immensely tall Halifax, when getting out of the car at Berchtesgaden, mistook the diminutive Hitler for a footman. He was about to hand him his hat and coat when an agitated von Neurath hissed into his ear, '*Der Führer! Der Führer!*' Fortunately his host had not noticed the gaffe. The meeting, in the morning and afternoon of 19 November, took three hours and its salient points are well attested by Ivone Kirkpatrick, Dr Paul Schmidt, Hitler's interpreter, and the handwritten pencilled notes covering three sheets of paper taken by Halifax himself, which he later worked up into a twenty-one-page report to the Cabinet. His diary of the visit also tallies in all essentials. These pieces of evidence all show that Halifax did the one thing which Eden had told him not to, and which Vansittart had warned would 'bring the European card-castle tumbling down'.[26] Moreover, he did it not once but thrice in the course of the conversations.

Halifax opened the discussion by complimenting Hitler on 'performing great services in Germany', especially in repulsing Bolshevism, and added, 'if the public opinion in England took up an attitude of criticism . . . it might no doubt be in part because the people of England were not fully informed' about what was taking place in Germany. This statement had the effect of

negating his earlier remark about British public opinion being offended by
Nazi treatment of the Christian churches and 'to perhaps a lesser extent'
the Jews and trade unions. He went on to assure Hitler that an 'Anglo-
German rapprochement would not mean an attempt to divide Berlin and
Rome'. Hitler answered with his customary line about the unfairness of
Versailles and went on to waffle in a pseudo-intellectual way about 'the rule
of higher reason'. But as Hitler had nothing substantial to offer, he cannily
allowed Halifax the floor.

Halifax then said what for Eden and Vansittart was the mistake but for
Chamberlain and him the message:

> All other questions fall into the category of possible alterations in the
> European order which might be destined to come about with the
> passage of time. Amongst these questions were Danzig, Austria and
> Czechoslovakia. England was interested to see that any alterations
> should come through the course of peaceful evolution and that
> methods should be avoided which might cause far-reaching disturb-
> ances.[27]

It was Halifax, not Hitler, who first mentioned by name the areas where the
Versailles Treaty might be reinterpreted to Germany's benefit.

Of course Halifax hedged his message with qualifying phrases such as
'possible alterations', 'might be destined', 'with the passage of time', etc.,
but Hitler had little difficulty in seeing through the diplomatic language.
Versailles had provided for Danzig to be a Free City under League jurisdiction; it stipulated that Austria could not enter into political union with
Germany; it created the new state of Czechoslovakia with borders drawn in
such a way as to leave three million German speakers citizens of it; and it
limited the size of the German armed forces. Halifax effectively told Hitler
that so far as the British Government was concerned, parts of Versailles
could be up for review, so long as force was not employed.

Once he had learnt all he needed to know, Hitler quickly changed the
subject on to such relative irrelevancies as the conduct of the British press,
the threat of British rearmament, the fatuity of the League, how as a
veteran of the trenches he could never want another war, the colonial
question, prospects for the abolition of the bomber and other much loved
hobbyhorses. Those with a taste for black humour will find Hitler's closing
comments before lunch exquisitely amusing. It must have taken either
great self-control or a total lack of sense of humour, a mere fortnight after
the Hossbach Conference, for Hitler to have kept a straight face whilst
earnestly informing his guest that, 'Germany herself sets great store by
good relations with all her neighbours,' and 'International order should be
built up not on force but on law.' Von Neurath, not to be outdone, added
that Germany was all in favour of international co-operation and took as
his example the (wholly farcical) Spanish Non-Intervention Committee.

Halifax asked whether further conversations might take place as to the details of a rapprochement, but Hitler shrugged this off. When after lunch Halifax returned to the theme, Hitler commented, 'One must also be able to wait ... in a few years today's problems might wear a quite different complexion.'

Hitler, who had been 'peevish' all day, was insufferably boorish during lunch. Kirkpatrick recorded how,

> From a social point of view the lunch was a frost. Hitler was ... in a bad temper, Neurath was ill at ease and Lord Halifax could only talk through an interpreter. I made ineffective attempts to get a conversation going, but they all collapsed pitifully under Hitler's determination not to play. Of course we broached the weather. Hitler at once closed this topic by snapping: 'The weather; the weather prophets are idiots.' ... We tried flying. Hitler retorted: 'Only a fool would fly if he can go by train or road.' The Hunting Exhibition came up. Hitler at once wrote off this topic ... somebody remarked that Hess had just had a child, a bonny boy. Hitler observed that the Austrian birth-rate was declining sharply ... it was of course due to ... Austria's forced separation from Germany.

Kirkpatrick's assessment was that 'he behaved throughout like a spoilt sulky child'.[28]

After this dismal lunch, Hitler told Halifax how his favourite film, *Lives of a Bengal Lancer*, was compulsory viewing for the SS as 'this was how a superior race must behave', and he lost no time in expounding his answer to the problems of India. 'Shoot Gandhi,' he told the ex-Viceroy, 'and if that does not suffice to reduce them to submission, shoot a dozen leading members of Congress; and if that does not suffice, shoot 200 and so on until order is established.' During this tirade Halifax 'gazed at Hitler with a mixture of astonishment, repugnance and compassion. He indicated dissent, but it would have been a waste of time to argue.'[29]

To his diary of the visit Halifax reported with candour:

> I can quite see why he is a popular speaker. The play of emotion, sardonic humour, scorn, something almost wistful – is very rapid. But he struck me as very sincere, and as believing everything he said ... we had a different set of values and were speaking a different language. ...
> As to the political value of the talk, I am not disposed to rate this very high ... there was little or nothing he wanted from us and he felt time to be on his side ... regards disarmament as pretty hopeless and in short feels himself to be in a strong position and is not about to run after us.

Despite all that, 'it would be unfortunate if, like a previous conversation, this talk could not be followed up'.[30] Halifax was probably referring to

Eden's meeting with Hitler of February 1934. For his part after Halifax left Hitler spoke contemptuously of 'the English parson'.[31]

The next day Halifax travelled to Göring's vast estate at Karinhall. Göring had his instructions and the details of the previous day's meeting had been related to him by Dr Schmidt. The Nazi intention was to employ what policemen today call the 'hard cop/soft cop' technique. Halifax was encouraged to believe that while Hitler was an unreasonable autocrat who breathed fire, Göring was the amenable pragmatist and gentleman whose position must be bolstered by further concessions. This ancient totalitarian form of deception, often still practised successfully on the West today, encouraged the democracies not to be too hard on Germany for fear of weakening the hands of 'moderate' elements. The Italians tried much the same thing with an 'anti-British' Mussolini juxtaposing himself against the equally spuriously 'pro-British' Count Ciano. This technique was to take in many Foreign Office experts and pay dividends until well into 1940.

Therefore, when Göring met Halifax, 'He dealt with precisely the same questions as Hitler had done, only with infinitely more diplomacy.... "Under no circumstances shall we use force," he said reassuringly.'[32] Even Göring's get-up, which consisted of brown breeches and boots all in one, a green leather jerkin and a belt from which was hung a dagger in a red leather sheath, completed by a green hat topped by a large chamois tuft, was calculated through its very absurdity to put Halifax at his ease by rendering the Reichsmarschall a semi-joke figure. It worked; in a much quoted passage long held to damn him, Halifax wrote of Göring:

> I was immensely entertained at meeting the man himself. One remembered at the time that he had been concerned with the 'clean-up' in Berlin on June 30th, 1934 [the Night of the Long Knives] and one wondered how many people he had been, for good cause or bad, responsible for having killed. But his personality, with that reserve, was frankly attractive, like a great schoolboy ... a composite personality – film star, great landowner interested in his estate, Prime Minister, party manager, head gamekeeper at Chatsworth.[33]

The 'soft cop' routine had been played to perfection.

After church the next morning, the 21st, pausing only to issue an anodyne statement to the press and to refuse to speak to the French Ambassador, Halifax lunched with second-rank Nazi leaders such as the Reichsbank President, Dr Schacht, where the subject was restoration of Germany's colonies. Despite having so recently heard how Hitler would deal with troublesome native leaders, he entered into consideration of which Crown territories might revert to German rule and under which conditions. In the afternoon Goebbels and his wife came to tea at the Embassy. When Goebbels asserted that the British press correspondents in Berlin were dishonest and unfair to the Nazis, Halifax replied that many had served there for years; had they suddenly become dishonest or why had Germany not complained earlier? 'Dr Goebbels retorted with a charming and shameless smile: "We did not complain in the past because Germany was not rearmed. We complain now because we are strong enough to do so."'[34] Halifax had felt disdain for British journalistic standards since long before the *Evening Standard* had almost wrecked his visit. It had after all largely been against Irwinism that Fleet Street had exercised 'the harlot's prerogative'. He thought it unpatriotic of papers to make an already tricky diplomatic position worse and his Indian experience, where he could and did close newspapers virtually at will, led to a degree of high-handedness.

At tea with the Reich's Propaganda Minister, Halifax 'welcomed [Goebbels's] desire to avoid the Press in either country making mischief... HMG would do everything in their power to influence our Press to avoid unnecessary offence.'[35] He told his diary after meeting Goebbels, 'I had expected to dislike him intensely – but didn't. I suppose it must be some moral defect in me.' To someone who had also been at the tea Halifax remarked, 'I couldn't rather help but like the little man.'[36]

For the Cabinet minister with a special reputation for being a good judge of men, Halifax had been badly taken in by the Nazi hierarchy. Butler called Halifax 'the arch human-handler',[37] but instead of 'squaring' Hitler he had, in fact, been squared by him. It was perhaps fanciful and even arrogant to expect that after spending three hours in the company of a stranger, especially one who doesn't speak the same language and is carefully weighing his words, one could have much hope of discovering his true intentions. But at the first Cabinet meeting after his return, he ventured the opinion that, 'The Germans had no policy of immediate adventure. They were too busy building up their country, which was still in a state of revolution. Nevertheless he would expect a beaver-like persistence in pressing their claims in Central Europe, but not in a form to give others cause – or probably occasion – to interfere.'[38] As with so many of Halifax's comments, everything was hedged with qualifications and at this distance it is impossible to know what emphasis he put on any particular word.

Eden then 'expressed great satisfaction with the way the Lord President had dealt with each point in his conversations with the Chancellor'.[39] Halifax brought up Hitler's hint of an abolition of bombers, Göring's belief that a war was 'inconceivable' and prospects for a colonial deal as part of a general settlement. This aspiration, for a 'General Settlement', was to become the Holy Grail for which Chamberlain and Halifax were to quest until the latter realized it to be a dangerous chimera. His ability to keep his eyes firmly fixed over the horizon had proved invaluable in India, where during Civil Disobedience he ignored setbacks in order to keep the ultimate end in sight. On returning from Berlin that ultimate end was a 'General Settlement' and following up the advances he believed he had made became the most important thing in politics for him.

Chamberlain told his sisters the visit had been 'a great success because it achieved its object, that of creating an atmosphere in which it was possible to discuss with Germany the practical questions involved in a European settlement'.[40] He continued, seeing Halifax as a human form of the questionnaire they had tried to use earlier: 'What I wanted Halifax to do was convince Hitler of our sincerity and to ascertain what objectives he had in mind and I think both of these objects had been achieved.' He was half right; Halifax had shown Hitler sincerity, but like the pre-First World War Naval Attaché in London, the German had instead deduced weakness. Discovering from Halifax that the British were willing to countenance changes in the post-Versailles settlement, Hitler saw only opportunities for the expansion of the Reich. There was not much between that and the assumption Hitler correctly made that Britain would not fight to uphold Versailles any more than she had fought to uphold Locarno twenty months previously. Halifax let Hitler see his chance.

10

Lines of Latitude

Halifax was fully conscious in the months which followed, during which he pressed for his visit to be used as a springboard for further and wider negotiations, of the extent to which his personal prestige was bound up in them. He had told the press on his last day in Berlin that, 'If we have succeeded in opening a door now, I hope we will not let it be closed again.' The King wrote with great warmth commending his diplomacy. With considerable personal and political capital invested in the idea of a 'General Settlement', the series of rebuffs that were to be dealt to his advances could only have been a blow to Halifax's ego and spirit. Their pathetically transparent excuses showed that the Nazis had no desire for a frontier-stabilizing revision of Versailles. Halifax's attempt to 'square' Hitler had failed. His conversion from being the handmaiden of appeasement to its eventual pallbearer was not primarily due to the notorious process by which politicians at the Foreign Office tend to 'go native', but rather to his anger and embarrassment at seeing all his efforts so brusquely rebuffed.

Halifax, ever the rationalist, knew the British Government was not to blame for the breakdown in relations with Germany. During his talks with Hitler he had gone as far as he could and probably further than he should. But until the true nature of Nazi diplomacy revealed it to be impossible, he interested himself intimately in the many advances the British Government made towards a 'General Settlement'. There was a widespread feeling that too many opportunities had been missed and that a pact would at least restrain the tempo, if not the final extent, of German revanchism. The Cabinet were firmly behind the policy and Eden did little to hinder it. It is interesting that even after their ghastly lunch Halifax should have had so little personal criticism for Hitler himself. Writing to Brabourne on New Year's Day 1938, Butler said that Halifax had told him 'that if Hitler had worn a dhoti he could have mistaken his mystical approach to life for that of Mr Gandhi'.[1]

In a memorandum written on his return, Halifax made the assumptions that '(a) we want an understanding with Germany (b) we shall have to pay for it in (c) the only coin we have, which is colonial rendition of some sort'.[2] He therefore called for a 'frank examination of what every nation may be able to put in the pot for general appeasement'.[3] Believing 'the colonial issue was the only vital question between us',[4] the Government started considering various visionary schemes for finding Germany a place in the sun. Having heard from Schacht at the lunch on 20 November that Germany wanted Togoland and the Cameroons as well as 'a chunk made up from Belgian Congo and Angola',[5] the British Government allowed this to form the basis of the schemes.

Halifax was a member of the Foreign Policy Committee, a crucial Cabinet sub-committee whose conclusions were virtually never overruled by the main Cabinet. It was to this body that, on 24 January 1938, Chamberlain announced his plans for colonial appeasement. These he dressed up as 'the opening of an entirely new chapter in the history of African colonial development'.[6] It entailed drawing two lines across Africa, one along the five degree line of northern latitude and the other along the Zambezi River. The area in between (roughly everywhere between the Sahara and South Africa) was to be governed by an international consortium, in which the Germans would have a major say and which would be subject to 'new rules and regulations' concerning free trade, native armies and submarine bases.[7]

By far the largest part of this vast territory did not belong to Britain at all of course, but to France, Portugal and Belgium. To this hitch Henderson airily assured Hitler that our closest and oldest allies would 'merely be informed' of the conversations and would in the end co-operate in such a settlement. Halifax, conscious from personal experience of the fury the plan would spark in those who did not wish to hand native populations over to Nazism, intended to 'present it in a form which would not excite opposition from our own public opinion'. He added in fluent Halifax-speak: 'It was more important to the world at large that war should be avoided than that the natives in the territories to be transferred should remain permanently in the position they had been in during the last 20 years.'[8]

Although a cynical policy, colonial retrocession, especially of other countries' colonies, would have been an extraordinarily cheap form of Danegeld. As it was, Hitler showed no real interest. Obscure African colonies were of little use to Britain and would have been of even less to Germany, as on the outbreak of war the Royal Navy could swiftly blockade them into surrender. So when Henderson, complete with his map of Africa, met Hitler on 3 March, he discovered that equatorial *Lebensraum* was actually far lower on the Nazi agenda than Halifax had been led to believe.

Higher on that same agenda, due largely to Hitler's inability to laugh at

77

himself, was the behaviour of the British press, particularly its cartoonists. Halifax's notions about press freedom are best illustrated by the speech he gave to the Indian Legislature in January 1931, in which he warned that, 'When the greater power of the press is diverted from its true functions to dangerous and destructive doctrine, Government can no longer stand aside.' Returning from Germany, Halifax wrote to Henderson lamenting, 'if only we can get the press in both countries tame'.[9] To that end he arranged meetings with Lord Southwood, proprietor of the *Daily Herald*, and Sir Walter Layton, Chairman of the *News Chronicle*.

He emphasized to these men how difficult their coverage of news from Berlin was making his job and played up the responsible side of their prerogative. The meetings had little effect and the next week he had to write to Southwood complaining about an 'unjustly' cruel cartoon of Hitler in his paper. The reply came back that 'the German character was intended as symbolic only' (which is hard to believe as it wore jackboots, a swastika armband, floppy black hair and a toothbrush moustache).[10] The cartoonist who most infuriated the Nazis was David Low, the brilliant New Zealander who drew for the *Evening Standard*. After lunch with Halifax at the flat of the *Evening Standard* chairman, Captain Michael Wardell, Low created the character Muzzler by merging the salient features of Mussolini and Hitler.

Halifax was also responsible for taking off the air a series of BBC broadcasts in which leading opponents of government policy, such as Harold Nicolson and Leo Amery, spoke on the colonial issue. In order to get the maximum kudos for this and other such acts of quasi-censorship, Halifax decided that Henderson should be instructed to make sure they became known in Berlin.[11]

Halifax has been severely criticized for this. One recently published study called him 'two-faced' over his letter of 23 March 1938, in which he told Major Milner MP that 'no attempt has been made by instruction, request or suggestion to prevent newspapers from expressing their considered views'.[12] However, a passage in Layton's unpublished memoirs relating his meeting with Halifax shows the way in which Halifax operated and how his answer to Milner was strictly speaking accurate: 'after carefully explaining to me that he had no intention of trying to influence me in any way, [Halifax] merely passed on a message at Goebbels's request addressed to myself'.[13]

Although the introduction to Wardell had been the idea of a well-connected friend, Halifax knew most of the press proprietors socially. He had known the Astors for decades. During the war he stayed at the Dorchester with Lords Camrose and Kemsley and sat in the same Cabinet as Lord Beaverbrook. It would have been more remarkable if he had not had words in their ears. He knew how to appeal to their patriotism and vanity. He emphasized their influence and urged them to exercise discretion and to· refrain from exacerbating international suspicions. If they responded and engaged in a self-censorship helpful to British diplomacy, it can hardly be blamed on Halifax. He had little time for journalists' opinions, no trust in their objectivity and was correspondingly thick-skinned about their attacks. This dismissive and cynical attitude towards the media is easily castigated, but is probably shared by the majority of modern politicians. Although any degree of interference sounds sinister to modern ears, it must be borne in mind that the Foreign Office then had almost total control over BBC output and what today looks like censorship would have in 1938 more closely resembled responsible stewardship. Halifax had long taken a fairly authoritarian line on press freedoms, telling his father in April 1930 how 'few things have given me greater pleasure than shoving out the Press Ordinance ... and I look forward with sober optimism to real improvements in consequence of again bringing the Press under control'.[14]

In the 26 November letter to his sisters, Chamberlain had thought that Germany 'would be prepared to come back to the League if it were shorn of its compulsory powers now clearly shown to be ineffective', adding that it would have greater influence 'if it were not expected to use force but only moral pressure'.[15] Halifax was in the forefront of attempting to change the deterrent nature of the League as a price for German readmission. In Cabinet on 15 December 1937, he suggested 'saying to the world that the original conception of the League of Nations as set forth in the Covenant was obviously impractical in present circumstances when important nations were standing out'. Eden and the Cabinet approved his motion to instruct the British representative at Geneva 'to suggest that membership of the League should involve a general obligation to consult', but only to take military action in the most extreme circumstances. This would have meant castration had the League not already shown itself to be a eunuch. There is no indication that these attempts made any impression on Hitler, whose castigations of the League were merely a stock part of his rhetorical repertoire and who applauded Italy's decision to leave it in December 1937.

Hitler's ploy to proffer the abolition of the bomber showed particular brilliance and malevolence. Spanish civil war experiences, where bombers were deployed against defenceless towns such as Guernica, suggested a hugely exaggerated potential for the weapon that Baldwin had assured Parliament would 'always get through'. The Prime Minister told his sisters, who were often far better informed than most Cabinet ministers, that he believed 'qualitative rather than quantitive restrictions on material' could be on the agenda. When von Neurath was pressed to explain precisely what Hitler had meant by the term 'humanizing air warfare', he admitted that limiting the number of the Luftwaffe's bombers might be 'difficult', but assured the Foreign Office that ultimately the Führer was keen to abolish them altogether. So potent was this come-on for Halifax that even after Germany absorbed Austria he was still able to write to Henderson asking, 'Is there any chance of their being willing to talk seriously about disarmament? . . . we might then conceivably get to something not unlike the general settlement we have always worked for.'[16]

Before the Berlin visit, Halifax had told Tom Jones to expect a return visit from Göring, probably using a shooting trip as the excuse.[17] There were also a number of efforts to persuade von Neurath to come over to continue the talks. Knowing that they had nothing to demand which they were not anyhow in the process of planning to take, the Germans saw no advantage in further discussions. They held out the prospect of a top-level visit until August 1939, even though on at least one occasion it looked likely that Göring would be coming over to stay at Sandringham.

Halifax was willing to a great degree to defer to Henderson's knowledge of Germany and the Germans. When in March 1938 a number of eminent people led by the Archbishop of York asked for advice on how best to pressurize the German Government into releasing Pastor Niemöller, he sent them Henderson's letter on the subject. This said that in the Ambassador's opinion Niemöller's interests would be best served if the international clamour ceased.[18]

Halifax's ability to keep the ultimate goal of the 'General Settlement' always in mind meant that he could endure unflinchingly the difficulties and setbacks along the way. He could commit the solecisms of inviting Göring to meet the Royal Family, turn a blind eye to Niemöller, muzzle Low, return colonies or revise the Covenant of the League, as he considered all these as dust in the balance beside securing a lasting peace for Europe. He was probably right to think the Germans absurdly sensitive and suffering from a massive inferiority complex. Questions of prestige, which sent opponents of his policy into fulminations, hardly mattered to Halifax at all.

Yet the last area in which the British Government sought to appease Germany mattered profoundly. Czechoslovakia could field between thirty and forty divisions, and had a strong and heavily fortified mountain frontier against Germany. It also possessed Skoda, the world's largest armaments factory. The very existence of this Slavic democracy was anathema to Hitler, who likened its shape and geographical position to a knife pointing into the heart of Germany. Its German-speaking minority, led by the former gym instructor Konrad Henlein, seemed to wish to join the Reich. In Britain feeling, insofar as people thought about the subject at all in 1937, depended on one's point of view about Germany and appeasement rather than on the intrinsic merits of the Sudetens' case. Chamberlain saw it in terms of his father's finest hour, believing 'the Germans want the same thing for the Sudetendeutsche as we did for the Uitlanders in the Transvaal'.[19] The analogy was largely spurious; Britain merely wanted representation and political rights for the Uitlanders whereas Hitler demanded the

Sudetens' incorporation into the Reich. At Versailles the Sudetenland, which had not been part of Germany for centuries, had been incorporated into the newly formed Slavic state in order to give it a defendable frontier and leave it a viable economic and military unit.

The same day that Hitler met Halifax, Henlein had written to Hitler formally embracing National Socialism and begging him to annex the Czech provinces of Bohemia, Moravia and Silesia.[20] Hitler neither acknowledged the letter nor even saw Henlein until March 1938. But on 7 December 1937, he did make an addendum to the Hossbach Conference to say that 'Operation Green' had become more likely than an attack on France, as he was sure the Western Powers would not intervene to help the Czechs. All this time Britain kept up pressure on the French to persuade the Czechs, with whom France had an alliance, to go as far as possible in appeasing the Sudetens. Czech attempts to conform were impressive. They accorded the Sudetens such special treatment that it began to threaten Czech national integrity, but on 29 November 1937 the Sudeten representatives walked out of the Prague parliament and the tempo of riot, unrest and tough Czech police action moved up several degrees. On the same day, Eden and Halifax met the French leaders. The agenda largely comprised a report of Halifax's visit and they pressed the French to find out what concessions the Czech President, Eduard Beneš, would make to the 'legitimate grievances' of the Sudetens.[21]

Appeasement of Germany was also given a significant boost by the treatment meted out to the Permanent Under-Secretary at the Foreign Office, the dashing and formidable Sir Robert Vansittart. As early as May 1933, Vansittart had warned of the threat posed by the rise of German militarism. Firmly in the anti-German tradition of the pre-Great War Permanent Under-Secretary Sir Eyre Crowe, 'Van', as he was universally known, used stark imagery and a highly individual written style to warn against the further appeasement of Germany. It was partly his opposition to Halifax's visit and his constant sniping later which finally convinced the Prime Minister and Eden to remove him. In order to avoid adverse press comment, they used that peculiarly British method of marginalization: promotion. From 1 January 1938, Vansittart occupied the specially created and ill-defined post of Chief Diplomatic Adviser, while the more amenable Sir Alexander Cadogan took his job but not his room, which Vansittart stubbornly refused to vacate. Vansittart was kept away from the decision-making process and was eventually also starved of documents until his position became that of a Jeremiah preaching doom from the sidelines.

This relegation has long been held against Halifax, but as Sir Orme Sargent told Lord Birkenhead in the 1960s, Vansittart

used a terrible style in his minutes to the Cabinet; violent, facetious and fizzling with bad epigrams and they simply would not read them.

He became a recognized bore; they became sick of his constant nagging, and in a few years he was not listened to at all ... his failure was almost as much to be blamed to his own temperament and methods as it was to the men who refused to listen. Had there been a different man as Permanent Head, a big man without hysterics and Van's lack of subtlety, he could have fought Horace Wilson.

The way in which national security needs should dictate strategy, which in turn ought to decide armaments levels, had, by late 1937, got badly out of synchronization. In one Cabinet debate on defence expenditure, Halifax pointed out that,

> In spite of all the efforts of the Foreign Secretary, the Prime Minister and others, we had arrived at a position which above all we had wished to avoid and in which we were faced with the possibility of three enemies at once. The conclusion which [Halifax] drew was ... that this threw an immensely heavy burden on diplomacy and that we ought to get on good terms with Germany.[22]

However, from 2 to 6 February 1938, Hitler made personnel changes at the top of the Nazi hierarchy which made getting on any sort of terms far more difficult. He personally took charge of the War Ministry and sacked the cautious and pragmatic generals Blomberg and Fritsch. The pliable von Neurath was replaced by the stridently anti-British Ribbentrop, whom his own Private Secretary described as 'a pompous non-valeur and yes-man to his wife and to Hitler'.[23] Hitler was tightening up his organization to meet the strains of coming adventures.

On 11 January, President Roosevelt asked the British Government for their views on his intention to make a speech advocating a conference to discuss the European situation. One commentator has described their rejection of this opportunity as 'the worst blunder by any British Government in recent times'.[24] In fact, Roosevelt's initiative was just yet another attempt at appeasement. The wordy American call for unanimous agreement on 'essential and fundamental principles which should be observed in international relations' constituted, as Roosevelt admitted, 'the only lines which, in the state of public opinion in the USA, are open to him'. With its emphasis on providing equal access to the world's raw materials, the whole scheme was likely to benefit the USA substantially and it is hard to see how the conference could have had any more lasting benefit than making Roosevelt feel good inside. An America which did not repeal the Neutrality Acts in 1940 when London was being blitzed and Europe enslaved was hardly likely to commit herself very far in early 1938.

At the Foreign Policy Committee meeting on 19 January, Chamberlain, supported by Halifax, Simon and Inskip, urged polite but firm rejection of the Roosevelt offer as inopportune and coming just as their best efforts were being made to appease the dictators. Britain was poised to open negotiations with Mussolini, a move Roosevelt opposed. Eden made resignation noises, but the subject was allowed to lapse. Eden, piqued at the decision having been taken when he was out of the country, took a rather more positive view of the efficacy of American intervention than his colleagues. He was angry that seemingly whenever his back was turned, as on his holiday in August 1937, Chamberlain and Halifax used the opportunity to pursue policies of which he disapproved. He was also irritated by rumours that the Prime Minister was pursuing a rapprochement with Italy behind his back, using Austen Chamberlain's widow, Sir Horace Wilson, the Italian Ambassador Count Dino Grandi and Conservative Central Office's Sir Joseph Ball as intermediaries. Eden was all for tough measures against Rome, but he was not so intransigent over Berlin. He told the Cabinet on 2 February that at Geneva 'he had found a considerable and very real desire for better relations with Germany'; a week later, he urged that conversations be started with Germany before Hitler's Reichstag speech of 20 February, which 'might express disappointment that nothing has been done to follow up the Lord President's visit'.[25]

It came as a shock to Halifax when he discovered that Eden was contemplating resignation over the question of the projected Anglo-Italian entente. After moments of crisis, Halifax, ever interested in having his side of the case told properly, often penned short diary reminiscences, partly for interest's sake and partly in tacit self-justification. The notes which cover the Eden resignation show how on Friday, 18 February 1938, he had a pleasant afternoon pigeon-shooting with local farmers at Garrowby. Returning home he found a summons to a Cabinet meeting for 3 p.m. the next day. 'I said goodbye to my day's hunting' and got to Downing Street to hear the Prime Minister recapitulate at length the background to the Government's Italian policy. He passed a note to Hoare asking, 'Why this rather boring lecture on history?', only to discover that a serious rift had developed between the Prime Minister and Foreign Secretary. The meeting had been called to decide between the former's desire to go faster towards talks with Italy and the latter's equally strong instinct to rein in.[26]

Chamberlain's case was both formidable and, for every member of Cabinet bar Eden, unanswerable. He emphasized that 'the main issue was not one of principle ... but rather of method, timing and whether the present moment was opportune or not'. After reminding them of the dangers involved in having all three Axis powers at Britain's throat at once, he pointed out the positive signs for an Italian entente, whilst not denying that Italy was like 'a hysterical woman' to deal with. It was 'criminal' not to grasp the chance as this was 'one of those opportunities which come at rare intervals and did not recur'.[27] It was a virtuoso performance and Eden's counterblast, that he would countenance informal talks in London but wanted nothing signed until Italian troops had actually begun to leave Spain, did not convince the Cabinet, which declared itself fully behind the

Prime Minister. Chamberlain is often criticized for staffing his Cabinet with grey yes-men. Though not a particularly inspiring bunch, they were hardly out of the ordinary for a British peacetime Cabinet. Very few ever stand alone as Cabinets. It is more often true that, say, the Postmaster-General in any given Cabinet will be an obedient and fairly competent stocking-filler.

When Eden made clear his intention to resign, the stage was left to Halifax to try to find a compromise. Eden stalked off to the Foreign Office, where Halifax and the President of the Board of Trade, Oliver Stanley, soon followed. There they found him with his three staunchest supporters, Jim Thomas, 'Bobbety' Cranborne and Oliver Harvey. The sight of the three advisers reminded Halifax of 'the corner of a boxing ring where the seconds received back the pugilist and restored his vitality by congratulations and encouragement'.[28]

After the Cabinet failed to reach agreement on the morning of Sunday the 20th, Halifax appointed a committee of Thomas Inskip, Oliver Stanley, Malcolm MacDonald and William 'Shakes' Morrison to join him and the two antagonists to try to find some formula under which Eden could rescind his threat. After an hour and a half the Cabinet reassembled to hear Halifax, who had unobtrusively taken on the role of honest broker, put forward a compromise solution. This was an arrangement whereby Italian troop withdrawals from Spain would have to form an integral part of the final agreement. Chamberlain agreed to this, but Eden asked for more time to consider. Chamberlain had neared the point where his own authority was coming under threat, but as he told his sisters a week later, 'after the repeated efforts of the Foreign Office to shake off conversations and to prevent my seeing Grandi I knew that the time had come'.[29]

The consultations and waiting finally ended at 7.35 p.m. when Eden returned to No. 10 to tell the special committee that he still wanted to go. He thought Halifax's compromise was the worst of both worlds and anyway unlikely to be accepted by the Italians. Halifax's blandishments and compromise solutions were all to no avail. Eden had other reasons for resignation than just disagreements over the timing of what he must have known was really an inevitable approach to Italy. Four days earlier he had told the Cabinet about the Nazi intrigues going on in Austria and warned that he 'did not want to put himself in a position of suggesting resistance which we could not, in fact, furnish'.[30] Eden saw the threatened *Anschluss* fast approaching and just as clearly saw that there was nothing Britain could do to prevent it. His own reputation as the Government's bright young hope would inevitably be compromised when Britain offered no more than supine resistance to the forcible union of the two German-speaking nations.

By resigning shortly before *Anschluss*, Eden avoided the opprobrium that would have been the lot of any Foreign Secretary, however robust. Pique over the Roosevelt plan probably played a part although, like *Anschluss*, it was not mentioned as a factor at that time. Halifax, who thought him 'overstrained and tired', believed Eden's motives to be

> partly subconscious irritation at Neville's closer control of foreign policy; partly irritation at his amateur incursions in the field through Lady Chamberlain & Horace Wilson; partly Anthony's natural revulsion against Dictators, which I have always told him is too strong inasmuch as you have got to live with the devils whether you like them or not; partly ... excessive sensitiveness to criticism of the Left.[31]

If Eden was overstrained and tired, it may have had something to do with the fact that every time he went on holiday Chamberlain and Halifax thought up new ways to appease the Italians.

At this point Oliver Stanley and Malcolm MacDonald started to consider whether they too ought to resign. 'The situation', Halifax recorded, 'was becoming Gilbertian.'[32] Action needed to be taken to stop the whole Ministry unravelling and Halifax advised Chamberlain to call another Cabinet. This produced general unanimity. During the course of the next day it became clear that Cranborne would resign with Eden but Stanley and MacDonald would stay on. This prompted Lady Cranborne to retort, 'the Stanleys have been trimmers ever since Bosworth field'.[33] (Another female Cecil, Lady Gwendolen, blamed Halifax for appeasement because Chamberlain was 'a poor old middle-class monster [who] could not be expected to know any better'.)[34] Halifax stayed on good personal terms with Eden despite the Edenite Harvey's estimation of him as 'though not an intriguer...[a] tiresome and a captious critic'.[35]

It was to be a full five days before Chamberlain offered, and Halifax accepted, the Foreign Secretaryship. As late as the 23rd, Butler believed 'they will appoint a whole time Foreign Secretary in the Commons and Halifax will as usual wish to keep out of the limelight'.[36] The reception of the news of Halifax's appointment was mixed; Churchill told the Commons that the appointment of a peer was 'derogatory' and the senior Labour politician, Herbert Morrison, wrote in the *Birmingham Post* that Halifax was 'a weakling who will merely be the servile instrument of an ignorant and reckless Prime Minister'. However, Balfour's niece Blanche 'Baffy' Dugdale noted in her diary that the Lord Privy Seal, Earl De La Warr, had said, 'Lord Halifax will count in Foreign Affairs,' and that Walter Elliot had 'said Lord Palmerston has come among us again'. As Cabinet ministers they were likely to have a keener appreciation of his importance in the Government than outsiders like Churchill and Morrison.[37]

Halifax was by now a figure of considerable weight in the Conservative Party, whose political instincts Chamberlain, always more of a Liberal Unionist than fully a Tory, respected. Chamberlain appreciated how Halifax was known, trusted and respected by elements of the Party to which he himself still had only limited access. One of Halifax's junior Private Secretaries, Valentine Lawford, believes 'a growing affection founded on experience shared, rather than any similarity of mind or ... political outlook, marked the relationship of Halifax to Chamberlain'.[38] The charge that Halifax was Chamberlain's poodle was born from the lack of instances of Halifax overtly standing up to his boss. But quite apart from the fact that he never did his best work in public, he fundamentally agreed with the policies being pursued. When the time came he was to show himself more than independent enough, but not in ways outsiders, and even some historians, have noticed.

On 23 February, Halifax discussed with Harvey the work involved in being Foreign Secretary, 'in case he accepted', saying he was 'very lazy and disliked work. Could he hunt on Saturdays?'[39] This was just the sort of chaffing that Halifax enjoyed and did not mean to be taken seriously. He had after all given up that very Saturday's hunting and did not expect his words to be taken down by his new Private Secretary, let alone later used in evidence against him. In fact, Halifax worked hard and, as Lawford recounts, used to 'work for long hours in solitude' on his speeches. Lawford has left a superb pen portrait of him as Foreign Secretary which bears repetition at some length:

> When Halifax moved he could be graceful and grave and shy simultaneously, like a tall water-bird wading in the shallows.... Architecturally, the upper half of his head resembled a dome which, since it rested on more than usually jutting ears, appeared elusively to taper towards the apex.
>
> The loftiness of the face as a whole could not cause one quite to forget an ever-present, questioning look in the eyes; and beneath a long upper lip the line of the mouth itself was expressive less of wit and irony than of a controlled and philosophical melancholy, innate and instinctive rather than acquired ... his back and legs were magnificently straight and he looked his best astride a horse. And for one who combined proconsular talents with a reputation for almost medieval saintliness, he seemed always ... refreshingly human and outdoor.... Halifax's clothes were well cut, well cared for ... and even when they were new they were slightly dated ... though his suits were sober he was not above brightening them discreetly with a spotted tie or a patterned silk handkerchief half falling from the pocket ... his writing was neat, personable, slightly pointed and sloping, suavely scholarly and easy running: the script of a don or a Dean ... in public affairs he was not by any means hopelessly otherworldly but practical and understanding and shrewd.[40]

There were only 173 executive officials in the Foreign Office in London in 1938 and at the top ranks they constituted a homogeneous social group. It was a magic circle which Halifax's new Under-Secretary, R.A. Butler, hoped to break. The Marlburian Butler wrote to the Wellingtonian Brabourne complaining of 'the old FO team where PPSs, Ministers and officials had all got OE ties and called each other by their Christian names and had exactly the same brains'.[41] In the Foreign Office of 1938, Eton could number amongst her sons Eden, Halifax, Vansittart, Cadogan, six of the eleven Counsellors, half the Private Secretaries and the Ambassadors to Berlin, Rome, Moscow, Warsaw, The Hague, Stockholm, Ankara, Bucharest and Athens.

It was standard Foreign Office practice that when a Foreign Secretary resigned so also did his three Private Secretaries. But Halifax surprised Oliver Harvey, Derick Hoyer Millar and Harold Caccia by asking them to stay on, asserting that 'Anthony had the same outlook as my own'.[42] This was all part of a conscious policy to show 'no change' to the outside world. Telegrams were sent to Paris and Washington to this effect with the intention of making Eden's resignation seem incomprehensible and slightly ridiculous. Vansittart lost no time in making his power bid, asking Halifax's permission for direct access to the Prime Minister. In order to protect Cadogan's position, Halifax refused. He also refused to take on a Parliamentary Private Secretary from the Commons, because as he explained to Sir Ralph Glyn, who had proposed himself, 'the PM will to a certain extent make himself responsible for dealing with Foreign Affairs there. I am a little disposed to fear that it would constitute a further complication if I were to establish my own channels of communication with Members.'[43]

Halifax brought to the Foreign Office a certain serenity and calm that the nervy Eden could never achieve. He had the shortest 'honeymoon' period of any Foreign Secretary. The day after Eden went, Cadogan wrote in his caustic but invaluable diary:

> Went to see Halifax about 11. He in 'temporary charge'. Tells me he hasn't been offered the post. I told him of dangers if he accepted. These were present to his mind & he may not accept. Talked to him about policy. Brave words butter no parsnips. Austria is gone: no good teasing Hitler.... Everything is very hateful.

Taking on the Foreign Office as the European card-castle was on the verge of tumbling was an act of genuine political bravery. He did it partly in the belief that a German rapprochement was, however unlikely, still possible. Three events coming in quick succession soon served to disabuse him of all but the dream of this.

Hitler's 20 February speech to the Reichstag covered sixty-three pages but nowhere made positive reference to better relations with Britain, except on terms Hitler knew to be unacceptable. Instead, he attacked 'the statesmen, politicians and journalists in our so-called democratic countries' for their 'rare mixture of arrogance and pitiful ignorance which more than once presumed to sit in judgement on occurrences in a nation'.[44]

General settlement plans were 'too vague and nebulous for me to express any opinion on them'. He cleverly connected the idea of a ban on poison and incendiary bombs with a suppression of anti-German papers, a price he knew Britain could not pay. This rambling, sarcastic and bombastic speech, if taken at face value, really ruled out anything but the law of the jungle for international relations. Halifax took the rebuff calmly, allowing as always a great degree of latitude when dealing with the speeches of dictators, which he considered were primarily intended for domestic consumption.

Halifax's choice of Butler as his Under-Secretary was characteristic. Halifax needed a spokesman in the Commons and the thirty-five-year-old Butler, whose father had been Governor of the Central Provinces during Halifax's Viceroyalty, was both highly intelligent and utterly committed to appeasement. There were then only two Foreign Office ministers, as against five today. Butler carried off the difficult task of defending the policy in the Commons without giving away a single unnecessary point. This was no easy task, as he was soon complaining to Brabourne:

> There is no 'line' on the subject of the L[eague] of N[ations] or of Spain; all questions to the latter have to be answered by reference to the Non-Intervention Committee, and all the former to a sort of vague idealism. From your experience of the House you will realize that neither of these lines gives the speaker any real chance in debate. Unless I keep pressing this point of view, the H[ouse] of C[ommons] is naturally forgotten in the business of conducting the S[ecretary] of S[tate]'s normal day.[45]

If Hitler's speech had not doused Halifax's ardour for a 'General Settlement', Henderson's meeting with him should have. At his first Cabinet as Foreign Secretary, on 2 March, Halifax had put conversations with Germany firmly on the agenda, leading off with the colonial scheme. 'The Holy Fox' hoped that 'one advantage of this plan was that it could be presented to the world not as handing back to Germany her former colonies as a right but as a new plan based on higher ideals'.[46] The next day, Henderson presented this and other ideas personally to Hitler as a basis for agreement. Hitler, only days away from his Austrian coup, was unable to respond meaningfully even had he so wished. Instead, he raved against the British press, Government and clergy and issued a threat to 'protect' the 'ten million' Germans outside the Reich 'even if it meant war'.

At the next Cabinet Halifax, with all he had worked for on the brink of collapse, recapitulated, as much one suspects for his own benefit as anyone else's, all the efforts the Government had made for peace. As well as the colonial idea, 'he had shown that the Government were willing to do what they could about the Press and BBC ... we had taken a reasonable line about Central Europe ... done our best to steady public opinion as to Austria ... used our influence in Czechoslovakia in favour of a settlement'[47] and taken up Hitler's own proposals on abolishing the bomber. He might have also added British silence over Goebbels's *Kulturkampf*, the 'shooting' invitations to Göring and efforts to revise the League's Covenant. Appeasement was always a proactive rather than a passive creed.

In the meeting he was due to have with Ribbentrop the next morning, Halifax proposed to show 'disappointment, reproach and warning' and

> make clear to the German Government the danger he saw in the expression that responsible German leaders were giving in public to German policy.... The last thing he wanted was to see a war in Europe but the experience of all history went to show that the pressure of facts was sometimes more powerful than the wills of men, and if once war should start in Central Europe it was impossible to say where it might not end or who might not get involved.[48]

This was the 'Guessing Position' and was originally initiated by Eden in his Leamington speech back in November 1936. Under it, Halifax told Harvey, 'Germany could never be sure that HMG would not intervene in Central Europe and the French would never be sure that we *would*, thereby discouraging both.'[49]

The situation in Vienna was desperate. The Austrian Chancellor, Dr Kurt von Schuschnigg, hoping to forestall what he correctly surmised were Austrian Nazi plans for a coup, proposed to hold a snap plebiscite on the question of *Anschluss*. Union of the two German-speaking nations was expressly forbidden by Versailles, but there were a large number of Austrians – we shall never know whether they constituted a majority – who wanted to join the Reich.

There was a crowd outside the Foreign Office on the morning of 10 March chanting 'Release Niemöller!' and 'Ribbentrop Go Home!' Once past it the Reich's new Foreign Minister heard Halifax's warning, delivered 'halfway between sorrow and anger'. In the course of this, Halifax asked that Schuschnigg be allowed to conduct undisturbed the plebiscite on Austrian independence announced for 13 March. He received no assurances from Ribbentrop and told Harvey and Cadogan the next day, 'The only thing they understand is force, a warning will be useless unless accompanied by a threat to use force, which we cannot do.'[50]

Halifax thought Schuschnigg's plebiscite 'foolish and provocative'[51] and it certainly gave Hitler the spur to order the Austrian Nazis to stage their coup in Vienna, which was swiftly supported by German troops. From the declaration of *Anschluss* onwards, life for Halifax consisted of a Via Dolorosa of crises interspersed by bloodcurdling rumours and eternal waiting on the Führer's next broadcast. The Nazis were skilled both in indirect aggression and psychological warfare. Although the Rhineland had been his baptism of fire, *Anschluss* was more painful for Halifax, so starkly did it repudiate all that on which he had honourably set his heart.

11

'Spring Manoeuvres'

The British Government first heard of the German invasion of Austria at an official luncheon at No. 10, Downing Street, on 11 March. It was being given, ironically enough, in honour of Ribbentrop. After twenty minutes of 'talking earnestly'[1] with his guest of honour about 'a better understanding and mutual contributions to peace', Chamberlain was handed a series of telegrams which established beyond doubt that German troops were crossing the Austrian border and *Anschluss* was under way. The Berlin War Ministry protestations that troop movements should be ascribed to 'spring manoeuvres' convinced no one.

As lunch ended Chamberlain invited Ribbentrop, Halifax and Cadogan into his study where, as he told his sisters, 'Halifax and I talked to him most gravely and seriously begging him before it was too late to ask his Chief to hold his hand. I don't think either Halifax or I expect any result to follow.'[2] Halifax, describing the news as 'intolerable', followed up the talk with a call on the German Embassy at 5.15 p.m. There he protested vigorously to the Reich's Foreign Minister, who still claimed that he had no idea what was going on.

Despite Schuschnigg's strangled cries, Halifax knew that he could offer no practical assistance. The Italians were conniving in the crime and the French were in the middle of yet another government crisis. There was no British continental army in existence and the Austrian army itself had not resisted; indeed, as *The Times* was to report, the German army was welcomed into Austria by a large proportion of the population. It has been said that the only shots fired in anger during *Anschluss* were by those Jews who committed suicide.

In his memoirs, written while on trial for his life at Nuremberg, Ribbentrop blamed *Anschluss* squarely on Halifax. He cited a comment by Halifax in 1937 that 'the British people would never consent to go to war because two German countries wanted to merge'[3] as evidence that Halifax had given Hitler the go-ahead. He further said that at the 10 March meeting in the Foreign Office, Halifax 'accepted the situation calmly and with composure' and, at the 5.15 p.m. meeting the next day, 'our conference was quite friendly. I found an opening to invite Lord Halifax to Germany, which he accepted.'[4] Other reports suggest that Halifax warned Ribbentrop that, 'if once war should start in Central Europe, it was quite impossible to say where it might not end or who might not become involved'.[5]

Certainly Chamberlain drew a very different conclusion from Ribbentrop of Halifax's culpability, lamenting to his sisters that, 'It is tragic to think that very possibly this might have been prevented if I had had Halifax at the Foreign Office instead of Anthony at the time I wrote my letter to Mussolini.'[6] Far from being the piece of astounding casuistry it sounds, this is quite possibly correct, for had Eden not held up Italian negotiations until Britain was trumped by Germany, the Italians might have acted to prevent *Anschluss*.

Meaningful negotiations with Germany were hampered by the terminal denseness of Ribbentrop, described by Chamberlain after the meeting in his study as 'so stupid, so shallow, so self-centred and self-satisfied, so totally devoid of intellectual capacity that he never seems to take in what is said to him'.[7] The Polish Ambassador, Count Edward Raczynski, remembers him as 'a self-made cheeky fellow who saluted the King in his jackboots'.[8]

In the Cabinet post-mortem on 12 March, Chamberlain could not resist a dig at the Austrian ex-President and 'recalled that Dr Schuschnigg had not asked advice before announcing the plebiscite which had caused so much trouble'.[9] It was snide self-justification such as this that makes Chamberlain the cold, harsh and unappealing figure he is to history. At the same Cabinet Halifax, exhibiting a trait of concern for 'the record' which was a recurring feature, wanted the British Ambassador in Italy, the Earl of Perth, to discuss *Anschluss* with Mussolini in order 'to have the fact on record that we made the approach'.[10] He was also authorized to protest in the strongest possible terms to Berlin. He well knew that this would have no effect, that *Anschluss* had been a major setback and that there were no practical steps Britain could have taken to stop it. Staying calm and avoiding histrionics was, as even Vansittart admitted, about the best that could be done. The worst would have been to let Schuschnigg believe Britain was about to help and thus encourage a bloody but doomed resistance. After the Cabinet Halifax persuaded the Labour Party leader, Clement Attlee, not to press for an early debate on *Anschluss* and then remonstrated with Dawson about the overtly pro-German tone of *The Times*'s coverage of the entry of German troops into Vienna.

As soon as the *Anschluss* was complete all eyes turned to Austria's eastern neighbour, Czechoslovakia. There was now a continuous fascist bloc from the Baltic to the Adriatic. *Anschluss* had rendered the Czech fortifications totally worthless. An invasion could now come from three sides or, if the Poles, Romanians and Hungarians were also to claim their pounds of Czech flesh, all four. As Halifax told the General Secretary of the Trades Union Congress, Walter Citrine, 'the Germans expected they could nip up the wasp waist, meaning that part of Czechoslovakia where the country narrowed and where German territory was on both sides'.[11] It was at a Foreign Policy Committee meeting on 18 March that Halifax put forward and won acceptance for the 'Guessing Position', which, once ratified by Cabinet, was announced in Parliament by the Prime Minister on 24 March and was to stay government policy for the next six months. Halifax defined it at that meeting:

> it could not be in our interests to see France overrun ... [but] ... we had entered into no kind of definite and automatic commitment [to Czechoslovakia].... This had the great advantage that we were able to keep both France and Germany guessing as to what our attitude in any particular crisis would be.[12]

The military position was clear, as Thomas Inskip, the Minister for Co-ordination of Defence, summarized:

> It seemed certain that Germany could overrun the whole of Czecho-slovakia in less than a week ... it was difficult to see how we could effectively exercise any military pressure against Germany in time to save Czechoslovakia. Our only really effective means of pressure would be a naval blockade, but this would take between two and three years to bring Germany to her knees.[13]

After this gloomy view Halifax looked at the alternatives:

> France was admittedly helpless in the air. Germany was in a strong position to hold up any advances by land.... Mr Winston Churchill had a plan under which the French army was to act on the defensive behind the Maginot Line and there detain large German forces while Czechoslovakia engaged Germany's remaining forces.[14]

But if for no other reason than that Germany had no intention of attacking the Maginot Line until the Czechs were safely defeated, Halifax thought 'This seemed to have no relation to the realities of the situation.' He questioned 'the assumption that when Germany secured the hegemony over Central Europe she would then pick a quarrel with ourselves',[15] and thought 'the more closely we associated ourselves with France and Russia the more we produced in German minds the impression that we were plotting to encircle Germany'. He then went on to doubt whether Hitler had 'a lust for conquest on a Napoleonic scale, which he himself did not credit'.

Chancellor of the Exchequer Sir John Simon observed that even if

Britain won a war against Germany, Czechoslovakia would not be reconstituted in its present form. The policy of attempting to bring Germany and Czechoslovakia to direct talks about the future of the disputed areas seemed no more than common sense. France was the key, for if she stood by the Eastern European commitments she had entered into after the Great War, Britain would have to bail her out. 'Was any useful purpose served', asked Halifax rhetorically, 'by treading on the landslide and being carried along with it?'[16] The alternative policy of attempting to bluff the Germans into thinking Britain would fight for the Czechs was too risky, as 'To undertake a commitment and to fail to fulfil it would leave us in a worse position, morally and materially, than if we had never assumed it.' Bluff and brinkmanship require a tight hold over public opinion and are thus primarily totalitarian weapons which democracies can only rarely use successfully.

It was Halifax's memorandum, dated 18 March 1938 and entitled 'Possible Measures To Avert German Action in Czechoslovakia', that the Foreign Policy Committee used as the basis for its discussion. In it he called for 'measures to stabilize Czechoslovakia vis-à-vis public opinion in this country and in the world generally'. He attacked Churchill's idea of a 'Grand Alliance' of all Germany's neighbours as giving Germany an excuse, opportunity and provocation for attack. Throughout the crisis, Halifax saw Churchill's concept as precisely the same type of unwieldy and dangerous weapon that Schuschnigg's threatened plebiscite had been. Halifax's alternative was the 'Guessing Position' plus 'an agreement with Italy sufficiently attractive to her in the long run to abandon the "axis"; that we should intensify our rearmament, particularly in the air; re-affirming the guarantee that we have already given to France'. 'The Holy Fox' also suggested that the Ambassador in Paris, Sir Eric Phipps, should see the French Government before 24 March to let it know the gist of the Prime Minister's proposed declaration about Czechoslovakia, but not sufficiently long before to allow it time to alter it.

In the back of Halifax's mind there was always the suspicion that 'France might consider that her interests would be better served by making the best terms she could with Germany, perhaps at our expense'.[17] It was a doubt that lingered until the moment in June 1940 when the prophecy was fulfilled. Halifax is often castigated for his attitude towards the French, under the assumption that by mistrusting them he weakened them, which made him further distrust them and so on until they were rendered demoralized and impotent. Put in its most contentious form by his Francophile Private Secretary Harvey, 'neither he nor the PM have such an abhorrence of dictatorship as to overcome their innate mistrust of French democracy and its supposed inefficiency'.[18] This is a non sequitur; why should Halifax's stance on dictatorship have closed his eyes to the glaring deficiencies of the Third Republic, with its interminable political crises, short-lived ministries, dodgy politicians, labour unrest and far-Left Popular Front?

Only a very few Britons – notably Austen Chamberlain, Churchill and Duff Cooper – had any time for the fretful and pusillanimous French leadership. The very concept of the Maginot Line, indicating an inflexibly defensive mentality, seeped into the French national psyche, completely shattered since Verdun, until despite their technical and numerical military preponderance over Germany in May 1940, they lost the ability to counter-attack. Just before Eden's resignation Halifax had been 'strongly against' closer staff contacts with the French and a month later he told the Foreign Policy Committee that 'the French were never ready to face up to realities, they delighted in vain words and protestations'.

It is important to bear Halifax's feelings about the French in mind when considering his train of thought on presenting his memorandum – effectively Czechoslovakia's death warrant – to the Committee. Harvey noted that his master was 'very suspicious of Soviet Russia.... He is much impressed by military weakness of France and ourselves.'[19] This tends to negate Harvey's damning assertion of four days later that, 'He easily blinds himself to unpleasant facts and is ingenious and even Jesuitical in rounding awkward corners in his mind.'[20] It is clear from the Cabinet minutes that Halifax, self-confessedly a layman in military terms, was deeply influenced by the Chiefs of Staff's report entitled 'Military Implications of German Aggression Against Czechoslovakia'. This document plainly asserted that 'no pressure which this country and its possible allies could exercise would suffice to prevent the defeat of Czechoslovakia'.[21] Halifax was right to describe the report as 'an extremely melancholy document, but no Government could afford to overlook it'.[22] He told the Committee that, after reading the report, 'whatever his sympathies and anxieties, he felt he was not in a position to recommend a policy involving a risk of war'.[23] He was simply not prepared to risk a world war, with all the implications that had for Britain's Empire and position in the world, in order to restore an already as good as defeated Central European nation for the protection of which Britain had no contractual obligations.

Instead, Halifax wanted to put pressure on the Czechs via the French to explore every avenue to mollify the Sudetendeutsche. He was the first to acknowledge that this was to be 'a disagreeable business which had to be done as pleasantly as possible'.[24] As nearly three-quarters of Czech trade went through Germany, it was well within the German ambit to defeat her southern neighbour by means of economic strangulation alone. Domestic political considerations had also to be factored into the equation. The 'Guessing Position' was felt to be the only policy likely to be 'generally approved by Parliament and the country' in that it struck the right balance between war-mongering and abdication of responsibility. So on 24 March Chamberlain announced that although Britain was not guaranteeing

Czechoslovakia, neither was she abandoning her, for 'if war broke out ... it would be quite impossible to say where it might end and what Governments might become involved. The inexorable pressure of facts might well prove more powerful than formal pronouncements.'[25] The statement's wording has a profoundly Halifaxian ring to it and perfectly encapsulated the 'Guessing Position'.

After the announcement Halifax interested himself closely in the second indispensable arm of his policy: rearmament. He turned up to his first Committee of Imperial Defence meeting of the year on 31 March with ideas and queries on subjects as diverse as anti-aircraft protection of vital areas, the overhauling of Alexandria harbour and the protection of oil supplies after an outbreak of hostilities. He complained that 'the gap between performance and desirability seemed large' and demanded that 'any action which could be taken should be taken'.[26]

The Committee of Imperial Defence, virtually in mothballs since the end of the Great War, swiftly became a major forum. At late as mid-December 1937, it had been possible for Old Harrovians Hoare and the Marquess of Zetland to prevent the deployment of air defences in the grounds of their alma mater. Hoare called the 'disfigurement of a Balloon Barrage depot with its unsightly hangars' nothing less than 'a catastrophe for Harrow as the centre of Harrovian life' and thus the Home Secretary and Secretary for India overruled the views of the Minister for Co-ordination of Defence and the Secretary for Air. The days of such cosy patronage were over.[27]

One of the first actions Halifax took on becoming Foreign Secretary in February 1938 showed his innate toughness. Information from King Paul of Yugoslavia had led Cadogan to surmise that there was a leak emanating from the Foreign Office code and encyphering department. This department was made up of 'a hotch-potch of old clubmen',[28] many of whom were Cadogan's friends of many years' standing. Knowing this to be the case, Halifax volunteered to do the job of sacking the entire department, guilty and innocent alike, saying, 'My mind is made up. Nothing can be done although I realize what I am doing is very unfair.'[29]

Days after *Anschluss* he organized with the Secret Intelligence Service 'a few preparatory steps taken in deadly secrecy by Section D to counter Nazi predominance in small countries Germany had just conquered or was plainly threatening'.[30] To this end he invited the Canadian newspaper magnate, Sir Campbell Stuart, to look into the uses of sabotage, labour unrest, inflation and propaganda. The quality of intelligence about Germany received by the politicians from the intelligence services was never particularly high in the inter-war period. The historian Wesley Wark has shown how the British secret service was 'understaffed, underpaid and could run very few agents abroad, while the cryptanalysts of the Government Code and Cypher School provided a disappointingly limited access to the coded radio traffic of both Hitler's Germany and Stalin's Russia'.[31]

For domestic propaganda Butler told Halifax of 'a little publicity committee for our work', which would 'see that the correspondence columns everywhere were well stocked with our arguments written by our friends'.[32] This committee was to consist of Reginald Leeper, head of the Foreign Office publicity department, Henry Channon MP, Butler's Parliamentary Private Secretary, and Halifax's Parliamentary Private Secretary and future biographer, the Earl of Birkenhead (son of Halifax's old antagonist). It was to be chaired by Butler himself. These weekly meetings of 'Rex', 'Chips', 'Freddie' and 'Rab' were not quite intended to develop into the dirty tricks department of Butler's old India Bill days, but Butler's memorandum did state that stories and speeches would be planted in the press and 'Winston's campaign should be watched'.[33]

During his visit to Paris in March 1938, Churchill certainly was watched, on Halifax's orders, by Sir Eric Phipps. Halifax read Phipps's report on Churchill's meetings with various French politicians to the Cabinet and instructed Phipps to warn the Frenchmen 'that the right source from which to ascertain British Government policy is the declarations of the British Government, rather than Winston's exuberant interpretations of it'. When Lloyd George visited France in March 1938, Phipps was also ordered to keep a close eye on him and after his return deprecate his influence to those French politicians the ex-Premier had met. Duff Cooper too was watched by the British Embassy on Halifax's orders when he visited America during the Phoney War.

As late as the spring of 1938, very little opposition to appeasement manifested itself within the mainstream Conservative Party. Although David Margesson, the Government Chief Whip, ran a fanatically tight ship, the Tory Party, long a bastion of individualism and pugnaciousness, stayed faithful to appeasement. It then continued to stay loyal to Chamberlain personally even after he had been discredited. Despite the tradition of discipline in the Party and a fear lest a split would let in the socialists, one is left with the conviction that the Tories supported Chamberlain and Halifax because they truly believed in their policy.

What opposition there was to appeasement amongst Conservative MPs was scattered, disorganized and never amounted to more than about thirty, or less than one-tenth, of the parliamentary Party. These grouped themselves around the up-and-coming Eden, or even Leo Amery, rather than the down and all-but-out Churchill. Of the latter, Chamberlain crowed to his sisters in March 1938: 'Everyone in the House enjoys listening to him and is ready to cheer and laugh at his sallies but he has no following of any importance.'[34] Eden's opposition to the Government was, to the exasperation of his friends, so muted that he was not really considered too disloyal by it.

Discussions about negotiations with Italy began as soon as Eden cleared his desk. Since November 1937 it had been the Chiefs of Staff's urgent desire 'to reduce the number of potential enemies'.[35] As the negotiations developed, Halifax deftly distanced himself from the redundant compromise solution he had hammered out back in February when attempting to forestall Eden's resignation. At his first Foreign Policy Committee meeting as Foreign Secretary, he devised the distinctly 'Holy Fox' ploy of placing 'Spain formally on the Agenda Paper for the Conversations, but . . . it should not be discussed. . . . He feared that if at any time we should be forced to publish documents and it then appeared that we had not placed Spain formally on the agenda, the Government would be severely criticized.'[36]

Although the actual negotiations were conducted in Rome between Count Ciano and the Earl of Perth, it was essentially Halifax's achievement. He was given a great degree of leeway by the Cabinet and in the tough negotiations which followed, the Cabinet tended to defer to him over solutions. It often looked as though the talks would founder altogether and he told Harvey in mid-March, 'we shall not get any performance out of them until Franco has won. So we are in a complete jam.'[37]

Pressing for a 'liberal and practical interpretation' of the Prime Minister's February undertaking not to sign an agreement before Italian 'volunteers' were leaving Spain, Halifax worked hard for what he hoped might eventually become a reconstituted Stresa Front. De jure recognition of Italian sovereignty over Abyssinia involved no overt action by Britain beyond adding 'Emperor of Ethiopia' to the King of Italy's title on Perth's credentials. Halifax learnt the Hoare–Laval lesson well and when stepping on public sensibilities over Abyssinia he trod carefully. But time was running out. Hitler was due to visit Rome in early May and the League meeting at which Halifax was to urge de jure recognition was due for the 12th. In the Foreign Policy Committee, Halifax proposed a wily way out of the 'volunteers' dilemma: 'we might try to persuade Count Ciano to agree to a token withdrawal of volunteers, say 1,000 from each side. In this event could we contemplate taking action at Geneva?'[38] Nothing came of this and the situation worsened. Attempts to bribe Haile Selassie failed and, in early April, Halifax also had to warn the Committee for Imperial Defence of the possibility of impending trouble in the Far East.

Despite many setbacks an agreement was signed on 16 April, to come into effect at an unspecified date in the future. Although this was Halifax's birthday, the day was chosen to maximize weekend publicity and because Halifax ruled out a Good Friday signing. The Agreement confirmed that Britain would accord de jure recognition of Italian sovereignty over Abyssinia in return for Italian troop reductions in Spain. It also reaffirmed the status quo in the Mediterranean and had provisions for the exchange of military information, Saudi and Yemeni integrity, non-compulsion of native armies in Africa, religious freedom in East Africa, free use of the Suez Canal, a substantial reduction in Italian troops stationed in Libya and a promise that all Italian troops would be withdrawn after the Spanish war ended. The King and the Cabinet warmly congratulated Halifax on his achievement. But this was no Stresa. The Agreement did not come into effect for seven months and the withdrawal of volunteers provision, intended as an inducement for the Italians to behave well over Spain, soon turned into a thorn in the British Government's side.

Under a journalist's hostile questioning on 12 July 1938, Halifax said of the Agreement:

> Let's be honest with ourselves about this; it cannot possibly succeed one hundred per cent, but even if it succeeds seventy or even eighty per cent that will be worth achieving. . . . Well, at any rate we have got as a result of the agreement the withdrawal of troops from Libya and the cessation of anti-British propaganda, and I do not think that these things are negligible.[39]

He was franker with Phipps to whom he wrote, 'Although we do not expect to detach Italy from the Axis we believe the Agreement will increase Mussolini's power of manoeuvre and so make him less dependent on Hitler, and therefore freer to resume the classic Italian role of balancing between Germany and the Western Powers.'[40] There was something in that: Italy did not enter the war in 1939.

The speech which Halifax delivered to the League Council on 12 May 1938 typified his pragmatic approach to politics. He said that there were two types of idealism: 'the ideal of devotion, unflinching but impractical, to some high purpose' and 'the ideal of a practical victory for peace'. He had 'no doubt that the stronger claim' was the latter. But the League Council, especially after an emotional speech by Haile Selassie, looked unlikely to accord Britain the unanimous support she required. So committed was he to his Agreement that at a Cabinet meeting at the end of March Halifax suggested that, 'we should initiate a discussion at the Council and encourage as many as possible of the other states represented thereon to support our views and should regard this discussion . . . as in fact setting our hands free to recognize Italian sovereignty in Ethiopia'.[41] In the event, only China and New Zealand voted against.

To proponents of the 'Guilty Men' thesis, Halifax's guilt included not only outdoing Hoare but also virtually conspiring for a Francoist victory in Spain. Michael Foot goes so far as to assert that Franco was a hero of Halifax's.[42] The evidence for this rests on one throwaway line about a suspicion of Ciano's that 'at heart I think he would be glad if Franco's victory were to settle the question'.[43] In fact, in common with most of the Foreign Office, Halifax merely hoped that the potentially destabilizing conflict in Spain would come to an end as soon as possible. He kept scrupulously neutral and the nearest he ever came to committing himself was in a telegram to Perth sent at a particularly tricky point in the

Anglo-Italian negotiations, when he told Perth to inform Ciano that 'Spain should not fall under the domination of a Bolshevik regime ... [but should establish] ... a government in Spain which might rally to itself the support of all reasonable elements'.[44] This is a far cry from any secretly pro-Falangist sympathies of which he is often accused but was always devoid.

Britain was not solely at fault over the Spanish civil war; when Halifax attempted to set up a committee to investigate reports of indiscriminate bombing of undefended towns, he met point-blank refusals from America, Sweden, Norway and Holland to take any part. The embarrassment to Britain increased as the Nationalists realized that they could attack British shipping with impunity. Between mid-April and mid-June 1938, some twenty-two out of the 140 British ships trading with the Republic were attacked and half of them were sunk or badly damaged. Twenty-one British seamen and, ironically enough, seven Non-Intervention Committee observers, died in the attacks.

Most galling of all, a British ship, *Dellroya*, was sunk off Gandia within the very sights of a Royal Navy warship. This prompted the American Ambassador to Madrid to remark that it was the first time in the long and proud history of her maritime power that the British Empire had conceded this special humiliation. It was easy to scorn the Government along these lines, and many in Parliament did, but in fact the Red Ensign was then in widespread use as a flag of convenience, especially by Greeks. Very few of those 140 ships were actually British-owned. They were trading (at good profit) with the Republic fully cognizant of the dangers. The extent of the sailors' personal responsibility for their fates may perhaps be likened to that of those Britons who, despite Foreign Office warnings, decided to continue to live and work in Beirut after 1982. Butler was probably correct when he told Brabourne that, 'the Elizabethan policy of the PM in not intervening in the war in order to save a small section of the Merchant Navy is perfectly understood by the ordinary British citizen'.[45]

At the Committee of Imperial Defence discussion on 11 April 1938 on the advisability of a continental capability for the army, that is the formation of a British Expeditionary Force, Halifax said that he 'was as anxious as anyone that the field force should not be sent ... but he hoped that we should not categorically say that in no circumstances would a field force be sent to the Continent'[46] as he wished to ensure the French continued to think that it might. Britain had no detailed plans for a large continental army, but rather planned to supply naval and air force contributions in any future conflict. The French were to stay invincible behind their revered Maginot Line whilst Britain, in yet another hangover from the Great War, attempted to blockade Germany into submission. There was thus no need, thought the Service Chiefs, Captain Basil Liddell Hart and most of the other military thinkers, for a large, unwieldy and expensive Expeditionary Force of the sort that went to Mons in 1914.

Outmanoeuvred by Germany, strung along by Italy, patronized by America, distrustful of Russia and wary of France, Halifax approached the summer of 1938 under no illusions as to the extent to which his country could do more than make 'the disagreeable business' of forcing Czechoslovakia to dismember herself 'as pleasant as possible'.[47]

12

The Czech Crisis

Munich was not a case of appeasement but of sheer blackmail. The series of crises and rumours about Czechoslovakia started in late May 1938 when two Sudeten farmers were shot by a Czech official. Hitler, as self-styled 'Protector' of the Sudetens, was suspected (wrongly as it turned out) of intending to use this incident as an excuse to invade. In the full-scale crisis which ensued, the Czechs mobilized on 21 May and Halifax telegraphed Berlin in the early hours of the 22nd warning Ribbentrop 'not to count upon this country being able to stand aside if . . . there should start European conflagration'.[1] He added that 'the experience of all history went to show that the pressure of facts was sometimes more powerful than the wills of man, and if once war should start in Central Europe it was quite impossible to say where it might not end, and who might not become involved'.[2]

Halifax's action in this opening round of the war of nerves brought him plaudits from Cadogan, 'H. is admirably balanced and calm and sensible. . . . He does *think*, and think *calmly*,' and from Chamberlain, 'I thank God for a steady unruffled Foreign Secretary.'[3] But it is now known that the whole '21 May Crisis' was not so dangerous a situation as it seemed at the time. Hitler had been briefed by his High Command that the Wehrmacht would not be ready for a large-scale war for at least another six months. The view of the crisis emanating from Fleet Street, of a firm West facing down a bona-fide Nazi threat, bore little relation to fact and infuriated the Germans. It also brought the attention of the British public to the Czech problem for the first time. Ignorance about Central Europe was widespread and fully reflected by MPs who spoke of 'Czechoslovenia' and 'Czechoslavia', and who sometimes mixed up Bucharest with Budapest in their speeches. Walking past No. 10, Downing Street, Jan Masaryk, the Czech Minister to London, remarked how he spent 'most of my official time . . . explaining that Czechoslovakia is a country and not a contagious disease'.[4]

Throughout the summer the Government clung to the 'Guessing Position' but at the same time examined ways to neutralize Czechoslovakia along Swiss or Belgian lines. The Germans, meanwhile, rearmed steadily and perfected plans for 'Operation Green'. By mid-July, the situation was judged sufficiently serious to use a German Princess, Stephanie von Hohenlohe, to help arrange a secret meeting between Halifax and Hitler's adjutant and former Great War commanding officer, Captain Fritz Wiedemann. The two met at Halifax's London residence in Eaton Square at ten o'clock on the morning of 18 July. Cadogan acted as interpreter, but no notes were taken. The discussion really only served to ascertain that Hitler thought a Göring visit to Britain undesirable, that he was serious about the Sudetenland, that he was 'still bitter' about press treatment of the 21 May crisis, that he was 'enraged' by Fleet Street and that he would give no promise to resolve the Czech crisis peaceably.

In his report a week later, Wiedemann wrote that Halifax had said he 'before his death would like to see as the culmination of his work the Führer entering London at the side of the English King amid the acclamation of the English people'.[5] This completely fails to ring true, not least because against the background of such a disappointing meeting Halifax would hardly have used such uncharacteristically expansive imagery. Wiedemann, on the other hand, had every incentive to attempt to put his efforts in the best possible light with his Führer. None the less, when in February 1957 the editor of a Danish paper wrote to the *Manchester Guardian* about the incident, Halifax, then aged seventy-five, decided to absent himself from Garrowby for the day and refused to take calls from the press about it.

The Wiedemann meeting was only one of a number of cases in which Halifax attempted to bypass Ribbentrop, who was thought malignly to distort any British message to Hitler. Accompanying the King and Queen on their state visit to France the next day, Halifax told Prime Minister Edouard Daladier and Foreign Minister Georges Bonnet about the Wiedemann visit. He only did this because a *Daily Herald* reporter had recognized Wiedemann at Croydon aerodrome and, therefore, he calculated that they would have found out about it anyhow. Halifax approved of the then French Government and arranged the Royal visit partly in order to bolster Daladier. The month before he had authorized Phipps to work against Daladier's rival, M. Paul Boncour.[6] It was from this Government that Halifax secured acceptance for his next plan to prevent the Germans taking precipitate action against the Czechs.

Lord Runciman was a National Liberal shipbuilding tycoon, who had been President of the Board of Trade in the MacDonald Government. Halifax had known him for many years and considered him ideal to head a mission to Prague to mediate on the Sudetens' case. He was selected primarily, as a Downing Street memo makes plain, because he 'could be relied upon to put the results across'.[7] His background, political career and Establishment credentials left him naturally capable of knowing exactly how London would wish him to act without the need for constant reference back home. It was a classic liberal rationalist move to try to ascertain the rights and wrongs of the Sudeten problem and to try to settle things accordingly. Halifax and Runciman did not see how it is perfectly possible to have insoluble questions in international relations, where any initiatives only serve to render problems yet more intractable. Soon after arriving in Prague, Runciman found himself caught on the rack of the never-ending wait for the next inflammatory Nazi announcement. Despite consistent assertions to the contrary, his very presence in Czechoslovakia committed the British Government in a way it had not been formerly; not least in that it would be humiliating were Germany to march into Prague with Runciman still deliberating there.

Still standing by his 'Guessing Position', Halifax was keen that Henderson should do his utmost

> to get it into the very thick heads of the Germans that if they insist on stepping on the string the gun was very likely to go off. It is our only chance as I see it of preventing them doing it – and it is a difficult line to ride, without exposing ourselves to humiliation if we don't go to war. And that, with you, I have no intention of doing over Czechoslovakia, if I can avoid it.[8]

This is not so very far from the bluffing posture that Halifax's detractors complained he failed to adopt. Henderson warned that next time, at a date generally expected to be in September, Hitler would be ready and this time there would be no repetition of 21 May.

Henderson believed that as Czechoslovakia was 'constitutionally and initially a mistake',[9] it should not be allowed to prejudice an Anglo-German understanding which 'means world peace for a generation at least'.[10] It was undoubtedly wrong to have an ambassador so sympathetic to the aspirations of the country to which he was accredited. Nevertheless, plenty of Britons in 1938 agreed with Henderson's diagnosis of 7 April that, 'it is morally unjust to compel this solid Teuton majority to remain subjected to a Slav Central Government in Prague'. Those who defended the status quo had not taken all the moral high ground. The right of national self-determination of peoples had been a Gladstone war-cry. It had for centuries formed a central part of the liberal political lexicon. As Lord Erskine so succinctly put it to his fellow Provincial Governor, Lord Brabourne, 'How can England fight to retain two million Sudeten Germans inside a country which they detest, or crush a large number of Poles and Magyars who are in the same boat?'[11] Furthermore, Henlein, in his speeches to the Royal Institute of International Affairs, cleverly emphasized how Moscow's 1935 pact with Prague had turned Czechoslovakia into 'Russia's aircraft carrier'. The Czechs, he warned, in a phrase well calculated to get his Chatham House audience nodding in agreement, were 'tainted' with 'the bacillus of communism'.

Halifax had not invented the policy of putting pressure on Prague to improve relations with their German-speaking minority. When he was Foreign Secretary, Eden had urged reform on the then Czech President, Thomas Masaryk, and his Foreign Minister, Dr Krofta. Vansittart too had promised Henlein he would raise the matter at the League. Sudeten propaganda in Britain was well organized, with lavish junkets arranged for British MPs. Using advanced public-relations techniques, the Sudeten Nazis took their British guests trout fishing in Bohemia and then around the unemployment-stricken parts of their industrial heartlands, effortlessly evoking sympathy for them and anger against Prague. A war in 1938 to prevent the exercise of Sudeten self-determination would have been as divisive in Britain as the one against the American colonists or the Boers. Certainly the Dominions, whose support had been so vital to the successful prosecution of the Great War, were totally opposed to any military action over Czechoslovakia whatsoever. The High Commissioners of Canada, Australia, New Zealand, South Africa and Eire vied with one another to distance their Governments from any actions of the British Government which could possibly lead to bloodshed.

Halifax is often criticized for not having read *Mein Kampf*. The Foreign Office did, in fact, have certain passages translated and circulated, but his not having ploughed through the whole of that contradictory and repetitive propaganda work was no great sin. *Mein Kampf* is essentially about Eastern policy. The author proposed, in his fantastically dull and convoluted way, friendship with Britain and a war for *Lebensraum* in the East. He was initially to follow precisely the opposite policy. The thrillers and detective fiction Halifax used to enjoy would have given him a better insight into Hitler's mentality than *Mein Kampf* ever could. In November 1939, the Queen sent him a copy with the message, 'I send you *Mein Kampf*, but do not advise you to read it through, or you might go mad and that would be a pity. Even a skip through gives one a good idea of his mentality, ignorance and obvious sincerity.'[12]

The first hint of a rift between the Prime Minister and his Foreign Secretary came in May 1938 over Halifax's modest plans to increase British and check German influence in Central and South-Eastern Europe. In a memorandum of 24 May, Halifax recommended that an interdepartmental committee be set up to consider the technical aspects of how to head off German hegemony in the region. 'We are now confronted', Halifax warned the Foreign Policy Committee on 1 June, 'with the probability that German influence would penetrate throughout the whole of Central and South-Eastern Europe in the economic sphere, leading to the likelihood of Germany dominating this great area in the political sphere.' He therefore proposed that 'an attempt should be made to check this process before it is too late'.[13]

Chamberlain refused to see Britain in such direct competition with Germany and feared that any small countries Britain attempted to help would lose no opportunity to defraud her. To his mind Eastern Europe was no more vital to British interests than Abyssinia had been, and it was ridiculous to expend resources trying to protect them. This exposed a fundamental difference of thinking between Chamberlain, who came up with a plethora of criticisms of the memorandum, and Halifax, who feared 'a stranglehold' was being established and who wanted to provide in London at least a limited *point d'appui* to counter Berlin. Halifax listed 'the growing activity of numerous German emissaries, the spreading of German culture, the encouragement of the German language, the facilities given to the youth of the smaller countries to receive their education in Germany,' etc., as evidence of this creeping influence.

The Prime Minister did not see an economically powerful Germany as 'necessarily a bad thing'[14] and thought it might even redirect her energies into peaceable channels. Halifax, in defiance of the very nostrum that brought the National Government into being in the first place, instead called for 'practicable schemes even if they were open to objections of financial or even economic orthodoxy'. He targeted the purchase of Balkan tobacco crops as a means of weaning countries away, fearing that otherwise 'they would undoubtedly drift into Germany's orbit'.

This advocacy of the use of Britain's financial muscle to help her strategic position was not confined to Europe. China was the world's largest producer of wolfram, a rare tungsten necessary for the manufacture of certain weapons. In April 1938, the Germans had been in negotiation with the Chinese to acquire their entire annual output. Britain received all the wolfram she needed, about 1,000 tons per annum, from Burma, but in 1937 alone the Germans bought 8,000 tons of it and were believed to have some 20,000 more stockpiled. Halifax's problem was how simultaneously to help the Chinese war effort, deny the Germans their ore and yet not antagonize the Japanese. His solution was a large-scale loan to help stabilize the Chinese currency and thus make them less dependent on German cash. He also added that, 'from the point of view of morality, China's case strongly appealed to him, and ... she might in the end succeed in defeating Japan'.[15]

That vain hope notwithstanding, Halifax felt that Japan would be too busy fighting China to take on any commitments against Britain. But the Foreign Policy Committee was unimpressed; Simon pointed out the vulnerability of Hong Kong and Chamberlain feared Britain would be subjected to 'intense Japanese hostility' should direct assistance be afforded to China. They might also have pointed out that the wolfram which Halifax intended to use as the security for any such loan was not only still under ground, but also under ground soon to be captured by the Japanese. One (sadly unnamed) Cabinet minister came up with the splendid suggestion that the British Government should so rig the world's wolfram market as to ensure that it broke even on the deal.[16] Though thwarted in his Chinese currency plans, Halifax seemed to his Private Secretary to be 'determined to push it through one way or another'.[17]

Chamberlain's lack of concern over German economic aggrandizement was only partly actuated by the hope that it would pull the teeth of Nazi military revanchism. He was also attracted by the idea that before too long Germany might come up against the Russians. To many Britons in 1938, Bolshevism, with its menace of global revolution, seemed to pose more of a threat to Britain and her Empire than Nazism, the racial philosophies of which promised an end to adventure once all ethnic Germans had been gathered into the Reich. The Russian Revolution, only two decades old, with its legacy of confiscations, regicide, atheism and massacres, aroused much the same emotions that Edmund Burke had felt about its French counterpart. When Halifax first entered the Cabinet, Britain had not yet recognized the Soviet Union. For all his supposed softness in India, Halifax had always been extremely tough in suppressing communist activity. Deep distrust of the USSR, which came naturally to Conservative politicians of the day, partly explains Chamberlain's and Halifax's reluctance to play the Red card in the Czech crisis and beyond.

Stalin's purges of June 1937 had decapitated virtually the entire Red Army officer corps. Five of the seven marshals and a majority of generals and colonels were shot in a spasm of Stalinist paranoiac blood-lust, exacerbated by some superb Nazi misinformation. Russia's inability to overrun Finland in 1940 shows how badly her offensive capacity had fared. Despite her 1935 alliance, Russia had no border contiguous with Czechoslovakia, which at the nearest point was over a hundred miles away. The Poles and Romanians, out of fear of Germany and acting on the well-founded premise that the Red Army had a tendency to overstay its welcome, denied Russia the right to go to Czechoslovakia's aid. Chamberlain also suspected that Stalin intended to trick the West into thinking Russia would fight, thereby encouraging a war with Germany from which he would then actually stay aloof. The British Ambassador in Moscow was convinced that effective Russian help was unlikely to appear at all. Chamberlain and Halifax decided that hundreds of thousands of British lives could not be put at risk on the strength of Stalin's sense of honour. With Poland and Romania, which had their own claims against Czechoslovakia, more likely to join the Germans than the Czechs and with Italy aiding and abetting Germany, who can say that they were wrong not to encourage Beneš to sacrifice his country on the altar of Western morality? Chamberlain told Walter Citrine that 'Czechoslovakia would be like Humpty Dumpty. He would have fallen off the wall and no one could put him back again.'[18]

A red herring almost as great as the Russian alliance was the notion that elements in the German High Command, given the right encouragement and signal, were on the verge of overthrowing Hitler. The accusation constantly levelled against Halifax is that by failing to support these 'good' (as the Foreign Office nicknamed them) Germans, the British Government threw away a chance of winning the war without fighting and instead contributed to the myth of Hitler's invincibility. However, although the 'good' Germans were brave, sincere and individually admirable, there were simply not enough of them. Nor did they have the support of the storm-trooper, who owed his allegiance directly to his Führer. When he visited Hitler, Halifax noted that 'so long as the Army and SS (20,000) and Police are well paid it is pretty difficult to see how the regime should be upset'.[19] It was Churchill who was star-gazing when during his meeting at Chartwell with Ewald von Kleist-Schmenzin, the generals' emissary, he discussed the coup that would bring 'a new system of government within 48 hours. Such a government, probably of a monarchist character, could guarantee stability and end the fear of war for ever.'[20]

Chamberlain told Halifax that von Kleist-Schmenzin reminded him 'of the Jacobites at the Court of France in King William's time and I think we must discount a good deal of what he says'. Much the same was felt to be true of the secret warnings of Theodor Kordt, the Chargé d'Affaires at the German Embassy, who begged Chamberlain to encourage the anti-Nazi resistance in Germany by refusing to negotiate with Hitler. It is highly unlikely that a leader as popular and well protected as Hitler could have been overthrown, however badly the Czech crisis went for him. If it had happened, no one would have been more delighted than Halifax, but British foreign policy could not realistically be conducted on such a flimsy hope. Although Halifax was willing to meet such anti-Nazis as Adam von Trott, which he did at Cliveden in June 1939 and later introduced him to Chamberlain, he did not believe they had or could be given the where-withal to replace the Nazi regime in 1938–40. In this, painful as it may be to admit it, he was probably correct.

It should have come as no surprise to anyone when Runciman finally came to report that, 'it has become self-evident to me that those frontier districts between Czechoslovakia and Germany where the Sudeten population is in an important majority should be given full right of self-determination at once ... promptly and without procrastination'. On 3 September, Henlein published his 'Carlsbad Programme', which amounted to a series of demands for Sudeten autonomy. Three days later, under Runciman's blandishments, Beneš acceded to them with a 'Fourth Plan'. Henlein was under orders from Hitler only to make demands to which Prague could not possibly concede. When instead Prague did concede them, a nonplussed Henlein had to turn to Berlin for guidance.

His embarrassment was saved by *The Times*, which the next day, 7

As a boy on Jessie

Hickleton Hall, near Doncaster

Marriage to Lady Dorothy Onslow at Clandon,
21 September 1909

Election leaflet of January 1910

'The Hampton Court of the North', Temple Newsam, near Leeds

With the Queens' Own Yorkshire
Dragoons, 1914

Garrowby, near York

Leaving Buckingham Palace with the newly appointed Home Secretary, William Bridgeman, and President of the Board of Trade, Sir Philip Lloyd-Greame, in October 1922

Sir Edwin Lutyens's Viceroy's House, New Delhi

Lord Irwin as Viceroy of India with the son of the Maharajah of Bharatpur and Richard Wood as train-bearers

Mahatma Gandhi, 'a relentless bargainer'

The Man Whose Policy is Backed by BALDWIN

DO YOU WANT GANDHI GOVERNMENT IN THE BRITISH EMPIRE?

P.T.O.

A leaflet distributed during the St George's, Westminster, by-election, March 1931

A family group from the early 1930s: from left to right, Lord Irwin, Lady Bingley, Lord
Bingley, Dorothy Lane Fox, Anne Wood, Charles Wood, Richard Wood; the second
Viscount is supported by Lady Irwin, with the dog Gyp in the foreground

'The time has come,' Herr Hitler said, 'to
talk of many things . . .'; Lord Halifax: 'But
not about colonies.' Herr Hitler: 'Hush!'
Punch, 24 November 1937

Berchtesgaden, 21 November 1937

Dr Paul Schmidt, Lord Halifax, Baron von Neurath and the Führer at Berchtesgaden

Foreign Policy Vaudeville Act: Chamberlain using Halifax to balance Nancy Astor, Lord Lothian and Geoffrey Dawson with Leo Amery, Sir Henry Page Croft and Colonel Blimp. David Low cartoon, *Evening Standard*, 10 December 1937

Sir Alexander Cadogan walking with Lord Halifax in Whitehall

September, published its notorious leader which speculated whether it may 'be worthwhile for the Czechoslovak Government to consider ... making Czechoslovakia a more homogeneous state by the secession of alien populations who are contiguous to the nation by which they are united by race'. The outrage produced by this unashamedly pro-German stance prompted Halifax to arrange a meeting that day with Dawson. They lunched together at one of Dawson's clubs, the Travellers', ostensibly so that Halifax could administer a rap over Dawson's knuckles. But as well as being old friends and allies, Eton governors, All Souls' Fellows, Yorkshiremen and High Anglicans, they were also fundamentally in agreement on the basics of the Czech situation. The new hoop through which Halifax was preparing to jump – after those of Swiss-style neutralization, liquidation of Czech alliances and the Runciman mission – involved the holding of a plebiscite of the Sudetens as to their future, the outcome of which would be a foregone conclusion. It did the Government little harm to have this idea semi-officially mooted by *The Times* before any firm decisions were taken. Dawson had made regular visits to the Foreign Office throughout Halifax's tenure and was even sent sensitive Foreign Office memoranda. In July, Halifax had asked Cadogan to sound Dawson out as to who should be the next Ambassador to Washington. Giving news to *The Times* early meant that Dawson could write his leaders and headlines in good time and Halifax could be sure of good coverage in the one paper foreigners read.

They read it because, for all the Foreign Office denials of 7 September, it was a quasi-governmental organ. A couple of letters from the Marquess of Lothian to Halifax in late May 1938 show how Halifax used the paper. Lothian had had no official status since his Under-Secretaryship at the India Office in 1932, but was a friend of Halifax's and had non-parliamentary political influence of a type seldom seen in today's politics. On 31 May, Lothian sent Halifax a draft of a letter to *The Times* which Halifax had suggested he write. In it he reiterated the 24 March 'Guessing Position'. The letter was never sent, but had it been any cognoscenti would have been in no doubt that it carried government approval.[21]

The symbiotic relationship Halifax had with Dawson, and their friendship, was not about to be derailed by an article which, although he deprecated it in Cabinet, was not too far from his own position. On returning from the lunch, Dawson sent a note to his deputy editor saying that Halifax had 'reported, as I expected, that the last paragraph of [the] leader this morning had disturbed his office, though he did not seem to dissent from it himself'. In his diary that evening Dawson wrote of how 'the FO went up through the roof – not so, however, the Foreign Secretary, who came to lunch at the Travellers' and had a long talk. He is as much in the dark as everyone else as to what is likely to happen next.'[22]

If *The Times* chastised the Czechs with whips, the French press chastized them with scorpions. They were yet more keen for a plebiscite to rectify the

Czech borders in Germany's favour. All this prompted Henlein to stage a clash with the Czech authorities, allowing him off Beneš's 'Fourth Plan' hook and sending the spiral of provocation and reaction still higher. Hitler's long-awaited speech at Nuremberg on 12 September, which was widely expected to announce military sanctions, turned out to be only the usual round of abuse against Beneš and paranoiac froth against 'the eternal Jewish Bolshevik fiend'. Those Sudetens who took it as an invitation to insurrection were promptly quelled. At Cabinet that day Halifax gave his diagnosis : 'he thought that Herr Hitler was possibly or even probably mad',[23] but was not bluffing.

On 13 September, the Prague Government declared martial law ; two days later, Henlein fled into Germany to place himself under Hitler's 'protection'. The situation was considered so desperate that Chamberlain and Halifax, with the subsequent concurrence of Simon and Hoare, decided to activate the plan Chamberlain had somewhat melodramatically codenamed 'Plan Z'. This entailed Chamberlain flying direct to Germany for a face-to-face meeting with Hitler. Writing to his sisters he boasted that it was 'so unconventional and daring that it rather took Halifax's breath away'.[24] Although in retrospect it seems fatuous to treat Chamberlain's personality as some sort of secret weapon, it was undoubtedly an imaginative move at a time when 'summits' were virtually unknown, air flight was still in its infancy and Chamberlain, who had never flown before, was seventy years old. No British Prime Minister had visited Germany since Disraeli attended the Congress of Berlin in 1878. With his ubiquitous wing collar and umbrella, Chamberlain has been easy to satirize as a fussy and procrastinating old woman. In fact, he enjoyed nothing more than to take swift and decisive action, such as when during the 1931 financial crisis he halted the flight from the pound overnight. He and Halifax had learnt well the Baldwinian lessons as to the political advantages accruing to those who seized the initiative.

When Chamberlain flew to meet Hitler at Berchtesgaden on 15 September, Halifax stayed behind as the only minister of sufficient stature to keep the likely waverers – such as Duff Cooper, Oliver Stanley and Lord Winterton – in line. It was also a shrewd calculation that by not taking Halifax it would be possible to exclude Ribbentrop from the meetings. At the Cabinet on Chamberlain's return it soon became clear that the Prime Minister had suspended all critical judgement of the Führer. To his sisters he was unbearably pleased with himself, saying Wilson had heard that Hitler was impressed by him and had said, 'I have had a conversation with a man ... and one with whom I can do business.'[25] He went on to tell them how the King 'was as excited as a boy' and that 'It was an idea after Father's own heart.... I am the most popular man in Germany !'[26] To the Cabinet he was thankfully slightly more restrained and commented primly on the paintings of nude women at the Berghof.

Announcing a 'new understanding between England and Germany', he said of Hitler that 'it was impossible not to be impressed with the power of the man ... his objectives were strictly limited ... when he had included the Sudeten Germans in the Reich he would be satisfied'.[27] Here was the hubris required by all the best tragedies before any eventual nemesis. Halifax was not as impressed as most of the rest of the Cabinet. Using a characteristic metaphor he confined himself to noting how

> it was undesirable to burn too much incense on the altar of self-determination. The most which he was prepared to say on the matter was that it was impossible to lead this country into a war against this principle ... he would fight for the great moralities which knew no geographical boundaries ... the theory of preventive war meant that we should have a bad war every twenty years in order to prevent a war from occurring five years later.[28]

Once Chamberlain had conceded the basic principle of a plebiscite, the details of conditions, time and extent of the transfer of populations had to be worked out. Halifax was very keen that in his next meeting with Hitler the Prime Minister should obtain the best possible conditions, especially for the timing of the transfers, which 'could not of course be effected at lightning speed'.[29] The seven hours of conversations with the French the next day were characterized by the usual manoeuvrings of each side to place the blame for coercing the Czechs on the other. It was also discovered that the French air force had only twenty-one aeroplanes which were equal to the most modern German machines. Finally, after midnight, it was agreed to send Beneš, in Cadogan's words, a 'pretty stiff' message from the two Governments 'telling him to surrender'[30] areas where German-speaking inhabitants constituted over fifty per cent of the population. The only European democracy to the west of the Rhine was about to be dismembered according to an Anglo-French plan subject to the approval of the German Chancellor.

13

'Changing Back into Men'

With Chamberlain due to return to Germany, this time to the spa town of Bad Godesberg, the Cabinet met on 21 September to consider the stance he ought to take. Having already agreed in principle to areas of over fifty per-cent German speakers reverting to the Reich, the British and French Governments were keen to see any transfers take place in a fair and orderly fashion. Halifax attached great emphasis to the manner in which the Anglo-French plans were carried out, not only for propaganda and domestic political reasons, but also because it provided a test of German goodwill. He increasingly found the hectoring tone and vicious methods of the Nazis as distasteful as their actual actions.

At Godesberg the next day, Hitler confirmed all Halifax's worst fears. After Chamberlain said that he had secured Anglo-French agreement to the Berchtesgaden proposals, Hitler butted in to say 'that he is sorry, since these proposals could not be maintained'.[1] He then declared his unequivocal support for the Polish and Hungarian demands, adding, 'no delay was possible . . . a settlement must be reached within a few days . . . either by agreement or force . . . by 1st October at the latest'.[2] He went on to draw a lurid picture of a Sudetenland in which 'whole villages were empty . . . the men had been arrested or conscripted . . . only the children left wandering uncared for in the streets . . . there were shooting affrays every night along the frontier'. For further effect he had an aide interrupt the meeting to report the massacre of Sudetens at the hands of the Czech police. Chamberlain's reaction to these histrionics and blackmail was utterly craven. The Birmingham businessman in him ought to have recognized that the house-painter was haggling, bidding for more than he needed in the expectation of being bargained down to what he would eventually accept. Instead, Chamberlain said he was 'disappointed and puzzled' by Hitler's new stance and complained that 'he had got what the Führer wanted without the expenditure of a drop of German blood . . . he had been obliged to take his political life into his own hands. . . . He had actually been booed at his departure today.'[3]

Unimpressed by these pathetic protestations, Hitler produced a map and demanded total Czech withdrawal from a boundary liberally drawn on roughly linguistic grounds. This territory had to be occupied by German troops 'at once'. Moreover, the plebiscites would be so gerrymandered that Germans who had left the Sudetenland since 1918 would be entitled to vote whereas Czechs 'who had been planted there' since then would not. He went on to refuse to make any promises to the rump of Czechoslovakia or to indemnify those Czechs who lived in the Sudetenland and wanted to leave before it joined the Reich. They were even refused a decent period in which to sell up and pack their bags.

The news of Hitler's iniquity and bad faith was relayed to Halifax by Chamberlain at 10.30 that night. At 11.45 the next morning, the 23rd, he received a more detailed account from Godesberg:

> Boundary he proposes is based on a language map and he has so drawn it to give the most favourable results to Germany . . . failing acceptance of his proposals, which he describes as a peaceful solution, he intimates that he will be obliged to seek a military solution and in that event he will draw, not a 'national frontier' but a 'military and strategic frontier'.[4]

This unadulterated blackmail marked the turning-point in Halifax's attitude towards Hitler and Nazism. The positive, Christian side of appeasement, that of balming wounds and righting legitimate grievances, was wholly absent from this crisis. Harsh calculations of military readiness, in which factors such as 'the shocking state of the French air force'[5] weighed most heavily, determined the outcome of the Czech crisis, rather than any residual sentiment towards Germany.

At 4 p.m. on the 23rd, Halifax telegraphed the British minister in Prague to inform the Czechs that the French and British Governments could not continue to take the responsibility of advising them not to mobilize.[6] Distance from Godesberg allowed Halifax a far better overall perspective than the Prime Minister, and after a dinner at the Foreign Office with a number of Cabinet colleagues that evening, Halifax drafted and sent a telegram to Godesberg at 10 p.m. which read:

> Great mass of public opinion seems to be hardening in sense of feeling that we have gone to the limit of concession and that it is up to the Chancellor to make some contribution . . . it seems to your colleagues of vital importance that you should not leave without making it plain to the Chancellor, if possible by special interview that, after great concessions made by the Czech Government, for him to reject opportunity of peaceful solution in favour of one that must include war would be an unpardonable crime against humanity.[7]

As with so many politicians and diplomats before the advent of opinion polls, when Halifax wrote of the 'great mass of people' he really meant his own opinion, together with that of whichever friends he had spoken to and newspapers he had read.

Hitler's fulminations, exaggerations and lies about the 'unhappy victims of Czech tyranny' only exacerbated distrust in the unflappable Halifax. Left behind in London he had become the primary focus for resentment against the Government's complicity in the bullying of the Czechs. He was inundated with letters, calls and visits from old friends whose opinions he respected, such as George Lloyd, Leo Amery, Oliver Stanley and the Warden of All Souls, all of whom urged him to forego any further coercion.

On his return on 24 September, Chamberlain met the Foreign Policy Committee at 3 p.m. and the full Cabinet at 5.30 p.m., where he reported his 'considerable shock' at hearing Hitler's rejection of the Anglo-French proposals. Nevertheless, he proposed to go along with Hitler's demand for an immediate transfer of all the territory, despite even Henderson and Wilson considering the proposals 'outrageous'. In advocating Hitler's timetable of total transfer by 1 October Chamberlain averred,

> Herr Hitler had certain standards ... he would not deliberately deceive a man who he respected and with whom he had been in negotiation, and he was sure that Herr Hitler now felt some respect for him. ... He thought that he had now established an influence over Herr Hitler.[8]

Against this outlandish vanity and gullibility Halifax confined himself to the remark that 'the British Government would be unwilling to urge further sacrifices ... the real difficulty lay in the fact that under Herr Hitler's proposals German troops would move in almost immediately'.[9] A member of the Runciman mission, Frank Ashton-Gwatkin, wrote in his diary that day, 'We have swallowed the camel but the gnat is beginning to buzz.'

At one o'clock the next morning Halifax woke up and found himself unable to get back to sleep. He normally slept soundly and never let affairs of state worry him outside office hours. But that night of insomnia, between 24 and 25 September 1938, was different. The conversation about the Godesberg terms he had had with Cadogan when the latter dropped him off at Eaton Square that evening rankled. As he lay awake in the darkness of his bedroom, Halifax had nine and a half hours of reflection before the next morning's crucial Cabinet on the issue of coercing the Czechs to accept the Godesberg terms. He had a long time to turn over in his mind all the possibilities that were open to him. It is not too melodramatic to pinpoint that night as the time that Halifax underwent his almost Damascene conversion from appeaser to resister. He had for some time been troubled that appeasement had imperceptibly turned into submission, and what had once seemed rational and decent now looked base and craven.

The extent of the conversion Halifax underwent that night is best gauged from Cadogan's diary. On 24 September, Cadogan had been horrified by the Godesberg terms and

> Still more horrified to find PM has hypnotized H who capitulates totally. . . . I gave H a note of what *I* thought, but it had no effect. . . . Cabinet at 5.30 and H got back at 8 completely and quite happily defaitiste-pacifist. He seemed to think the Cabinet were all right. I *wonder*! . . . Pray God there will be a revolt. Back to FO after dinner. H got back from No. 10 talk with Labour about 10.30. Drove him home and gave him a bit of my mind, but didn't shake him. I've never before known him make up his mind so quickly and firmly on anything. I wish he hadn't chosen *this* occasion! I know there is a shattering telegram from Phipps about position in France : I *know* we and they are in no condition to fight : but I'd rather be beat than dishonoured.

Phipps's telegram, which read 'All that is best in France is against war, *almost* at any price,' urged the Government not to encourage the 'small but noisy and corrupt war group' in France.

Cadogan clearly played a pivotal role in Halifax's conversion. The next morning Halifax chided his Permanent Under-Secretary: 'Alec, I'm very angry with you. You gave me a sleepless night. I woke at 1 and never got to sleep again. But I came to the conclusion that you were right.'[10]

He decided to act on his misgivings and, even at the cost of disloyalty to Chamberlain, start unwinding the policy with which his name had been synonymous. It was an act of considerable intellectual as well as political bravery and self-confidence. The nearest thing to it was his unswerving advocacy of the Dominion Status Declaration nine years earlier, but even that did not amount to such a complete reversal of opinion. His ability to effect this transformation was partly due to the fact that, as his Assistant Private Secretary Ivo Mallet noted: 'Halifax had not Chamberlain's obstinate conviction of the rightness of his own judgement.'[11] All depended on his perception of what Hitler's real aims were, and Halifax had a few days earlier telegraphed Butler at Geneva to say that Chamberlain was making a supreme effort at Godesberg to remove a German grievance and it would constitute a test of German sincerity. That test Hitler had signally failed.

Halifax's entire career to date had been concerned with finding the *via media*. The Whiggish view that there was a rational solution to all problems and all that was needed was to find a modus vivendi comfortable to all parties was deeply ingrained in his character and personality. A necessary precondition to that view of the world were rational parties who sincerely wanted to reach solutions. Here at last was an opponent who had proved himself unwilling to entertain compromise, was endemically incapable of keeping promises and who interpreted even the desire to negotiate as a sign of weakness in his enemy. On 22 September, Halifax had asked of Cecil of Chelwood, 'if in fact events show that [Hitler] had reached already the decision to attempt at this moment the execution of a policy much wider than that of finding a remedy for the grievances of the Sudetendeutsch'.[12] If such was the case, Halifax knew that without immediate decisive action he would go down in history as idiotically naïve and ineffectual.

Halifax appreciated that the reasons Hitler gave for his Godesberg demands – 'evasion and delay on the part of the Czechs' – were bare-faced lies. He also knew that Chamberlain now admired and trusted Hitler, as his embarrassing performance in Cabinet that afternoon had shown. Halifax would have to have been superhuman not to have let personal political calculations enter his reasoning. For he knew himself to be in a very strong position, both inside the Government and out. Having parted with one Foreign Secretary that year Chamberlain could not afford to lose another. The Cabinet discussion prior to Halifax's 'public opinion' telegram showed the Prime Minister steadily losing Cabinet support. Chamberlain was seventy years old and the other contenders for the premiership, such as Simon, Hoare and Inskip, were either too closely connected with Chamberlain's policy or of insufficient stature for the succession.

Nor was there any obvious contender outside the Government, Eden being too young and Churchill far too unstable. Neither had much of a following in the Party; the 'Eden Group' were mistrusted and contemptuously referred to as 'the Glamour Boys'. Halifax always had a keen awareness of his limitations, but his political instinct would have told him that should he turn against appeasement he could present an ideal counterpoise to the Prime Minister in Cabinet. He was anyhow already beginning to be treated as such; that very day four members of the 'Eden Group' had written to him about coercing the Czechs. When back in July a friend, Victor Cazalet MP, had told him that at Mrs Blanche 'Baffy' Dugdale's dinner a number of MPs had all wanted him as the next Prime Minister, Halifax had jokingly offered Cazalet the post of his Parliamentary Private Secretary in any future Halifax ministry.

It came as a harsh shock to Chamberlain when, at the 10.30 a.m. Cabinet, Halifax came down firmly against any further pressure being put on Czechoslovakia to accept the Godesberg demands, even if war should result. In the words of one spectator, the War Minister Leslie Hore-Belisha, Halifax 'gave a fine moral lead'.[13] To Chamberlain's mounting apprehension Halifax asserted that he now 'felt that a moral obligation rested upon us in consequence of the concessions which Czechoslovakia, on British advice, had agreed to make'.[14] He went on to declare that

he had found his opinion changing somewhat in the last day or so. . . .
Yesterday he had felt that the difference between acceptance of the principle of last Sunday's [Berchtesgaden] proposal and the

[Godesberg] scheme now put forward ... did not involve a new acceptance of principle. He was not quite sure ... that he still held that view ... there was a distinction in principle between an orderly and disorderly transfer with all that the latter implied for the minorities in the transferred areas ... he could not rid his mind of the fact that Herr Hitler had given us nothing and that he was dictating terms, just as though he had won a war but without having had to fight.[15]

Halifax then dropped his circumlocutory late-Victorian form of expression and bluntly told the Cabinet of the

ultimate end which he wished to see accomplished, namely, the destruction of Nazi-ism. So long as Nazi-ism lasted, peace would be uncertain. For this reason he did not feel that it would be right to put pressure on Czechoslovakia to accept. We should lay the case before them. If they rejected it he imagined that France would join in and if the French went in we should join them.[16]

Adding further to the Prime Minister's already acute discomfort, Halifax went on to advocate calling Hitler's bluff, for

He also remembered that Herr Hitler had said that he gained power by words not by bayonets. He asked whether we were quite sure that he had not gained power by words in the present instance and that if he was driven to war the result might be to bring down the Nazi regime.[17]

This concept of war as a positive instrument for Hitler's overthrow was one Halifax was to reiterate over the coming months.

The implications of this dramatic and well-articulated volte-face were not lost on any of the twenty-one politicians sitting around the Cabinet table that morning. Halifax 'concluded by saying that he had worked most closely with the Prime Minister throughout the long crisis. He was not quite sure that their minds were still altogether at one. Nevertheless, he thought it right to expose his own hesitations with complete frankness.'[18] As soon as he had finished the speech Chamberlain sent him a pencilled note, which amounted almost to a resignation threat:

Your complete change of view since I saw you last night is a horrible blow to me, but of course you must form yr opinions for yourself.
It remains to see what the French say.
If they say they will go in, thereby dragging us in, I do not think I could accept responsibility for the decision.
But I don't want to anticipate what has not yet arisen. N.C.

To which Halifax replied: 'I feel a brute – but I lay awake most of the night, tormenting myself, and did not feel I cd reach any other conclusion at this moment, on the point of coercing Cz. E.' Chamberlain jotted a typically acerbic reply: 'Night conclusions are seldom taken in the right perspective. N.C.'[19]

A second exchange of notes later on in that meeting saw Chamberlain repeat his refusal to lead a Government which encouraged the Czechs to resist. This was subtle word-play. There was no question, at least in Halifax's mind, of inciting the Czechs and French to refuse the terms. Halifax's next note to Chamberlain made his stance perfectly clear: 'I should like the Czechs to agree on the facts – but I do not feel entitled to coerce them into it.'[20] Senior Government ministers were then invited to give their views. Hailsham, Stanley, Elliot, Earl De La Warr and Hore-Belisha all came out in support of Halifax. The Marquess of Zetland, Inskip, Simon, Hoare, Leslie Burgin and Ernest Brown followed Chamberlain.

Halifax later showed Inskip a letter he had received from a junior minister, Lord Winterton, which warned that further coercion of the Czechs would result in at least three ministerial resignations. So it is probable that Halifax's intervention headed off a major Cabinet split. At his summing up, a clearly rattled Prime Minister chose his words carefully. He acknowledged 'there had been some difference of opinion, as was only to be expected ... [but] it was important that the Cabinet should present a united front'. Bowing to the dissenter's pressure, he advocated merely 'putting before Czechoslovakia all the considerations which should properly be borne in mind in reaching a decision'.[21] The revolt had succeeded.

Halifax followed up his Cabinet performance when he returned to the Foreign Office. Conclusion (g) of the Committee of Imperial Defence's meeting of 15 September had been to send ten officers from the War Office to France to work out the detailed arrangements for the dispatch of an Advanced Air Striking Force to France. Inskip had held this up as it was felt that the publicity attendant on a visit of such a large body of officers would be bad for Anglo-German relations. The minute that 'On the 25th September the Secretary of State for Foreign Affairs intimated that it was no longer necessary to postpone Conclusion (g)'[22] is yet another indication of Halifax's change of stance. In her diary that day 'Baffy' Dugdale said that the Minister of Health, Walter Elliot, 'gave me the feeling that the Rubber Stampers are changing back into Men – and he hinted that Lord Halifax is coming over to them'. Duff Cooper delightedly recorded that Halifax's speech 'came as a shock to those who think as I do'.

The reason why more has not been made, in the vast Munich bibliography, of Halifax's change of heart is because it fails to fit into either side's interpretation. Churchillian historians, content to portray Halifax as Chamberlain's henchman, play it down or ignore it altogether. Apologists for appeasement tend to concentrate on his earlier zeal for the policy and overlook this later heresy. Halifax's own memoirs are also partly to blame. He gave the impression that he was scrupulously loyal to Chamberlain throughout and forbore to mention his opposition to the Godesberg terms.

Indeed, his only mention of Munich was the extraordinary remark that, 'The criticism excited by Munich never caused me the least surprise. I should very possibly have been among the critics myself, if I had not happened to be in a position of responsibility.'[23]

It was during the crisis that Halifax made one of his few recorded jokes. When a journalist asked him whether the constant late-night crisis meetings were wearing him out, he replied, 'Not exactly. But it spoils one's eyes for the high birds.'[24] On one page of his Garrowby scrapbooks for the period he stuck the advertising circular received by him and his neighbours from the makers of Titan Air Raid Shelters. On the next is a profile cut out from the left-wing paper *Tribune*, which described him as 'smug, unctuous ... platitudinous, pious ... no outstanding ability ... arrogant ... snobbish ... a piqued small-minded imperialist prig [who] battered and bludgeoned [India] ... whose history was in the van of civilization while his own ancestors were still submerged in the crapulous slime of barbarism'. The very fact that he specifically kept this abusive snippet to show his children and grandchildren tends to suggest that he was not as dour or self-important as critics have so often depicted him.

On the afternoon of 26 September, there emanated from the Foreign Office a press communiqué which read: 'if in spite of all efforts made by the British Prime Minister a German attack is made upon Czechoslovakia the immediate result must be that France will be bound to come to her assistance, and Great Britain and Russia will certainly stand by France'.[25] The genesis of this tough message, known as 'The Leeper Telegram', has been disputed. In 1947, Churchill wrote to Halifax asking him for confirmation that he was in the room while the document was drafted. Halifax answered that it was he, rather than Churchill, Leeper or anyone else, who was responsible for having it sent. He added, 'greatly to my surprise, Neville was much put out when the communiqué appeared and reproved me for not having submitted it to him'.[26] The fear that any tough action might be 'provocative' was a part of the mentality of appeasement of which Halifax was now keen to divest himself. Harvey's diary entry for 29 September shows how far he had come: 'H is by no means persuaded that we are going to get out of this wood. ... He has lost all his delusions about Hitler and now regards him as a criminal lunatic. He loathes Nazism.'

At 7.30 p.m. on the 27th, having been turned out of the Cabinet room by electricians rigging up sound equipment for a Prime Ministerial broadcast, Chamberlain, Halifax, Cadogan and Wilson adjourned to Wilson's office. There Halifax was shown Wilson's draft of a telegram to Prague, which effectively called on the Czechs to let German troops move immediately into the Sudetenland up to Hitler's Godesberg lines. This was an attempt to bounce Halifax into doing the opposite to that which he had advocated at the Cabinet meeting on the 25th. 'H played up against it,' wrote Cadogan that night; instead, it was the old and hard-pressed Prime Minister's turn to feel the strain. 'Poor PM (quite exhausted) said, "I'm wobbling about all over the place", and went in to broadcast.'

It was in that speech that Chamberlain told the British public 'how horrible, fantastic, incredible it is that we should be digging ditches and trying on gas masks because of a quarrel in a faraway country between people of whom we know nothing'. This statement was all the more disgraceful coming from the son of the greatest imperialist of them all, and from the leader of a country which in its past had thought nothing of committing troops to theatres as far distant as Kabul, Peking and Zululand. Geographical obscurity and the level of public awareness of the local peoples had never before stopped Britain doing what she thought right or necessary.

By the time the Cabinet convened at 9.30 p.m., Halifax was under enormous pressure to go back on his nocturnal decision. The Chiefs of Staff, to whose opinion he usually deferred, emphasized the Services' unfitness for hostilities. Phipps continued to relay warnings of French opposition to war. Malcolm MacDonald reiterated the Dominions' total reluctance to fight. Chamberlain used Henderson's reports from Berlin to assert that Hitler would not be shaken from his Godesberg demands. Yet despite all this, Halifax stuck to his position and warned that he would 'feel the greatest difficulty' in sending Wilson's draft telegram.

To hinder the telegram's despatch he used the hackneyed but serviceable excuse that action had to be closely co-ordinated with the French. But his underlying objection was still the moral one. He argued that

> The suggestion amounted to complete capitulation to Germany.... He realized that, if we did not adopt this suggestion, the consequences to Czechoslovakia and to many other people might well be very grievous. Nevertheless he did not feel that it was right to do more than to place before M. Beneš an objective account of the position ... there was a much greater difference between the Franco-British proposals and the German [Godesberg] Memorandum than one of time, method and degree. We could not press the Czech Government to do what we believed to be wrong.[27]

He also pointed out the domestic political difficulties attendant on seeming to take the German side against the essentially innocent Czechs.

Chamberlain, having failed to bend Halifax to his will, was forced to conclude that 'the Foreign Secretary had given powerful and perhaps convincing reasons against the adoption of his suggestion. If that was the general view of his colleagues, he was prepared to leave it at that.'[28] Wilson's draft telegram was scrapped. Instead, the Royal Navy was mobilized and for the first time war looked the more likely outcome than peace. Just as the Cabinet ended, Halifax's strong stance seemed to be vindicated when Chamberlain was brought a letter from Hitler promising that German troops would go no further than the agreed areas, that the plebiscite would be free and fair, and that Germany would guarantee the rump of Czechoslovakia. Hitler was being stretched on a rack of his own making; he had promised the Nuremberg rally that he would have the Sudetenland by 1 October and could not now afford to lose face. Signals such as the Leeper Telegram made Hitler wonder whether 'Operation Green' was not about to land him in a war on two fronts, without the aid of Italy or Japan and before his fortifications in the west were complete. Indications inside Germany suggested that, whereas his people would react with glee to a bloodless victory over Czechoslovakia, the prospect of another large-scale European war was deeply unpopular.

The manner of the announcement of Hitler's invitation to Chamberlain to Munich in order to renegotiate the Godesberg terms was so dramatic that it has given rise to (unfounded) accusations of stage-management. At 3.30 p.m. on 28 September, Halifax was sitting in the Peers' Gallery in the Commons watching the Prime Minister below recount in detail the events of the last few days. The House was packed and the atmosphere as tense as only the imminence of a cataclysmic war could create. Suddenly Cadogan appeared and handed a message to Halifax, who read it and hurried down to behind the Speaker's Chair, where he sent it to Lord Dunglass, the Prime Minister's Parliamentary Private Secretary. He passed it to Simon, who had some difficulty in attracting the Prime Minister's attention. When he did succeed in passing it on, Chamberlain scanned it in silence, taking some time to digest its meaning but betraying no surprise on his face. After asking Simon whether he ought to announce its contents, he then said, 'I have something more to tell the House,' and announced that Hitler had invited Mussolini, Daladier and him to Munich the next day. The Commons erupted into unprecedented scenes of relief and jubilation.

This euphoria was to grip the nation and continue undiminished throughout the next week. It was a hysterical outpouring of emotion and during it Chamberlain flew to Munich and returned with an agreement significantly better than Godesberg and roughly analogous to the original Anglo-French proposals. Czechoslovakia was still to be stripped of the Sudetenland but in a phased operation with safeguards and under international jurisdiction. The scenes of enthusiasm which welcomed Chamberlain's return to Heston aerodrome, in which Halifax fully participated, prompted Orme Sargent to remark that one might have thought that Britain had won a great victory rather than betrayed a small country.

Chamberlain was unable to resist milking the occasion for all it was politically worth. The son of the man who raised aloft the two loaves in Bingley Hall, Birmingham, knew the power of the stark visual image. The 'photo opportunity' he masterminded, in which he waved a piece of paper in the September breeze, was truly inspired. To that end, and almost as an afterthought, before leaving Munich he had asked Hitler to sign a banal one-page document which stated the desire of the British and German peoples never to fight one another again. Like the vow of a teenager suffering from his first hangover never to touch alcohol again, it was as virtuous a sentiment as it was swiftly forgotten.

Chamberlain made a shrewd calculation when he had William Strang, a Foreign Office official, draft the document. For most people the 'piece of paper' became the physical manifestation of the peace he had brought back, rather than the actual Munich Agreement itself. It managed to dwarf the real issue, which everyone anyway preferred to forget, which was the awful fate of ruined Czechoslovakia. It was also to have another, unintended, use a year later, when it gave to the British people that sense of personal outrage necessary to steel them to half a decade of deprivation and bereavement. In that sense the 'piece of paper' was to the Second World War what 'plucky little Belgium' had been to the First: the vital tangible reminder of the duplicity and cynicism of the enemy.

14

Whispers at the Triumph

During the triumphs of Ancient Rome, the victorious general would have a slave in his chariot whose duty it was constantly to whisper in his ear reminders of his mortality. In the drive back from Heston aerodrome to Downing Street, Halifax performed much the same function for Chamberlain. Even as flowers were thrown into the car and people leapt on to the running board to shake the Prime Minister's hand, Halifax advised Chamberlain not to capitalize on his coup by calling a snap general election, as Conservative Central Office urged, but rather to widen the Government by offering the Labour and Liberal leaders seats in Cabinet. It showed amazing rectitude on Halifax's part, 'with the cheering of the crowd still in their ears',[1] to refuse to take advantage of circumstances which, had Chamberlain demanded a mandate for Munich, would have afforded him a victory on the scale of 1931 or 1935. Chamberlain deflected Halifax's suggestion by referring it to Sir Horace Wilson, whom he could rely on to be hostile. His vain old head turned by the adulation, Chamberlain could not understand why Halifax should even desire a broader-based Government now that he had brought back peace.

Halifax's ultra-rational and dispassionate demeanour has long been held against him, but in the heady days after Munich it served his country well. Lady Mosley was correct in saying that when Chamberlain landed, Halifax cheered so much one could see his tonsils, but the relief of any man with three sons of service age would surely have been as great.[2] On 4 October, the Duchess of Beaufort invited the Halifaxes to Badminton 'now that we can breathe again'.[3] But this sense of relief did not prevent Halifax suspecting that when the Prime Minister declared he had secured 'Peace with Honour', he had in fact achieved nothing of the sort. Ten years later he told Churchill how Chamberlain's boast had 'made me shiver when I heard it'.[4] He thought the presentation of the Agreement as some sort of quasi-victory over Germany was a dangerous fiction. When later the dawn was to be proved false, Halifax's reticence and relative anonymity – he did not go on any of the three flights to Germany – stood him in good stead. Staying out of the limelight at Munich kept him out of the spotlight later.

At the first Cabinet meeting after the Prime Minister's return, Halifax made only the most perfunctory congratulations, his sole contribution being the distinctly downbeat observation that, 'it would be desirable that the Cabinet should have the opportunity to reflect on the many important questions that were raised by the Prime Minister's visit to Munich, and that at a later date there should be an opportunity for further discussion of these matters'.[5]

The stark divergence between the way Chamberlain presented the Munich Agreement in the Commons and Halifax's report of it to the Upper House was marked enough to excite comment at the time. The Prime Minister hailed his achievement as a triumph of restraint and dignity and spoke of 'the winning back of confidence, the gradual removal of hostility between nations until they could safely discard their weapons', etc.[6] Meanwhile, in the Lords, the Foreign Secretary took pains to enunciate the eleven ways in which Munich had been an improvement on the Godesberg demands, but called the outcome only the better of 'a hideous choice of evils'. Whilst the Commons heard Chamberlain discuss eventual disarmament, Halifax told Their Lordships that 'one of the principal lessons of these events is that the diplomacy of any nation can only be commensurate with its strength, and if we desire this country to exercise its full influence in world affairs, the first thing we have to do is to ensure that it is in all ways fully and rapidly equipped to do so'.[7]

It was not in Parliament or in front of the newsreel cameras but in his correspondence with old friends that Halifax's true feelings are best ascertained. When Amery saw Halifax the day Chamberlain returned, he noted that although the Foreign Secretary 'put up such defence as he could . . . he obviously wasn't very proud of the result'.[8] In answer to a critical letter from a school and Christ Church contemporary, Lord Francis Scott, he wrote on 18 October:

> No one I imagine can think that the arrangements made at Munich were anything but the choice of the lesser of two horrible evils . . . with the development of the air the capacity of this country as it existed in the XIX century, based on sea power, to do the cosmopolitan policeman no longer stands . . . we have not been as wrong and unprincipled as you think . . . a hideous choice of evils. . . . I could not have prevented a worse fate for Czechoslovakia . . . and if I had sought that remedy, it would have been at the price of immeasurable suffering imposed on the world, and the probable disruption of the British Empire, which may yet perhaps be a rallying point of sanity for a mad civilization.[9]

The very day after Chamberlain landed, Harvey recorded how Halifax 'told me he thought it was a horrid business and humiliating, no use blinking the fact, but yet better than a European war'. Harvey thought 'His position has been most difficult ... he can certainly claim a large share in preventing the PM going even further in his concessions.'[10]

Duff Cooper's resignation did not impress Halifax, whose attitude was that as everyone was on the same side, resignation was virtually indistinguishable from self-indulgent abdication of responsibility. He thought of it in much the same terms as his father's reason for not leaving the Anglican communion: one had been placed in that part of the line of battle and therefore ought to stay put and do one's best. Harold Caccia believed that after Munich 'Halifax did go through a hideous period, but if he ever considered resignation he might have thought: "If I resign it will weaken the Government and Britain. It might bring the Government down, and we should have had the socialists, who were hopeless." '[11]

At the second Cabinet after Munich, Halifax unveiled the hawkish stance he was to adhere to throughout the forthcoming year. Saying how he 'was much impressed by the need for doing something urgently'[12] for Czechoslovakia, he persuaded the Cabinet to give her £10 million to help with the refugee problem, and to offer it that day rather than the next month as Chamberlain preferred. He also called off the Lord Mayor of London's projected visit to Berlin and Rome. Far more importantly he came out in strong support of Walter Elliot's call for an intensification of the rearmament programme.

There was a discernible hiatus in British foreign policy in the weeks immediately following Munich. The problem of devising a coherent strategy is best illustrated by Cadogan's inability even to be able to set out a skeleton draft of a paper on the subject: 'I only know the one we have followed is *wrong*.'[13] Since his first major speech as Foreign Secretary, in which he had pleaded, 'do not let us exaggerate our differences. The country today needs all the unity it can find,' Halifax had laid great emphasis on national unity in crisis. To that end, after seeing Eden on 11 October, he wrote Chamberlain a long letter again listing the advantages of offering Labour, the Liberals and dissident Conservatives places in the Government: 'My instinct therefore does on the whole lead me to feel that this is the psychological moment to get national unity and that, if for any reason it is not taken, it may be a long time before another occurs.'[14]

It was a call he was to make at regular intervals throughout the year, to Chamberlain's ever-increasing chagrin. Halifax cannily presented this in terms of Chamberlain's own self-interest. To appear desirous of building a national consensus would be popular with public opinion, Halifax argued, so 'whether it succeeded or failed it would have a value'.[15] Chamberlain merely complained, 'Now one of my colleagues, and a very important one, is pressing me to broaden the base of the Cabinet. ... I am not prepared for the sake of what must be a sham unity to take on as partners men who would sooner or later wreck the policy with which I am identified.'[16] Baldwin, who kept a close eye on politics after his retirement, spotted the Prime Minister's increasing isolation within the Cabinet. Out walking with a former Private Secretary, Lord Hinchingbrooke, on 14 October, he remarked: 'When I was Prime Minister I always had Neville, as Ramsay [MacDonald] had me, to interpret my views to the Cabinet and carry them along. The trouble is, Neville has nobody.'[17]

For a man who had not himself had to fight an election since 1910, Halifax kept more of a weather eye on the electoral implications of policy than the Prime Minister himself. In his weekly letters to Ida and Hilda Chamberlain, their brother crowed about the huge majority the Conservatives would win in the election which had to be held before November 1940. Halifax was not so sure; the Munich glow did not take long to pall and in by-elections the Conservatives lost Dartford to Labour on 7 November, Bridgwater to an Independent ten days later and only held Oxford City with a greatly reduced majority. The limited Cabinet reshuffle of late October, which Halifax had hoped would be drastic, did nothing to strengthen the Government.

It was in the crucial field of rearmament that Halifax's about-turn was most dramatic. As a former War Minister he could not have been surprised at the way military weakness had limited Britain's options in the Munich crisis. Writing to Phipps on 1 November, he acknowledged that 'it would be fatal for us to be caught again with insufficient armed strength'. The minutes for the Cabinet, Foreign Policy Committee and the Committee of Imperial Defence all show Halifax consistently in favour of taking a tougher line than Chamberlain in every matter relating to defence. As he told Phipps on 28 October, he expected 'very shortly to reach conclusions that would greatly speed up our rearmament'.[18] Over policy towards France, too, Halifax began to pursue a more hawkish line. Whereas earlier in 1938 he had authorized Phipps secretly to intrigue against the anti-dictator French Foreign Minister, Paul Boncour, after Munich he urged Phipps to encourage the French greatly to increase their rearmament programme.[19]

On 20 October, only three weeks after Munich, the question arose in the Committee of Imperial Defence as to whether to recall the gas masks that had been issued to the public during the crisis. Had Munich really been considered to have won peace in anyone's time it would have been only sensible to take back the masks. A long discussion was brought to a close by Halifax pronouncing somewhat curtly that the masks should be left with the public.[20] Equally revealing about the way his mind was working was a discussion there five days later, in which the decision had to be made as to how many capital ships, under the terms of the Anglo-German naval treaty, Britain would forecast she would possess by the end of 1942. Hoare, keen not to anger Germany, suggested sixteen. Halifax, past worrying about provoking Hitler and more keen to impress him, plumped for nineteen. Once again he got his way.

Halifax was, in the most gentlemanly manner possible, uncompromisingly asserting himself. On 3 November he demanded, and got, a second battalion posted forthwith to Shanghai. A fortnight later he called for each local authority in the country to set up a 'War Emergency Committee'. He advocated the removal of the ban on munitions under the Export Credit Guarantee Scheme so that public money could be used to insure friendly countries' arms purchases. In the teeth of Chamberlain's opposition he championed calls for the setting up of a Ministry of Supply to co-ordinate the rearmament effort. He advocated the immediate compiling of a National Register to facilitate national service. Chamberlain's letters to his sisters betray definite signs of petulance at his colleagues' zeal. 'A lot of people seem to be losing their heads,' he complained to them in late October, 'and talking and thinking as though Munich had made war more instead of less imminent.'[21]

Late October 1938 also saw a Foreign Office file distributed which called for the dissemination of anti-Nazi propaganda within Germany, specifically of pamphlets containing the latest speeches of Chamberlain and Halifax. On 5 November, Halifax noted his support for this initiative and two days later asked Cadogan to arrange for suitable material to be made available.[22]

In the wider debate on British strategy, Halifax played a crucial role in dislodging the Government from its long-established reliance on 'limited liability'. Kirkpatrick had returned from Berlin in mid-December with a rumour that Hitler was planning a surprise air-strike against London on or near 21 February. According to the telegram Halifax dashed off to Roosevelt, Hitler was engaged in a fit of megalomaniac loathing against Britain and the attack might come at any time. Colonial demands might provide the *casus belli*, or alternatively an attack on France 'in aid of' Italy. Major diplomatic approaches to Brussels and Paris were undertaken and the Chiefs of Staff were ordered to draw up a swift report. The anti-aircraft batteries stationed at Lichfield were promptly moved to Wellington Barracks, where the staff of the German Embassy in Carlton House Terrace could not help but notice them. This crisis gave the spur to those who thought it was time for a rethink of British defence posture and Halifax gave 'determined backing' to Hore-Belisha's plans to return to a British continental military commitment. Although Halifax had his doubts about the rumours – which did, indeed, turn out to be disinformation planted by German anti-Nazis in order to stiffen the West – he was not above using them for an end he wished anyhow to pursue.

In late 1938 and early 1939, the Chiefs of Staff concluded that a future war would necessitate a major British military contribution on the continent. At the time only two divisions were earmarked for France, and those primarily to obviate the understandable French accusation that Britain was willing to fight to the last Frenchman. Halifax saw that both military necessity and Anglo-French relations required the smashing of this last great totem-pole of British post-war military thinking. Britain could no longer merely produce the air and naval contingents and leave the bulk of the land fighting to France. Lurking in his mind was also his old fear that the French were possibly willing, in the last resort, 'to stand aside while Germany attacked us'.[23]

Hand in hand with any such continental commitment went the need for Staff talks with the French, and also if possible with the Belgians and Dutch. On 26 January 1939, Halifax signalled his conversion by informing the Committee of Imperial Defence that, 'For a long time he had tried to think that a war of limited liability was possible, but now he was convinced that we should abandon such a concept . . . we should extend our industrial requirements . . . in these times it was necessary to think on wider lines than a few months before.'[24] He went on to advocate tripling the British Expeditionary Force, doubling the Territorials and instituting immediate wide-ranging Staff talks and full military conscription.

Chamberlain and Simon opposed these measures, both on financial grounds and because they saw Staff talks as symptomatic of the pre-1914 mood they were trying at all costs to avoid. At the Foreign Policy Committee on 26 January 1939, Halifax pressed for the adoption of the Chiefs of Staff's advice that a German attack on Holland or Belgium should be taken as a British *casus belli*, and that this should be communicated to Berlin forthwith. He even said that Britain should be prepared to go to war for Switzerland. The 'close and intimate Staff conversations' he wanted held with the French High Command 'would serve no useful purpose unless they proceeded on the basis of a war against Germany and Italy in combination . . . he did not believe that if there was a leakage it need necessarily have any detrimental consequences'.[25] Indeed, far from pushing Mussolini further towards Hitler, the knowledge that the Western Allies were planning to devastate Italy in the event of his joining Hitler might concentrate Il Duce's mind wonderfully. Deterrence, rather than accommodation, had become Halifax's watch-word. He cut through the debate on whether Staff conversations with the French should also include the Near and Far Eastern theatres by asserting that, of course, they should 'embrace every factor with which France and ourselves would be concerned'.[26]

The *Kristallnacht* pogrom during the night of 9/10 November shocked even a Foreign Office hardened to news of Nazi brutality. *Picture Post*'s photographs of smashed Jewish shops led public opinion, already showing its doubts about Munich, to react sharply. Halifax had, as he put it in a letter to a close friend many years later, 'always been rather anti-Semitic'.[27] Although inexcusable, especially in a practising Christian, it was an anti-Semitism of the relatively mild form common to a number of his social contemporaries. The viciousness and bloodshed of *Kristallnacht* was symptomatic of an altogether different species of anti-Semitism, and Halifax was genuinely revolted by it. He convened a special meeting of the Foreign Policy Committee to declare that, 'The happenings in Germany of the last few days following on from the sequence of events since Munich had made the position very difficult.'[28] He then produced a digest of 'a number of recent reports from highly confidential sources', which he claimed had proved their worth during the Munich crisis and now 'all tended to one and the same direction'. We now know that much of the information came from intercepts of German diplomatic radio traffic between London and Berlin.[29]

From the way Halifax employed secret information throughout his political career, it is unsurprising that the 'direction' these reports tended was the one in which he had wanted the Government to go. The memorandum, prepared by a Foreign Office official named Gladwyn Jebb, postulated that Germany was on the verge of bankruptcy and was likely to follow a 'grandiose programme of expansion towards the Black Sea, Turkey and India'. Nazi Party officials were openly discussing the splitting up of the British Empire. Hitler had been heard to remark, 'If the English have not got universal conscription by the spring of 1939 they may consider their world empire is lost.' An extension of German power in South-Eastern Europe was to be expected and 'Germany is arming to the limit'. Halifax, using the report and *Kristallnacht* to illuminate his arguments, further emphasized his total about-face on appeasement. After saying that 'the crazy persons who had managed to secure control' of Germany were trying to pick a quarrel, he enunciated what he hoped would become the new policy: 'The immediate objective should be the correction of the false impression that we were decadent, spineless and could with impunity be kicked about.'

He then propounded the need for double shift working in the aircraft production factories and supported calling off the contemplated Anglo-German discussions on colonies, 'until that Government either mended their ways or ceased to be Nazis'. He initiated a discussion on what 'positive action' could be taken to help the Jews in Germany without making their position still worse. Western Australia and British Guiana were briefly considered as possible homelands. During all of this Chamberlain was frankly unsympathetic and at times thoroughly unhelpful, confining himself to remarks such as 'we were not in a position to frighten Germany' and 'There is no suggestion that Herr Hitler contemplated any immediate aggressive action.' He deprecated Halifax's secret reports as less precise than the ones received the previous summer and only agreed to action to help the Jews, 'to ease the public conscience', and only so long as it did not include economic sanctions against Germany.

Chamberlain poured cold water over Halifax's idea for a compulsory National Service Register. Halifax preferred this to a voluntary system because of the 'enormous moral and emotional effects [it would have] here and abroad',[30] where it would be seen as 'the organizing of an entire nation to meet an emergency'. Against the combined opposition of Chamberlain, Runciman, Simon and others – and with virtually no support from the rest of the Committee – Halifax was overruled.[31] He nevertheless stuck to the campaign and fought it with increasing vigour over the coming months, as other ministers came around to his point of view. Harrowing reports of the Nazis' treatment of the Jews continued to pour in. In December 1938, Harold Caccia sent him details of 'an old woman whose face had all been slashed and cut, and ... an old woman in Dusseldorf who had been trampled to death'.[32]

Writing to the Organizing Secretary of the Anti-Nazi Council on 12 November, Churchill suggested that Halifax be invited to speak to a luncheon being given by the anti-appeasement Focus group, saying, 'I do not think he is as far gone as the Prime Minister.'[33] Halifax accepted the invitation and after the event, which took place on 9 February 1939, Churchill thanked Halifax for attending and commented, 'I am sure your speech, and the frank talk which followed, did good.' Halifax kept in touch with Churchill throughout the Munich crisis, lunching with him on occasion at the latter's home in Morpeth Mansions.

On 16 November 1938, the Anglo-Italian treaty was finally implemented after 10,000 Italian troops were withdrawn from Spain. They left behind 12,000 men in the Littoria Division as well as pilots, artillerymen and enough NCOs to train four Nationalist divisions. Halifax wanted to hold out for more concessions, but it was felt unwise to attempt to pursue that line simultaneously with the tougher stance he had adopted against Germany. When it became clear that Franco was set for victory, Halifax soon started to encourage him to be as independent as possible from his erstwhile fascist allies. This policy, although open to criticism, was none the less ultimately to prove successful.

The Chamberlain–Halifax visit to Paris of late November 1938 fulfilled a range of objectives. It strengthened Daladier and provided an opportunity to urge faster rearmament on him. It also allowed Halifax to receive assurances to allay his nagging fear of what the French might do in the event of a German attack on Britain alone. Franco-Italian relations were at a low ebb, with quasi-official demonstrations in the Italian parliament calling for the annexations of Nice, Savoy and Corsica. The British visit to Paris also cleared the way for an eventual visit to Rome some time in early 1939. Chamberlain, in his vanity, also saw it as a chance to, in his own words, 'give the French people an opportunity of pouring out their pent-up feelings of gratitude and affection' towards him. To that end, he told his sisters, he made sure to pull down the carriage window, 'so that people might have some chance of looking at me'.[34] He was deluged with presents from fishing rods to a Bechstein grand, and one old Greek peasant woman asked for a splinter off his umbrella for her crucifix. The effect of such international adulation upon even a naturally modest man would have been incalculable.

15

'Nothing for Nothing'

With the increasing dichotomy of their views, it was inevitable that the hitherto close relationship between Prime Minister and Foreign Secretary should become strained. As early as 12 October 1938, Harvey noticed Chamberlain's 'very odd behaviour vis-à-vis H'.[1] Harvey admired the way Halifax 'showed no annoyance (which he would not be human if he did not feel)' at the way the Prime Minister had hogged the limelight during Munich.[2] The sympathy between the two had always been primarily political rather than social. They went fishing together every so often, but Chamberlain's interests in music and bird-watching did not coincide with Halifax's in hunting and shooting. Halifax did not visit the ballet until he was in his seventies (when he found it pleasant, but immodest). Their senses of humour were different too; Halifax's may have been ironic and corny but Chamberlain's was much worse. One of Lord Dunglass's duties as Parliamentary Private Secretary was to cut the 'cringe-making' puns out of the Prime Ministerial speeches.[3]

Despite great personal respect for his abilities and although he would have baulked at putting it in those terms, Halifax was coming round to Duff Cooper's view that Chamberlain had about as much chance of 'squaring Hitler' 'as Little Lord Fauntleroy would have of concluding a satisfactory deal with Al Capone'.[4] Halifax disliked Chamberlain's method of dealing with criticism by constantly pointing to the demagogy, self-seeking or ignorance of his opponents. Although Halifax was scrupulously loyal in front of officials, by January 1939 Harvey had 'a hunch that [Halifax] finds [Chamberlain] more trying than he admits'.[5]

Halifax's loyalty and natural reticence, as well as the discreet nature of the official minutes, make it impossible to ascertain the true level of Halifax's ire in the months following Munich. Intended solely to record what was agreed, the Cabinet minutes use code phrases such as 'after much discussion' when they often mean 'after much argument'. The initialling of internal Foreign Office files meant only that the documents had been read and not that the opinions expressed therein were approved. Halifax was remarkably taciturn in his marginalia, usually confining himself to a single small 'H' and the date, written in the Secretary of State's red ink. A useful method of approach with minutes is to 'job backwards': by reading the conclusions of any particular discussion first and then looking to see who initially used the language or brought up the idea finally adopted, it often becomes clearer who was holding sway. In the period after Munich it is astounding, even given the historical context of Foreign Office primacy in government decisions, how often Halifax's opinion was deferred to – even on issues totally unconnected with foreign affairs.

Events were moving against appeasement and among the Westminster and Whitehall cognoscenti it was known to be he who was leading the move inside the Government. By November 1938 Halifax was in a particularly strong position. The American journalist, Gram Swing, believed: 'Lord Halifax stands to some extent above the political battle. He is the one man in the Cabinet in London whose resignation if it were offered on an issue of principle could bring down the Government.'

Cadogan thought Halifax was contemplating resignation in late November 1938 and for that reason hesitated to inform him of information which implied that No. 10 was sending signals to the Germans without the Foreign Office's knowledge. An MI5 officer named Rill had told him that George Steward, the Chief Downing Street press officer, had been having conversations with Dr Fritz Hesse of the German press agency. Intercepted messages from the German Embassy to Berlin showed Steward to be greatly exceeding his brief. Cadogan noted in his diary on 28 November that should Rill confirm the suspicions, 'I shall have to talk to H about it. Don't want to as he's getting rather fed up and I don't want to give him reason for resigning.' The next day Rill confirmed the facts and Cadogan duly told Halifax, who arranged a meeting with Chamberlain for six o'clock that evening. Halifax believed Chamberlain's protestations of innocence and agreed that Wilson should have a word with Steward. As Cadogan suspected Wilson of complicity anyway, this was hardly a satisfactory outcome, but the incident died without issue.

The next rupture came when Chamberlain was due to address the Foreign Press Association's annual dinner on 13 December 1938. He afterwards complained, 'I had a message from Halifax that he didn't like the speech as he thought it laid too much stress on appeasement and was not stiff enough to the dictators.'[6] Halifax had a passage he wanted inserted, but Chamberlain refused because he had not enough time and anyway he thought it would give offence in Rome. 'H. who lives in the calmer atmosphere of the House of Lords doesn't realize how upsetting it is to receive that sort of message just as one is about to go into action.'[7] Although Halifax later congratulated Chamberlain on the speech, it was noticed that the tough parts of it were received with applause and the appeasing parts in virtual silence. Butler noted 'a slight tiff. N. C. is extremely bad at not showing such speeches in time to H. . . . this is the sort of occurrence which lay behind his parting with Anthony.'[8] But Halifax was no resigner and as events moved in such a way further to discredit appeasement, so his political position vis-à-vis the Prime Minister strengthened, to the latter's evident annoyance.

Suspicions that Chamberlain was slipping back into his old ways were revived by the flight of Montagu Norman, the keenly pro-appeasement Governor of the Bank of England, to Berlin in the New Year to stand godfather to Dr Schacht's son. Chamberlain had agreed to the visit, which though personal could probably also be seen in a political light. But, as Harvey fumed, 'No word of this reached H, no attempt to ask his permission either by Norman or by the PM . . . a further case of the PM's policy of working behind his Foreign Secretary's back and keeping a side-line out to the dictators.' When Halifax read about the visit in the papers, he had Cadogan write to Norman to warn him not to engage in any serious talks. This infuriated Norman but did the trick.[9]

None of this deflected Halifax, who had a remarkable capacity for staying calm and receiving annoyances and setbacks with equanimity and quizzical good humour. The resignation thoughts came not from policy disagreements with Chamberlain, for he was getting his way on most of them, but from sheer weariness with the lack of rest and the mood of constant crisis. It never affected him so seriously as to make him consider going, although doleful looks and mutterings about how much he would prefer to be at Garrowby were fairly common form. His early life had given him a toughness that was to see him through, although there was a streak of self-pity which he would leaven with excruciating humour. Jasper Rootham, one of Chamberlain's Private Secretaries during this post-Munich period, remembers a typical example when Halifax was looking out of the window at No. 10 just prior to going into a Cabinet meeting which was likely to carry on all afternoon. He remarked on how much he would like to be in the country and bemoaned having to work on weekends, especially when the sun shone. But when the time came for him to go into the meeting, he brightened up and quipped, 'Well, here I go into Society – as the oyster said when the Duchess swallowed him!'[10]

Halifax's workload was as diversified as it was heavy. The international subjects on which files circulated around the Foreign Office ranged from 'Japanese Salmon Poaching off the Alaskan Coast' to 'Claims against the Nitrate Corporation of Chile'. They could be as obscure as 'Details of the Liberian Budget' or as improbable as 'Leading Swiss Personalities'. As Foreign Minister of an imperial Great Power, Halifax found far more in his red boxes than just Anglo-German relations with which to deal. The subjects could at times become esoteric; one file dealt with British investigations into whether or not Hitler had opened a Dutch post office account and another with allegations that President Beneš had stashed £2 million away in the Stamford Hill branch of Lloyds Bank.[11]

In mid-December, Halifax told the Cabinet that the Germans were spending £5 million per annum on propaganda as against Britain's £50,000. 'The matter was urgent,' he warned them, so he 'trusted the Treasury would not look too jealously upon minor items of expenditure'[12] for the schemes he had in mind to rectify the situation, such as short-wave broadcasting of propaganda from Luxembourg and Liechtenstein. Rumours and counter-rumours were rife and for every relatively accurate analysis of future German intentions there was a totally misleading one. It was surprising that Halifax did not get more blasé about the secret reports he was receiving. The Chairman of the Joint Intelligence Committee, Victor Cavendish-Bentinck, has said that Halifax took 'rather a gentlemen-don't-read-one-another's-mail' attitude towards intelligence matters, but it might be more accurate to say that he used it sparingly and usually only as illustration for opinions which he had already formed and needed ammunition the better to present.[13]

Long on the interventionist and high spending side of the Conservative Party, Halifax found it less difficult than many to override the fiscal objections raised by Simon and the Treasury against rearmament. He argued that abnormal circumstances called for abnormal borrowing and felt 'the present level of tension could not last indefinitely and must result either in war or the destruction of the Nazi regime'.[14] At that point the President of the Board of Trade, Oliver Stanley, added that Halifax 'had expressed what many of them were feeling'.[15]

It would be as easy as it is misguided to condemn Simon and the Treasury's reluctance to finance all Halifax's expenditure requests. A trade depression in 1938 had seen a serious falling off in tax revenues, defence spending produced substantial deficits and the balance of payments looked bleak. Income tax and interest rates were at their highest levels since 1914, vast defence loans stretched borrowing to the limit and weakened the pound precisely at the time that gold or Sterling was required to pay for imports and munition raw materials. There was a genuine fear in the Treasury that should Sterling collapse, Britain would be faced with a crisis as great as that of 1931. Massively increased defence spending was inflationary and thus a recipe for higher wage costs and reduced exports. The man who was to become Minister for Co-ordination of Defence in January 1939, Lord Chatfield, remembered how 'There *was* a definite belief that we were heading for financial dislocation, loss of credit, the danger of inflation.'[16]

Halifax had been halfway through his Viceroyalty at the time of the Wall Street Crash and so was not party to the counsels that had to face such shattering Great Depression phenomena as the decline of shipbuilding to some seven per cent of its pre-Great War figure and the reduction by two-sevenths of British textile production. He was not continually haunted, as were Chamberlain, Simon and Hoare, by the memories of 1931, the crises that had brought them to power and very largely kept them there. The long (i.e. two- or three-year) war that was expected would once again require Britain to become 'the arsenal and paymaster of freedom'. As Simon never tired of pointing out, financial strength was an essential war material too.

None the less, Halifax boldly advocated that economic orthodoxies could be flouted in the present emergency. He led the campaign to use British commercial and financial resources to counter German economic and commercial penetration of Central and South-Eastern Europe. This once again led him up against Chamberlain, Simon, Hoare and other strong voices in Cabinet, and further accentuated the dichotomy between his strategic thinking and theirs. When the decision had been taken to set up the Interdepartmental Committee in June 1938, Chamberlain had expressed the view that German economic hegemony over Eastern Europe might not be all bad.

Cadogan expressed much the same view as Chamberlain even as late as mid-October 1938, thinking, 'We must cut our losses in Eastern Europe. Let Germany, if she can, find her *Lebensraum* and establish herself, if she can, as a powerful economic unit. I don't know that that necessarily worsens our commercial and economic outlook. I have never heard that Mr Gordon Selfridge ruined Harrods.'[17] Neither did Butler afford any support for Halifax, explaining to Lord Erskine how 'it is important to give [Germany] something to do. People here are horror struck with the idea of Germany extending her economic influence into the Danube Basin, but I cannot help thinking she is pre-eminently suited to exert such influence.'[18] Halifax took the view diametrically opposed to this complacency. He held out no great hopes of countering German expansion in the region – trade with it amounted to sixteen per cent of German exports against only three per cent of British – but in certain well-targeted and high-profile areas he considered it worth the effort to offer a counter-poise to Berlin.

Whereas Chamberlain feared the dangers of being seen to be attempting to 'encircle' Germany, Halifax now welcomed the chance of forcing Germany to face the prospect of a war on two fronts. Poland and Romania could not be left to Germany's mercy. It was generally understood that there was little the West could realistically do to protect the rump of Czechoslovakia that was left after the wrenching away of the Sudetenland. Roger Makins, a Foreign Office official attached to the commission which had been set up to see fair play in the carve up, told Butler on 18 October that he was 'able to do little more than watch the constriction of the rabbit by the boa; after a few preliminary struggles the rabbit decided that its only hope of continued existence was to submit to the embrace. Czechoslovakia will in future be little more than a German colony.'[19] Halifax was determined to do everything in Britain's power to prevent the rest of South-Eastern Europe slipping down the boa's throat.

The genesis of the guarantees to Poland and Romania can be found in these strategic and economic debates of late 1938 and early 1939, in which Halifax was the chief proponent of the 'forward' policy. Chamberlain was deeply sceptical about his Foreign Secretary's expensive and, he thought, ultimately doomed schemes. Halifax's refusal to allow Germany a free hand in South-East Europe amounted to a reversion to the mainstream of traditional 'balance of power' foreign policy, abandoned after Versailles, of active involvement to prevent any one power dominating Europe. Chamberlain's commitment to the post-Versailles concept of avoiding continental entanglements was coming under severe pressure from his Foreign Secretary.

As early as May 1938, Halifax supported Turkish requests for £10 million in industrial credits from the British Government, as well as a £6 million credit to buy British-built warships. In an opening salvo in what was to be a long struggle against the Treasury, Halifax argued that with Austria and Hungary in Germany's pocket, the lines of communication to India and the Far East would be fatally compromised should Turkey be the next to fall. Therefore, he maintained, details about the commercial viability of certain 'loans' ought to be subordinated to overall strategy. A fortnight after Munich he advocated the purchase of 200,000 tons of Romanian wheat against 'grave objections' from the President of the Board of Trade, who vigorously argued that Britain had no need for it. Halifax stressed that the German Economics Minister was shortly due to arrive in Bucharest. The wheat deal would, he argued, have 'symbolic value disproportionate to its intrinsic worth'.[20] It went through.

On 7 December 1938, the Cabinet agreed to amend the Export Guarantees Act in order to facilitate uneconomic political credits to deserving countries. At the Foreign Policy Committee the next day, Halifax championed schemes for the import of Greek tobacco, credits for Greece, purchases of Romanian oil and wheat on a regular basis, construction projects on the Black Sea and the increase of British trade with Yugoslavia, Hungary and Bulgaria. When it came to persuading Lord Dulverton, the Chairman of Imperial Tobacco and an old friend, to use Greek tobacco in his blends, Halifax came up against an immovable obstacle. The Government was told that Greek tobacco was so pungent it could not be stored in the same warehouses as other tobaccos and the slightest whiff of it would immediately be recognizable to Imperial's highly discerning customers. Undeterred, Halifax proposed Imperial be indemnified with taxpayers' money for their purchase of the crop, even if subsequently they found they had to burn it. It should not have taken Lord Runciman's business acumen to highlight the inherent absurdity of the idea and point out that 'it might be best and cheapest in the long run' just to give the Greeks the money direct.[21]

Whitehall obstruction of Halifax's schemes was hitherto fairly easily overcome; the Foreign Office was pre-eminent among the government departments and Halifax was a talented departmental warrior with a wide circle of acquaintance amongst senior civil servants, especially in those departments where he had previously served. His support for higher defence expenditure won him the approbation of many in the War Office, Admiralty and Air Ministry. However, the tobacco saga did not involve these, whereas it did seem to range the rest of Whitehall firmly against him. The Dominions Office warned of an outcry from Rhodesia were Imperial to buy from Greece instead. The Board of Trade warned that as Cordell Hull, the American Secretary of State, came from a tobacco-growing state, he would not take kindly to a decrease in American tobacco exports. The Treasury thought that the Turks might become disaffected and demand compensation in more financial credits. Finally one minister warned that should it be leaked that the Government had adulterated the smoker's cigarette for such overt political reasons, 'there would be an uproar from the public which would be quite uncontrollable'.[22] Even this did not discourage Halifax, who warned the Foreign Policy Committee on 10 May that refusal to purchase even part of the crop would mean 'Greece would be discouraged and disgruntled and less willing and able to withstand German pressure'.

He consulted a banker friend, Rex Benson, who helped work out a complex international trading system, the losses of which, expected to run to approximately half a million pounds, would be borne by the taxpayer. It is clear from Benson's diaries that negotiations had already been going on for some time. Three weeks earlier Benson had met the Overseas Trade Minister, Robert Hudson, to discuss

> the formation of a company to carry on three-cornered trade with help of Export Credits e.g. we buy from Turkey or Greece their tobacco or figs for re-sale to Finland or Scandinavian countries who have sterling balances to pay for the manufactured goods and machinery which we want to sell to Turkey and Greece.[23]

Chamberlain, unconvinced, complained that the Government 'would take all the risks while Messrs Benson and their associates were to take the profits', if any.[24] Simon called the proposal 'a gamble, if not a ramp' and came down heavily against the use of public money in 'so speculative, hazardous and dubious a venture'. In the face of such opposition, Halifax was fortunate to win a reprieve for his scheme, which was referred back to the relevant departments. Every penny for political credits had laboriously to be eked out of an unwilling Treasury and the tenacity Halifax showed over it was commendable.

He was equally hard-nosed about the visit he and the Prime Minister were to make to Rome on 10 January 1939. Just prior to his departure

Halifax told the Cabinet that 'our main principle should be "nothing for nothing". We should make no concession to Signor Mussolini unless he would help us to obtain the detente which it is our policy to obtain.'[25] Chamberlain had significantly higher hopes than that; he wanted "something for something". . . . Signor Mussolini could be persuaded to prevent Herr Hitler from carrying out some "mad dog" act.'

The meetings were perfectly civil but completely unproductive. They attended athletics displays, walked along corridors lined with soldiers dressed in black who saluted with drawn daggers, and went to the opera. They met the King of Italy and the Pope and had long conversations with Il Duce and his son-in-law and Foreign Minister, Count Ciano. They ascertained that Italy was perfectly content in the German camp and in no mood to stray. The Italians had long broken the British diplomatic codes, tapped the Embassy telephones, duplicated keys to the Ambassador's despatch box and bribed the stoker whose job it was to burn the Embassy's waste paper. Indeed, the Ambassador only discovered that the keys to the Embassy safe were also in Italian hands when, instead of secret documents, the spy could not resist stealing his wife's tiara. All confidential conversations between Halifax and Cadogan during the visit had to take place after precautions which we only know to have been absurd, but sadly not precisely how absurd.

A friend wrote to Leo Amery that, towering over their hosts, 'our tall black-coated Ministers looked like a couple of undertakers' mutes'.[26] Although they could hardly have helped their heights, neither looked as ridiculous as Ciano, who gave the fascist salute with his heavily brocaded hat perched at a jaunty angle and a silly grin on his face. Even before the British contingent left, Ciano was on the telephone to Ribbentrop to assure him that nothing had come of it. On returning home Chamberlain described it as a 'truly wonderful visit',[27] but Halifax merely used the opportunity correctly to assess Italy as 'what it has always been, a lightweight outfit, no raw materials, no stamina to face a modern war'.[28]

A snippet from the memoirs of the Ambassador to Turkey, Sir Hughe Knatchbull-Hugessen, illustrates the general view of ennui and frustration Halifax so often felt about his job during this period. During a half-hour conversation before returning to Ankara from leave, 'We studied the map of Europe, which Halifax took out and spread on the table, remarking as he did so, "What a bloody place it is."' He might have found the job tiring and dispiriting, but he was impressing some of those elements at the Foreign Office who had hitherto been hostile. His change of attitude certainly had a great effect on Oliver Harvey, who wrote on 17 February: 'We may have trouble with the PM before too long! . . . [Halifax] is carrying his line more and more – it is close to A.E.'s. He is almost unrecognizable from the H of a year ago. He says bluntly, "No more Munichs for me." '[29]

16

'Halt! Major Road Ahead!'

The already substantial and ever-widening gap between Chamberlain and Halifax's perception of the future of Anglo-German relations became even more apparent on 19 February 1939, when the former wrote to Henderson about his hopes for effecting a Franco-Italian rapprochement and then starting disarmament and colonial discussions with the Germans. Halifax later told Henderson he found all this 'rather optimistic. I do not myself think there is any hope of making sense of any colonial discussions ... unless and until your German friends can really show more than smooth words as evidence of friendly hearts.' A week later Chamberlain complained that his critics said that the Government had come round to their way of thinking, 'and I am not sure if Halifax were alone he would feel it necessary to deny this'.[1]

Halifax's pragmatic and unsentimental approach to international affairs is well attested by the position he took in the debate over whether and when to recognize General Franco. On 8 February, he told the Cabinet, 'it was clear that General Franco was going to win the war and he thought that the sooner this country got on better terms with him and made up lost ground the better'.[2] Ignoring Republican pleas, he then cajoled the French into jointly recognizing the Nationalist Government on 27 February. This has since been taken to demonstrate Halifax's covert desire for a fascist victory in Spain, but in fact only illustrates his readiness to face facts and try to make the best of them. Typical of the way his mind worked was his refusal to help fleeing Republican refugees whilst they were still in Spain, yet advocating sending them humanitarian aid as soon as they reached the French border.

Meanwhile, the differences between Prime Minister and Foreign Secretary were becoming easily discernible to Whitehall insiders. Shortly after Easter 'Rab' Butler asked in his diary:

Whence comes the present drive away from the policy of appeasement? The Foreign Office is certainly surprised and gratified by the energy with which this has been prosecuted. I have decided that the determination comes from Halifax himself. Sometimes he has moved the Cabinet by what at first sight appear to be rumours. . . . But whatever the methods it is clear that Halifax is determined to set up a counter force to Germany and that he is going ahead single-mindedly.[3]

Although that diary entry, quoted in his autobiography, *The Art of the Possible*, sounds like approbation for Halifax, in fact Butler made it clear to friends in late January 1939 that 'his views were those of the PM rather than those of Halifax'.[4] For all his brains in his 1950s and 1960s heyday, it is hard to see Butler as a sympathetic figure in the 1930s. He took to appeasement with an unholy glee not shared after *Anschluss* by anyone else in the Foreign Office. His extreme partisanship against members of his own party, his relish for back-room deals and his almost messianic opposition to Churchill make Butler, as even his own heavily weeded papers are unable to prevent, seem a thoroughly unattractive figure.

Halifax's growing split with Chamberlain led Harvey to canvass his name to almost everyone he came across in February and March 1939 as the next Prime Minister. On 22 February, Eden told Harvey he would like to serve as Leader of the House of Commons under a Halifax Premiership, adding that Baldwin also thought the combination possible. At dinner with Lord Birkenhead on 2 March, Harvey noted Churchill himself 'is well pleased with H but does not trust the PM'.[5] At varying intervals over the next few weeks Harvey canvassed Oscar Cleverly, the Prime Minister's Private Secretary, Jim Thomas, Lord Hinchingbrooke MP, Seymour Berry, the acting editor of the *Daily Telegraph*, and others about Halifax, receiving a generally positive response from all of them. But his master was no more an intriguer than a resigner and he would have been furious had he known that his Private Secretary was hawking his name around London in this way.

Despite possessing Job's patience, even Halifax found the next series of events difficult to bear. Largely because of intelligence reports that Germany was in deep economic trouble, early March 1939 saw an absurd resurgence of optimism amongst the appeasers. Chamberlain, who when he consulted anyone was advised by Wilson, Simon, Butler, Dunglass and Henderson, took on an absurdly rosy view of the future. Halifax, who now by dint of situation as well as inclination spent his time with Cadogan, Harvey, Vansittart and Sargent, saw little to justify this new mood. On entering the Foreign Office on the morning of 10 March, he noticed a suspicious unanimity in the newspapers' sanguine reporting on the state of Anglo-German relations. When he asked about this, he was shocked to learn that Chamberlain had the night before personally given an extensive press briefing on foreign affairs to all the parliamentary lobby correspondents. Although Wilson had seen Cadogan at 4 p.m. the previous evening, he had not seen fit to mention it.

David Keir, political correspondent of the *News Chronicle* and former chairman of the parliamentary lobby correspondents for 1938, was present at the briefing and kept detailed notes of exactly what the Prime Minister had said. 'Generally speaking,' he had told the assembled journalists, 'I think the foreign situation is less anxious and gives me less concern for possible unpleasant development than it has done for some time.' He went on to talk of his hopes for 'some agreement about disarmament', adding, 'we should remember all the time there is going on … a great deal of interchange between Germany and this country, not all of it of an official character, but of an unofficial or semi-official, which is of a very different nature'.[6] The painstaking work which Halifax and his Office had undertaken since Munich to show a tougher face to Germany lay in tatters. Even so much as to mention the word 'disarmament' sent precisely the wrong signals to Berlin. Cadogan pointed out that for the Prime Minister to speak of settling Franco-Italian relations would merely cause suspicion in France, where it would be thought Britain was trying to do a deal, whilst encouraging the Italians to increase their demands. The references to 'interchange' of 'an official or semi-official' character sounded suspiciously like the Montagu Norman and George Steward contacts with the Germans, which Chamberlain had promised Halifax were innocent and unauthorized.

'Halifax,' according to Harvey, 'though he did not show it, was annoyed and asked to see the PM. We then heard that he had left for Chequers last evening!... Of course the rumour has started that H and the PM no longer see eye to eye.'[7] So he wrote a letter which, though it was couched in typically polite and friendly terms, made his message clear:

> I fear that the publicity given to the hopes of early progress in disarmament – which however desirable I cannot regard as probable – will not do good in Germany at this moment. They will be encouraged to think that we are feeling the strain, etc., and the good effects that the balance you have up to now maintained between rearmament and peace efforts is tilted to our disadvantage.... You know that I never wish to be tiresome or take departmental views!... but none the less I think that when you are going to make such a general review about foreign affairs it might be helpful and well if you felt able to let me know in advance that you are going to do it, and give me some idea of what you had it in mind to say.[8]

The reply from Chequers was charm itself. 'My dear Edward,' the Prime Minister began, 'your rebuke is most delicately conveyed and was fully merited. I can only say 1. mea culpa. 2. I was horrified at the result of my talk to the Press which was intended only as a general background but was transcribed by them verbatim. 3. I promise faithfully not to do it again.' The apology contained not a word of regret about the substance of his talk, to which he stubbornly adhered. Harvey recorded that on receiving the apology, Halifax was only 'half-convinced'. Harvey thought the briefing was intended as a reply to a recent speech Halifax had made, and which No. 10 had complained was too tough, in which the Foreign Secretary had likened Britain's message to Germany to the T-junction road-sign which read 'Halt! Major Road Ahead!'. Chamberlain's mood of optimism led Hoare to make a cocksure speech to his Chelsea constituents and Simon into confident predictions which they were very soon deeply to regret. For less than a week after Chamberlain's lobby briefing there were German troops in Prague.

At the meeting held at 11 a.m. on 15 March, Halifax could tell the Cabinet nothing more about the sudden German invasion of the rump of Czechoslovakia than they could read in the early edition of the *Daily Telegraph*. Apparently, as a result of an agreement between Hitler and the new Czech President Emil Hacha, the Czech army stayed in barracks. The Cabinet was instead used to work out a formula whereby the Government could back out of the guarantee of Czechoslovakia signed at Munich. They came up with the ingenious device of declaring that since the Slovak Diet had declared itself independent, no such state as Czechoslovakia legally existed when the Germans went in. When Halifax got up to present that sophistry in the House of Lords, it was not a proud moment for him or for Britain. However, in that Cabinet meeting he did point out the central message of Prague was that Hitler did not intend his Reich merely to be an Aryan stronghold as some had been led to think, but was on the way to becoming an empire like any other. He

> thought it was significant that this was the first occasion on which Germany had applied her shock tactic to the domination of non-Germans. . . . He also stressed that Germany's attitude in this matter was completely inconsistent with the Munich Agreement. Germany had deliberately preferred naked force to the methods of consultation and discussion.[9]

It was decided to cancel the Oliver Stanley and Robert Hudson visits to Berlin, but not to recall Sir Nevile Henderson. Henderson had largely lost Halifax's confidence by this stage, partly because of Lady Halifax's estimation of him as a 'light-weight'.

Prague left Halifax, who had resolutely refused to take part in the spirit of optimism of the previous few days, in an even stronger position vis-à-vis his Cabinet colleagues. The effect on public opinion of Germany's latest example of unprovoked aggression was a seismic shift away from Chamberlain's position and towards his. The day after Prague the Conservative Foreign Affairs Committee called for national service, all-party government and a Russian alliance. The first two of these had long been championed by Halifax, who was also swiftly coming around to the third. For a great many Britons Prague marked the point at which war began to seem inevitable. Due to mark his seventieth birthday with a major speech in Birmingham, Chamberlain turned to Halifax to help draft it.

Despite Chamberlain's slight change of emphasis, it is inconceivable that a guarantee would have been given to Poland had Halifax not been Foreign Secretary. Had almost any of the other Cabinet ministers been in the job, Chamberlain would have been able to view Prague as a setback instead of being forced to see it as a major reversal. For between Munich and Prague Halifax's 'Godesberg' view of Hitler was vindicated as plainly as Chamberlain's 'Munich' view was discredited.

On the afternoon of 17 March, the Romanian Minister in London, Virgil Tilea, visited Halifax with the highly perturbing news that the Germans had dictated an economic ultimatum to his country, the tenor of which was indistinguishable from a political ultimatum. Coming only two days after Hitler's seizure of Czechoslovakia, this must have looked to Halifax exactly like the 'mad dog' act that Chamberlain had spoken of back in January. As Harvey ushered Tilea into the Foreign Secretary's room, he informed Halifax that Walter Elliot had phoned to say that through Robert Bernays, the Romanian Princess Marthe Bibesco and the President of the Romanian Council, he had heard that this report was indeed accurate.

Halifax immediately telegraphed almost every friendly European power – France, Poland, Russia, Turkey, Greece and Hungary – to inform them of the news and to ask for their reactions. When the German Ambassador, Herbert von Dirksen, called the next day to complain about some remarks Duff Cooper had made about Hitler, Halifax 'fairly let him have it'.[10] He told Dirksen that, 'if Germany committed an act of naked aggression on Roumania, it would be very difficult for this country not to take all the action in her power to rally resistance against that aggression and to take part in that resistance herself'. This amounted to an oral guarantee of Romania and reflected Halifax's fury. Dirksen was understandably taken aback, for it transpired from a cable from the British Ambassador to Bucharest the next day that the ultimatum had been a misunderstanding, or possibly even a hoax.

At the post-mortem Cabinet on the 18th, Halifax thought it as well to go ahead with consideration of how Britain would respond should something of the sort really happen. Somewhat disingenuously he said, 'he was not certain whether the telegrams had all been despatched,'[11] whereas they had actually gone out nineteen hours previously and replies had already begun to come in. One scholar has interpreted this as 'conveniently obscuring the fact that he had acted without consulting the Cabinet'.[12] Ever present in his calculations was the knowledge, fully supported by the Chiefs of Staff, that with the vast oil, gas and grain supplies of Romania, Germany could negate the effect of a naval blockade of Germany. He was also deeply concerned lest the fall of Romania, coupled with Bulgaria's pro-German sympathies, meant a direct route for Germany to the Mediterranean. The only way to protect Romania was by ensuring that, in the event of a German attack, Poland and Russia would come to her aid. Romania was allied to Poland, but felt only fear and suspicion of her eastern neighbour. As early as 18 March, Halifax was insistent that Romania was vital to Britain's defence. Even Chamberlain was forced to agree that, should she be attacked, Britain would 'have no alternative but to take up the challenge'.[13]

Halifax's entire standpoint on the question of going to war against Germany had altered as radically as so many of his other assumptions. No longer was it the unimaginable disaster that had to be avoided in all events. He had inserted a passage into the Birmingham speech which had envisaged war as preferable to dishonour and at the post-Tilea crisis Cabinet he went so far as to suggest 'a war which did not have immediate and conclusive success, might have important internal reactions in Germany'.[14]

All through this period Halifax kept up the pressure on Chamberlain to widen the Government, telling Harvey in late March how 'it had become nearly impossible to carry on diplomacy now without a non-party government'. Harvey replied by urging his master to usurp the Prime Minister, telling him on 26 March how,

> if an all-party government were formed under your leadership it would be acceptable to all. You are now regarded in all quarters as the most obvious successor to the present PM in spite of the H[ouse] of L[ords] difficulty. What is required is a very drastic remodelling of the government, many old ministers retiring to make way for new blood and for those representing the other parties in the new administration.[15]

At the Foreign Policy Committee of 27 March, Halifax made it clear that as Britain seemed to have to choose between Poland and Russia he thought she should opt for Poland. He thought little of the Red Army's capacity for offensive warfare, said her air force was obsolete and predicted chaos in her supply arrangements. The Polish army, on the other hand, consisted of fifty divisions 'and might be expected to make a useful contribution'. He added

> that there was probably no war in which France and ourselves could prevent Poland and Roumania from being overrun. We were faced with a dilemma of doing nothing or entering into a devastating war. If we did nothing this in itself would mean a great accession to Germany's strength and a great loss to ourselves of sympathy and support in the United States, the Balkans and in other parts of the world. In these circumstances if we had to choose between two great evils he favoured our going to war.[16]

Even his earlier beliefs about the stability of the Nazi regime came under revision. 'The real issue', he told the Cabinet uncompromisingly, 'was Germany's attempt to obtain world domination ... we were the only country who could organize such resistance ... the sooner we united the better. Otherwise we might see one country after another absorbed by Germany.'[17] He then went on to discuss the desirability of an alliance with Russia, Poland, Turkey and America. This was almost to the word what Churchill was advocating in his press articles at the time. When Churchill sent Halifax his 'Memorandum on Sea Power', which predicted that Japan would 'clean us out of all our interests' in Hong Kong and Shanghai and called for plans to be drawn up to look into how to win naval control in the Baltic, Halifax answered, 'I find my thoughts going very much with yours.'[18]

Far from being, as Malcolm Muggeridge portrayed him, Chamberlain's faithful Sancho Panza, Halifax was the first politician in the Government to see what was happening and the major force in steering the way from an appeasing to a resisting tack. As well as glorifying those who went into the Wilderness (and so abdicated responsibility for the nation's affairs), there ought to be some recognition for Halifax, who stayed on and took the hard decisions, tackling from the inside the ghastly business of pre-war decision-making. Churchill's time 'in the Wilderness' (his characteristically melo-dramatic phrase for the same fate as many other politicians have had to undergo) was neither imposed on him, nor the result of his opposition to appeasement.

Halifax could cajole, outwit and manoeuvre with the best of West-minster's insiders. Cancelling Stanley's projected visit to Berlin, ordering the indefinite closure of the Anglo-German Fellowship Society, setting up the nucleus of what was to become the Special Operations Executive and advocating the deportation of sixty-one Nazi officials working in London, were only a few of the dozens of sound but unsung actions he took in March 1939.

The logic of protecting Poland and Romania only made sense if there was some agreement with the Soviet Union, which would have to provide the logistical support, armaments and eventual back-stop to any war in the East. On this Chamberlain was a definite drag on policy. He had 'the most profound distrust' both of Russian motives and their ability to mount an effective offensive. If there had to be a choice 'he would prefer Poland, Romania and Finland as allies to Russia.'[19] By 27 March, Halifax had to bow to this potentially disastrous situation. Poland and Romania had said that public association of Russia with the scheme would weaken it, and similar indications had been received from Finland, Yugoslavia, Italy, Spain and Portugal. One of the major accusations levelled at Halifax for concluding a Polish guarantee without a concomitant understanding with Russia was that it tied London's hand whilst freeing Moscow's. Stalin was left secure in the knowledge that a German attack in the East meant help from the West. A German attack in the West, however, was a war from which he could stand aside.

At the time of Munich one of the most cogent and frequently used arguments against guaranteeing Czechoslovakia was that the decision between peace or war would pass out of British hands and into those of foreigners. The Cabinet minutes are full of examples of both Chamberlain and Halifax using this argument to good effect. By guaranteeing Poland and closing off their options, they did precisely what they had denounced six months earlier. This was not, as it has been portrayed, Grand Strategy by Panic. Neither was it the cynical laying of a tripwire in order to bring a declining Empire to war without incurring political opprobrium for having started it. It was instead the result of Halifax's conviction that Hitler should no longer be kept guessing as to Western intentions; rather he should be left in absolutely no doubt that further aggression could not be tolerated.

On 25 March, the whole issue was gone into at length in Halifax's huge room in the Foreign Office, where the overriding consideration was simply that, 'H feels adherence to Poland is essential to any effective scheme to hold up Germany in event of aggression. . . . What we want to secure is the certainty of a war on two fronts.'[20] To that same end Halifax four days earlier had told the French Foreign Minister Bonnet,

> it was now a question of checking German aggression, whether against France or Great Britain, or Holland, or Switzerland, or Roumania or Poland, or Yugoslavia or whoever it might be ... what was vitally necessary was to assert the general position as quickly as possible. That would be a danger signal to German and Italian aggression and at the same time a rallying point for the smaller nations.[21]

The intellectual argument for the guarantees had been won. All that remained was to see what quid pro quo the Poles were willing to make and whether it was possible to conclude a secret treaty with Russia to come to Polish or Romanian aid in the event of a German attack. The Secretary for War, Leslie Hore-Belisha, recorded in his diary for 28 March:

> After lunch I went straight to the House and saw the PM in his room. He told me Halifax was insistent that some forthright action should be taken as immediate evidence that we meant business in resisting aggression. An announcement of a bigger military effort on our part would be the most convincing gesture we could make in the present tension.

The then Polish Ambassador to London, Count Raczynski, wrote of the Polish guarantee, 'this momentous act was performed with courage and a remarkable sense of timing. It is not certain who was responsible, but probably it was Halifax.'[22] In a letter to some American friends Victor Cazalet believed, 'it is generally thought that Halifax has been the moving spirit in the Cabinet for both the guarantees and conscription. He is the only man who has any real influence with Neville.' Eden told Halifax's official biographer long after the war, 'Something had happened between the Tuesday (of Prague) and the Saturday (of Birmingham) and he thought it may have been a demarche by Halifax.'[23] 'Chips' Channon had no doubt at all. Writing of Halifax in his diary on 25 August 1939, he remarked, 'The Polish guarantee was his pet scheme and his favourite god-child.'

The issue between Poland and Germany – the German demand for the Polish Corridor and Danzig – ironically represented the Reich's strongest case so far. Danzig was eighty per cent German and the Corridor had been one of the more outlandish provisions of the Versailles Treaty. But for Halifax the issue had long moved beyond the rights and wrongs of individual claims and towards the 'great moralities' which he had declared his willingness to fight for at the time of Munich. The fear which materialized in late March was that Poland might disclaim Danzig and allow herself to be neutralized in return for not fighting, thus chalking up yet another bloodless coup for Hitler.

It took a great deal to persuade Chamberlain that the Polish guarantee meant anything less than the certainty of war at some later date. He rightly suspected that it would stiffen Polish resolve not to treat with the Germans. He thought it inevitable that the European balance was going to shift towards Germany in what was, after all, her own economic hinterland. In anticipating gradual Nazi penetration from Poland to the Mediterranean, Halifax was the first minister of the period to expound what was later to become the 'domino theory' of international power politics. But even by mid-1939, a lot of dominoes needed to fall before the Mediterranean became open to German cruisers. Halifax had long since decided that Britain would not allow Hitler a free hand in Eastern Europe and all he required was an opportunity finally to push Chamberlain into making the projected guarantee.

Just as Halifax used the Tilea episode to stiffen Chamberlain's Birmingham speech, so he employed another equally false rumour to effect the major policy reversal of the establishment of a serious British commitment in Eastern Europe. The timing could not have gone better for him. After a Cabinet on 29 March, at which he had declared 'this country should do what it could to strengthen the will to resist aggression and to give support to those who were prepared to resist aggression',[24] he received a visit from the Berlin correspondent of the *News Chronicle*, Ian Colvin, whom Lord Lloyd had sent over. Colvin gave Halifax, Cadogan and Leeper 'hair-raising details of [an] imminent thrust against Poland'.[25] Cadogan, by then virtually immune to such amateur warnings, was not convinced.

Leeper later described what happened:

Colvin said his piece. Halifax was most impressed, and it was evident that he was itching to do something definite. He got onto the telephone to Neville and told him that he *must* see Colvin. The upshot of this was the British guarantee to Poland. Halifax would not have used such an instrument as a Press Correspondent if he had not badly wanted to do something.[26]

The tale Colvin repeated to Chamberlain amounted to little more than anecdotal evidence about an army victualler receiving increased orders, but as Chamberlain told his sisters on 2 April,

> on the same day we got the same talk from quite another source of this week-end swoop and the thought that we might wake up on Sunday or Monday morning to find Poland surrendering to an ultimatum was certainly alarming. We then and there decided that we should have to make [the guarantee declaration]. . . .[27]

Halifax stayed up till 1 a.m. drafting the announcement. Having got nothing substantial from either the Poles or the Russians, he was still willing to go ahead with what amounted to a declaration that the use of force over Danzig would result in a full-scale European war. At the next morning's Cabinet he hoped to offset criticism by calling it 'an interim measure' and predicted that it would 'help to educate public opinion in Germany'. Throughout the meeting the Prime Minister left no doubt as to the authorship of the guarantees, referring to them throughout as 'the Foreign Secretary's proposals'.[28] He found Halifax's tough draft of the announcement hard to accept, believing it 'should end up on a somewhat less defiant note',[29] but he went along with the substance. After the Cabinet which approved the principle of the guarantees, Horace Wilson informed the Foreign Policy Committee that, as there were only fourteen extra German divisions on the Polish border, it was highly unlikely that Colvin's thesis was correct. But Chamberlain, convinced by then of the need for the new policy, did not want to admit this to the Commons as it 'would cut away the justification for the declaration'.[30] Halifax had so built up the momentum behind the change in policy that its original *raison d'être* was felt to be almost irrelevant.

Cadogan was right when he called the guarantee 'a frightful gamble' and many valid criticisms have been made of the policy both by Lloyd George and Churchill at the time and many historians since. It did constrict British and French freedom of manoeuvre, tying them into an inherently dangerous situation. It also strained Dominion loyalty and presented the Germans with a superb propaganda coup. But despite this, when Chamberlain told the House of Commons at 2.45 p.m. on 31 March 1939 that, in the event of a German attack on Poland, 'His Majesty's Government would feel themselves bound at once to lend the Polish Government all support in their power', Britain had at least and at last put an end to the disastrous 'Guessing Position'.

17

The Peace Front

The Polish leader, Colonel Josef Beck, arrived in London on 3 April 1939 and stayed for four days to tie up the details of the guarantee. His agreement to make it reciprocal was of limited use to Britain as there was little likelihood of Germany attacking Britain before Poland. Beck, who Chamberlain thought had 'a sly look and an equivocal reputation',[1] refused to countenance any public understanding with Russia. This was partly out of fear of Germany's reaction, partly for domestic political reasons and partly due to mistrust of the Soviets. It proved a setback to Halifax's hopes for any effective 'Peace Front' against Germany.

The British Government has regularly been accused of negotiating with Beck in bad faith, as they had no real intention of coming to Poland's aid in the event of war. But an undated note by Halifax in his papers, which seems to be a commentary on the 1952 publication of the official *Documents on British Foreign Policy* for 1939, asserts that

> neither the Polish Government nor the Roumanian Government were under any illusions as to the measure of concrete help that they might expect from Great Britain in the event of Hitler choosing war. For them, as for us, the guarantees were the best chance, and indeed the only chance, of warning him off that decision.

However, Halifax was wrong; the Poles did – however illogically and unreasonably – expect help. Here was a deterrent with no inherent power to deter. Concern to avoid retaliatory bombing in the west and the immutable geographical fact of Poland's isolation in the east meant that the Chiefs of Staff never seriously considered aiding Poland. She was a more distant country of which we knew even less. Halifax had attached British foreign policy to the cause of a nation whose name was synonymous with tragedy and which had spent much of the previous two centuries being partitioned thrice and under a foreign yoke.

In May 1939, the Polish Ambassador in London, the dapper, charming and aristocratic Count Raczynski, asked Halifax for a £60 million line of credit for his country to buy essential war materials. Simon, the Chancellor of the Exchequer, blocked this by pointing out that gold stocks were being strained to their utmost; £68 million had already been granted to Turkey, Russia, China, Romania, Czechoslovakia and Egypt. He starkly warned that further depletion would mean 'a reduction of the time for which we could feed our people during a war ... we should not be able to maintain the fight ourselves for long'.[2] Chamberlain sided with Simon, and on 17 May the two of them sent a message requesting Halifax to contact the visiting Polish emissary, Colonel Koc, and 'make it clear that it is no use to come over expecting gold or Sterling'. Throughout the summer of 1939, Halifax pressed for the Polish loan, sending on to Chamberlain the letters of the British Ambassador to Warsaw, Sir Howard Kennard, which detailed the Polish army's woeful shortage of modern weaponry. When Raczynski complained about the debate over Danzig which was being conducted in the letters column of *The Times*, Halifax told Dawson that 'he should now be definitely relieved if the correspondence could be closed'.[3] It was.

The day Beck left London the news came through of the Italian invasion of Albania. It was Good Friday. Halifax was in a three-hour church service and Chamberlain was fishing in Scotland. Halifax immediately supported Churchill's call for an early recall of Parliament, cancelled his Garrowby weekend and convened a meeting of ministers for 11.30 a.m. the next morning. Despite being chaired by Simon, Halifax did all the talking. He said he was not about to abandon his pro-Italian policy because of Mussolini's action in a country which had for a century been an Italian satellite and was moreover almost ceded to her altogether at Versailles. His greatest concern was that an attack on Greece, probably via Corfu, was planned, which led him to propose that Britain should guarantee both Greece and Turkey, whilst simultaneously somehow attempting to 'keep Italy in play'.[4] Halifax considered the integrity of Greece and Turkey, lying at Britain's imperial jugular, to be equally as vital to British interests as were Poland and Romania. In a conversation with Churchill on 6 April, Halifax agreed that Yugoslavia might also be a worthy recipient of yet another guarantee.

Although it undoubtedly disturbed the international waters, '*le jeu Albanais*', as Mussolini ordered the Counsellor at the Italian Embassy in London to inform Halifax, '*ne vaut pas le chandelle*' of Anglo-Italian relations. Halifax used it as an extra argument in his ceaseless campaign for increased economic aid to Greece and Turkey, and even the Greek tobacco question resurfaced. On 13 April, he secured Chamberlain's consent for a joint Anglo-French guarantee to Greece and Romania. Halifax justified these (by now seemingly indiscriminate) Balkan commitments by reasoning that

Britain would probably anyway be drawn into war in the event of attacks on these countries, and it was just as well that the dictators realized this. He was also keen to safeguard British prestige both in the Balkans and in America, stay as close as possible to France, and deny Romania's great oil and wheat resources to Germany. To foreigners, such as the Turkish Foreign Minister, who were expressing disbelief that the Western Powers would ever take a stand anywhere, the guarantees came as a salutary lesson. Halifax may have wondered whether he had gone too far, though, when the Liberian Ambassador solemnly requested a British guarantee of Liberia.

Thanking Harvey for an overview of the international scene in mid-April 1939, Halifax commented:

> We are some way yet off from automatic all-round collective security: though we may get somewhere near it through present alliances and guarantees. We have not yet produced a tolerably workable plan for revision of frontiers. If free agreement is not forthcoming what remains except force or the threat of force?[5]

This problem of how to revise the unworkable Versailles frontiers without recourse to the law of the jungle had occupied much of Halifax's time and thought since he had relinquished departmental duties in December 1935. Nazi aggression had tended to make the problem more, rather than less, urgent, until in the post-Munich period it became clear that the inherent rights and wrongs of the Nazi claims had been subsumed by the bullying and threatening methods they used to pursue them.

On 19 April, the Cabinet was faced with the problem of how to mark Hitler's fiftieth birthday. Halifax proposed that the British Chargé d'Affaires in Berlin should decline to subscribe to the traditional Corps Diplomatique present and it was also agreed to excise the customary 'health and welfare' good wishes from the King's congratulatory telegram.[6] This official reticence did not prevent Britons such as the Duke of Buccleuch and Lord Brocket from flying to Berlin to attend the celebrations. Throughout the period Halifax was deluged with letters from a number of the nation's grandest aristocrats imploring him to return to appeasement. Although they differed over details, their general line was that Germany bore no ill will towards Britain per se and ought to be allowed a free path eastwards to fight Russia. To these people the Polish guarantee was a disastrous error. Another constantly recurring feature in the letters was the belief that war with Germany would be ruinous to Britain's place in the world and only Jews and communists would benefit. Halifax, who had himself roughly subscribed to almost these views as recently as 1937–8, wrote back long and polite letters, courteously explaining and defending his policy.

He knew these correspondents socially; indeed, he had been the Marquess of Londonderry's fag at Eton. Responding to him, and others such as the Dukes of Westminster and Buccleuch and the Marquess of Tavistock (soon to become the Duke of Bedford), who still implored him, well after the war had begun, to revive friendship with Germany, Halifax stuck rigidly to the Government line. When Tavistock published his correspondence with Halifax in *Fate of a Peace Effort* in 1940, it did nothing to embarrass Halifax but instead turned the author into a pariah. Anti-war or pro-Nazi letters from less well-born correspondents were passed on to Special Branch.

On 11 April, Harvey wrote to Halifax reminding him how, 'you said the other day that you wanted to gain time because every month gave us 600 more aeroplanes'. As the spring of 1939 turned into summer and his hopes for stable and peaceful co-existence with Germany ebbed away, Halifax was determined to win as much time as possible for the rebuilding of Britain's air defences. Every month that he won for peace he considered a victory in itself and running concurrently with this holding action was his insistence on increasing the pace of rearmament, especially in the air. On 17 April, the pushy but talented War Minister, Hore-Belisha, tried to enlist Halifax's support for a scheme to conscript Territorial Army Anti-Aircraft groups and found to his delight that the Foreign Secretary wanted to go still further and preferred universal conscription. Halifax thought offensive, as opposed to merely defensive, conscription would send a more apposite message to Berlin and Paris.

Halifax was perfectly prepared to indulge in some light deception of Chamberlain if the occasion required; on 17 April, he told Hore-Belisha, just after he had been shown some War Office papers advocating immediate partial mobilization, that he 'would speak to the PM about the WO papers and that he would not mention how he got hold of them'.[7] It is also instructive that Hore-Belisha, on the verge of resignation, should have chosen Halifax to show the papers to, in direct contravention of an order from No. 10 not to allow Cabinet ministers to see them. At the meeting Hore-Belisha requested at 6.50 p.m. on 17 April, Halifax 'said that he had good reason to believe that conscription was the only course that would have any effect on Germany. He asked me what I thought of the idea of inviting Attlee, TUC leaders, Churchill and others to attend the CID.'[8]

Chamberlain had pledged never to introduce peacetime conscription, but was willing to employ the sophistry that, 'while we are not actually at war, it would be a mockery to call the present conditions "peace"'.[9] In Cabinet on 24 April, he announced 'a limited measure of compulsory military service in a form which would [not arouse] irreconcilable opposition from the working classes'.[10] Halifax went further and called for the immediate declaration of a national state of emergency and the calling up of the Territorials and Army Reservists. He emphasized the vital necessity of training civilians for the 'Air Defence of Great Britain' programme. He had to withdraw the state of emergency suggestion the next day after consideration of the ill effects it would have on financial confidence and because it was estimated that it would only take two days for the Reserve and Auxiliary Forces Bill to pass through Parliament.

On 27 April, against opposition from the Trades Union Congress and much of the Labour Party, compulsory military conscription was introduced for twenty and twenty-one year olds. Hore-Belisha exclaimed in his diary that evening, 'Another complete volte-face – Munich, appeasement – collective security, Pact with Poland, etc.; Ministry of Supply and now Conscription!' Without exception each had come as a result of the constant pressure Halifax exerted on the Prime Minister and elements of the Cabinet.

On the same day on which Britain announced conscription, Hitler denounced the Anglo-German naval agreement of 1935. Halifax took this calmly, arguing for a tough statement to be issued as he was anxious about the way British actions were being reported by German propaganda. He also thought it probable that the Germans had been cheating on its provisions anyway. War rumours abounded, but he told the Cabinet that these were 'part of a technique designed to keep us in a state of constant alarm'.[11] The imminent surprise bombing of the Fleet was a favourite scare story and in May precautionary measures were taken to prevent the King and Queen, who were travelling to Canada, being intercepted and kidnapped by the nearby pocket battleship *Deutschland*.

As Chamberlain became progressively isolated within the Cabinet, his political alienation from Halifax deepened and became more publicly perceivable. *The Week* led with an article on 29 March which postulated that 'talk of a Government under Halifax has revived. It appears to be true that ... Lord Halifax has within the last three days committed himself more definitely than ever before to opposition to the policy of Mr Chamberlain.' The magazine's report of 'rebels' supporting Halifax and canvassing the Labour leadership in his favour were probably no more than a combination of rumours about Harvey's king-making efforts and *The Week*'s innate mendacity. However, it does tend to show the extent to which the Chamberlain/Halifax split was becoming widely enough known to be commented on.

It was during this period that Halifax considered replacing Henderson, whom he correctly felt to be over-sympathetic to the Germans. He also took action to marginalize his arch-appeasing Under-Secretary, Butler. The diary of the engaging if sybaritic 'Chips' Channon, Butler's Parliamentary Private Secretary, recorded how 'Rab is annoyed that he has not been more consulted over the Polish guarantee and thinks that Halifax, who is veering away from the PM, intends to keep him in the background.'[12] Butler was right: on the day the guarantees to Greece and Romania were about to be agreed, Halifax, walking across the Park to No. 10 with

Butler, reproached him: 'I suppose you are coming to give the PM moral support.'[13] Channon considered that 'Halifax is weaned away from Neville now on many points . . . and the PM still feels more mentally at home with Rab than with anyone.' By 28 May, Chamberlain was so isolated over his opposition to a Russian alliance that he complained, 'the only supporter I could get for my view was Rab Butler and he was not a very influential ally'.[14]

In June 1939, Butler wrote a character study of Halifax in which he noted how many of the Foreign Secretary's metaphors came from the chase, adding somewhat petulantly,

> In the case of the Polish guarantee a jump from a dangerous main road had suddenly to be made over a high hedge in cold blood, to be followed by a series of fences. . . . These the Cabinet took under urgent pressure from Halifax who used every means, such as journalistic reports, to show the danger of not taking action.[15]

Butler also noted how Halifax regularly saw Churchill, Eden and Labour leaders, walked to the Foreign Office in the mornings with junior MPs 'and sees discreetly other figures outside the Office'. In the original manuscript the word 'figures' had originally been 'followers'. Halifax was quietly building up a constituency. One of the 'followers', Victor Cazalet, used to walk with Halifax to the Foreign Office every Wednesday morning giving him the political gossip he needed (and enjoyed) so much. Despite his sepulchral reputation, Halifax, in Oliver Lyttelton's opinion, 'had the nobleman's love of gossip. He knew every potain de ville, and also enjoyed producing his own titbits.'[16]

Halifax's engagement diaries for 1939 record private lunches with Churchill and Eden and, no longer wedded to Chamberlain's vision, he spoke emphatically of the 'unsatisfactory state of the internal situation' and made no secret of the fact that he wanted a national government.[17] After a lifetime in politics and coming from the same Victorian aristocratic background as Churchill, it was natural that, though on different sides of the political divide, Halifax and Churchill should often rub shoulders socially and discuss good-naturedly the topics of the moment. There was far more cross-fertilization of ideas and contact then than would be expected in politics today.[18] After the war Rex Leeper remembered how Halifax

> was big-minded, and raised no objection to his continued association with Eden while he was serving him. One day when Rab (a convinced Chamberlainite) was there and the question of consulting Eden arose, Rab said, 'I don't think it matters what Anthony thinks,' and Halifax replied, 'I do.'[19]

He also stayed in close touch with his old mentor, Stanley Baldwin. Driving to Victoria to take leave of the Romanian Foreign Minister on 26 April, Halifax insisted to Harvey that '*he* was as much responsible for foreign policy as the PM'. Harvey replied 'that was so but the Left did trust H & they believed that the recent change of our policy and its stiffening was due to his influence.... India ... had put him on a pedestal from which he could not be knocked off.'[20]

It is astonishing how often, despite the almost constant state of crisis, Halifax was able to find time to lunch and dine with friends. Almost every lunchtime he would go to the Savoy Grill, Le Normandie, the Dorchester, Quaglino's or some other fashionable restaurant, with Lady Halifax if she was in London or family friends such as Lady Nina Balfour, Geoffrey Dawson, Lady Oxford, Lady Maureen Stanley, Walter Monckton, Lady Alexandra Metcalfe or his daughter Anne. He attended the All Souls Gaudy in June and motored down to Eton with Dawson for Fellows' meetings there. Nevertheless, of the thirty Foreign Policy Committee meetings between 14 November 1938 and 1 September 1939, Halifax was present at all but one. Indeed, the only crossings out in his diary are for minor political speaker meetings and a dinner at the German Embassy on 30 March. This does not imply laziness, so much as a more relaxed life than would be possible for a Foreign Secretary today, as well as a tendency not to be rattled by events and a natural affinity for the company of charming and intelligent women. Lord David Cecil put it best when he said, 'Edward was purely Edwardian in his love of purely decorous flirtations in which he played the part of instructor and adviser.'[21] Sometimes Lady Halifax and he would have picnic lunches together on the great desk in his room in the Foreign Office.

Chamberlain's nightmare of the division of Europe into 1914-style opposing blocs became significantly more real in the spring of 1939. On 12 May, Britain signed a mutual assistance pact with Turkey; ten days later, Germany and Italy signed a ten-year alliance, the 'Pact of Steel'. The next day Parliament approved the White Paper on Palestine, by which the Mandate was committed to independence by 1949 and which so restricted Jewish immigration that it was ensured a reasonable reception from the Arab states. The White Paper indicated a step back from the promises made to the Jews by the Lloyd George Government in the 1917 Balfour Declaration. Although Palestine was strictly speaking outside Halifax's immediate departmental province, relations with the Arab states were not, and although he remained on good personal terms with Chaim Weizmann (who also stayed at the Dorchester during the war), Halifax was always more keen not to offend the Arabs than to honour British commitments to a Jewish national homeland in Palestine. On the questions of banning Arab land sales to Jews and the creation of a Jewish brigade, Halifax took the official government line as laid down by his friend the Colonial Secretary, Malcolm MacDonald. On 30 November 1939, Weizmann wrote to him to protest that 'just at a time when almost two million Polish Jews are completely crushed under the Nazi occupation regime, Great Britain should impose an absolute bar on the entry into Palestine of even those of them who have managed to escape'. Halifax's rather lame answer came a full three weeks later: 'we are putting our whole energy into a life-and-death struggle with Nazi Germany, the persecutor of Jewry in Central Europe, and by ridding Europe of the present German regime we hope to render a supreme service to the Jewish people'.[22]

The major event, however, was Halifax's victory over Chamberlain on the question of an alliance with Russia. The fact that the Russian negotiations have not yet been seen by historians in the context of a struggle between Halifax and Chamberlain is partly because of the way they were conducted and partly because Halifax's constantly reiterated pessimism as to the efficacy of the alliance almost mirrored Chamberlain's own. His antipathy and distrust of the Soviets sometimes led him to extraordinary lengths. In July 1939, Queen Mary heard from the Brazilian Ambassador that he was shortly due to be recalled. This meant that as the next longest-serving ambassador's wife, Mrs Ivan Maisky would become the 'doyenne' of the diplomatic corps, whose duty it was to introduce new ambassadresses to all the others. Halifax took steps to see to it that the Brazilian Ambassador stayed. The Brazilians, not unreasonably, did not believe that it was because Senor de Oliviera was so good. In the end, 'private soundings' were taken with the Brazilian President which resulted in Mrs Maisky being denied her treasured post.[23]

As early as 18 April, the Russian Foreign Minister, Maxim Litvinov, had tendered an eight-point proposal for a tripartite military alliance with Britain and France. Superficially attractive, this was enthusiastically welcomed by Churchill, the French, Lloyd George, the Labour Party and the press as a last great hope for peace. With a friendly Russia, it was argued, Germany would not dare attack Poland for fear of a real war on two fronts. Halifax has long been lambasted for being dilatory and doubtful over the offer. He has also been censured for not visiting Moscow personally to negotiate and sign the agreement. He has even been accused of cavilling at the idea of an alliance because the Soviets were atheists. However, as the 1952 note in his papers explains, the Polish and Romanian fear of Russia was at least as great, and probably greater, than their fear of Germany. Poland had been at war with Russia as recently as the 1920s. The Litvinov proposals provided for a joint guarantee of all the states bordering Russia between the Baltic and the Balkans. But they also demanded the amendment of the Polish–Romanian Pact to excise references to the Soviet Union. Harvey summed up the view of many in the Foreign Office at the time when he told Halifax's official biographer: 'No one thought the Russians were any good or would last more than a fortnight.'[24]

Halifax took his time in answering what he agreed with Cadogan were mischievous proposals. His overriding concern was to prevent a diminution of Polish and Romanian confidence in the West. He also wanted to ensure that in the event of a German attack, Russia would provide at best assistance and at worst benevolent neutrality. So he concocted an alternative set of proposals under which Russia unilaterally guaranteed her neighbours. As the negotiations progressed it became clear that, far from his being a potential ally, Stalin displayed a paranoia, short-sightedness and territorial greed that could turn Russia into a hostile neutral or even an enemy. As early as 3 May, Halifax warned the Cabinet of the possibility of an entente between Russia and Germany, however outlandish that must have sounded at the time. Fear of such an outcome was later to become the major spur for Halifax to keep the negotiations going.

It was not only Poland and Romania that were averse to entering into defence arrangements with the Soviet Union; Halifax had indications that Britain's friendly relations with Turkey, Greece, Spain, Italy, Portugal, the Vatican, Finland, the Baltic republics, Yugoslavia, America and Hungary would also suffer. His ideal scenario was for a Russian pledge to give help in such a form as might be acceptable to Poland and Romania. All his diplomacy during the summer of 1939 was devoted to that end. But Beck's obtuseness allowed him to see no further than Danzig and his guarantee. Halifax was not prepared to threaten Poland with a withdrawal of the guarantee any more than he was willing to allow Russia to snap up the three Baltic states as the price of an agreement. So talks with the increasingly suspicious Soviets wore on.

The Russian Ambassador, Ivan Maisky, was an unattractive figure, whose intrigues with Lloyd George, Churchill, Hugh Dalton and other opposition figures was well known to the Government through the tap MI5 kept on his telephone. Jasper Rootham well remembered his own embarrassment and Chamberlain's great diffidence when he presented the Prime Minister with the verbatim transcripts of the conversations Maisky had been having with Churchill.[25] Maisky's mendacity is well illustrated by a passage in his memoirs in which he affected to remember how, during the Blitz, 'thousands' of East Enders in the shelters would spontaneously burst into singing the 'Internationale' at the sight of him. The fact that Halifax found it hard to deal with this sly and cynical envoy was blamed on religious difficulties, whereas in fact the problem was the Russian's own personality. Lady Halifax, to whose beautiful nature all attest, remembered how after an official luncheon at the Dorchester with Maisky and his wife in 1940,

> just as they were leaving, a bad daylight raid began and we saw a bomb explode on the other side of the Park, where the Russian Embassy is situated. I had a rather wicked pleasure in drawing their attention to the location and I could see a good deal of uneasiness on

their part. He was a funny little man with a face like a rosy apple, and she looked like a man dressed as a woman. Indeed many people said she was a man.[26]

The Chiefs of Staff had such a low opinion of the advantages of Russian friendship that in one report they considered it did not even offset the disadvantages of Spanish enmity. But heightened agitation in Danzig, which Halifax feared would declare itself part of the Reich and thus bring Polish retribution and German reprisal in quick succession, forced him to look again at the Russian proposals. By 17 May, he was prepared to countenance extended Staff conversations. Two days later the issue came to a head when the Russians formally turned down Halifax's alternative plan and insisted on the original full tripartite alliance. It was at this point that the ways of the Prime Minister and Foreign Secretary once again diverged. Cadogan noted on 20 May that, 'PM says he will resign rather than sign alliances with Soviet. So we have to go warily. I am, on balance, in favour of it. So, I think, is H.' The Cabinet decided to postpone a decision until after Halifax had visited Geneva to speak to the Russian and various other delegations at the League of Nations.

On the way to Geneva, Halifax told Harvey that despite Chamberlain's reluctance, 'many in the Cabinet favoured it. He himself took the view that we had gone so far that the little more would not make that much difference.'[27] On 21 May, Chamberlain bitterly informed his sisters how 'some of the members of the Cabinet who were most unwilling to agree to the alliance now appear to have swung round to the opposite view'.[28] Writing from Geneva, Halifax reported that he had been unable to move the Russians off the tripartite position and, moreover, the French were insisting on it as well. More dubiously he told the Prime Minister: 'Poland had raised no objection, the Dominions were divided.'[29] With everyone but Butler ranged against him Chamberlain retreated.

Returning from Switzerland on 24 May, Halifax received a letter at Le Bourget which said that the Prime Minister had relented. He would swallow the Russian desiderata so long as they could be covered with the fig leaf of League respectability. At a meeting later that morning the grounds on which Halifax declared his support for a Russian deal proved almost entirely negative. He was concerned at the embarrassment should talks break down, felt it vital to head off the possibility of Russo-German rapprochement and welcomed the domestic political advantages such a pact would bring the Government. He had no objection to linking the agreement to some spurious League verbiage so long as it did not water down the final outcome. Chamberlain's fear that a pact would 'provoke' Hitler was answered by Halifax with the assertion that, in fact, the absence of a solid bloc was far more likely to achieve that.

The most enthusiasm Chamberlain was able to raise was a reluctant admission that he 'thought it impossible to stand out against' the new mood.[30] The League of Nations dressing was a ploy to offset the attacks from assorted Roman Catholics, foreign governments and right-wingers, who were expected to be outraged by this dalliance with Bolshevism. What made Halifax change his mind so decisively between 19 May – when he told the Foreign Policy Committee that he had the strongest possible distaste in acquiescing to Soviet 'blackmail and bluff' – and 24 May, when he commended the Pact to the Cabinet? As so often with him part of the answer lay in the domestic political scene: a Russian alliance would play well in Parliament and the press. He could also see the propaganda advantages of a bold and imaginative step that would radically alter German perceptions. But it was the spectre of a Russo-German entente which provided the ultimate spur. The draft Anglo-French treaty of 27 May was Halifax's brainchild in all but the references to Article XVI of the League Covenant, which came from No. 10.

The negotiations themselves ran through June and July and on into August. They were detailed, hard-fought and complex. Complete lack of trust on both sides meant that every ambiguous interpretation had to be clarified and every eventuality discussed. The talks got badly bogged down over the question of 'indirect aggression' in the Baltic. This presupposed a scenario in which a pro-Nazi coup in one of the three republics established a government which then 'invited' in German troops. This thrust would side-step Poland and would not therefore trigger the British guarantee. In an ominous move on 3 May, Stalin replaced the Jewish and cosmopolitan Foreign Minister Litvinov with Molotov, whom Halifax thought like 'a rather buttoned-up secondary school master'[31] and Cadogan described rather more forthrightly as 'an ignorant and suspicious peasant'.[32] After the failure of the negotiations Halifax wrote to the Viceroy, Lord Linlithgow, explaining the breakdown as being 'partly, I think, because they were double crossing us all the time, but also, I am prepared to admit . . . because they were genuine in their fear of indirect aggression through the Baltic countries on which we, suspecting motives, were sticky'.[33]

The assertion, so often made, that had Halifax gone to Moscow in person the outcome would somehow have been any different is little short of fatuous. He was correct in thinking that the Russians would have failed to be impressed but would instead have interpreted any high-level visit as a sign of weakness. Early June saw the relatively junior Foreign Office official, William Strang, sent out to Moscow to negotiate as the Ambassador, Sir William Seeds, was suffering from 'flu. The talks dragged on slowly and became particularly intractable both over definitions of 'indirect aggression' and the problem of what Russia would do in the event of a German attack in the West. Halifax's patience ebbed as the Russians produced endless objections, which served only to reveal the depths of

Stalin's paranoia and duplicity. Understandably terrified, in Moscow's murderous political atmosphere, of committing himself too far on any point of substance, Molotov slowed proceedings by continually referring all substantial matters back to his chief.

The twin facts of Poland's geographical position and Britain's guarantee put Molotov in a strong position. Britain would have to fight, whereas the Soviet leadership had little inclination to be dragged into a war for Belgium or Switzerland. On 26 June, Stanley told the Foreign Policy Committee that the latest idea of a pact which did not include the direct promise of Russian support for Poland 'would serve no useful purpose, it was, in fact, no pact at all and would deceive nobody'.[34] Halifax replied that the only consideration was to conclude any pact, however unsatisfactory, in order to forestall Russia and Germany partitioning Poland between them yet again. At the end of the meeting he approved a draft to Molotov naming those states whose independence the tripartite pact ought to guarantee. The sheer extent of it shows how far Halifax was willing to go to deter Germany. The prospective candidates for the role of *casus belli* numbered no fewer than nine: Estonia, Finland, Latvia, Poland, Romania, Turkey, Greece, Belgium and the Netherlands.

Despite Halifax's repeated and sincere attempts to find agreement with the Russians, the talks stuck on the issues of 'indirect aggression', Polish and Romanian recalcitrance, and Russian reciprocity of guarantees in the West. Halifax was not willing to countenance allowing the Red Army to stay in barracks in the event of a German attack on Holland if London got bombed as a result of some Nazi-engineered coup in Latvia. When it became clear that agreement was unlikely, he encouraged Staff talks, but only in the expectation that they 'would drag on and ultimately each side would expect a general undertaking from the other. In this way we should have gained time and made the best of a situation from which we could not escape.'[35] Morality alone prevented the Chamberlain Government from taking the other available course: allowing Russia to annex the nascent Baltic republics.

Throughout these negotiations the outmanoeuvred Chamberlain had been a carping critic, pleased when Halifax was at last getting 'fed up' with Molotov. 'I would like to have taken a much stronger line with them all through,' he told his sisters on 15 June, 'but I could not have carried my colleagues with me.' By 23 June, he was lamenting that he was being forced to carry Halifax's can: 'it is rather hard that I should have to bear the blame for dilatory action when if I wasn't hampered by others I would have closed the discussions one way or another long ago'.[36]

Throughout the summer and early autumn of 1939, Halifax continued to press for economic aid to Britain's friends in the Balkans. He supported the Turkish request for £15 million in credits, believing it fatal that his Anglo-Turkish agreement should break down for mere financial reasons.

He went so far as to propose to the Foreign Policy Committee that every cigarette sold in Britain should be required to contain a small amount of Balkan-grown tobacco as, 'in present circumstances, it was not right to assume that we could continue indefinitely with the minimum of interference with existing habits'.[37]

January 1990 saw the release of documents from 1939 which were hitherto embargoed under the Fifty-Year Rule. These provide yet more evidence that Chamberlain contrived to encourage further 'private' contacts with Germans during the summer of 1939, still with the ultimate object of securing a 'general understanding'. The historian Arthur Bryant, who is best known for his middle-brow but patriotic histories of England, wrote to Chamberlain, a collection of whose speeches he had recently edited, on 11 June 1939, asking him to meet Dr Kurt Blohm, a desk officer in the British section of the foreign affairs department of Nazi headquarters, whose direct superior was Walter Hewel, Hitler's Staff officer. This was refused, but Chamberlain allowed Bryant to be informed 'entirely unofficially' that 'he should certainly go to Germany'. This was to be 'on his own authority and there must be no suggestion in any quarter that he was going at the request of the PM or that he had been in touch with the PM. For that reason it would be undesirable for the PM to see him.' Others, such as a Mr Tennant of the Anglo-German Friendship Society, were also in semi-official contact with various prominent Germans at the time and Sir Horace Wilson was even moved to comment that 'it won't do to have too many people at the job, even if they begin by going to different quarters there'.

In the memorandum of a secret meeting which took place when Blohm flew over to England, Bryant described himself as 'one of the few Englishmen who may still be thought ... sympathetic to the German point of view'. Just how sympathetic is apparent from a letter from Bryant to Blohm dated 3 July 1939, which insisted that, 'except for a few intellectuals who have no power ... there is no inherent enmity to Germany'. Indeed, Bryant believed that should Hitler show 'some patience and magnanimity' over Poland, 'he would be regarded at last in England for the great man he is'. The historian then went on to describe to the former Hitler Youth leader how 'it is surprising how often one hears common folk over here ... speaking ... of what the Führer has done for his own people and what he might do for the world' should he embrace peace. Bryant went on to describe Hitler, and this in July 1939, as 'the great German whom fate raised up to rescue his people from the miseries and humiliations' of Versailles and 'the man who, alone among the leaders of mankind, has endured all the sufferings and trials of a common soldier – and who to my eyes seemed almost like the German unknown warrior risen from the grave'. Whatever else Mr Bryant may have been, it is quite clear he was precisely the wrong sort of person to send to Germany to warn Nazi officials that Britain meant to stand by Poland, surely the one message which it was imperative to drum into the German mind. Bryant told Chamberlain how, in conducting such a meeting with the high-level Nazi official, he was 'conscious that it will mean risking my professional career'. He need not have worried; he had forgotten the protection the Fifty-Year Rule would afford his reputation for the rest of his lifetime.

Bryant took Chamberlain's hint and went to Salzburg to meet Hewel. He told No. 10 that he would do this 'at my own expense ... [and] appear as an ex-serviceman without even the smallest official connection ... ostensibly to collect additional material for my book'. In two meetings on 11 and 12 July, Bryant discussed the world situation in detail with Hewel, who reported back to Hitler after both meetings. At the first meeting Bryant heard how Hitler 'had never promised to respect the integrity of Czechoslovakia under all circumstances'. To this novel interpretation of Germany's guarantee to Czechoslovakia at Munich, Bryant, the author of *Our Island Story*, was reluctant 'to lose the purport of my talk in argument' and so he 'did not pursue this'. If Bryant really thought Hewel – who knew of his Chamberlain connections and who picked up his hotel bill – did not know he was in contact with Downing Street, he was being naïve. Certainly Chamberlain minuted to Wilson that Bryant's account had 'an air of frankness and even naïveté'. Hewel told Bryant that the Germans had found documents in the Foreign Ministry when they marched into Prague dating from early summer 1938, which had led Hitler to believe that the British had been bluffing all along during the Czech crisis.

Chamberlain's underlinings and marginalia in this hitherto secret document are instructive and show how far the scales had fallen from his eyes since Prague. When Hewel said Germany desired only 'her rightful place in partnership with [Britain] as a world power', the Prime Minister annotated: 'This only means free hand in E and S.E. Europe.' To Hewel's comment that 'only the previous night, Hitler had been speculating in conversation about what would have happened if Britain had accepted his earlier offers of collaboration on a basis of equality,' Chamberlain commented briskly, 'He never made any.' To Hewel's report that Hitler had been 'obsessed' with Polish press attacks, Chamberlain repeatedly underlined the word with his blue pencil and noted in the margin 'characteristic'. He had to face the fact that, as he put it in a memorandum to Wilson, Hewel's comments 'obviously can't, and aren't, intended to form the basis of a general understanding'. Only at that stage did he order Wilson to show the file to Halifax.[38]

Halifax had, meanwhile, been taking precisely the opposite tack and discouraging people from visiting Germany. When in July 1939 General Sir Hubert Gough received an invitation to attend the Nazi Party Day rally in Nuremberg, he asked the Foreign Office whether or not he ought to attend. Halifax had Harold Caccia telephone Lady Gough to say that the question was far too sensitive for any official steer to be given, but, as an internal memorandum put it, 'whether the General ought to go or not would no doubt greatly depend on what he thought the effect of his presence at Nuremberg would be – that in turn would depend on who were the other English guests'. It was a form of words such as this which were used to convey Halifax's true feelings on the matter, and the Goughs duly turned the invitation down.[39]

Seeing the difficulties she faced in Europe, the Japanese lost little time in capitalizing on Britain's discomfort in the East. The murder on 9 April of a Japanese agent by two Chinese terrorists in the British concession of Tientsin, eighty-five miles south-east of Peking, provided them with the perfect opportunity to promote discord. Two other Chinese were implicated in the plot, but the British refused to hand over the four men to Japanese 'justice', despite knowing them to be guilty and having previously promised to do so. The Japanese press and Government began sabre-rattling. The British Consul at Tientsin and Sir Robert Craigie, the British Ambassador in Tokyo, cabled Halifax for instructions, but had to watch the situation deteriorate as they waited for his answer. Halifax knew that to return the men meant their certain deaths, but Tientsin, with its large British community and interests, was well behind Japanese lines and out of the range of any conceivable protection.

Halifax dithered for two whole months before reaching his decision. Although he had always discounted the chances of a clash with Japan, he knew the seven capital ships the Admiralty estimated would be the minimum required to fight Japan could be stripped from neither the Mediterranean fleet nor home waters without presenting Hitler with a tempting opportunity for a surprise attack. The length of time Halifax took in making up his mind allowed an ugly situation to develop in Tientsin. Britons of both sexes were publicly strip-searched and humiliated at bayonet point whenever they entered or left the Concession.

By the time Halifax came up with a policy, the Japanese had decided both to blockade the city and to raise their demands from the handing over of the men to the effective ending of British sovereignty over Tientsin. The Japanese press hit ever more strident notes, which prompted retaliation by the British press. Meanwhile, the Concession slowly ran out of food and other vital provisions. Halifax's complaints to the Japanese Ambassador went unheeded and he found himself having to steer between the Scylla of a war Britain could not fight and the Charybdis of the international humiliation of a climb-down. It was a godsend both for German propaganda and domestic opponents of the Government. Sir Oswald Mosley told a crowd of 20,000 at a rally at Earl's Court that Halifax's 'particular genius' over Tientsin was that 'when you are walking down the street and someone comes up and gives you a hard kick up the backside you can pretend not to notice it'.[40]

The situation continued to be acute until August and was only saved when Halifax gave Craigie total discretion to reach whatever accommodation he could with Tokyo. In a brilliant display of diplomatic initiatives and media manipulation, Craigie eventually worked out a formula which, albeit at the cost of the terrorists' lives, protected the Concession and steered Britain clear of war. The crisis had highlighted the reluctance of America to help Britain out of her difficulties in the Far East, and Halifax was starkly reminded of Britain's debilitating weakness in the region. Although Halifax came out badly from the incident, he did at least show the acumen, first developed in India, to allow the man on the spot as much leeway as possible, in this case with successful results.

For his stance towards Germany, however, Halifax was beginning to win plaudits from unexpected quarters. Churchill used the speech to propose Halifax's health at a dinner of the 1900 Club on 21 June to show his appreciation of the way Halifax had steered the Government away from appeasement:

> Let me tell you that when we have drunk your health tonight it will be a sign that in principle there are no differences between us. We have all, from various standpoints, accepted the policy which you and the Prime Minister have now proclaimed. If differences remain, they will only be upon emphasis and method, upon timing and degree.[41]

When in late June the owner of the *Observer*, Lord Astor, confided to Halifax plans for a press campaign on Chamberlain to include Churchill in the Cabinet, Halifax was 'for having Winston in'. The news led Lord Camrose, the owner of the *Daily Telegraph*, to support the scheme and within a week the call had also been taken up by the *Manchester Guardian*, *Yorkshire Post*, *Daily Mirror*, *Evening News*, *Star* and *News Chronicle*.[42]

On 29 June, Halifax delivered a speech at Chatham House which amounted to the clearest warning yet to Germany that Britain was neither bluffing nor willing to put up with further blackmail. He told his audience that

> the threat of military force is holding the world to ransom, and our immediate task is to resist aggression. I would emphasize that tonight with all the strength at my command, so that nobody may misunderstand it. . . . Hitler has said that deeds, not words, are necessary. That is also our view.

As he said to Henderson, the speech was intended to 'convince the Germans once and for all that we have reached the limits of unilateral concession, that we should fight to prevent aggression'.[43] The speech was recorded and listening to it one is immediately struck by the near silence which met any hint of softness ('we are ready to co-operate') compared with the loud applause, table-thumping and 'Hear!, Hear!'s which greeted firmness ('we must be prepared to fight', etc.).

His voice was an authoritative bass. He pronounced the letter 'r' as 'w', which made phrases such as 'Crusade for Christianity' sound slightly comic. However, the overall effect, with the very minor speech impediment which was the last remains of a stutter he had managed to master in adolescence, was to make his voice sound interesting.[44] His long pauses, huge height, long face and old-fashioned dress made him a figure of impressive authority. The speech was enthusiastically received. Cadogan called it 'a moving paraphrase of "We don't want to fight, but by Jingo if we do,"'[45] and Harvey believed it 'created a great impression here and abroad for its firmness. All at home approve it, including Labour.'[46] One statement which received tumultuous applause was Halifax's hope for a successful conclusion of the negotiations with the Soviets (which he pronounced 'Soviettes'). But here he knew himself to be on far shakier ground.

18

'A Good Conscience'

Halifax is frequently criticized for the way in which the military mission sent to Russia on 5 August took so long to get there. This is held as evidence of his lack of commitment to the cause. For by the time the leader of the mission, Admiral the Honourable Sir Reginald Aylmer Ranfurly Plunkett-Ernle-Erle-Drax, got his Anglo-French team (and his name) to Moscow, a full six days had elapsed. The mission could not have flown directly without refuelling somewhere in Germany, which was felt to be impossible, and Halifax was unwilling to send a cruiser through the Baltic in case it implied to the Russians that Britain was desperate. In the end they chartered a very old thirteen-knot merchantman, but not before General 'Pug' Ismay had suggested they go by bicycle.

At his briefing with the Prime Minister and Foreign Secretary before he left, Admiral Drax was told that should he perceive the Russians not to be interested in closing the deal, he should try to drag the negotiations out, if possible, until the October snows came to Poland. It is easy to see Drax, whose published works include *A Handbook on Solar Heating* and *World War III : Some Pros and Cons*, as something of a joke figure. In fact, he turned out to be a fine negotiator who skilfully parried Marshal Klementi Voroshilov's questions about Polish defences and French attack plans, which in the end were asked for very different reasons from those envisaged.

Stalin's calculations had crystallized into a decision which Halifax's presence in Moscow, British assent to the Russian definition of 'indirect aggression' or even Puck-like fleetness of foot from Drax would have done nothing whatsoever to alter. Hitler, in choosing to outbid the democracies, seemed to offer Stalin far more than an uneasy peace and security. His scant regard for other nations' independence meant he could give Stalin half of Poland, the three Baltic republics and the even more inviting prospect of a war in the West from which Russia could stand aloof. The Chamberlain Government cannot be blamed that through a combination of Hitler's cunning and cynicism and Stalin's greed and short-sightedness a deal was struck at a higher price than Britain and France could ever have paid. Stalin, who needed time both for the five-year plan and in order to rebuild his army, could not envisage anything more inviting than a long and exhausting, preferably trench, war between his enemies. During the Battle of Britain, Maisky used to add up the numbers of the German and British aircraft shot down in the same column. Maisky's accusation, inexplicably spread by Butler, that Halifax opposed a Russian alliance out of distaste for her atheism is shown to be hollow by the reply Halifax gave to a letter from Lord Alfred Douglas, (the seventy-year-old 'Bosie'), who had complained that a Russian alliance was blasphemous. In it he stated that Russia was not so immediately menacing to Christianity and the cause of peace as was Germany.[1]

The news of the Molotov–Ribbentrop Pact came as less of a shock than has been supposed; there were a number of indications that an entente was in the offing. Dining with Halifax the night it was signed, a friend noted Halifax's extraordinarily sanguine view that, 'in our agreement with Poland both we and they have always discounted Russia, so materially the situation is not so enormously changed'.[2] Although the USSR of the 1930s was by no means the superpower it later became and was economically backward, militarily decapitated, politically isolated and notoriously untrustworthy, Halifax was either putting on a brave face or showing foolhardy bravado if he really thought Stalin's decision had not materially changed the situation for the worse. His guess for the likely outcome was either 'a quick seizure of Danzig alone or Danzig and the Corridor and the Poles not fighting, some hold they will be bellicose for the last minute only'.[3] The Germans, who had for years waxed highly indignant about being 'encircled', had themselves at one stroke pulled off the encirclement of their next item of prey.

When Halifax signed the Anglo-Polish Agreement at 5 p.m. on 25 August, he sent yet another unequivocal message to Hitler that Britain meant to stand by Poland. Considering the bleak circumstances facing the Poles, it was a brave and poignant act. Since grabbing Teschen off Czechoslovakia at Munich, Poland had been deeply unpopular in British governing circles. Halifax was among the first, at the time of the guarantees, to overcome this distaste for Polish opportunism. 'During this anxious time', wrote the Polish Ambassador of the period after 25 August 1939, 'I called almost daily on Lord Halifax whose confidentiality I had gained and who from time to time showed clearly that he shared my own view of the situation.'[4]

Halifax would take notes of Raczynski's comments to use as ammunition in Cabinet when putting the pro-Polish point of view. 'Halifax himself did not doubt for a moment', continued Raczynski, 'that any attempt to patch matters up had been out of the question since the conclusion of the

German–Soviet Pact.'[5] He ignored the plea from Göring's friend and envoy, Birger Dalherus, that he should find an opportunity to postpone the signing, telling the Cabinet the next day that to do so would make Britain's friends suspicious and her enemies 'feel that we were likely to give way to pressure'. Letters from the public poured into the Foreign Office with Heath Robinson ways of solving the dilemma, such as by the construction of bridges and tunnels across the Corridor. There was even one ingenious scheme to deflect the Vistula River via Lithuania.

Despite the enormous psychological, moral and political pressures on him, Halifax showed great resilience and strength of personality. He agreed with Cadogan that the crisis was if anything less stressful than Munich had been because the prospect of war with Germany was not so militarily catastrophic in 1939 as it would have been in 1938. The strains of the crisis did not show. Inskip's diary entry for 25 August marvelled that 'Halifax, after a long day, including a speech in the House of Lords and a broadcast at 9.30 p.m., seemed as calm as usual, with the air of a rather languid weariness which never quite deserts him, unless he has something to tickle his sense of humour, which is never far off.'[6] At dinner with Lady Alexandra Metcalfe on 22 August he was 'entrancing and charming, might have no cares', and two days later Lord Crawford was astounded 'that at the supreme moment of crisis one of the protagonists could so completely detach himself'.[7] This detachment was largely due to his ability 'always to see the other point of view, which made decision so much more difficult but when the agony was over and the mind made up, the position was much securer and more impregnable'.[8]

Accusations that Halifax was planning another Munich over Poland are completely unfounded. The Swedish businessman, Birger Dalherus, flew backwards and forwards between London and Berlin over the next fortnight in an attempt to engineer one, but was told only that the guarantee still stood. For all of his changing taxis in Piccadilly, cars in a Soho garage and using the back door into No. 10, Dalherus only discovered the British Government sticking to its position throughout the crisis. Dalherus was not the ideal shuttle-diplomatist because of his doubtful loyalties and inability to get to the point. But he was deemed a useful way of bypassing Ribbentrop and the Wilhelmstrasse diplomatic bureaucracy, encouraging Göring in his opposition to war and slowing Hitler's plans, all with no great risk to Britain. He was never the conduit for any important policy initiatives and the Foreign Office official whose job it was to ferry him around, Frank Roberts, was right to consider him 'never enormously important'.[9] Cadogan saw him as a source of information about German intentions and even then complained that he 'didn't add much to what we know'.

The entry for 25 August – the day of the Anglo-Polish Pact – in Lady Cadogan's diary reads : 'A[lec] says Edward H keeps repeating to himself

"Do you really think this means war?" Halifax found it hard to believe that Hitler could be so delinquent as to ignore a deterrent as plain as the Polish guarantee. But the subtle change in German propaganda since Prague – which tended now to concentrate on the British embarrassments in Tientsin, Moscow and Palestine – heralded a sinister change in German policy. No longer was 'encirclement' railed against in order to engender in the German people a sense of grievance; instead, the enemy's setbacks were highlighted to boost morale and convey the feeling of invincibility.

Dalherus met Halifax at Downing Street at 11 a.m. on 26 August and told him that the Anglo-Polish Agreement had been perceived in Berlin as a challenge. He proposed that Halifax write to Göring to 'calm their wrath'. An anodyne note was prepared which reiterated Britain's desire for a peaceful settlement to the Danzig question. Halifax thought it 'platitudinous'[10] and it went no way towards placating Hitler, who was woken up that night to meet the returned Dalherus. Hitler rambled on for an hour and a half, on two occasions becoming 'violent and excited'.[11] He merely repeated the totally spurious proposals he had earlier given to Henderson. He had already postponed the invasion of Poland once and did not want to be forced to do so again. The proposals were therefore nothing more than a list of impossible demands and irrelevant statements, the most ludicrous and patronizing of which was his offer to guarantee the British Empire. Raczynski recorded how the news of this last insult brought a 'contemptuous grimace' to Halifax's face.[12]

In the light of Hitler's 'proposals', the attempt by Ciano to institute a general peace conference was considered by Halifax to have only the slimmest chances of success. It was nevertheless another way to gain the time needed for world, and especially American, opinion to mobilize against Germany's aggressive aims. It might also provide Hitler with a way to climb down from the rash promises he had made his followers concerning Danzig. A conference would give Hitler pause to consider the ill effects the Russian Pact had had on his Japanese, Italian and Spanish allies. Halifax took the idea so seriously as to consider the stance Britain should take at such a conference, deciding on an exceedingly tough one. It was perhaps inevitable that enemies should portray his enthusiasm for the conference idea as a mixture of naïveté and willingness to castrate Poland with another Munich-type agreement. When Harvey told him this fear was widespread in the Foreign Office, 'he said we needn't worry – he had it all in his mind & we mustn't be suspicious of any attempt to rat on the Poles'. To which Harvey 'assured him we had no doubt of *him*'. The clear implication being that Chamberlain and others were more suspect.[13]

It is also untrue to assert, as so many have done, that the appeasers' earlier pusillanimity led Hitler to calculate that he could invade Poland without war. When they met on 28 August, Hitler told Henderson that he fully realized the West was not bluffing. The Germans had tapped the

Halifax–Henderson telephone connection and also intercepted a report from the Yugoslavian legation in Warsaw to Belgrade, which referred to a letter from Halifax to Beck assuring the Pole that Britain would stand by the guarantee. Although Hitler misinterpreted the *type* of war he was starting, he could have been under no illusions that his invasion of Poland would inevitably bring war with Britain. By Tuesday 29 August, Halifax allowed himself a little cautious optimism. Walking across the Park to Parliament he agreed with Harvey that 'Hitler was now in a fix'.[14] Halifax was keen to 'get into negotiation and then be very stiff and then Hitler would be beat'. At lunch with the Halifaxes at the Rubens Hotel, Lady Alexandra Metcalfe heard that 'there is still a possible solution such as Danzig to be a free city inside the Reich. Edward thinks if we can keep Hitler talking for 2 more days the corner will be turned.'[15] An intelligence officer named David Boyle arrived that afternoon with good news. The nature of this is not known, but as he had been sent to Berlin specifically by the head of the Secret Intelligence Service, Admiral Sir Hugh Sinclair, who had two days earlier told Cadogan of serious dissensions in the German General Staff, it is reasonable to assume the news concerned a possible revolt in the High Command.

Halifax's hopes for a favourable outcome faded when he learnt the next day of the German demand that a Polish emissary with full negotiating powers be immediately sent to Berlin. This was precisely the method Hitler had used to take the rump of Czechoslovakia. Halifax told the 11.30 a.m. Cabinet that the line was to be 'at once firm yet unprovocative'.[16] When Dalherus telephoned Göring from Cadogan's office, Halifax ordered him 'to rub into Göring that it was essential that any proposals Hitler may make should not be couched in the form of a diktat ... we were prepared to do our best in negotiation only if it really was negotiation and not dictation on the Czecho-Slovak model'.[17] Halifax had, as one of his Private Secretaries put it, 'reached the limit of what he thought could be sacrificed for peace'.[18]

Late that afternoon Halifax told Hore-Belisha he was in favour of expediting mobilization and would support him against any Prime Ministerial obstruction. The authorities were keen to get on with evacuation, as much to avoid the mass panic, looting and demoralizing expected to follow the bombing of London as for any humanitarian reasons. To the Dominions Secretary, Halifax demanded that the ever-appeasing Dominion High Commissioners must not tone down one of his draft statements. 'No!' he told Inskip, 'it is meant to be firm and even sharp ... the High Commissioners only see part of the picture.' He then used the method to justify himself that had so infuriated Birkenhead and Butler, saying that he had secret information from Düsseldorf that the crowd was pulling down Nazi posters.[19] As late as the evening before the invasion Halifax believed there was still a chance for an Italian-sponsored conference to revise Versailles. But he was not prepared to put pressure on the Poles to part with territory before such a conference took place. On 31 August, lunching with Cadogan and a couple of junior Cabinet ministers, he 'was optimistic and even used the simile of "the first view of the beaten fox" in reference to the Führer'.[20]

At dawn the next morning, Friday 1 September, 'the beaten fox' sent fifty-seven air-supported divisions deep into western Poland, using a new method of warfare called *Blitzkrieg* to sweep aside the ill-equipped and badly positioned Polish army. He did this in the full knowledge that Britain and France would declare war but having calculated that with Russia on his side, Czechoslovakia in bondage and America on the sidelines, Polish resistance would be extinguished before a war on two fronts had time to develop. As master of Central Europe there would then be plenty of time to negotiate peace with the Western Powers.

Halifax first heard of the invasion when Cadogan called on him at 9 a.m. He summoned the (ironically enough anti-Nazi) German Chargé d'Affaires, Theodor Kordt, to No. 10 to ask whether the reports were accurate, adding that if true it was 'a most serious situation'.[21] Immediately afterwards he saw Count Raczynski in the Private Secretary's office and assured him that, given verification of the reports, 'we should have no difficulty in deciding that our guarantee must at once come into force'. The German disinformation machine insisted that Poland had invaded Germany, that it was only a border incident and that only military targets were being attacked. At the first Cabinet at 11.30 a.m. nothing in the nature of the immediate aid stipulated by the Anglo-Polish Agreement was so much as discussed. Instead of a ringing clarion call for succour to Poland, Halifax told the meeting that as there was no very definite information as to what hostile action had taken place in Poland, it was desirable not to take any irrevocable action until they had a better idea of what was going on. Some weeks later, he was savagely brought up to the realities of the situation when the Great War hero, General Carton de Wiart VC, who had been stationed in Warsaw at the time, met the Halifaxes by chance at Le Normandie restaurant. Invited over by their mutual friend, Sir Arthur Penn, the Halifaxes were sickened to hear 'the horrible account of the German invasion, the bombing and machine-gunning and the murdering of the poor Poles'.[22]

The decision not to go to war either that day or the next shows an aspect of Halifax's psychological make-up that was to re-emerge with even worse consequences for his reputation eight months later. His ever-rational mind told him that the Chiefs of Staff had no plans to render Poland effective assistance anyhow; hence it made little difference whether Britain failed to help Poland on 1 September or on the 3rd. If those extra hours could give Mussolini time to pressurize Hitler to halt and hold a conference, while at the same time British evacuation and other war measures were expedited before Hitler had an excuse to bomb London, it seemed to Halifax folly to throw them away.

He failed to take sufficient cognizance of the ill-effects such a delay would have on public and Conservative Party morale. Being seen to be dragged reluctantly into war a full fifty-five hours after the German invasion was inevitably deleterious to the Government's standing. The logistics of putting the nation on a war footing did require some delay. The Minister for Co-ordination of Defence requested time before any ultimatum was sent. During the meeting, Dalherus called from Berlin with yet another proposal. Although he was probably himself sincere, the Swede was being used by Hitler to confuse and disorientate the British Government. Halifax obtained Cabinet approval to a reply that was 'stiff' and stressed the fact that 'the only way in which a world war could be stopped would be if the German troops left Polish territory'.[23]

The next problem was synchronization of the ultimata with Paris. The French wished to avoid giving the impression of being dragged into war by Britain and said they wanted to declare war before London. Halifax preferred simultaneous announcements. France's evacuation programme took longer than Britain's and Bonnet had more faith in Ciano's ability to pull off a coup, so the French were a definite brake on the declaration of war. Once the Advanced Striking Air Force had been sent to France, the conscripts called up, seventeen Emergency Bills passed through all their stages in Parliament on 1 September and evacuation begun, all the declaration of war really amounted to was a green light for the Germans to start bombing London. The tardy response to Hitler's crime, though not as honourable as an immediate declaration, was eminently practical. The demand for all German troops to vacate Poland, which Halifax stuck to in his many conversations with Bonnet, Ciano and Dalherus, seems to betray a startling ignorance of the nature of modern warfare. Friday 1 September ended with the Cabinet content merely to send Berlin a warning rather than an ultimatum.

The next morning, Saturday the 2nd, Cadogan walked with the Halifaxes through the gardens of Buckingham Palace (to which the King had, as a special favour, given Halifax a key) and noticed that the purple autumn crocuses were out. On arriving at the Foreign Office they learnt that no answer had been received to the warning. This may have been partly due to Henderson's equivocal presentation of it. The French did not want any ultimatum delivered until noon the following day; moreover, they wanted a forty-eight-hour time limit attached, with no declaration of war until Thursday the 5th. At 2.35 p.m. Halifax received a call from Ciano proposing a five-power conference between Britain, Germany, France, Italy and Russia. He said that Ribbentrop had indicated to the Italian Ambassador in Berlin that Hitler had not turned the idea down but wanted until noon the next day to consider it. Halifax adhered strictly to the original demand for a German withdrawal. Knowing that Simon was about to make a statement in the Commons, Halifax and Harvey rushed over to Parliament and caught him just before he rose. With the statement safely postponed, Halifax returned to speak to Bonnet, who had committed himself more deeply to Ciano's proposal than he admitted. Halifax promised to convey Bonnet's feelings to the Cabinet. All the time the German war machine churned through western Poland.

'I never remember spending such a miserable afternoon and evening,' wrote Halifax later.[24] The Cabinet met at 4.15 p.m. in 'an extremely difficult mood'. While he had been phoning the European capitals, the Government had been brought up against the enormous weight of public and parliamentary opinion, which was moving heavily in favour of giving Hitler no more time or chances. When Halifax argued in Cabinet for Bonnet's proposal for a further delay 'if this would facilitate discussion of a conference',[25] he found himself in a minority of one. Instead, the Cabinet resolved on a midnight ultimatum and authorized Chamberlain and Halifax to settle the terms of this communication and of the statements to be made in Parliament that afternoon. The next few hours were spent in a hectic series of telephone calls. To Phipps in Paris Halifax said that naval dispositions rendered French hopes for a long expiry time unrealizable. At 6.38 p.m. Halifax rang Ciano urging him to put pressure on Berlin to withdraw from Poland and attend a conference, adding however that such a withdrawal was an essential precondition.

When the House of Commons reconvened at 7.30 p.m., the declaration details and timings had still not been agreed with Bonnet. The lack of hard news fed rumour and the House exploded with resentment after Chamberlain failed to announce the declaration of war. When the deputy Leader of the Labour Party, Arthur Greenwood, rose to speak, Leo Amery cried out, 'Speak for England!' Greenwood told the House that 'Every minute's delay now means . . . imperilling our national honour.' The whole performance disgusted Halifax, who thought it 'showed democratic assemblies at their worst' and never fully forgave those Cabinet ministers who believed he and Chamberlain were scheming for another Munich. He told Chamberlain that he 'found their behaviour intolerable' and said the Prime Minister 'had the temper of an archangel' to put up with it.[26]

Having heard their decision for war at midnight flouted by Chamberlain, the Cabinet resolved to impose their will on him and Halifax. Led by Simon they indignantly went on what one of their number later called a 'strike', refusing to leave one of the rooms in the House of Commons until another Cabinet meeting was called. It is a sign of his unflappability that even at that moment of crisis Halifax went home to change into black tie to go to a dinner he still believed he could have at the Savoy with his wife and Geoffrey Dawson. Cadogan was actually halfway through dinner with his wife when he was called to No. 10 to finish it there with Mr and Mrs Chamberlain, Wilson and Halifax.

Immediately after Chamberlain sat down in the Commons, Halifax had his speech telegraphed to Henderson to pass on to 'certain quarters', meaning Göring via Dalherus. There was no response. Half an hour later the Cabinet deputed Simon to go to No. 10 to demand another Cabinet meeting. Any slim hopes Halifax might have entertained at 4.15 p.m. for a conference were utterly doomed by the time of the 11.30 p.m. Cabinet. It was quite clear that the Cabinet wanted war, even without any declaration from France. Seeing their mood Halifax did not attempt to champion the Italian option any further; probably by then he had himself completely lost faith in Ciano's ability to deliver. Ribbentrop blamed Halifax for rejecting the Ciano proposal, writing from his condemned cell six years later that it looked for some time on 2 September that peace might be saved.

Chamberlain was badly shaken by his reception in the Commons and after being advised by the Chief Whip, David Margesson, that the Government could not survive another such meeting of Parliament, the decision for war was forced upon him. With a violent thunderstorm outside, the Cabinet debated the timing and length of the ultimatum, finally agreeing on Simon's suggestion of 9 a.m. the next morning with a two-hour expiry. Returning to the Foreign Office with Ivone Kirkpatrick at 1.30 a.m., Halifax ill-temperedly told Dalton that war would be declared the next day, but once all the relevant telegrams had been sent Kirkpatrick remembered he

> seemed relieved that we had taken our decision.... He called for beer, which was brought down by a sleepy Resident Clerk in pyjamas. We laughed and joked, and when I told Lord Halifax that news had just come in that Goebbels had prohibited listening to foreign broadcasts he retorted: 'He ought to pay me to listen to his.'[27]

The next morning Halifax got into the Foreign Office at 10 a.m., but found, as he put it in his diary, 'There was nothing to do.' This is an astounding remark for the British Foreign Secretary to make exactly one hour before the outbreak of the Second World War. Dalherus called Frank Roberts twice between Halifax's arriving at the Foreign Office and the expiry of the ultimatum, the second time to suggest that Göring wished to fly to England. Pausing only to turn this offer down flat, Halifax walked through the crowds to No. 10. When by 11.12 a.m. it was clear that no official answer had been received from Berlin, Chamberlain went on the air. He and Halifax then drafted the statement to Parliament that was to be made at noon, finishing just as an accidental air-raid warning went off at 11.50 a.m. While Halifax announced the declaration of war in the Lords, Churchill told the Commons that 'our hands may be active, but our consciences are at rest'.

Britain's clear conscience was a vital war asset, won partly through her Foreign Secretary's endless efforts to secure peace, even after his own personal hopes had dwindled to nothing. Total war guilt once again smeared Germany's name and the credit for making this so plain to the world must go primarily to Halifax. As Simon wrote to him as war broke out, 'you have struggled for peace *devotedly* to the last minute and the last ounce, and it is largely due to you that we all go into this horrible business with a good conscience. The country, and history, will give you thanks.'[28] Simon was wrong; because of their misunderstanding of his motives, neither has yet done anything of the kind.

19

'Atmosphere of Frustration'

No great outburst of joy met the declaration of war, as it had in 1914. The Prime Minister's announcement was distinctly downbeat and regretful, referring more to his own disappointment than to the necessity of defeating Germany. In his post-Munich letter to Lord Francis Scott, Halifax had written of trying to crush Germany that, 'after the experience of the last twenty years, I confess that it is not an end that has ever seemed to me to be practical politics'.[1] When in February 1940 the Halifaxes heard a preacher in Grosvenor Chapel say they were fortunate to be living at that hour and privileged to be called upon to fight for such great issues, they 'felt that this was putting it a bit higher than we could easily make our own'.[2]

With Russia, Italy and Spain neutral, and Chamberlain actively hostile to American involvement for fear of the influence it would have at the peace conference, the war began as a distinctly parochial affair. Japan, still reeling from the implications of the Molotov–Ribbentrop Pact, had so cooled her anti-British stance that at the 4 September Cabinet Halifax could talk about the possibility of attempting to revive the 1902 alliance. Halifax deserves credit for the way in which the inherently hostile Governments of Italy, Spain and Japan perceived it in their best interests to stay on the sidelines in September 1939. This was not a world war. It was, moreover, hard to see how it could be a winnable war. The invasion and subjugation of Germany was a total impossibility in 1939. That was only finally achieved by the combined British, Russian and American armies after six years of war. What then was the alternative?

Poland withstood twenty-five days of torment before the Germans entered Warsaw. On the fourteenth day of her agony the Russians moved in from the east to occupy the third of Poland secretly awarded her by the Molotov–Ribbentrop Pact. Halifax, anxious not to clash with Russia, refused to register anything more than a mild protest. The British guarantee only covered attacks on Poland from the Germans. In the west Belgium declared her neutrality, the French arrayed themselves behind the Maginot Line and the British Expeditionary Force only arrived on the continent on 30 September.

With a numerically far inferior air force, Halifax thought it inadvisable to start trying to bomb Germany into submission. He knew that every day which passed before the Germans bombed Britain meant more uninterrupted work in the aircraft production factories. He was concerned that Britain should therefore not be the first 'to take the gloves off'. Often mistakenly believed to have been motivated by naïveté, or even cowardice, this actually made sound strategic sense. Basil Liddell Hart's diary for 27 August mentions Dawson's information that 'Halifax was determined to put a check on the bombing campaign, which could lead to no real issue except useless mutual damage'.[3]

He also knew that the peace offer Hitler might have had in mind could hardly be proffered after London had been bombed. So long as the Allies did nothing to discourage the Germans to dream of a Western peace, British aircraft production could continue apace. To that end Halifax at least seemed seriously to entertain all the peace feelers that came out of Germany, whilst sternly opposing any moves to initiate the bombing of Germany. The reason this stance is treated with such ridicule today can largely be put down to Sir Kingsley Wood's asinine remark that the RAF could not bomb the Black Forest because so much of it was private property.

The night Hitler's expected peace offer came through, on 6 October, a friend who had been dining with Halifax heard how,

Hitler's speech today makes negotiation not impossible, but the way to do so without causing a cry of 'appeasement again' is definitely difficult. He must be proved wrong and not the victor, he would have to give up a lot, thereby humiliating himself, retire partially from Poland, create an independent Czech State, give up half his air force ... and lots more.[4]

These were far from Hitler's expectations of being allotted the overlordship of Central Europe in return for Britain's securing her massive maritime empire.

Hitler's hopes of extorting a profitable peace were dashed when Chamberlain broadcast his rejection of the offer on 12 October. He explained that experience had shown that Hitler's word could not be trusted. In the Cabinet debates at the time, Halifax thought that anti-Göring propaganda ought to be damped down since 'our real object was to destroy Hitler'. Churchill half agreed with the objective of setting Göring against Hitler and used the analogy of Göring possibly playing the role of General Monck. A friend noted Halifax's reasons for confidence:

Turkey is okay, Italy is swinging our way, Japan looks better and Russia is keen to trade with us. Edward does not think that Hitler intends at present to violate Holland or Belgium, nor does he want to hurl himself against the Maginot Line as he is hoping always to drive a wedge between us and the French.[5]

A young Tory MP called Somerset de Chair took notes at the 1922 Committee meeting on foreign affairs which Halifax addressed on 25 October. He records Halifax's 'eyes somewhat bloodshot from overwork, his black coat hanging very square, his left sleeve very thin. He smiled occasionally with a slow, charming smile when he made a joke'.[6] Halifax began modestly by admitting how the very fact of war could be counted as the failure of any Foreign Secretary. He was nevertheless relieved that Hitler had not tried to negotiate with Poland, as it would only have led to accusations of 'a second Munich'. He was greeted with loud 'Hear!, Hear!'s when he averred that Britain had been right not to have bought a Russian agreement with the freedom of the Baltic republics.

The avoidance of war with Russia was a cardinal point in Halifax's Phoney War diplomacy. He was not about to have the achievement of whittling Britain's opponents down to Germany alone wrecked by having also to oppose the Soviet Union. He answered de Chair's question as to whether a Russian attack on Bessarabia would trigger the British guarantee to Romania by admitting that 'we should be very reluctant to have to implement our guarantee in that direction'. There were around 250 backbenchers packed into the committee room and de Chair felt Halifax acquitted himself extremely well.

Although ministers found ludicrous reasons for optimism – Halifax told Inskip on 8 September that Mussolini was dying of syphilis and needed five daily injections in the heart – there were also plenty of genuinely encouraging signs.[7] Halifax believed, in common with most other ministers and the Chiefs of Staff, that the German economy and morale were intrinsically weak and that the navy's blockade would take a relatively short time to tell. If Munich, in the common cliché, 'bought' a year for rearmament, the Phoney War also bought an extra eight months. Time, as Halifax told his friend the Ambassador to Washington, Lord Lothian, was as much on the Allies' side after the war had started as it had been before it. This would be thrown away were Britain to resort to what he called 'beastly' or 'frightful' warfare such as aerial bombing. So when the RAF flew over German territory on 19 September, all they dropped were propaganda leaflets. Halifax was sceptical about the efficacy of these and tended to agree with Noël Coward's view that they were presumably an attempt to bore the Germans to death.

Once Poland fell it was not easy to see how the war would develop. Asked on 23 September about war aims, Cadogan found some difficulty in formulating any. 'We could no longer say "evacuate Poland" without going to war with Russia, which we don't want to do! I suppose the cry is "Abolish Hitlerism". What if Hitler hands over to Göring?! ... What if Germany now sits tight?'[8] After he confided these doubts to his wife, she wrote in her diary, 'Rather difficult to ask the British Empire to wage war if we don't know what we are fighting for.' Cadogan, a decent, harassed man, finally decided on 7 October that the removal of Hitler was the major, if not the only, war aim. Scepticism was rife and a week after war broke out Chamberlain admitted, 'what I hope for is not a military victory – I very much doubt the possibility of that – but a collapse of the German home front'.[9] The day before Cadogan had found the King 'rather depressed and a little défaitiste'.[10] A limerick which did the rounds in the Foreign Office during the Phoney War went, with reference to Chamberlain:

> An elderly statesman with gout,
> When asked what the war was about,
> In a Written Reply,
> Said 'My colleagues and I
> Are doing out best to find out.'[11]

With so little enthusiasm or direction from the highest echelons of Government and society, it was not surprising that some influential voices were raised against continuing the war at all. Halifax, keeping his personal views strictly for his family, close friends and later his diary, took a leading role in outmanoeuvring the quite formidable domestic opposition to the war. On 12 September, Lord Hankey, the former Cabinet Secretary, wrote to him warning of a 'somewhat defeatist and pacifist' meeting that had been held the night before at the Duke of Westminster's home, Bourdon House, in Davies Street. The Duke of Buccleuch had attended, as well as Lords Rushcliffe, Arnold and Mottistone.[12]

A second meeting there a fortnight later was better attended: a number of MPs turned up, as well as Lords Noel-Buxton and Harmsworth plus a few clerics. The anti-war memorandum discussed and approved there ended by asserting that 'London is, terribly, the best aerial target on the face of the earth.' The thought must have been particularly terrible for 'Bendor' Westminster who owned so much of it. Once other pro-peace patricians such as the Marquesses of Tavistock and Londonderry and Lords Brocket, Darnley, Ponsonby and others are taken into account, it is hard to escape the conclusion that a pro-peace Cabinet might have been the most aristocratic in composition since that of the Duke of Grafton.

The presence of so many peace-mongers in the House of Lords took all Halifax's political wiles and powers of diplomacy to keep them in check during the Phoney War. After one debate in December 1939, the Earl of Crawford remarked in his diary, 'For some time past we have had regular debates in which the defeatists have been most prominent ... the mugwumps ... have had everything their own way ... Halifax ... made the most decisive pronouncement since the war began. His voice was firm and non-apologetic.'[13] In February 1940, Halifax successfully refused Lord Ponsonby's call for a secret session of the Lords to discuss peace by daring him to make public his reason for demanding it.

It was by no means principally among the upper classes that there was such opposition to war. In the three days after Hitler's 6 October peace offer, more than three-quarters of the 2,450 letters received on the subject at No. 10 were in favour of stopping the war. After a peace initiative by the monarchs of Belgium and Holland in November 1939, some 14,000 letters of support were received by the former Labour Party Leader and pacifist, George Lansbury. Lloyd George, George Bernard Shaw, the Independent Labour Party, some senior Church figures, Captain Basil Liddell Hart, the still substantial pacifist movement and a number of prominent people in the City and the business world manifested their desire for an early negotiated peace.

There has long been a tradition of domestic opposition to wars, indulged in some cases to almost ridiculous lengths of tolerance. Burke supported the American colonists in 1776, Gladstonian liberals criticized many of the colonial wars of the nineteenth century, Lloyd George opposed the Boer War and Ramsay MacDonald conscientiously objected to the Great War. The powerful 'Stop the War' movement represented a serious problem for Chamberlain, who said that he had 'always been more afraid of a peace offer than of an air raid', and who 'did not want an offer which would be sufficiently specious to encourage the peace-at-any-price people'.[14]

The peace feelers, even after Chamberlain's categoric rejection of 12 October, continued to arrive on Halifax's desk at regular intervals. Halifax wrote to Lothian on 21 November: 'We are almost daily recipients of peace feelers from various quarters in Germany.'[15] These 'various quarters' were believed to be comprised of official Nazi sources, an increasingly independent Göring and groups of anti-Nazi conspirators. Halifax went on: 'None of these produce any very positive proposals and, indeed, as things stand at present, I think it would be impossible either for us or the French to enter into discussions of any proposals with the present Govt of Germany ... all our present information goes to show that if Hitler decides to overrule contrary advice, the country as a whole would no doubt follow him.'[16] The murky area of possible peace negotiations has spawned an entire cottage industry for academics. It has also proved an irresistible attraction for cranks, frauds, fantasists and political extremists. Situated in the twilight world between intelligence-gathering, disinformation and diplomacy, it is hard to distinguish truth from falsehood and even the most bona-fide information seems open to differing interpretations.

The matter is made more complex by the long time-limits imposed on some of the Foreign Office files – no less than seventy-five years in some cases. Although it is possible from a number of other sources to ascertain how far Britain and Germany were from making peace in 1939–40, the complete story will not be told until the files are declassified in January 2016. This secrecy has fuelled a level of speculation which, ironically enough, the documents themselves probably do not warrant. In 1946 the story of Britain's lone stand in 1940, without thought of parley, was considered by the authorities to be so much of a national asset that official papers which tended to question it were closed.

The perennial accusation is that Halifax wished to surrender to Hitler in 1940. In 1989 alone there were two separate spates of correspondence in the *Sunday Telegraph* on the subject. The truth was that although during the Phoney War Halifax felt no objection to hearing what proposals Hitler had to offer, he was resolute in refusing them, believing that Britain could win the war without apocalyptic expense of blood and treasure. After the defeat of Britain's European allies in May 1940, however, his stance changed to wishing actively to solicit a peace offer as he could not see how the war could be won by Britain alone. This offer would have meant a redrawing of the map of Europe but would not affect Britain's independence, military capacity or freedom of manoeuvre. Never did he so much as consider surrendering to Hitler. His stance towards the dozens of sometimes bizarre Nobel Peace Prize hopefuls was, as with Dalherus, that he would never reject the opportunity to listen. With air rearmament at a critical stage and all hope of a two-front war lost, it was common sense to try to gain time.

Halifax was supremely conscious of the overriding necessity of buying time for rearmament, the blockade of Germany and for world pressure to build up on her. In his scrapbook albums at Garrowby there is a hitherto unpublished note dating from the last week of the Phoney War which illustrates this position perfectly. Ever the diligent curator of his own reputation, Halifax had afterwards annotated it, 'Cabinet 6th May 40. Exchange of notes with Winston C after I had suggested one way to gain time was to delude the Germans by peace talk!' The content clearly indicated that at some point in the Cabinet discussion, Churchill, perhaps stunned by the very concept of 'peace talks', had accused Halifax of high treason. Halifax immediately sent a note to Churchill in his own defence: 'You are really very unjust to my irresponsible ideas. They may be silly, are certainly dangerous, but are not high treason. I dislike always quarrelling with you! But most of all on "misunderstood" grounds. E.' On which Churchill wrote underneath and passed back: 'Dear Edward. I had a spasm of fear. I am sorry if I offended. It was a very deadly thought in the present atmosphere of frustration. You could not foresee this. Forgive me. W.'[17]

Virtually no advance, however amateur, was considered too spurious to be investigated by the Foreign Office. At the very least they hoped it might yield some information about the state of feeling in Germany. A number attained the level of high farce. On 21 January 1940, Göring held a meeting with the prim and worthy Bishop of Oslo, at which the prelate asked earnestly, 'If you could choose would you rather have peace or victory?' The Reichsmarschall replied, 'Peace, absolutely peace,' adding with a chortle that, of course, he 'should very much like to have victory first!' He was nevertheless able to convince the Scandinavian that he could 'see the vision' of peace.[18]

There were so many amateur and professional contacts between the protagonists in the various neutral countries that one is left with the impression that it must have been hard to get to the bar in any Swiss café during the Phoney War for all the spies discussing peace terms with one another. The British diplomats would listen with equal patience to the official German representatives as to the anti-Nazi conspirators. Once they got the two mixed up when, at Venlo in Holland in November 1939, they believed they were talking to the latter when in fact the 'conspirators' were Gestapo agents. As a result, two British spies were kidnapped and taken over the German border for interrogation. Some peace conversations were sublime, such as Putzi Hanfstaengl's plan to offer Göring the Order of the Garter if he would overthrow Hitler. Others were as ridiculous as Princess Stephanie Hohenlohe's contention that Himmler was a secret monarchist and could be persuaded to overthrow Hitler and become Kaiser.

The list of Anglo-German contacts in 1939 and 1940 is as impressive in length as it is insubstantial in content. Lords Darnley and Tavistock discovered a set of terms via the German legation in Dublin in January 1940, but Halifax's letters to Tavistock on the subject were so non-committal that they did not even require censorship before Tavistock published them in 1940. A small group of Labour MPs under the leadership of Richard Stokes, inexplicably calling themselves 'the Salvage Corps (Darning Needles) Ltd', continued to bombard Rab Butler with calls for peace even after the start of the Blitz. Stokes himself brought back a German offer from Franz von Papen, the German Ambassador in Ankara. A Dutch mountaineer called Visser also brought one back from him in November 1939.[19] The head of the German Secret Service, Admiral Canaris, talked to the Papal Nuncio in Berne about peace terms. An American Quaker, Malcolm Lovell, passed on some he had received from the German Embassy in Washington to the British diplomat Neville Butler. The Chief Justice of Sweden discussed them with another British diplomat, Sir Victor Mallet.

A certain Mr Anthony Gibbs returned from The Hague with a set of terms in April 1940. The head of the German Foreign Office, Ernst von Weizsäcker, offered to fly Karl Burckhardt of the League of Nations to Berlin in a Red Cross plane to receive some.[20] The anti-Nazi Baron von Thyssen told Britain's Vatican envoy, D'Arcy Osborne, about some in February 1940. When Lady Halifax visited Rome the same month, the

Pope used the opportunity to send a message to her husband about 'a just peace, but a solid and durable one,'[21] and there were literally dozens of other such meetings all of varying degrees of legitimacy and intrigue.

Some tend to sound as outlandish as the results of a game of Consequences, such as when the Great War spy Sir William Wiseman met Princess Stephanie Hohenlohe in the Mark Hopkins Hotel in San Francisco in 1941. He said to her that he had come to listen. She said to him that Lord Halifax was the leader of the British 'peace party', and the consequences were that as J. Edgar Hoover's FBI bugged the whole conversation nothing came of it. All these feelers must be subjected to the same inexorable logic dictated by the military situation. Up to 10 May 1940, Halifax consistently reiterated the facts that Britain had a war-winning strategy, time was on her side, Hitler's promises were worthless and unless either the German Government or the military situation changed drastically the war would continue. It was inconceivable that the master of Central Europe would accede to the Allied demands for a free and independent Poland and Czechoslovakia. Halifax even curtailed Dalherus's visits after 17 October, although this was partly out of embarrassment at having to explain them to the French. On 13 December 1939, Halifax met a Swiss named Mr Bondi, who, Cadogan reported, had 'a scheme for Göring to bump off Hitler and form a Government!' Talking this over with Cadogan the next morning, they came to the only sensible conclusion: 'Let them get on with it, and I will then render my judgement!'[22]

This myriad of contacts during the Phoney War meant little and led to nothing. Halifax's view of one such meeting in late November 1939 was typical and reinforces the evidence of the note of 6 May 1940 in the Garrowby album: 'If there is anything in it,' Halifax told Field Marshal Gort, 'you had better explore it . . . in any case, it is useful as a time-gainer.'[23] The continual emphasis placed by Halifax and others during this period on the possibility of an internal coup against Hitler seems quite ludicrous today. The undermanned and underfinanced Secret Intelligence Service led Halifax to believe that Hitler was weak, whereas in fact he was phenomenally popular amongst Germans throughout the first half of 1940. Having not slipped up once since the Rhineland crisis of 1936, Germans credited Hitler with almost superhuman powers of political instinct and timing. After the successful subjugation of Denmark, Norway, Belgium, Holland and France, they proved quite willing to add military genius to his other attributes. For all the amazing bravery of those Germans who plotted to kill him, they were always a tiny minority whose chances of pulling off a successful coup were minimal.

One of the many files at the Public Record Office which is closed until 2015 is believed to relate to the contacts between an Englishman, J. Lonsdale Bryans, and Ulrich von Hassell, a leader of the anti-Nazi resistance. It seems that Halifax trusted Bryans to make contact with von

Hassell principally because he was the great-nephew of Lord Grimthorpe, a friend of his father's. Bryans was also an Old Etonian member of Brooks's to boot. Having met von Hassell's son-in-law by accident in a café in Rome in October 1939, Bryans was encouraged by Halifax to keep in contact and had some forty clandestine meetings, which came to a halt with Germany's invasion of Norway in April. Halifax – codenamed Signora Manassei – was directly involved and via Bryans promised the conspirators that Britain and France would certainly take no advantage of any anti-Hitler coup to launch an assault on Germany. This promise was easily given as the Allies had no serious plans to attack Germany anyhow. Halifax considered that although Bryans was 'clearly a lightweight',[24] the talks, as with so many others, 'can do no harm, and may do a lot of good'.[25] Halifax was willing to offer inducements to what he called 'the Göring tribe' for a reasonable peace and seems to have stuck to Cadogan's line that the principal war aim was the personal removal of Hitler and his replacement with someone who could make a trustworthy peace. It seems from the notes of his conversation with Bryans of 8 January 1940 that Halifax believed the Reichsmarschall could be included in that category.[26]

Throughout the vast correspondence Halifax was forced to have with British proponents of a negotiated peace, there recurs one factor as Halifax's central and overriding argument. Cadogan noted on 6 December 1939 that although Halifax evidently hankered after peace, he could feel nothing but utter distrust of Hitler. Hitler was not sufficiently honourable – in Halifax's view simply not enough of a gentleman – to keep his word. The lesson learnt on the sleepless night of 24/25 September 1938 had principally been one about Hitler's aims and integrity. All that had taken place since then had served to confirm him in the view of Hitler he had then formed.

Even if a compromise solution were hacked out between the two countries, what, as he put it to the Earl of Lytton in November 1939, would happen then? If there were a peace conference,

> Everyone would be expected to demobilize ... we should be expected to lift our blockade and we should know all the time that, if Hitler refused to accept what we thought reasonable, he could very probably start again more easily than we could ... and that meanwhile our position would have greatly weakened.

The smaller neutrals 'might go for peace at any price', while the Russians and Italians would be no help and the Americans would probably not attend.[27] Halifax therefore did his best to defeat those, such as the Pope, the Dutch and Belgian monarchs and especially President Roosevelt, who made offers to meditate for peace.

A hitherto unpublished letter written by Halifax on 10 November 1939 shows the way his mind was working two months into the war; it is a far cry from the 'hankering' for peace of which he is accused and explains why he was unwilling to get embroiled in hypothetical discussions regarding the future relationships Germany would have with her eastern and southern neighbours:

> To define your war aims precisely as people want would mean for me, if I spoke all my mind, that I wished to fight long enough to induce such a state of mind in the Germans that they would say they'd had enough of Hitler! And that point is not really met by talking about C.Z., Poland and all the rest of it. The real point is, I'm afraid, that I can trust *no* settlement unless and until H is discredited. When we shall achieve this nobody can say, but I don't think any 'settlement' is worth much without![28]

The converse side of Halifax's policy of 'buying time' whilst keeping the Russians and neutrals content was opposition to any vigorous activity against Germany, except over the blockade. This refusal to countenance Britain being the first to resort to bombing soon brought him up against the one member of the Cabinet who saw the war in terms significantly different from his.

20

Restraining Winston

The national saviour image of Winston Churchill in 1940 is so deeply ingrained into the British psyche as to make any criticism of his conduct during that year sound almost blasphemous. At the outset of that annus mirabilis, however, he was not considered the splendid personification of British glory he was to become later on in it. Rather he was seen by many in society and the Conservative Party as a political turncoat, a dangerous adventurer who, in his own words, had 'ratted and re-ratted' by twice crossing the floor of the House. Although some thought him a delightful rogue who lacked political judgement, there were those who considered him unscrupulous, unreliable and unattractively ambitious. A letter from Lord Erskine to Lord Brabourne during the Munich crisis may be a robust but not untypical Establishment reaction, and refers to 'that arch war-monger and self-seeker Winston Churchill'.[1] In an age which, far more than our own, tended to judge people according to their lineage, it was remembered that the Churchill family had certainly contained more than their fair share of cads.

His colleagues worried about the enormous consumption of alcohol, few appreciating how weak he mixed his whiskies and soda or that he actually performed better in the constant state of slight intoxication that his all-day drinking induced. Halifax once complained to a friend during the Phoney War how Churchill's 'voice oozes with port and the smell of the chewed cigar'. Lady Halifax, who came from a family of heroic drinkers, understood the benefit Churchill gained from it. She later recalled an occasion when she sat next to him at a dinner:

> At the start of the meal I immediately plunged into conversation on my other side, as I well knew that during the first two courses Winston would be silent, grumpy and remote and conversation would be uphill work. But mellowed by champagne and good food he became a different man, and a delightful and amusing companion.[2]

Churchill's wit and oratorical ability was not enough to overcome severe doubts about his judgement. The 'gift of the gab' reputation did as much harm as good amongst traditional Conservatives ever distrustful of genius. On the very day Churchill became Prime Minister, Rab Butler drank a doleful bottle of champagne with John Colville, the Prime Minister's Assistant Private Secretary, Dunglass and Channon, during the course of which he described Churchill as 'a half-breed American whose main support was that of inefficient but talkative people of a similar type, American dissidents like Nancy Astor and Ronnie Tree'.[3] (It is not recorded how Channon took this reference to his countrymen; he probably thought himself so thoroughly Anglicized that it did not apply to him.)

Even Churchill's famous radio broadcasts were not universally admired until the Blitz. They had too much of the ham actor to them and in the Phoney War the events they described simply did not match up to the hyperbole employed. It was not until after the Fall of France that Britain's predicament rated the sort of rhetoric Churchill had been using throughout his political life. During the Phoney War, a friend of Halifax believed many were 'shaken by his unwise remarks and a little shocked by the "first rate turn" attitude that his broadcasts give'.[4]

The strange dress, ridiculous hats, heavy drinking and pronounced speech impediment did little to encourage the Tory old guard to respect him for much more than having been proved right about the German threat. Even on that issue it was alleged, though wrongly, that the most substantial of the inter-war reductions in Defence Estimates took place under his Chancellorship of the Exchequer from 1924 to 1929. The years in the self-imposed Wilderness had been punctuated by disastrous campaigns over India and the Abdication, which turned what following he may have had in 1929 into a tiny disaffected rump by 1939. Just before war broke out, Lord Hardinge, an ex-Permanent Under-Secretary at the Foreign Office, ex-Viceroy of India, father of the King's Private Secretary and as near a personification of the British Establishment as it is possible to get, commented to Lord Erskine:

> There are I believe a fair number of people who think and say that in these times Winston ought to be in the Government, but why? Look at his past history: give him credit for not having dismissed the fleet in August 1914, but after that: Antwerp, Dardanelles, Denikin Expedition, Treasury (change to Gold Standard), India Bill, and his attitude in the Abdication. Could anybody have a worse record? But we are a forgetful and forgiving people.[5]

Sir Alan Lascelles, the King's former Assistant Private Secretary, summed up the prevailing sentiment when he said: 'The sad truth is that Winston did not like gentlemen.'[6]

Churchill's natural dynamism, fuelled by his concern lest a lack of action might encourage peace talk, led him to adopt forward and energetic stands on all issues concerning the war. He made it perfectly clear that the price of his unswerving political support for the Prime Minister was the right to interest himself in every aspect of the war. This brought him up against Halifax, who, very much the senior in Cabinet and skilled in the ways of the Government from which Churchill had been absent for a decade, invariably got the better of him in departmental battles. Despite the obloquy heaped on Halifax for his caution and his role in restraining Churchill during the Phoney Way, the creative tension between the two served Britain very well in the end.

One has to piece together the evidence for Halifax's relationship with Churchill with care. Halifax, who sent handwritten notes and rarely kept copies, 'weeded' his private papers thoroughly before donating them to the University of York.[7] Many more discussions between Churchill and Halifax took place, particularly in and around Cabinet time, than were recorded or recalled.

The first clash came soon after Chamberlain invited Churchill into the War Cabinet. Churchill 'stigmatized as odious the conduct of the Roumanian Government'[8] for imprisoning the fleeing Polish Government in accordance with German wishes. He said that he thought Britain should try to extend the conflict throughout the Balkans. Halifax replied with a precision and practicality that must have infuriated the First Lord. It was not in British interests, he said, to have Germany invade Romania. Polish resources, gold reserves, ships and manpower could as easily be mobilized under another government as under the one that had been interned. He categorically repudiated Churchill's Balkan ideas, pointing out what little difficulty Germany would have in overcoming one Balkan country after another in 'a series of additional cheap victories'.[9] The Chiefs of Staff supported Halifax. Had Churchill had his way, friendly Turkey might have fallen and Italy probably would have come in against the Allies far earlier than she did.

In late October, Halifax dampened down Churchill's enthusiasm for military action against Eire for her refusal to allow the Royal Navy use of various ports. Churchill believed that as a member of the Commonwealth, Eire (which, as the Irish Free State, he had been instrumental in founding) was legally 'At War but Skulking'[10] and he therefore toyed with the idea of the forcible seizure of the ports. Halifax was horrified at the implications of this scheme and, in conjunction with Eden, pointed out the disastrous impact it would have on Ireland as a recruiting ground, American public opinion, naval commitments, German propaganda and de Valera's political position vis-à-vis Sinn Fein.

As if antagonizing the Irish were not enough, Churchill's well-known and obscurantist views on India, if put into practice, would have put paid to

Lord Halifax as Foreign Secretary in 1940, photographed by Cecil Beaton

Chamberlain leaves for Berchtesgaden, seen off by Sir Alexander Cadogan, Sir Horace Wilson, Lord Halifax and R. A. Butler

Oliver Harvey and Anthony Eden walking in St James's Park

Benito Mussolini, Count Ciano and Neville Chamberlain in Rome, January 1939

Taking the salute in Rome

The Cabinet, September 1939. Top left to right, Sir John Anderson, Lord Hankey, Leslie Hore-Belisha, Winston Churchill, Sir Kingsley Wood, Anthony Eden, Edward Bridges; bottom left to right, Lord Halifax, Sir John Simon, Neville Chamberlain, Sir Samuel Hoare, Lord Chatfield

Relaxing with their grandchildren at Garrowby on leave from Washington, 1942

Exchange of notes with Winston C. Cabinet May 6.40 after I had suggested that one way to gain time was to delude the Germans by Peace talk!

You are really very unjust to my irresponsible ideas. They may be silly, an certainly dangerous, but are not high Treason.

I dislike always quarrelling with you! but most of all on 'misunderstood' grounds.

E

Dear Edward I had a spasm of fear. I am sorry if I offended. It was a very deadly thought in this present atmosphere of prostration. You ct not foresee this. Forgive me. W.

'Exchange of notes with Winston C. after I had suggested that one way to gain time was to delude the Germans by Peace talk!', Cabinet, 6 May 1940

Chancellor of Oxford University, with his son Peter as train-bearer

Franklin Delano Roosevelt

The problem: hunting with the Plunket Stewarts in Philadelphia, March 1941

The solution: 'De-icing
Edward', a photo opportunity
out west

With the Hon. Angus
McDonnell

Halifax and Churchill on the steps of the British Embassy in Washington, August 1941

the then Viceroy's attempts to reconcile Congress to the war. Here, too, Halifax was on strong enough ground to block Churchill's ideas for India, which he continued to do throughout 1940.

In late November 1939, Halifax managed to get his man rather than Churchill's appointed as head of the Secret Intelligence Service. Once again the decision seems to have been taken on social and political grounds as much as professional. Stewart Menzies had been President of Pop and Captain of the Eton XI, was in the Life Guards and White's, and had married Earl De La Warr's daughter. Lady Cadogan's diary records that her husband was not convinced that Menzies 'was quite good enough to succeed the Admiral, but everyone likes him enormously'.[11] Margesson, too, supported Halifax's candidate and at the crucial meeting on 28 November Halifax 'played his hand well and won the trick'.[12] In the end, Menzies proved a highly successful 'C' whilst Churchill's protégé, Admiral Godfrey, merely succeeded in 'putting people's backs up'.[13]

By Christmas Eve 1939, when Chamberlain's gout started playing up, Harvey noted how Halifax was still the favourite to succeed Chamberlain, though some doubted whether he could hold down the job. Churchill was 'a good second, but everyone is nervous of his instability. Recent naval successes have, of course, put his shares up.'[14] These 'successes' were part of a relentless propaganda campaign Churchill waged throughout the Phoney War, culminating in his claim to have sunk half the U-boat fleet when the true figure was actually eight per cent. It was only when Churchill intruded in Foreign Office business that Halifax's feelings of amused resignation towards his old boss and sparring partner turned into exasperation. By November 1939, he was butting into internal Foreign Office business to the extent of asking in Cabinet when the Ambassador to Brussels was going to be replaced.

It was his broadcast to the neutrals on 21 January that snapped Halifax's patience. The speech was a disaster. Churchill had described the neutrals as each hoping the German crocodile would eat his neighbour in the hope of it devouring him last. In the Foreign Office E. H. Carr drew up an eight-page digest of the negative reactions of various neutral governments. The Ministry of Information complained the next morning that the speech had set back their efforts in wooing over the neutrals by a full three months. Although Halifax's protests to Chamberlain, Churchill and the Cabinet were dignified and restrained, the true state of his feelings was that, 'It is incredible that a man in his position should make such gaffes. His bragging about the war at sea is followed every time by some appalling loss (last time two destroyers).'[15] Churchill's charming apology – 'Asking me not to make a speech is like asking a centipede to get along and not put a foot on the ground'[16] – was just enough to blunt Halifax's indignation.

Halifax, unlike a number of more junior ministers, was not in the least overawed by Churchill, and had not been since marching into his room in the Colonial Office in 1921. When Cadogan complained that 'it's silly of everyone to go on funking Winston', he did not include Halifax, who used to advise other ministers to win Churchill's respect by standing up to him. Halifax started a daily diary on 31 January 1940, and when in early February at a Supreme War Council meeting in Paris Churchill came into Halifax's bedroom wearing a dressing-gown at 7.30 a.m., he noted, 'what an extraordinary creature he is, but I must say the more I see of him the more I like him. It is the combination of simplicity, energy and intellectual agility that is so entertaining.'[17] Churchill's practice of keeping unusual hours was soon to irritate Halifax, whose habits were regular and who liked to be in bed by 10.30 p.m. Churchill, who slept for an hour almost every afternoon of the war, was able to stay working till the early hours. Halifax suspected that he used the late nights as a way to tire out and browbeat Service Chiefs and ministers. He also resented the way Churchill's loquacity tended to draw out Cabinet meetings.

The Soviet invasion of Finland in late November 1939 prompted cries of indignation from press, public and Parliament. With yet another innocent neutral violated by the totalitarians, there were calls for the Allies to go to Finland's aid. These grew louder as the Finns fought back heroically and even won initial victories over the numerically vast Red Army. Apart from the logistical problems involved in supplying a country so close to the Soviet Union and Germany, Halifax's rational mind whilst sympathizing with Finland appreciated the underlying problem. He was not about to sacrifice his policy of minimizing the number of Britain's enemies in a spasm of self-righteousness. 'God', he reminded Victor Cazalet on 13 April, 'made Finland much nearer Russia and Germany than England.'[18] At the time of the Russian attack on Poland ('a stab in the back for which there could be no possible excuse'),[19] he had told Lord Salisbury that his policy was to try to drive a wedge between Russia and Germany. When Churchill came up with a scheme by which Britain and France would reinforce Finland via northern Norway and Sweden, thereby cutting off the Germans from their vital ore supplies in Sweden's Gällivare orefields, Halifax secured Chamberlain's opposition. After he blocked a similar plan to prevent the transfer of the Swedish iron ore from Narvik to Germany by sending a flotilla to intercept, Halifax wrote to Churchill to say, 'I have too great a respect for you, and for all that you bring to this business of saving civilization, to feel other than uncomfortable when my mind does not go with yours.'[20]

Churchill's plan would have violated the sovereignty of both countries, who had forbidden Allied troops the right of entry out of fear of the Russian and German reaction. Halifax firmly rejected any plan which might have involved Britain in going to war with two Scandinavian countries in order to aid the third. He cannily refused Maisky's request for him to act as mediator between Moscow and Helsinki, correctly seeing it as a ploy to get

Britain to put pressure on Finland to sue for peace. Although some fairly small-scale aid was sent, Halifax considered it wasteful to send large-scale help when military equipment was so desperately needed at home. On hearing of the Russo-Finnish peace treaty of 12 March 1940, he allowed himself 'some feeling of thankfulness at not having got an expedition bogged down where it could not be maintained.... I don't believe anything in the long run would have made much difference. But I certainly shall not say this in public.'[21]

By the time Roosevelt's confidant and friend Sumner Welles visited London in March 1940, at the end of his whistle-stop tour of European capitals to explore the possibility of Roosevelt acting as a peace-maker, the British Government was in a pugnacious mood. Halifax was quite prepared to pump Welles for information about the mood in Berlin, but to Welles's talk about disarmament he was adamant that 'it is more true that disarmament follows confidence than that confidence flows from disarmament'.[22] The Foreign Office crib sheet sent to the King for his meeting with Welles read more like a Ministry of Information propaganda briefing. It listed three obstacles to peace of which the first was Germany's 'deliberate policy of extermination in Poland'.

The sacking of the dynamic War Minister Leslie Hore-Belisha in January 1940, at the time blamed on Chamberlain and various generals, seems also to have been partly the work of Halifax and the King. The Channon and Chamberlain diaries both make it quite clear that the impetus for removing Hore-Belisha came directly from Buckingham Palace. George VI was prompted to act by the criticisms of the Minister he had heard from Lord Gort and others on a visit of inspection to the British Expeditionary Force. Hore-Belisha, whom the generals had nicknamed Horeb Elisha, was, as Chamberlain admitted, a man of 'courage, imagination and drive', who had faithfully carried out the Government's military reforms in the teeth of great opposition from the military. This had prompted a vicious whispering campaign against him, which made no specific charges. When, months later, Halifax was out riding with Valentine Lawford on Wimbledon Common and they passed Hore-Belisha's house, Halifax mentioned how he had disliked the way Hore-Belisha would send for General Gort when Chief of the Imperial General Staff to talk to him from his bed.[23]

Halifax's malign influence in the affair of Hore-Belisha's sacking began at about the time that, under pressure from the King and some army elements, Chamberlain had decided to move Hore-Belisha to the Information Ministry. Halifax had hoped one of his two old friends Walter Monckton or George Lloyd would get Information. It was Cadogan who persuaded Halifax that Hore-Belisha's Jewishness would, in his words on the matter to Sir Horace Wilson, be 'catastrophic' at Information. He thought it would be a boon for Goebbels and would have a bad effect on the isolationists in America. After the 11.30 a.m. Cabinet on 4 January, with Hore-Belisha totally unaware of what was going on and due to meet Chamberlain an hour later, Halifax told Chamberlain that Hore-Belisha's appointment to Information 'would have a bad effect on the neutrals both because HB was a Jew and because his methods would let down British prestige'.[24] He suggested that perhaps Hore-Belisha could go instead to the Board of Trade. There was a certain irony in this, for in May 1937 Margesson had advised Chamberlain that his Jewishness precluded Hore-Belisha from the Board of Trade and that he could only think of the Health Ministry as being suitable for him.

Halifax's theory that the appointment of a Jew to Information would somehow 'discount the value of the Ministry in American eyes' had already been dismissed as baseless by the veteran Ambassador to Washington and former Permanent Under-Secretary at the Foreign Office, Sir Ronald Lindsay. Nevertheless, Chamberlain wavered; 'If I had known earlier of Edward's views', he complained to his sisters, '. . . I should have left H. B. alone.' In the event, he bowed to Halifax's judgement and offered Hore-Belisha the distinctly inferior Trade post. Hore-Belisha refused it and resigned from the Government altogether. The part Halifax played in the affair and the argument he used were wholly discreditable. Both as a devout moralist and an opinion-former, Halifax ought to have been able to rise above the 'club' or 'social' anti-Semitism that was such an unattractive but common feature of his less enlightened contemporaries.

Altogether more cerebral and tolerant was Halifax's speech to the undergraduates of Oxford in the Sheldonian on 27 February 1940. Speaking as Chancellor of the University and Foreign Secretary, it was both a spirited defence of the values of Christian civilization and a personal contribution to the debate on war aims. Entitled 'The Challenge to Liberty', it ended with a call to arms of almost Churchillian tones:

> . . . be so proud of the race to which you belong that you will be as jealous of its honour as you are of its safety, and that you will fight for both with equal determination. The struggle will be arduous, it may be long, and it will certainly demand of our nation that it should withhold nothing that may contribute to our strength.

He was severely criticized in private by Max Beaverbrook and others for the great emphasis he continually put on religion in his speeches and what the American Ambassador, Joseph Kennedy, contemptuously referred to as 'all that God stuff'.

His enemies derided these speeches as so much sanctimonious cant. In fact, he was fulfilling a crucial role. In expecting people to be prepared to sacrifice their way of life, even sometimes their homes and family, they had to be convinced that the cause was morally and spiritually – as well as merely politically – just. Throughout the history of human conflict, it has been necessary for people to know that God is on their side. Churchill's wartime speeches appealed to patriotism, History and national honour. Halifax's reputation for piety and responsibility helped provide another, religious, ingredient which cynics were and are wrong to deride.

As the winter turned into spring, Halifax became more confident that in the one area that mattered more than any other, the air, there were significant signs of improvement. 'What they cannot as yet succeed in understanding', he wrote of the dictators in April 1940, 'is that we are much less frightened of them jumping out on us now than we were at the time of Munich.'[25] In a meeting of Lord Salisbury's bellicose Watching Committee that month, he again expressed his conviction that nothing should be done that might precipitate attacks on the aircraft factories, which were daily improving Britain's chances of survival. Halifax's interests were never confined to the field of foreign affairs. He was opposed to the silencing of church bells except in the event of invasion, arguing that German parachutists were far more likely to land at dawn than at five to eleven on a Sunday morning. He wanted a special form of peal set aside to denote invasion.

When, on 16 February, Churchill gave him ten minutes to decide whether HMS *Cossack* could stop a German ship, *Altmark*, carrying British prisoners to Germany, Halifax let him go ahead, regardless of the consequences of the violation of Norwegian neutrality. Churchill appreciated this, commenting to his naval advisers at the Admiralty, 'that was *big* of Halifax'.[26] The capture was, in Halifax's words, 'a very fine performance, and quite in the Elizabethan style'.[27] The Russo-Finnish peace had put paid to Churchill's schemes of taking the Swedish orefields with the excuse of reinforcing Finland. His next idea for cutting off this vital raw material for Germany's munitions industry was the mining of the Norwegian harbours from which the ore-carrying ships sailed. Halifax assented to the scheme not so much for its practical value, of which he held severe doubts, as for the salutary effect it would have in Germany.

At 7 a.m. on 9 April, Halifax was woken to hear that Germany had invaded Denmark and Norway. His initial reaction was amazingly one of relief: 'It eases our path immensely vis-à-vis the Scandinavian position.'[28] Although as late as the day before even Churchill had been doubtful about the chances of German intervention, it was Chamberlain who took the brunt of criticism for his assertion of only five days earlier that in not having attacked for six months Hitler had 'missed the bus'. This joined a good number of other phrases to prove his ability of saying the wrong thing at the wrong time. It was this capacity which, more than any mistaken operational decisions, was finally to bring him down.

The only significant intervention Halifax seems to have made in the Norwegian débâcle came at the beginning of the operation when he advocated attacking Trondheim as well as Narvik in opposition to the First Lord's advice. In pressing for an attack on the larger and more southerly town, Halifax gave priority to political rather than purely military considerations and was being more ambitious than Churchill himself. By this bold manoeuvre he hoped to bolster Norwegian resistance, make the Germans 'wonder a bit' and dissuade Mussolini from attacking Greece or Yugoslavia. 'The Holy Fox' also hoped that by blocking the Trondheim/ Oslo rail link the Germans would be forced to invade Sweden in order to protect Gallivare from the British troops in Narvik, thereby bringing Sweden into the war on the Allied side.[29] At the same meeting he approved the mining of Swedish harbours on the understanding that this was vigorously denied by the Admiralty. After the Chiefs of Staff decided against his Trondheim plan, Halifax withdrew to let Chamberlain and Churchill fight the campaign. No military strategist, he had to admit to a meeting of ministers on 2 May, the very day on which the British started ignominiously to evacuate Norway, that he was not competent to decide whether Trondheim should have been attacked or not.

Blame for the débâcle centred principally on Chamberlain despite Churchill, as First Lord of the Admiralty, having been much closer to the operational side. Halifax was angered by the great efforts he detected were 'being made to represent the Norwegian business as the result of timid colleagues restraining the bold, dashing and courageous Winston. As a matter of fact the exact opposite would be at least as near the truth.'[30] Whatever the truth all parties knew that the parliamentary debate on the Norway defeat would give the Government's opponents a chance to criticize the Prime Minister. Few guessed it would also give them the opportunity to bring him down.

21

'The Unpersuadable Halifax'

The revolt against the Chamberlain Government at the end of the two-day debate on the Norwegian campaign was a case of parliamentary spontaneous combustion. Though an embarrassing setback, the failed expedition was not of itself sufficient reason to bring down a government which had until so recently enjoyed almost total political mastery. Historians' attempts to find long-term underlying causes for the coup have met with little success.

There was a degree of uneasiness about the continuing inactivity on the Western front and much resentment against various personalities in the Government, especially Sir Samuel Hoare and Sir John Simon. The decisions not to bomb Germany or to aid Finland had angered some of the more bellicose spirits on the back-benches, but until the debate began the Government Whips had no inkling that the majority (which was normally around two hundred) would fall substantially. The fact of war rendered Chamberlain's prestige as a man of peace suddenly useless, or worse than useless, but he nevertheless still enjoyed great respect in the country. Indeed, there was a certain resentment that Labour's refusal to serve under Chamberlain robbed him of the opportunity and legitimacy that a truly national government would have had to galvanize the whole country and to wield the powers over industrial policy and citizens' rights necessary for Total War.

The Norway debate, far from being the result of a groundswell of outraged opinion against prevaricating government, was primarily a parliamentary event intended to rebuke Chamberlain, which his own personality and the nature of Westminster politics turned into a full-scale coup. The essential ingredients necessary for such a situation – inflammatory speeches, incessant intrigue, high-profile and well-timed desertions, and most of all disinclination of Tory back-benchers to display their confidence in Chamberlain – were all present in abundance on the evenings of 7 and

8 May 1940. Halifax's deft stewardship of the House of Lords prevented the insurrection spreading to the altogether more quiescent red benches, but all he could do was hear in disgust of the reverses suffered by the Government in the Lower House. Neither he nor Chamberlain had thought the debate would 'amount to much', but he was still keen that Chamberlain should deflect criticism by asking Labour to join the Government. To that end he had held a private meeting with Herbert Morrison on 6 May. According to John Colville's diary, the quid pro quo was to be the dropping of Simon, Hoare and Kingsley Wood. Morrison declined Halifax's offer, if offer it was, preferring to hang on for the greater prize.

The following two days saw the spectacle of the House of Commons at its most theatrical, powerful and merciless. The Hansard report of the debate reads more like the script of a West End play. Indeed, Penguin published it soon after in paperback. Sir Roger Keyes, hero of the 1918 Zeebrugge raid, arrived in his Admiral of the Fleet's uniform with its six rows of medal ribbons, to denounce the handling of the Norwegian campaign. The mood of the House turned against Chamberlain when he made the error of trying to treat the debate as any other, calling on his 'friends' in the House to support him when it came to the division. This was correctly portrayed as a blatant attempt to win the debate through a narrow and conventional appeal to party loyalty. 'I have my friends in the House' must rank alongside 'the very midsummer of madness', 'Peace for our time' and 'Hitler has missed the bus' as yet another of his catastrophic catch-phrases.

Lloyd George, who had waited more than seventeen years for his revenge, told Chamberlain that the best sacrifice he could now make for his country was to hand over the seals of office. He went on to describe Churchill, who had to defend the Government's record the next day, as an air-raid shelter protecting his colleagues from blame. This image left Churchill, in the words of one spectator, 'like a fat baby swinging his legs on the front bench trying not to laugh', and effectively negated Churchill's later efforts to defend Chamberlain's Government.[1] Leo Amery's famous philippic, all the more powerful for coming from a Birmingham MP, was a masterpiece from one not noted as a particularly talented speaker. He sensed the mood of the debate dramatic enough to end with the peroration Cromwell had used when dissolving the Rump Parliament: 'You have sat too long here for any good you have been doing. Depart, I say, and let us have done with you. In the name of God, go!'

Halifax received a report of all this from Lady Alexandra Metcalfe, who had spent the evening attempting to watch the debates in both Houses and who likened moving from the Commons to the Lords to 'going from Twickenham to St Paul's'.[2] After a hurried dinner on the second day, Halifax went to the Commons to hear Churchill do his best winding up for the Government. Churchill lost his temper with the Labour MP Emanuel Shinwell and failed to convince his friends amongst the Tory dissidents to support the Government. Halifax then watched with horror as the division was taken, and Labour members taunted Chamberlain with cries of 'Missed the bus!', 'Get out!' and 'Go, in the name of God, go!' One of the Conservative rebels, Harold Macmillan, started to sing 'Rule Britannia' with Lord Winterton until they were silenced by furious Chamberlainites. In the end, forty-one Conservatives voted against the Government and some fifty abstained. Despite this, Chamberlain won the division by 281 to 200, a Government majority large enough under peacetime circumstances for it to survive.

But the moral weight of the debate had gone badly against the Prime Minister, who rightly felt that the personal antipathy against him was too great for the national unity necessary in wartime. Although the majority of Tory MPs had stayed loyal to him, going dutifully through the Aye lobby, they had been elected back in 1935 on the platforms of anti-socialism, collective security and sound finance, all issues which had long since been subsumed. The rebels had included a number of influential and well-known names, including Duff Cooper, Hore-Belisha, Robert Boothby, Lord Winterton, Lady Astor, Lord Wolmer, General Spears, Ronald Tree and Harold Nicolson as well, of course, as Amery and Keyes. Many back-benchers had considered it no bad thing for the leadership's knuckles to be rapped over Norway, but had no idea that Chamberlain would be forced to resign. Furthermore, few had given any consideration as to who should succeed him.

During the second day of the debate, Chamberlain had the opportunity for a short talk with Halifax in his room behind the Speaker's Chair. There he made it clear that should he be forced to resign he wanted Halifax to take over. After the debate a friend noted how Halifax

> was amazed at the personal animosity to the PM. We discussed the chances of his having to take on that ghastly and thankless job. He thought it would never work, the difficulty of the Lords and Commons being impossible and having someone to deputize for you would always be unsuccessful. He dreaded the thought.[3]

The next morning, Thursday 9 May, the Government managers responded to their nominal victory but moral defeat in the time-honoured way. The Whips tried to discover from the dissenters what price the Government would have to pay for the recovery of their support. Chamberlain's canny and prescient Parliamentary Private Secretary, Lord Dunglass, brought leading back-benchers to No. 10 to discuss their grievances and openly intimated to anyone still prepared to listen that Simon and Hoare might be sacrificed to appease the rebels. Dunglass had been the first to recognize the threat to Chamberlain and even before the debate had asked Butler to persuade Halifax to take on the Premiership should it go badly for the Prime Minister. Salisbury's Watching Committee met to decide that

Chamberlain had to go, but it expressed no preference as to his successor.

Chamberlain saw Leo Amery and offered him the choice of either the Chancellorship of the Exchequer or the Foreign Secretaryship. Amery refused. It is not known what Halifax thought of his job being hawked around to safeguard Chamberlain's political future in this way, or even if he was ever told. Only when it became clear that the rebels had refused all concessions was Margesson forced to inform Chamberlain that he could not continue as Prime Minister. Those who abstained would, it was feared, enter the No lobby in any future confidence motion and those MPs serving in the armed forces were on balance expected to join them. After a frantic early morning of meetings and telephone calls Chamberlain knew, by the time he sent for Halifax at 10.15 a.m., that the revolt had become a revolution.

When they met, Chamberlain told Halifax that all parties had to be brought into the Government immediately, although Churchill, still furious with Labour after the debate, had been doubtful about it the night before. As all-party government was precisely the policy he had been pushing since before Munich, Halifax was enthusiastic. He also appreciated that the chances of Labour agreeing to serve under Chamberlain were negligible. Halifax knew perfectly well what was coming when Chamberlain then offered to serve under him. Halifax 'put all the arguments that I could think of against myself', concentrating, he said, on the 'difficult position of a Prime Minister unable to make contact with the centre of gravity in the House of Commons'.[4] It was an argument he had used ever since January 1939, when he referred to a Halifax Premiership as 'impossible because of his being in the Lords'.[5]

Chamberlain did not argue that constitutionally Halifax would be allowed to sit in the Commons, but instead made the far more dubious prediction that in a coalition government there would be little opposition anyway. The drift of the conversation left Halifax with a bad stomach-ache, but he did not rule out the idea altogether. Instead, 'I told him again, as I had told him the day before, that if the Labour people said that they would only serve under me I should tell them that I was not prepared to do it, and see whether a definite attitude could make them budge.'[6] So far Halifax was standing faithfully by his captain, but with the crucial proviso: 'If it failed we should all no doubt have to boil our broth again.'

This 'broth-boiling' sounds suspiciously like the initial refusal which he used throughout his political life to reinforce the invaluable public image of an inherently modest man, indifferent to high office, but dragged there by friends for his country's good. Unsurprisingly, considerable cynicism has been expressed about this, which has been viewed as at best a disingenuous pose and at worst a political ploy. The truth is more complex. Halifax knew from recent experiences that his principal role, especially with Chamberlain discredited or removed, had to be to restrain Churchill as war leader. This was likely to have been a major topic in his conversation with Chamberlain at the 10.15 a.m. meeting. As Butler recorded after Halifax returned from it:

> He told me that he felt he could do the job. He also felt that Churchill needed a restraining influence. Could that restraint be better exercised as Prime Minister or as a Minister in Churchill's government? Even if he chose the former role, Churchill's qualities and experience would surely mean that he would be 'running the war anyway' and Halifax's own position would speedily turn into a sort of honorary Prime Minister.[7]

For a man with a keen instinct for where power lay and how it worked, Halifax was not about to be lured into political impotency by the title of Prime Minister. He would have had no objections to becoming Prime Minister under other circumstances. Eden certainly thought that Halifax would have liked the job.[8] He refused the Premiership not because he was unambitious but because he knew he would be in a better position as Foreign Secretary to dissuade Churchill from disastrous over-reactions. He would still be the heir apparent and most influential Cabinet minister. It was a shrewd calculation and was the real reason that Butler 'saw that, in truth, Edward did not really want the Premiership, was indeed bent on self-abnegation'.[9] Halifax simply calculated that he would be in a more powerful position standing behind the throne than sitting on it. Also, as he put it in a highly confidential letter to a friend on 13 May, 'I don't think WSC will be a very good PM though I think the country will think he gives them a fillip.'[10]

One factor could spoil Halifax's plans: the Labour Party, which at that moment was holding its annual conference at Bournemouth. If, because of old grudges and the bitterness of the exchanges during the Norway debate, they proved unwilling to serve under Churchill, there might have to be some 'broth-boiling'. Early that morning Halifax had received a note from Butler about two conversations Butler had had the night before with Dalton and Morrison. They had said that the Labour Party

> would come into the Government under you but not under the PM or in the company of Simon ... that is the view that he and his friends hoped I would pass on to you.... Dalton said there was no other choice but you. Churchill must 'stick to the war' and Anderson has not been sufficiently 'built up'. He saw no objection to the Lords difficulty.[11]

The very mention of the uncharismatic Home Secretary, Sir John Anderson, shows the paucity of credible third candidates: even Amery was considered by some, although interestingly no one seems to have proposed Eden. The ever-present fear of Lloyd George – Britain's Pétain-in-waiting – grabbing power was a spur to action for all parties. Attlee told Brendan Bracken on the first evening of the debate that he was quite prepared to serve under Halifax. *The Times* carried a letter on the morning of 9 May from the young Labour candidate and All Souls Fellow, A. L. Rowse, advocating Halifax as Prime Minister. Halifax's Viceroyalty, reputation for solidity and good personal relations with the Labour leadership all paid dividends just when he himself had come round to the decision not to take the Premiership.

His continual references to his peerage as the major obstacle were largely a blind. He had obviously given the matter some thought. On 6 October 1939, he explained to Lady Alexandra Metcalfe that

he would not take the Premiership if offered, his reason being that not being in the Commons made the position too difficult.... Winston would have the difficult job of being the Leader without the cachet of PM. Situations would be bound to arise in which the PM in the Lords got irritated by what was being said in the Commons. The question of posts to be filled would have to be done ... without knowledge of the proper men available, therefore he would be dependent on other men's advice and if those difficulties were surmounted by getting him a safe seat in the Commons he felt he was too tired to start that racket again.[12]

The intriguing reference to a 'safe seat' being provided – as had been the nineteenth-century practice when Prime Ministers lost their own in general elections – implied that Halifax knew it might be constitutionally possible for him to re-enter the Commons. The reasons he gave Lady Alexandra in October 1939 were substantially the same as he gave Chamberlain seven months later, but examination shows them to amount to little. When Halifax told Butler he knew that he could do the job, he was speaking no more than the truth. He had been responsible for 320 million people as Viceroy, had been the closest colleague to both the previous two Prime Ministers, and was perfectly at ease with the pressures and responsibilities of power. The peerage objection was so transparent as to almost make one suspect that it may have even been a 'straw man' argument raised solely by Halifax in the hope and expectation that it would be knocked down. However, by May 1940 he had a genuine reason for not wanting to take the Premiership, but decided to employ the old arguments. The reason Chamberlain did not try harder to persuade Halifax at the 10.15 a.m. meeting was that he fully understood Halifax's decision to restrain Churchill from below rather than above.

The King, possibly because he lacked the Prime Minister's and Foreign Secretary's political wiles, lost no time in pronouncing that Halifax's peerage could be put 'into abeyance'. The influential All Souls Fellow, Sir

Arthur Salter MP, saw 'no insuperable obstacle. The needs of the country must override every technical consideration and if necessary an Act of Parliament could give him a place in the Commons."[13] Dalton had already intimated that on neither constitutional nor egalitarian grounds would the Labour Party oppose Halifax's return from the Lords. It was ironic that back in 1919 it had been the young Hon. Edward Wood who had successfully moved for the rejection of Waldorf Astor's bill to allow the surrendering of peerages, after Astor's father had accepted a peerage partly in order to stymie his own son's political career.

There can be little doubt that at the time of the 10.15 a.m. meeting on 9 May Chamberlain believed it to be possible for a peer, under certain circumstances, to sit and to speak in the Commons. John Colville's diary for 28 December 1939 reads:

> The PM has another attack of gout and is worried by the prospect of not being able to carry on if these attacks increase in number and violence. Meanwhile very secret soundings are being taken regarding the possibility of an enabling bill to allow a peer to speak, but not vote in the Commons, so that Lord Stamp can succeed Simon as Chancellor of the Exchequer.

Any result of these soundings would be as applicable to Halifax succeeding Chamberlain as Prime Minister as to Stamp ousting Simon as Chancellor. They were taken by Sir Horace Wilson, who consulted the parliamentary legal adviser, Sir Granville Ram, emphasizing it was intended solely 'as a special ad hoc war measure'. Ram advised that it was the House of Commons's privilege who may enter and speak in it and a resolution of both Houses would be constitutionally sufficient.[14] It is not known whether Halifax knew about the plot to remove Simon, but Chamberlain was certainly informed by Wilson of Ram's findings.

It was precisely in situations such as that which prevailed on 9–10 May 1940 that the political role of a constitutional monarch comes most prominently into its own. Here too Halifax was on very good ground. The King and Queen were far closer to him than to any other senior politician of the day. In an earlier age he might have been described as a 'favourite' courtier. The Woods had served the Royal Family in a personal as well as a political capacity for over a century. The King and Queen used to dine à quatre at their home in Eaton Square and Lady Halifax was one of the Queen's Ladies-in-Waiting. On George VI's death in 1952, the bereaved Queen thanked 'such old and dear friends as you and Dorothy'. The loan of the key to the Buckingham Palace gardens and the recent offer from the Queen for Halifax to use the summer house there were made as a friend rather than as Foreign Secretary. Halifax's important, if sotto voce, influence in the Abdication crisis had been unwaveringly on the side of the Yorks, whereas Churchill had been the most prominent 'King's Man'. Sir Alan Lascelles, the King's Assistant Private Secretary, remembered how, 'When Chamberlain fell the King felt that he should send for Halifax. Alec Hardinge knew that Winston was the man, but had a hard job selling him to the King as the Queen was very anti-Winston.'[15]

Insofar as it is possible to ascertain the Royal Family's politics at this period, it is clear that they were totally in sympathy with Halifax's. It has been said of George VI that he had the political views of a moderate and politically uninterested London clubman. After the ladies had withdrawn at a dinner at Windsor Castle in April 1938, the King had confided to Butler that 'he liked Halifax's telegrams' and generally 'seemed friendly to the present regime'.[16] As late as the end of February 1939, Hardinge wrote to Halifax expressing the King's disappointment that 'a number of Jewish refugees from different countries were surreptitiously getting into Palestine and he is glad to think that steps have been taken to prevent these people leaving their country of origin'.[17] During the press campaign to have Churchill readmitted to the Cabinet in July 1939, Chamberlain sat between the Duchess of Kent and the Queen at a dinner in Buckingham Palace and the Prime Minister recorded how 'neither left me in any doubt' as to their opposition to the idea.

George V had threatened to abdicate in 1935 had Britain gone to war with Italy. Edward VIII was a keen appeaser and as Duke of Windsor had visited Berchtesgaden in October 1937. Until the Blitz the Royal Family were as lukewarm about the war as anyone in the higher echelons of government. The Queen wrote to Halifax on 1 April 1940 declining his request for her to broadcast to the neutrals until such time as she was able

> to assure myself . . . that anything we intend to do in a warlike manner in the near future is absolutely honourable and right. Because I do not feel that I can talk of high ideals and the right ways of life, if at the same time the neutrals are accusing us of not keeping our word. We *must* beat the Germans, but the neutrals won't like it whilst it's going on! If they *do* mind very much, a broadcast from me might do more harm than good.[18]

After Chamberlain's resignation she wrote to him saying how

> deeply I regretted your ceasing to be our Prime Minister. I can never tell you in words how much we owe you. . . . During these last desperate and unhappy years you have been a great support and comfort to us both, and we felt so safe with the knowledge that your wisdom and high purpose were there at our hand. I do want you to know how grateful we are, and I know that these feelings are shared by a great part of our people. . . . You did all in your power to stave off such agony, and you were right. Your broadcast was superb. My eldest daughter told me

that she and Margaret Rose had listened to it with real emotion. In fact she said: 'I cried, Mummy.'[19]

This affection and support was readily transferred to Halifax, whom the Queen Mother remembers as 'a very delightful, wise, rather saintly man with a splendid sense of humour and a remarkable understanding of his beloved Yorkshire heritage'.[20]

Because he knew the final decision rested with the King and Chamberlain and that both the Labour leadership and the vast bulk of the Conservative Party were favourable to him, Halifax entered the 4.30 p.m. interview in the certain knowledge that the Premiership was safely his for the taking. Twenty years later Margesson told Beaverbrook that he had advised Chamberlain 'that the House of Commons would prefer Halifax'.[21] However, at a lunch back on 25 February, Halifax commented on the talk about a Churchill premiership that, 'inasmuch as the situation would only arise if the war was going badly, he would, in those circumstances, probably be exactly what the nation needed'. Halifax, who was still suffering from his psychosomatic stomach-ache, had another compelling reason for not accepting the Premiership, however the broth boiled. A week earlier, asked about whether an attack on Trondheim might have been more effective than one on Narvik, he was forced to admit that he was not competent to answer the question. Even by the end of the war he readily admitted to a friend that he was a 'layman' in all things military.[22] Despite his brief spell as War Minister, he knew himself to be bored by and only semi-literate in matters of military strategy. He recognized this lacuna to be disastrous in a wartime Premier. Churchill, on the other hand, thrived on war and was fascinated by it. He was stimulated by everything to do with the clash of arms and carried his military responsibility with ease.

It may also be that Halifax was tired and unwilling to return to the bear-pit of the Commons to face the sort of serious personal criticism and scrutiny he had seen Chamberlain put through the night before and from which he had been absent during the last fifteen years. There is almost something more immensely impressive and inversely grand about having been offered the Premiership only to refuse it. He might also have been encouraged by the almost universal expectation that Churchill's ministry was going to be short-lived. Churchill was not being offered the Leadership of the Conservative Party and so was only Prime Minister on sufferance in much the same way as Lloyd George had been from 1916 until 1922. Notwithstanding the brief Norway clamour, the majority of Conservative MPs were still loyal to Chamberlain. Halifax had no cause to think that that Thursday afternoon would be his last and only chance for the Premiership.

When Churchill entered the Cabinet room for the interview, it was only three days after he had had his 'spasm of fear' and had accused Halifax of 'high treason'. For him the meeting was all or nothing.

There are a number of differing accounts of what happened during the interview. By far the most famous is that given by Churchill eight years later at the end of the first volume of his history of the Second World War. In it he implies Halifax acquiesced out of embarrassment and contrition and only after a long silence in which the two wills clashed, Churchill's emerging triumphant:

> I have had many important interviews in my public life, and this was certainly the most important. Usually I talk a great deal, but on this occasion I was silent. Mr Chamberlain evidently had in mind the stormy scene in the House of Commons ... when I had seemed to be in such heated controversy with the Labour Party. Although this had been in his support and defence, he nevertheless felt that it might be an obstacle to my obtaining their adherence at this juncture.... As I remained silent, a very long pause ensued. It certainly seemed longer than the two minutes which one observes in the commemorations of Armistice Day. Then at length Halifax spoke. He said that his position as a Peer, out of the House of Commons, would make it very difficult for him to discharge the duties of Prime Minister in a war like this. He would be held responsible for everything, but would not have the power to guide the Assembly upon whose confidence the life of every government depended. He spoke for some minutes in this sense and by the time that he had finished it was clear that the duty would fall on me – had in fact fallen on me.[23]

In this version, in which Halifax is supposed to have lectured Chamberlain and Churchill 'for some minutes' on the most basic facts of the British constitution, Halifax almost blurts out his refusal, from embarrassment and politeness, and possibly in the vain expectation that Churchill would reciprocate. Sir William Deakin, Churchill's research assistant and fact-checker for the book, believes that Churchill was 'hamming up' his account of the interview, which, because of its dramatic qualities, has inevitably become the accepted version. 'The passage is typical of him,' says Deakin; 'he used to dictate and often from a source ... here it's Feiling's *Life of Chamberlain* ... he's being amusing, it's not to be taken seriously.' He chivalrously adds that Churchill's errors as to the date and time of the interview, and even in excluding Margesson from it altogether, were his rather than Churchill's fault.[24] Nevertheless, these lapses of memory must inevitably cast doubt on the accuracy of Churchill's account, which ought to be read as literature, rather than as a factual account of what actually took place. Churchill would frequently repeat the anecdote to Colville and others, adding elements of the tale as time went on, so that by the time he came to write it down a full eight years later it had acquired the barnacles of exaggeration which adhere to every well-sailed story.

The account Cadogan received that same afternoon and the one Halifax himself wrote up the next morning make no mention of this gladiatorial atmosphere to the meeting. It is altogether more believable, if less dramatic, than Churchill's:

> The PM, Winston, David Margesson and I sat down to it. The PM recapitulated the position, and said that he had made up his mind that he must go, and that it must either be Winston or me. He would serve under either.... David Margesson said that unity was essential and he thought it impossible to attain under the PM. He did not at that moment pronounce between Winston and myself, and my stomach-ache continued.
>
> I then said that I thought for all the reasons given the PM must probably go, but that I had no doubt at all in my own mind that for me to take it would create a quite impossible position. Quite apart from Winston's qualities as compared with my own at this particular juncture, what would in fact be my position? Winston would be running Defence, and in this connection one could not but remember how rapidly the position had become impossible between Asquith and Lloyd George, and I should have no access to the House of Commons. The inevitable result would be that being outside both these vital points of contact I should speedily become a more or less honorary Prime Minister, living in a kind of twilight just outside the things that really mattered. Winston, with suitable expressions of regard and humility, said that he could not but feel the force of what I had said, and the PM reluctantly, and Winston evidently with much less reluctance, finished by accepting my point of view.[25]

All the other available evidence, especially Cadogan's contemporary diary entry, tends to suggest that when Chamberlain once again asked Halifax, as the senior minister present, whether he would be willing to become Prime Minister, Halifax made an unprompted, immediate and sincere act of self-abnegation and went on to commend Churchill. As Churchill later told his Chief Whip James Stuart, 'For once I did not have to argue my case.'[26]

Neither Chamberlain's nor Halifax's letters or diaries mention a silence. Margesson, in correcting the proofs of a friend's book on 1940, approved the sentence: 'According to Margesson, the silence was in fact a short one, broken almost immediately by Halifax urging Churchill's greater fitness for leadership in war.'[27] Halifax sensed that the times called for giants. He drew the obvious parallel of the disastrous relationship Asquith had with Lloyd George in the Great War. The historian in him might just as easily have presented the far more felicitous Pitt–Newcastle partnership of an earlier age. Halifax's overt reason for refusing was not simply that he would not have access to the Commons. He also mentioned 'Winston's qualities as compared with my own *at this particular juncture* [author's italics]'. For the rest of his life he derived quiet amusement from the way Churchill agreed with his prognosis 'evidently with much less reluctance' than that shown by Chamberlain.

A year later Halifax told the story of the interview to his friend and Private Secretary Sir Charles Peake, by which time it had changed dramatically and came complete with the famous silence, 'which he did nothing to break', making an appearance for the first time.[28] In this account, Margesson did much of the talking and plumped for Churchill, after which Halifax agreed the whole country wanted him, and Churchill was supposed to have replied, 'Edward, Edward, allow me to congratulate you. You have spoken better than I have ever heard you.' This account ought to be seen in its context of the post-Blitz realization that Churchill had proved himself a success.

Churchill's accounts became ever more convoluted as time went by and Colville remembered one favourite version in which Chamberlain was supposed to have asked Churchill the trick question of whether he saw any problem with having a peer as Prime Minister.[29] The British Ambassador in Cairo, Sir Miles Lampson, recorded a different version given him 'in the greatest secrecy' by Cadogan in August 1942, in which Halifax, 'who really wanted the job', replied modestly and Churchill had brusquely insisted that he had the better qualifications.[30] Two similar versions appear in Robert Bruce Lockhart's diary in August 1942, one from Randolph Churchill and the other from Malcolm MacDonald. Randolph glorifies his father for bluntly telling Halifax that he wouldn't be captain of his own ship, while MacDonald asserts that Churchill said, 'There is only one possible Prime Minister and that is me.'[31]

The objectivity of all the later versions are highly suspect. All those written later than a week after the event took place – and especially that written over half a decade later – are, in this instance at least, next to useless as historical evidence for anything beyond establishing what the raconteur thought about the principal characters at the time of telling. Nothing can cast doubt on the central fact that with the ultimate political prize in his grasp, Halifax acted selflessly and put his country before his father's dreams and his own ambitions. A hitherto unpublished note which he wrote on Foreign Office paper from the Dorchester that same evening confirms his state of mind at the time. To Lady Alexandra Metcalfe, to whom he had during lunch that day explained the full situation, he wrote, 'My dear Baba, a line to tell you that I have hopes of things working out so that you will not be more frightened of me than you have hitherto! And at the same time procuring good broad results.'[32]

This was no piece of bravura from Halifax, who never once later expressed a word of regret for his decision. Writing on 13 May he told a friend, 'The instinct for self defence is so strong in all the lower animals! I simply don't think it would have been at all a tolerable position for me to get into,' and hinted that there were 'other reasons which I will give you when we meet'.[33] Talking to the historian Kenneth Rose in March 1952, he said that Chamberlain's plan to make him Prime Minister in 1940 'was a stupid idea for a variety of reasons'.[34]

Despite the interview on the 9th, Chamberlain had not given up all hope of persuading Labour to join his Government, and after the 4.30 p.m. interview Churchill and Halifax went outside to sit together in the garden and wait until Attlee and Arthur Greenwood arrived. The Labour leaders were then asked by Chamberlain whether they would serve under either the present Prime Minister or another. As the minority party they were not about to be allowed to choose which Conservative they preferred, but it is clear from statements made at the time that they would have been equally prepared to serve under either Halifax or Churchill. Returning to Bournemouth to consult their colleagues, they promised to telephone the answers as soon as they had arrived at a decision, but warned Chamberlain it was unlikely the Party would agree to serve under him.

In the meantime, at dawn on Friday, 10 May 1940, Hitler unleashed his *Blitzkrieg* on the West. He attacked Belgium and Holland in a bid to outflank the Maginot Line and deal a knockout blow to France. Halifax was woken at 6 a.m. with only enough time to digest the news before the Dutch Ambassador appeared on his doorstep for tea, sympathy and a message of support. Hard on the Dutchman's heels came his (recently deneutralized) Belgian counterpart. The attack did not come as that much of a surprise; in a letter which went out to all British missions less than a week before, Halifax had warned that it 'seems likely ... we are shortly to meet the full force of a German onslaught on ourselves'.[35] After Cabinets at 8 a.m. and 11.30 a.m. Chamberlain announced that he considered the new military situation to have so changed the political one as to justify postponing his decision to resign. At this point one of his closest supporters, Sir Kingsley Wood, who had the day before changed sides to back Churchill, bluntly told Chamberlain that he could no longer hold on to the Premiership. Samuel Hoare, whose political career depended on Chamberlain, noted that at that crucial moment, 'No one said anything in the Cabinet except me. Edward quite heartless.'[36] Halifax most probably felt, even if he was not so disloyal to say it, that the German attack made it more rather than less imperative for Chamberlain to hand over to Churchill.

Upon receipt of Labour's final decision not to serve under Chamberlain, one final effort was made to persuade Halifax to change his mind. Dunglass telephoned Channon to ask Butler to persuade Halifax to accept the Premiership. When Butler duly called round to Halifax's room in the

Foreign Office, he found the Foreign Secretary had gone to the dentist. Halifax's junior Private Secretary, Valentine Lawford, who was later blamed by Channon for not passing on the message, believes that he did, but Halifax 'brushed it off, in favour of going to see the dentist – as the easier course!'[37] Although Halifax did have to see the dentist twice in two months in late 1939, he would hardly have left the Foreign Office if he had been at all amenable to these last-minute approaches.

When Chamberlain went to Buckingham Palace, George VI 'accepted his resignation and told him of how grossly unfairly I thought he had been treated and that I was terribly sorry that all this controversy had happened. We then had an informal talk over his successor. I, of course, suggested Halifax, but he told me that H was not enthusiastic.... I was disappointed over this statement, as I thought H was the obvious man.'[38] Chamberlain's assertion put paid to Colville's and Butler's hopes for the 'unlikely chance of the King, who (remembering perhaps the Abdication) is understood not to wish to send for Winston, being able to persuade ... the unpersuadable Halifax'. Queen Mary even wrote to Colville's mother to encourage her to persuade her son not to serve under Churchill, and when Halifax met the King and Queen by chance in Buckingham Palace gardens the next day, 'The Queen spoke very strongly about the House of Commons behaviour. The King ... was clearly apprehensive of Winston's administrative methods.'[39] He told Halifax, 'I was sorry not to have him as PM.'[40]

Churchill kissed hands in the evening of 10 May, but the immediate political result of his coup was a backlash, which Cadogan called the 'morning after feeling', against him by the 'respectable' wing of the Conservative Party, who started to realize that the Conservative rebels and Opposition parties had stolen a march on them despite their vastly superior numbers in the Commons. The Secretary of the 1922 Committee, Maurice Hely-Hutchinson, told Butler on 13 May that he estimated three-quarters of the parliamentary party were willing to put Chamberlain back in power. Certainly when the ex-Prime Minister entered the Chamber that day it was to a roar of approval, whereas virtual silence from the Tory benches greeted Churchill's entry. This experience had such a salutary effect on the new Prime Minister that he stayed deeply conscious of his political weakness for almost the whole of 1940. Amongst friends he used to refer apprehensively to 'the louder cheer'. As late as July 1941, a full eight months after Chamberlain's death, Churchill felt it necessary to appoint George Harvie-Watt as his new Parliamentary Private Secretary to strengthen his connections with the Chamberlainites in the Commons.

After referring to Chamberlain's louder cheer in a letter to Baldwin on 14 May, the veteran political commentator J. C. C. Davidson wrote of Churchill, 'his appointments are heavily criticized in private ... the crooks are on top, as they were in the last war – we must keep our powder dry!' Halifax thought Churchill had been incredibly rough in his record of handling those he was going to drop! Merely a message through his secretary! And in two cases at least that I know the person concerned saw it in the paper or heard it on the wireless. I think even in war things should be done different to that. He's an odd creature.[41]

By 14 May, most of the new Government had been announced. Halifax was unimpressed with the new War Cabinet, which included Attlee and Greenwood in the place of Simon, Hoare and Kingsley Wood. His only comment was, 'Certainly we shall not have gained much in intellect.'[42] He found himself the colleague of a number of people, such as Beaverbrook, Dalton and Bracken, for whom he could barely conceal his distrust and dislike. 'It's all a great pity,' he said to Butler on the 14th, inviting the inevitable reply that that was because he had not taken the Premiership himself. Halifax snapped back, 'You know my reasons, it's no use discussing that – but the gangsters will shortly be in complete control.'[43] In a letter to Hoare – who had been unceremoniously sacked – Lord Hankey summed up what a great many in the Establishment were thinking: 'The only hope lies in the solid core of Churchill, Chamberlain and Halifax, but whether the wise old elephants will ever be able to hold the Rogue Elephant, I doubt.'[44] Halifax doubted too, but having sacrificed the highest political prize in British politics, he pledged himself to the task.

22

Churchill as Micawber

The Rogue Elephant was the first to acknowledge himself to be, in fact, a caged animal, the prisoner of Chamberlain's majority in the Commons. He wrote to Chamberlain on 10 May to say, 'To a large extent I am in your hands.'[1] Halifax received a similar letter, which thanked him for the 'chivalry and kindness with which you treated me', adding, 'with your help and Neville's I do not shrink from the ordeal'.[2] At the end of it, as a handwritten afterthought to the typescript, Churchill wrote, 'and you will of course lead the House of Lords'. Halifax had no intention of taking on such a time-consuming and tendentious commitment – a fact of which he thought Churchill was fully aware. It prompted him to remark to himself: 'I told him this was quite impossible and he must think again. I have seldom met anybody with stranger gaps of knowledge, or whose mind worked in greater jerks. Will it be possible to make it work in orderly fashion? On this much depends.'[3] Instead, Halifax advised Churchill to appoint Inskip, by then Lord Caldecote, as although the obvious candidate 'Bobbety' Cranborne was one of his 'greatest friends', Halifax felt 'he is apt to be a little petulant'.[4]

Churchill was not put forward as Leader of the Conservative Party as it was feared that to deprive Chamberlain of that post as well might have turned the Chamberlainite back-bench Tory resentment into open revolt. Churchill's coup was only precariously maintained and even during the Blitz he was keenly aware of how weak were his supporters and how strong his potential detractors in the 1935-elected House of Commons. It was not until much later in 1940 that his genius as a war leader made him politically secure. On 13 May, Halifax was already complaining at the way Churchill had kept the Cabinet up until midnight and 1 a.m. on the previous nights, 'but I hope we have cured him of that! I could not remain on such terms.'[5]

The spring of 1940, wrote Graham Greene in *End of the Affair*, 'like a corpse was sweet with the smell of doom'. The German breakthrough at Sedan on 14 May had been swiftly exploited and despite superior numbers of tanks the Allies were flung back in confusion. Nowhere could the front stabilize and, on 20 May, Hitler first scented victory when he heard that his advance columns had reached Abbeville and the Channel, trapping twenty British and French divisions north of the Somme. Military historians may debate where the blame for the débâcle should lie, but by 24/25 May the British Government had to face the prospect of total military collapse on the continent. French counter-attacks from the south were turned with ease by the Germans, whose reinforcements moved up quickly to capitalize on earlier successes.

Halifax's diary shows that he was in no way rattled or defeatist about the news. He took Churchill's admonitions to the Cabinet to keep up morale. Sir Llewelyn Woodward described how he and the Turkish Ambassador were in the FO just after France fell and met Halifax coming downstairs. 'He was perfectly calm and apparently unmoved.'[6] He was aided in this by the iron control he could exercise over his emotions which meant, as one old friend told his biographer, 'at times of great stress he was incapable of showing his pain or emotion'.[7]

After the failure of a major French push across the Somme, Halifax lamented on Saturday 25 May:

> I cannot see how we can hope to join over the gap. Meanwhile valuable time is slipping away and the mystery of what looks like the French failure is as great as ever. The one firm rock on which everyone was willing to build for the last two years was the French army and the Germans walked through it like they did through the Poles.[8]

That same day, the Chiefs of Staff circulated a top-secret memorandum to the Cabinet entitled 'British Strategy in a Certain Eventuality'.[9] That 'eventuality' – potentially too demoralizing even to be referred to by name – was the surrender of France and defeat of the British Expeditionary Force. The intelligence services suspected Germany would not even wait for the French capitulation before mounting an immediate assault on the British Isles.

The Chiefs of Staff's report concluded that Germany might crush British resistance by 'unrestricted air attack aimed at breaking public morale, starvation of the country by attacks on shipping and ports and occupation by invasion'. This came to Halifax, who was fully conscious of his own shortcomings in matters of strategy, as a shock and a spur. The Chiefs, estimating that 'it is impossible to say whether the UK could hold out in all circumstances', believed ultimate victory would 'depend entirely on Pan-American economic and financial co-operation'.[10] As Halifax knew that this was unlikely to be forthcoming, he that same day formulated an appeal to Roosevelt. The telegram was never sent, but the draft survived in the

Prime Minister's papers and illustrates the circumstances in which Halifax feared Britain could be forced to sue for peace. From its position in the Prime Minister's files, it was presumed by Valentine Lawford that the undated and unsigned document was written on 25 May.[11] In the controversy over peace proposals it also shows the way Halifax hoped Britain could escape her predicament with her independence, Empire and honour intact.

After a brief explanation to the President of the gravity of the military position, the draft made various prognostications as to what the future held. After the fall of France Halifax supposed,

> It would be natural for Hitler to say that he would include Great Britain in his peace offer but only on terms that would ensure our not taking revenge, which would leave this country entirely at his mercy and which we of course could not accept. There is of course the possibility that he on his side, and also Mussolini, may not wish to see indefinite continuance of a struggle with all the damage which, although we may be hit harder, it would still be in our power to inflict upon Germany and Italy.

At this point Halifax hoped Roosevelt would step in, suggesting,

> If you ... say to Hitler that, while you recognize his right to obtain terms that must necessarily be difficult and distasteful to those whom he defeated, nevertheless terms which intended to destroy the independence of Great Britain and France would at once touch the vital interests of the US, and that if such insisted upon, you thought it inevitable that the attempt would encounter US resistance, the effect might well be to make him think again. If you felt it possible in the event contemplated to go further and say that, if he insisted on terms destructive of British independence and therefore prejudicial to position of US, USA would at once give full support to GB, effect would of course be all the more valuable.[12]

With the prospect of total defeat looming, Halifax also hoped to resurrect the channel, which had proved helpful at the time of Munich and by which he had hoped to prevent war in September 1939. The approach to Mussolini was intended to run along similar lines as that to Roosevelt. The Italian Ambassador, Giuseppe Bastianini, was 'well-mannered, conciliatory ... not at all extremist'.[13] When Lord Phillimore met him on 20 May, he seemed enthusiastically in favour of a British approach to Germany via Rome. Phillimore informed Butler, whose notes emphatically state that, 'Hitler would listen to him [Mussolini] and him alone, even now.' It was believed that Mussolini was biding his time, looking for the best opportunity to declare war on the Allies. He had ignored a flattering appeal from Churchill of 16 May ('I declare I have never been the enemy of Italian greatness nor at heart the foe of the Italian law-giver'),[14] but in Cabinet on the morning of 25 May Halifax had more encouraging news. Vansittart had been approached by a Signor Paresci, the Press Attaché at the Italian Embassy, who intimated that a fresh approach would not be rebuffed. Churchill authorized Halifax to pursue the matter further, saying that he 'saw no objection to an approach of the character suggested' so long as it was not made public.[15] No mention was made of any German angle and Halifax rationalized his stance by saying: 'Very likely nothing might come of all this. Nevertheless, even if the result were merely to gain time, it would be valuable,' and as it was in line with French policy they 'would certainly be pleased'.[16]

But Halifax was always sceptical. As late as 23 May he had told Kennedy that Mussolini had no influence on Hitler, although this may have just been part of the effort to convince Roosevelt that if he wanted peace in Europe there was no real alternative to prompt and decisive American action. None the less, he met Bastianini on the afternoon of 25 May, ostensibly to attempt to work out a formula under which Mussolini could be persuaded to stay neutral. It was estimated that an Italian invasion of France would tie down at least ten French divisions in the south-east of France just when they were most needed against the Germans in the north-west. There were two totally different Allied plans for action with regard to Italy that were over the next three days to be constantly mixed up and confused with one another. To make matters worse, some politicians, including Halifax, later pretended to be referring to one when it was in fact the other, and after the war they denied the existence of one of the plans altogether. The first was the plan to bribe Mussolini to stay out of the war and the second a scheme to attempt to persuade him to intercede with Hitler to procure reasonable terms for a permanent cease-fire. The two were, of course, mutually contradictory; the first being designed to facilitate the more successful waging of the very war which the second was intended to bring to an end.

It is clear from the account of the Bastianini conversation which Halifax sent to Sir Percy Loraine, the British Ambassador in Rome, that, in however roundabout a way, discussion of the neutrality option soon turned into consideration of the mediation possibilities. Halifax requested that Mussolini act as an honest broker at a conference to revise Versailles. In the crucial passage of the despatch Halifax said he told Bastianini, 'I had always thought, if any discussions were to be held with a view to resolving European questions and building a peaceful Europe, that matters which caused anxiety to Italy must certainly be discussed as part of a general European settlement.'[17] The term 'matters which cause anxiety to Italy' was diplomatic language for her demands for various outposts such as Suez, Gibraltar, Malta, Tunis and Djibouti. She was also thought to be casting covetous glances in the direction of British Somaliland, Algeria,

Corsica, Uganda and even Kenya. 'Signor Bastianini then said that he would like to know whether HMG would consider it possible to discuss general questions involving not only Great Britain and Italy but other countries.' Halifax answered: 'It was difficult to visualize such wide discussion while the war was still proceeding.' To which Bastianini replied that, 'once such a discussion was begun, war would be pointless.'[18]

Halifax went on to tell the Ambassador 'that Britain and France would never be unwilling to consider any proposal made with authority that gave promise to a secure and peaceful Europe'. With German forces rampaging through the open French and Benelux countryside, this statement could only mean Mussolini's pressure on Hitler to offer reasonable peace proposals. Bastianini agreed with Halifax that his master would have 'an absolutely vital part to play' and 'was always ready to help in securing a wider European settlement because he saw the solution of Italian problems only within the framework of the solution of all the problems of all other European countries'.[19] It is obvious which other European country was being referred to; indeed, if, as was later claimed by Halifax and others, this conversation was solely concerned with keeping Italy neutral, that statement would have been so banal as to be virtually meaningless.

The Whig in Halifax saw war as a means of obtaining specific and limited objectives. Just as the dynastic wars of previous centuries were fought over territories such as Alsace-Lorraine or Nice and Savoy, so he believed Hitler's victory at Sedan could be rewarded by certain concessions, with Mussolini picking up the odd *pourboire* for good behaviour. He had seen from the Great War what damage was done both to victors and vanquished by total war. The demand for 'unconditional surrender' from Germany was not adopted as policy until 1943. Until then it was taken for granted that the war would end through some sort of negotiated settlement. Wars fought for ideas, in which nations exhausted themselves and risked their own extirpation in pursuit of the enemy's annihilation, were completely alien to Halifax's nature. Hitler had clearly won the first round in what could be a decade-long struggle, and it seemed only common sense to Halifax to attempt to obtain at least a breathing-space along the lines of the Treaty of Amiens. If this could save the British Expeditionary Force and much of France, so much the better.

If such a peace had to be bought at the price of some colonies, Mediterranean possessions, French overseas territory and maybe the de jure ratification of Hitler's de facto conquests in the east, Halifax saw the deal as potentially worth looking into. Churchill likewise, although partly in order to keep as much of his War Cabinet with him as possible, expressed his willingness to examine a peace along those lines. What neither of them would for a moment consider was a situation in which Britain lost her navy, air force, Empire, independence or ability to wage war in the future. To this (distinctly un-eighteenth-century) threat Halifax was totally firm, thereby incidentally proving baseless accusations that he was willing to 'surrender to Hitler'.

Halifax differed from Churchill over a number of points which provided the conjectural basis for the debates in the War Cabinet over the next four days. Churchill said that he believed that America would soon be providing vital aid over the coming months. In fact, no American declaration of war came or really even looked like coming until after Germany had declared war on America in December 1941. No significant aid arrived in Britain until after she had proved she was going to survive. The timing of this crisis could not have been worse for Britain, coming as it did six months before the Presidential elections, in which both candidates vied with one another to distance themselves from the suggestion that American boys might be sent to die in foreign wars.

Churchill's hope, which Halifax also shared, that the German home front was shaky was also impossibly optimistic. The Nazi hold on German public opinion was probably stronger in May 1940 than at any point before or after. The blockade, on which British strategists had pinned a good deal of their hopes during the Phoney War, was no longer viable, now that Germany was able to call on supplies from Brest to Vladivostok. With Italy about to declare war, the British Expeditionary Force near capture and Paris in chaos, there was little that the Allies could offer Hitler which he was not already in a position to take. As can be seen from his draft telegram to Roosevelt, Halifax hoped that Hitler might consider peace in order to avoid a bruising and indefinite continuation of hostilities.

Any peace terms, Halifax reasoned, were more likely to be acceptable with France still in the war, the British Expeditionary Force at liberty and the Allied aircraft production factories still intact. He considered that if negotiations were to be conducted at all, the sooner they started the better any likely terms would be. Churchill felt precisely the opposite. He believed that Hitler had to be shown he could not invade Britain and that better terms were more likely to be won only when that had been proved. His superior feel for Hitler's psyche made him realize that until the Führer had either avenged Versailles or met sufficient resistance, he would not be open to reasonable discussion. He probably knew that the grounds he gave his colleagues for optimism – about the likelihood of an American declaration of war, the level of expected American aid, the German home front, the blockade, the effects of bombing on enemy morale, the French army, the comparative strengths of the RAF and the Luftwaffe, and even the weather – were demonstrably thin, but he also knew that Halifax provided no viable alternative.

Churchill's superior grasp of history let him put his faith in a combination of a short stretch of water and the sheer bloody-mindedness of the British people. Almost all the rational arguments were on Halifax's side and even though Churchill, for the reason of the effect it would have on

British morale as much as any other, was right to block his plans, he had no alternative strategy for winning the war. As it stood the war was unwinnable and insofar as Churchill had any policy as Britain went into the Blitz, it was that of Mr Micawber hoping to survive until 'something turned up'. Without Hitler's Himalayan blunders of declaring war on both Russia and America in 1941, the war might well have stayed unwinnable for Britain.

Although Halifax considered his interview with Bastianini to have been 'not unsatisfactory', Cadogan's Private Secretary, Gladwyn Jebb, heard later that afternoon from Signor Paresci that because Halifax had brought no specific proposals and avoided giving 'geographical precision' as to exactly what the Italians could expect to pick up, the interview had 'raté' (miscarried) completely. At 11.15 p.m. that night, Halifax saw Jebb and sent him back to Paresci to try to create a better impression.[20]

On Sunday 26 May, just as the Halifaxes were getting ready for church, No. 10 called to say that the French Prime Minister was making a surprise visit and there would be a 9 a.m. Cabinet. At that meeting Halifax reported his conversation with Bastianini, adding, 'we had to face the fact that it was not so much now a question of imposing a complete defeat on Germany but of safeguarding the independence of our own Empire and if possible that of France'.[21] Tientsin, his own Viceroyship and the experiences of the last war had left Halifax keenly aware of the strains that already existed in the overextended and hard-to-defend Empire. He correctly surmised that another long war would sound its death knell. After a service at Westminster Abbey, Halifax lunched with Chamberlain and they returned together to the Cabinet scheduled for 2 p.m. There Churchill reported his lunchtime conversation with Paul Reynaud, who had painted the blackest of pictures. With fifty French divisions facing 150 German, the French commander, General Weygand, did not think resistance could last much longer. Churchill suggested that Halifax go over to keep Reynaud company at Admiralty House, where he, Chamberlain and Attlee followed shortly afterwards.

Reynaud's memoirs allege that he went to London to get certain concessions 'in order to prevent Italy falling on us'.[22] In fact, according to Chamberlain's diary, 'Reynaud said Mussolini might find in the enquiry a proposal for a European settlement.'[23] 'European Settlement' became the standard linguistic formula for an approach to Germany. Halifax agreed, saying that Mussolini should be reminded that an Allied collapse could not be good for Italian independence, 'but if he would use his influence to get reasonable terms which did not menace our independence and offered a prospect of a just and durable settlement of Europe we would try and meet his own claims'.[24]

Reynaud, who had earlier said he was willing to offer Mussolini Tunis and Djibouti, said that any approach would be useless without 'geographical precision'. Churchill was highly sceptical, but did say that 'if we could get out of this jam by giving up Malta and Gibraltar and some African colonies he would jump at it. But the only safe way was to convince Hitler he couldn't beat us.' Halifax 'argued there could be no harm in trying Musso and seeing what the outcome was. If the terms were impossible we could always reject them.'[25] This seemingly eminently sensible approach was, in fact, deeply fraught with danger. Halifax must have realized that there would be enormous harm in approaching Mussolini had the British public somehow found out. The damage it could do to morale might have been so great as to make it hard for Britain to reject terms when they arrived. It was also assuming much of Mussolini, that he had enough influence over his fellow dictator to dissuade Hitler from fulfilling his dream of avenging Versailles. Hitler's view was that Mussolini might be a Roman, but his people were Italians.

The escape from Dunkirk was helped immeasurably by Hitler's decision to halt his Panzers on a high ridge to the west of the city at noon on 24 May and not give them orders to move off until 1.30 p.m. on the 26th. This failure utterly to crush the British Expeditionary Force had no link with peace negotiations but was an operational decision emanating from Hitler's need for reinforcements, desire to give the troops some rest after a fortnight's solid campaigning and fears of a trap in Dunkirk. It took the German High Command some time to realize from intercepts and aerial reconnaissance that the British were intending to quit the field altogether, a process which began on 26 May.

When the time came for Reynaud to leave, Churchill was forced to sum up that 'we would try to find some formula on which Mussolini would be approached but we must have time to think'.[26] When Reynaud got back to France, he told his colleagues that only Halifax understood the situation. After his departure the fifth and last member of the War Cabinet, Arthur Greenwood, was sent for. Cadogan and a secretary turned up a little later to attend the continuing discussion on the Italian proposals. The meeting was 'rather jumpy', with so many secretaries entering and leaving with messages that Halifax likened the atmosphere to that of Waterloo Station.[27] Churchill was evidently as keen as Halifax not to give Reynaud any reason to lose heart, even though, as Chamberlain believed, 'it was plain from his attitude that he had given up all serious thought of fighting'.[28] Halifax's own stance was almost as pessimistic as Churchill's; 'I do not myself think it will do any good,' he wrote of the proposed approach to Rome in his diary on 26 May, 'but I do not want to give the French an excuse for complaining.'[29] The French angle was a constant factor militating against outright rejection of either plan.

The minutes of the meeting, which lasted until 6 p.m., show Churchill fearful that any terms would prevent Britain from completing her rearmament programme. This prompted Halifax to reiterate that if that was the case they could always be rejected, but it would not be 'in Herr Hitler's interests to insist on outrageous terms. After all, he knew his own internal weaknesses. On this lay-out it might be possible to save France from the wreck. He would not like to see France subjected to the Gestapo.'[30] Greenwood 'saw no objection to this line of approach being made to Signor Mussolini'.[31]

In the opinion of Greenwood and Chamberlain, Mussolini was probably 'out to get' all or some of Malta, Gibraltar, Suez, Somaliland, Kenya and Uganda. Halifax thought this an excellent reason for not giving 'geographical precision' to which territories would in the end be handed over. He did repeat his view that 'if we got to the point of discussing the terms of a general settlement and found that we could obtain terms which did not postulate the destruction of our independence, we should be foolish if we did not accept them'.[32] The War Cabinet invited Halifax to draw up a draft of his projected communication with Italy for consideration at the next meeting.

That afternoon Halifax circulated the memorandum, entitled 'Suggested Approach to Mussolini'.[33] This purported to represent Reynaud's proposal for 'a direct approach to Mussolini'. Close examination of the vocabulary used, which matched word for word the language Halifax had employed in the previous Cabinet, the Bastianini interview and his own diaries, show how the memorandum was principally composed of Halifax's own ideas. It was a blueprint for the Italian mediation option:

> If Signor Mussolini will co-operate with us in securing a settlement ... we will undertake at once to discuss, with the desire to find solutions, the matters in which Signor Mussolini is primarily interested. We understand that he desires the solution of certain Mediterranean questions: and if he will state in secrecy what these are, France and Great Britain will at once do their best to meet these wishes.[34]

Considering the support he gave the mediation plan even before Reynaud's visit of 26 May, it was misleading for Halifax constantly to portray the approach as being solely due to the 'insistence' of Charles Corbin, the French Ambassador. His diary was intended for circulation among family and close friends and was often slightly coy or even disingenuous for that reason. At the 11.30 a.m. Cabinet meeting on Monday 27 May, Halifax announced that King Leopold of the Belgians was considering suing for a separate peace, which would result in a bare left flank for the British Expeditionary Force. The day before, the Chiefs of Staff reported that 'supposing Germany gained complete air superiority' and 'if with our navy unable to prevent it, and our air force gone, Germany attempted an invasion, our coast and beach defences could not prevent German tanks and infantry getting a firm footing on our shores. In the circumstances envisaged above our land forces would be insufficient to deal with a serious invasion.'[35] They also predicted that should the Luftwaffe press home its night attacks on Coventry and Birmingham, it would be able to bring work in the aircraft production factories to a standstill. As for bombers, they added, 'numerically the Germans have a superiority 4 to 1'.[36] Churchill vigorously disputed these gloomy figures and had a more sanguine set drawn up. He argued that the overall ratio was closer to five to two and, with the RAF shooting down German planes at a rate of roughly three to one, 'the balance was on our side'.[37]

At dinner the previous evening Churchill had taken great pains to convince Halifax that the war in the air could be won, enlisting Beaverbrook to impress Halifax with the extent of the air rearmament programme and Lindemann to cast doubt on the Air Ministry's figures. It has been pointed out that as Churchill's concern over the figures for aircraft numbers did not affect the military position and as they were not for publication, they could have no propaganda value: 'Churchill was trying to influence those who were aware of the figures, and most likely the Foreign Secretary in particular.'[38]

When at the 11.30 a.m. Cabinet Halifax brought up Lothian's latest telegram from Washington, in which the Ambassador mooted the idea of buying American goodwill by the cession of various British territories in the Western hemisphere, Churchill made a remark very different in tone from the supplicatory telegrams he was sending Roosevelt and the generous references to America in his speeches. 'The United States', he said bitterly, 'had given us practically no help in the war and now that they saw how great was the danger, their attitude was that they wanted to keep everything which would help us for their own defence.'[39] Ciano's meeting that day with the American Ambassador in Italy saw Roosevelt's appeal to Mussolini turned down flat. Ciano commented unequivocally of Il Duce, 'it is not that he wants to obtain this or that; what he wants is war, even if he was to obtain by peaceful means double of what he claims, he would refuse'.[40]

London could not know Ciano's private views and, after the long morning session, the Cabinet had to be resumed at 4.30 p.m. for further consideration of the proposed Anglo–French approach. For this item the five-man War Cabinet was augmented by Sir Archibald Sinclair, the Air Minister, in his capacity as Leader of the Liberal Party. Churchill had cunningly included Sinclair on the grounds that the issue required all-party agreement. Sinclair, who had served in Churchill's battalion in the Great War, was known to be a keen, if somewhat sycophantic, supporter. Using Halifax's memorandum of 26 May as the basis for their deliberations, the conversation soon turned into a wide-ranging and hard-hitting argument between Halifax and Churchill. In his diary Halifax called it 'a long and rather confusing discussion about, nominally, the approach to Italy, but also largely about general policy in the event of things going really badly wrong in France'.

The French Ambassador in Rome had ignored Halifax's strictures against giving any 'geographical precision' and specifically mentioned to Ciano that Tunisia and Algeria were available to Italy. But by then it was too late. Chamberlain had changed his mind overnight and come out against the plan. Sinclair was against it altogether, as were Attlee and Greenwood. Churchill thought the approach 'futile' and put forward a compromise which was politically astute enough to command the allegiance of both Chamberlain and the Labour and Liberal members. He proposed to wait for two to three months until the situation was clearer. In the words of the Cabinet minutes, Halifax then spoke of certain 'rather profound differences of points of view which he would like to make clear'.[41] In his own diary Halifax put it more frankly: 'I thought Winston talked the most frightful rot, also Greenwood, and after bearing it for some time I told them exactly what I thought of them.'[42]

Halifax wanted a declaration from France that they would fight to the end for their independence and to use this as a bargaining chip against the Germans. Secondly, 'He could not recognize any resemblance between the action proposed, and the suggestion that we were suing for terms and following a line which would lead us to disaster.'[43] He leapt on Churchill's admission of the day before that he 'would be thankful to get out of our present difficulties on such terms, provided we retained the essentials and the elements of our vital strength, even at the cost of some cession of territory'. Halifax took advantage of Churchill's attempt to be as moderate as possible, the better to sell his policy to the War Cabinet, and in particular to carry Chamberlain with him.

The War Cabinet debates of 25 to 28 May 1940 have too often been portrayed as a supine Halifax willing to make a craven peace versus a heroic Toby Jug Churchill confident of final victory. Close examination of the evidence shows them to have been nothing of the sort. They were actually conducted between an ultra-rational Halifax hoping to get authorization to obtain peace terms that were in no way destructive of British independence and the yet more realistic Churchill who would not mind hearing or even accepting reasonable terms, but who wanted to do nothing to solicit them for fear of the effect it would have on morale. Churchill implied that he was not fighting so much for victory as for better terms in the near future.[44]

Halifax accurately assessed Churchill's plan, which as the Chiefs of Staff's report of the day before showed, 'meant that the future of the country turned on whether the enemy's bombs happened to hit our aircraft factories'.[45] He added yet again that 'he was prepared to take that risk if our independence was at stake; but if it was not at stake he would think it right to accept an offer which would save the country from avoidable disaster'.[46] Halifax was angry at the way Churchill twisted and misrepresented his arguments; it was on this as much as on the peace issue that he then issued a resignation threat, and said of Churchill and Greenwood that, 'if that really was their view, and if it came to the point, our ways would separate'.[47] He was incensed by the way Cabinets, which were designed for sober and mature reflection, had instead to hear harangues in which romanticism and illogicality vied for the upper hand.

The hyperbole which did so much to stiffen the public morale in 1940 struck Halifax as melodramatic and best reserved for public broadcasts. He had heard it all throughout his political life and it smacked to him of the histrionic and dangerous posturing which illustrated all the famous Churchillian lack of judgement. To those immune to Churchill's aura, the exuberance and childlike enthusiasm were reminiscent of nothing so much as Toad of Toad Hall. Halifax was keenly aware that the imminent onslaught probably spelt the end of Britain's Empire and way of life and he also – probably wrongly – thought it may have been avoidable. To read the Chiefs of Staff's horrific prognostications was bad enough without having one member of the nation's highest deliberative body giving spirited impressions of Harry at Harfleur. Halifax's constant repetition of his utter opposition to capitulation was totally genuine, but he saw nothing particularly heroic in going down fighting if it could somehow be avoided. Cadogan, who had been in at the last hour of the meeting the day before, also found Churchill 'too rambling and romantic and sentimental and temperamental'.[48]

Halifax had considered resignation in the past. Cadogan had thought him near it at Munich; it was one of Halifax's favourite refrains to say that if anyone else thought they could do his job any better they were welcome to it. Just before the Norway debate, he had told a friend that should Chamberlain be forced to resign, 'he will go too, as he identifies himself with his policy, so how could he remain?'[49] He had repeated the assertion on 13 May after Churchill had called two late-night Cabinet sessions. But his threat on 27 May had a strong effect on Churchill, who could not afford to see his Government so publicly, swiftly and fundamentally split, especially on what was bound to be publicly perceived as the issue of peace or war. Of course Halifax knew this too, rendering the exercise more of a warning shot than a serious intention to go.

On reception of the threat, Churchill 'surprised and mellowed'[50] and made a concession: 'If Hitler was prepared to make peace on the terms of the restoration of German colonies and the overlordship of Central Europe, that was one thing. But it was quite unlikely that he would make such an offer.'[51] Pressing home this advantage Halifax asked whether, if Hitler offered such terms, Churchill would be prepared to discuss them. In order to avoid seeming intransigent, Churchill was forced to reply that 'he would not join France in asking for terms; but if he were told what the terms offered were, he would be prepared to consider them'.[52] Both men agreed that Britain would not send a delegate to meet Hitler should Paris fall and that 'the issue which the War Cabinet was called upon to settle was difficult enough without getting involved in the discussion of an issue which was quite unreal and was most unlikely to arise'.[53]

After this Cabinet Halifax asked to see Churchill in the garden of No. 10 for a private talk. He there repeated his resignation threat and Churchill 'was full of apologies and affection'.[54] Returning to tea at the Foreign Office, Halifax was urged by Cadogan not to 'do anything silly under the stress' of Churchill's penchant for rhetorical flourishes and historical allusions, which, Cadogan assured him, 'probably bore you as much as they do me'.[55] Two days later, Cadogan noted in his diary on a different issue: 'WSC rather theatrically bulldoggish. Opposed by NC and H and yielded to a reasonable extent. Fear relations will become rather strained. This is Winston's fault – theatricality.'[56] However much annoyance he had shown, though, Halifax had no intention of resigning. Indeed, the more Churchill hectored, the more convinced he was of the necessity for him to stay. Eventually he contented himself with confining his exasperation to his diary: 'it does drive me to despair when he works himself up into a passion of emotion when he ought to make his brain think and reason'.[57]

23

'Foredoomed to Failure'

At a meeting of the full Cabinet at 10 p.m. that Monday 27 May, Churchill announced the imminent capitulation of Belgium. Calais had fallen and the Chief of the Imperial General Staff said that the British Expeditionary Force was in 'the most serious peril'. By the time the War Cabinet reconvened at 11 a.m. the next morning, Tuesday 28 May, the Belgians had surrendered and although 11,400 British soldiers had been rescued, a quarter of a million men were trapped. Admiral Sir Roger Keyes warned the Cabinet both of the efficiency of German bombing in breaking Belgian resistance and the RAF's inability to pierce the German fighters' protective shield. Churchill read out the Draconian terms Germany had imposed on Belgium and conveyed the intimation that equally unreasonable ones might be expected for Britain. This sense of futility was further strengthened by Halifax's news that Mussolini's response to the Roosevelt approach, which had run along roughly Anglo-French lines, had been 'entirely negative'.[1]

It was thus in an atmosphere pregnant with the sense of impending doom that the War Cabinet met at 4 p.m. on the 28th to reconsider the Italian option, insofar as it still existed. The Ministry of Information was fearful that the public might panic: there were rumours of an immediate invasion via Norfolk and Eire, Mosley had been arrested, crackdowns on anti-war activity and potential fifth columnists were implemented, and plans were laid to evacuate the Royal Family and the Bank of England's gold to Canada. Further to exacerbate matters, Lothian had telephoned at 2.10 a.m. the day before to report a distinctly unhelpful conversation with Roosevelt, who, 'thinking aloud', had said that 'if things came to the worst' the Royal Navy should be prevented from falling into German hands by sailing to Canada, whereas the Royal Family should go to Bermuda as 'the American republics may be restless at monarchy being based in the American continent'.[2] Far from the potential saviour Churchill publicly portrayed him, the American President was beginning to look like a shifty pawnbroker sorting through the remnants of the British Empire to see which items caught his eye.

Despite the ever-gentlemanly tone of the minutes, there can be no doubt that the debates of 27 and 28 May were conducted in a tough, heated and gladiatorial atmosphere, principally between Halifax and Churchill, who sat directly opposite one another across the Cabinet table. If during the relative peace of the Phoney War Churchill had accused Halifax of 'high treason', it is reasonable to assume tempers got frayed when the very existence of the Empire was at stake. When the War Cabinet met in the Prime Minister's room in the House of Commons at 4 p.m. on the 28th, it was the fifth time the subject had been discussed in three days. Positions had hardened against the proposal.

Halifax again repeated his formula that 'we should be prepared to say that we were prepared to fight to the death for our independence, but that, provided this could be secured, there were certain concessions that we were prepared to make to Italy'.[3] This was illogical and had either Halifax or the Cabinet minutes been more intellectually honest they would have added 'and Germany'. Churchill reiterated his belief that any talks constituted a 'slippery slope'. He wanted Britain to think about peace terms only after the German invasion had been repulsed.

At no point was Churchill so incautious as to prophesy ultimate victory over Germany; he merely argued for a 'wait and see' policy in the hope that after two or three months of fighting better terms might be forthcoming. Halifax profoundly disagreed with this hypothesis, believing that terms would be better with France still in the war, however precariously, the British Expeditionary Force free and the Allied aircraft production factories unbombed. The debate was not a moral clash between resister and defeatist but rather a sharp disagreement between different perceptions of the present and future state of likely negotiating strengths. Churchill's course did carry with it the possibility of ultimate victory should Hitler blunder, but also the more likely spectre of national annihilation.

Sinclair and Attlee, though silent during much of the earlier discussion, now sided with Churchill; Chamberlain had long since given up hope for Italian mediation but wanted the rejection phrased in such a way as to give the French minimum disappointment. Halifax was unable to see the harm which could be done by listening to the German terms, whilst fully appreciating that there was little Hitler could want that he was not in a position to take. He failed sufficiently to take into account the devastating effect suing for peace would have had on the morale of the British public, let alone the problems in resuscitating that morale and resolution if negotiations broke down. Churchill estimated the chances of receiving reasonable proposals as a thousand to one against. It was Chamberlain's summing up against pursuing the scheme 'at the present time', although accepting that the climate might change 'even a week hence', that led the Cabinet, with Halifax's dissent but with no formal vote taken, to reject what was still euphemistically termed 'Monsieur Reynaud's' plan.[4]

It was not until after Halifax had already been outgunned that Churchill pulled the coup which completely outmanoeuvred him and laid to rest any serious possibility of peace negotiations for the rest of 1940. The meeting adjourned at 6.15 p.m. for Churchill to meet those ministers not in the War Cabinet. War Cabinet ministers held these meetings regularly (Halifax called them 'Children's Hour') and took it in turns to appraise the ministers of developments, but Churchill had called this one specially. Speaking to the twenty-five of them, Churchill summoned up all his powers of rhetoric and gave one of the great virtuoso performances of his career. Several of his listeners, such as Duff Cooper, Cranborne, Lloyd, Beaverbrook and Amery, largely owed their positions to him, while others such as Dalton and Kingsley Wood were more recent additions to the Churchillian fold. After his oratorical performance, about the fighting at Dunkirk and the prospects for Britain, and his final flourish that, 'We shall go on and we shall fight it out here or elsewhere, and if at last the long story is to end, it were better it should end not through surrender but only when we are rolling senseless on the ground,'[5] none but the most hard-bitten cynic could fail to applaud.

It is likely that they knew something of the disagreements in the War Cabinet and with Churchill's speech aimed directly against talk of peace it is reasonable to assume that most ministers would have guessed that was in part what the speech really referred to. Dalton certainly had an inkling; in his account of the meeting he blamed Chamberlain ('the Old Umbrella') for wanting 'to run very early'.[6] The Churchill peroration painted a bright picture of Britain's chances of survival, did not dwell on the Chiefs of Staff's report and was calculated to appeal more to the heart than the brain. The ministers were bound to applaud even if some, like Sir John Reith, found the speech 'dramatic, unreal, insincere'.[7]

What Churchill did not do was present an accurate picture of Halifax's position, which was not for 'surrender'. Instead, he portrayed a Britain which sought terms as a 'slave state ... Hitler's puppet ... under Mosley or some such person', even though this was precisely the outcome Halifax had all along sought to avoid. His sanguine remarks about the likelihood of early American involvement were starkly at odds with his more honest assessment to the War Cabinet of the day before. Nothing had happened in the subsequent twenty-four hours to justify Churchill's comment to the ministers outside the War Cabinet that the USA 'might even enter the war' should Britain be seen to stand alone.[8]

When the rest of the War Cabinet – none of whom had been at the meeting – reassembled at 7 p.m., Churchill played up the enthusiastic reception he had received, rubbing it in to Halifax that 'he did not remember having ever before heard a gathering of persons occupying such high places in political life expressing themselves so emphatically'.[9] At this, and in view of Chamberlain's change of heart, Halifax gave up the unequal struggle and only briefly mentioned the plan in his diary as 'perfectly futile after all that has been attempted'. The 'wait and see' policy, which was quite distinct from 'victory at all costs', had won. Churchill's telegram to Reynaud that night said that, 'without excluding possibility of an approach to Signor Mussolini at some time, we cannot feel that this would be the right moment'.[10]

It is not surprising that Halifax's stance has been misinterpreted so widely since May 1940 as even at the time there were those who thought, with John Colville, that 'there are signs that Halifax is being defeatist'.[11] The jittery and highly strung mood of a Whitehall attempting to come to terms with disaster accounts for a good deal of this suspicion, for which there is no other evidence. The same day Colville wrote of his 'defeatism', Halifax himself was writing to Beaverbrook and Morrison pointing out seven 'striking examples of misdirected effort and waste' in Britain's war effort and calling for immediate remedial action on issues as diverse as replacing male with female official chauffeurs and the combating of private extravagance and waste. A 'defeatist' would hardly have bothered to press for the calling up of all non-skilled workers under forty years of age or investigations into the efficiency of government sub-contracting.[12]

The motives ascribed to Halifax by his detractors have been faint-heartedness, a continuing fondness for appeasement, a desire to protect his property, cowardice and even incipient treachery. The real reason was that he believed it was not too late to cobble together a deal that might have left intact the Allied armies in the field. There was nothing ignoble about the desire to safeguard Britain's Empire and independence. Only later in the war did Hitler take on the fully diabolical image as the incarnation of evil, to countenance parley with whom was blasphemy. Until June 1940, the BBC still referred to the dictators as *Herr* Hitler and *Signor* Mussolini.

Churchill's instincts proved correct. Halifax had attempted to bring logic and reason to a problem long since devoid of either. A truce would only have led to another conflagration, probably within the decade and with a Germany in possession of radar, rockets and possibly even nuclear weaponry. Halifax was right to think that there was nothing particularly patriotic in adopting a 'death or glory' attitude if the odds were on the former, any more than there was anything treacherous about attempting honourably to shorten a war Britain was clearly losing. As it had been the Italians who had made the first intimations, it was understandable that Halifax should have erroneously believed that Mussolini was amenable to suggestions.

Intelligence reports continued to encourage the belief that the Nazis were suffering from a degree of popular opposition to the war within Germany which simply did not exist. The German nation was proud of their victorious army's seemingly unstoppable advance and was enthusiastic to avenge 'the humiliation of 1918'. Halifax was also wrong in thinking that France's continuation in the war was vital, or even necessarily advantageous, for Britain. In fact, she was to prove so much a dangerous drain on resources, especially in the air, that when France finally surrendered, Air Chief Marshal Dowding actually went down on his knees and thanked God.

The collapse of France led to a seismic shift in Britain's war aims. For all Churchill's broadcasts – which still never fail to bring a lump to the throat half a century later – survival rather than victory had to be the aim. In his confidential communication to ministers of 29 May (incidentally the first day Halifax carried a gas-mask), Churchill wrote only of the Government's decision 'to continue the war till we have broken the will of the enemy to bring all Europe in his domination'.[13] Peace terms could always be entertained once the invasion had been repelled. Britain had gone to war for Poland, but any plans for restoring freedom and independence to Poland and Czechoslovakia were shelved, as it so turned out, for ever. The Prime Minister's telegram to the Dominions of 27 May was even more circumspect, saying of the decision to 'carry on fighting' that 'this view is of course without prejudice to consideration of any proposals that might hereafter be put forward for a cessation of hostilities and subject to developments in the military situation'. This is distinctly not so ringing a phrase as 'victory at all costs' or 'We shall fight on the beaches'.

To see this critical period in the black and white of the treacherous Halifax versus a heroic Churchill is simplistic and unhistorical but, partly one suspects because of the British predilection for blame and betrayal, it is this perception which has survived to impugn Halifax's patriotism to this day. The Micawber 'wait and see' policy lasted all summer. Britain waited for five years and saw final victory, albeit at appalling cost, and ruin for her standing in the world.

In October 1942, Sir Orme Sargent wrote to Halifax about the way the events of 25 to 28 May 1940 ought to be portrayed in Sir Llewelyn Woodward's official history of the war. Halifax, who as early as February 1941 had shown disquiet about this, replied with a staggering lack of candour. He asserted, 'There was certainly never the idea in the mind of HMG then or at any time of asking Mussolini to mediate terms of peace between them and Germany,'[14] and went on to imply that it had been solely neutrality from Italy and never mediation with Germany that had been the subject of the Bastianini conversation and subsequent Cabinet discussions. Taking advantage of the refusal to grant 'geographical precision', Halifax insinuated that the most Britain had been willing to offer Italy was a seat on the board of the company which administered the Suez

Canal. 'The Holy Fox' could hear the hounds baying for his reputation, but he could lay only the faintest of false trails.

He was not alone. Churchill wrote in *Their Finest Hour* how, 'Future generations may deem it noteworthy that the supreme question of whether we should fight on alone never found a place upon the War Cabinet agenda ... we were much too busy to waste time upon such academic, unreal issues.'[15] In fact, future generations might find it just as noteworthy that there were five meetings, some of which went on for as long as four hours, solely on that very subject. Indeed, it would have been an astonishing and disgraceful dereliction of the Cabinet's duty to safeguard the Empire if there had not been.

An internal Foreign Office memorandum commenting on Sir Percy Loraine's post-mortem of the affair shows how Halifax set out to minimize the issue only a matter of days afterwards: 'The short point seems to be that all our efforts during recent weeks were foredoomed to failure: but I don't think that the ambassador would suggest that their failure has done much harm, would he?' he asked. Referring to the encouragement given to Roosevelt to contact Mussolini, Sargent answered, 'On the contrary it would have done harm in the USA if we had not made these efforts.'[16] Loraine had included the statement that 'Historians ... may approve the generous gesture, but as a step in the conduct of the war I think it is a mistake.'[17] He was undoubtedly right about seeing it as a mistake, but woefully wrong about the way most historians have so far interpreted the affair.

24

'Common Sense and Not Bravado'

Rarely can a Cabinet decision have been so swiftly vindicated as that of 28 May 1940. The very day after Churchill's rejection was telegraphed to Reynaud, Halifax heard from Loraine that Italy was preparing to declare war forthwith. Ciano had added that Mussolini would not even be deflected by the offer of Tunis, Algeria and Morocco. The news coincided with that of the wonder of the Dunkirk evacuation. On 30 May, some 77,000 men were reported to have been saved and in the following five days over 300,000, virtually the entire British Expeditionary Force, were brought home to man the defences of Britain, albeit without any of their heavy equipment. Halifax was as astounded as anyone by Dunkirk, which he thought 'must have been exactly like Cowes Regatta in the dark'.[1]

The Cabinet of 1 June saw Halifax abandon his conciliatory approach to Mussolini. He proposed that Ciano be told that on the Italian declaration of war, RAF bombers would start the devastation of the industrial regions of northern Italy. He also suggested Mussolini's son-in-law be informed that Air Commodore West, the former Air Attaché in Rome who had 'intimate knowledge' of the targets, would be put in command of the bomber force. Halifax used the opportunity to inform the Cabinet of his talk with Joseph Kennedy about a plan to acquire a number of American destroyers. The claim which Churchill later broadcast – that the Destroyers-for-Bases deal were two simultaneous and largely unrelated expressions of each nation's high regard for each other – was a useful fiction to hide some very tough transatlantic bargaining.

Chamberlain proved as loyal to Churchill as Churchill had been to him. Although the Labour Party and some Conservative rebels had blocked him from the Chancellorship of the Exchequer, he was found many diverse tasks as Lord President of the Council – from setting up various secret service offshoots to broadcasting reassuring statements about the chances of invasion. With his record for untimely remarks, any prediction from him which deprecated the chances of invasion should have had any reasonable person out into the garden burying the silver. Halifax continued to provide constructive criticism. Sometimes he would be driven almost to despair by the Rogue Elephant. 'I have never seen so disorderly a mind,' he told his diary on 30 May; 'I am coming to the conclusion that his process of thought is one that has to operate through speech. As it is exactly the opposite of my own it is irritating.'

For the rest of May and throughout the first half of June 1940, the British Government was subjected to harrowing appeals from the French for more air support for the Battle of France. Since 14 May, Air Chief Marshal Sir Hugh Dowding had opposed Reynaud's pleas for more fighters and he was soon supported by the Air Minister Sir Archie Sinclair. By 2 June, Halifax found himself in the van of the movement, supported by the Air Ministry and the Chiefs of Staff, to send only the barest minimum across the Channel. 'Winston would like to send more than the air experts agree,' wrote Colville,[2] and it took until 8 June for the experts, supported by Halifax, to persuade the Francophile and ever-optimistic Prime Minister not to allow any more than eight out of the fifty-three RAF fighter squadrons to stay in France. Halifax once again took the expert advice, correctly recognizing that every plane lost in France was one less to fight the fast-approaching Battle of Britain.

Returning from a snatched weekend at Garrowby, his first in months, Halifax discovered that Mussolini, like a hyena looking to scavenge from the kill but not participate in it, had declared war from midnight on 10 June. The naval Staff at once asked whether they could start sinking Italian shipping before that time, to which Halifax 'without any hesitation' assented.[3] The Italian news was offset by Sir Robert Craigie's success in signing an agreement in Tokyo which ensured peace in the Far East.

On 13 June, Halifax flew with Churchill to Tours for what turned out to be the last meeting of the Supreme War Council. There he found nothing but chaos and incompetence: 'Streets and roads packed with refugees, motor cars and mattresses, people sitting about forlornly in the street and pouring with rain. A pretty desolate scene.'[4] At that meeting Reynaud painted a picture of the fall of France which for one of those present, General Edward Louis Spears, 'evoked the pathetic, rather sordid police photograph of a murder'.[5]

Spears's superb account of the meeting tells how

Halifax, immensely tall, debonair, thin and loose-limbed, seemed interested in things happening above our heads ... his long figure curled like a question mark.... His good hand ... was under his chin, his mouth slightly open. His general attitude conveyed as it always does an impression of extreme courteousness and attention. His expression seemed slightly tinged with scepticism. I thought this was how this

High Anglican would listen to a sermon on modern miracles in a Roman Catholic church.

But Reynaud had no miracles to report. When he begged for France to be released from her 28 March obligation not to make a separate peace, Churchill refused and, according to Spears, 'Even Halifax, like the dove in spring, assumed a livelier hue.'

The British delegation then went out into the garden and there 'Beaverbrook and Halifax at once expressed complete support for Churchill'.[6] After walking three abreast around the tiny garden of the Tours prefecture for twenty minutes, the British delegation returned to the table. Churchill told Reynaud, who was probably hoping that Halifax would moderate Churchill's position as he had on 26 May, that his views 'were certainly shared by the whole British Government' and advocated French guerrilla action in metropolitan France and then continued resistance from Algeria. 'At all events Britain would fight on. She would not alter her resolve: no terms, no surrender. The alternatives for her were death or victory.'[7] It is possible that Halifax was specifically taken along to that meeting to prove to Reynaud that there really was no other view in the British Government to which he could look for salvation.

Back in London the next day, Halifax saw the Dominion High Commissioners, who wished to discuss the peace offer Hitler was widely expected to be about to make. He told them that their plan to encourage the United States to guarantee the results of any peace conference was 'almost inconceivable, and that if it did take shape it would mean that for his own reasons Hitler wanted a settlement, which would also mean that there would be reasonable time to consider what seemed to me at present a totally unreal hypothesis'.[8] He then went over to No. 10 to tell Churchill what had passed. This is simply not a man about whom conspiracy theorists would have one believe that he was, only three days later, plotting to contact Berlin behind Churchill's back to look for a peace offer.

On 17 June, what had always been referred to in secret papers as 'A Certain Eventuality' (presumably without consideration of the ambiguity attached to the word 'certain') came to pass and France finally collapsed. The First World War hero, Marshal Pétain, replaced Reynaud as head of the French administration. Pétain's appointment of the Anglophobe Admiral Darlan as the Naval Minister excited British fears that the powerful French navy might fall into German hands, with disastrous results for the Royal Navy's primacy. At noon on 17 June, hopes that Pétain might continue the struggle from abroad were dashed by his announcement that he was staying in France and suing for peace.

Some time that afternoon or early evening while out walking in St James's Park, Butler quite by chance met the Swedish envoy in London, Björn Prytz. Prytz was an honest and popular figure in London diplomatic circles, a businessman who knew Britain intimately and who had been Sweden's minister since 1938. Talking over the dangerous turn events had taken, Butler invited Prytz back to his room in the Foreign Office to continue the conversation. There is nothing suspicious either in their original meeting – people used to come across one another in the Park with great regularity – or in the fact that Butler took no notes of the conversation, as he did when speaking to foreign diplomats, for this was purely an informal conversation. However, the report of the conversation Prytz sent back to Stockholm at 8.20 p.m. that evening set in train a series of events that was to excite suspicions which exist to this day.

Prytz telegraphed to his country's Foreign Minister, Christian Gunther:

> Britain's official attitude will for the present continue to be that the war must go on, but [Butler] assured me that no opportunity for reaching a compromise would be neglected if the possibility were offered on reasonable conditions and that no 'diehards' would be allowed to stand in the way in this connection.... During the conversation, Butler was called in to see Halifax, who sent me the message that 'Common sense and not bravado would dictate the British Government's policy.' Halifax added that he realized such a message would be welcomed by the Swedish Minister, but that it should not be interpreted as 'peace at any price'. It would appear from conversations I have had from other members of parliament that, if and when the prospect of negotiations arises, possibly after 28 June, Halifax may succeed Churchill.[9]

The crucial sentence ascribed to Halifax – 'Common sense and not bravado will dictate the British Government's policy' – was not relayed in Swedish but in English because Prytz had made a note of the exact words. Much has been made of the telegram, with conspiracy theorists seeing in it a treacherous attempt to obtain peace terms behind Churchill's back and Butler apologists trying to explain it away in terms of a misinterpretation of what Butler had really said. In fact, the conversation was a candid assessment from Butler of the way he viewed the 'wait and see' policy of 28 May, combined with a shrewd look at the weakness of the 'half-breed American' Churchill's coalition. Halifax's summons of Butler was entirely coincidental and his message, if message it was, was not meant as a hint to Stockholm to initiate peace feelers in Berlin.[10]

Prytz's telegram arrived in Stockholm at an unfortunate time. The Swedes were under great pressure from Germany to allow their transport facilities to be used to send armaments to German forces in Norway. The very day after the telegram arrived in Stockholm, Ribbentrop made a particularly threatening demand along those lines. The Swedes later blamed the telegram for their pusillanimity over the transport concession, and reasoned that if Britain did indeed seek peace, she would not be in any position to punish Sweden for her blatantly non-neutral transit arrangements.

Instead of making discreet enquiries in Berlin, the Swedish Foreign Minister proceeded to advertise the Butler conversation to his Cabinet colleagues, the Foreign Affairs Committee and the Swedish ambassadors in five European capitals. He also sought further explanation from Sir Victor Mallet, the British minister in Stockholm, who was understandably mystified by the whole affair, coming as it did only hours after Churchill's defiant 'Finest Hour' speech. Mallet reported Gunther's version of Prytz's telegram back to Halifax on 19 June and asked for further instructions. The next day Halifax drafted a telegram to Mallet in his own hand, which he was careful to get counter-signed by Butler and approved by Cadogan. In it he denied that any hint was intended and put the blame squarely on Prytz for exaggerating any 'polite message' and mistaking 'courage and wisdom' for 'common sense and not bravado'.[11] There the affair might have ended had not two members of the Swedish Foreign Affairs Committee leaked a garbled version of the story to the Stockholm correspondent of the *News Chronicle*.

Although Mallet managed to get to the journalist in time, it was felt that Butler ought to meet Prytz again to agree a common line. They met on 21 June, but did not discuss what had actually passed between them at the original meeting four days before. The *News Chronicle* leak in no way vitiated the statements in Prytz's original telegram, it merely served to cloud the issue. It is fatuous to suppose, as so many have done, that the Prytz affair was an attempt to engineer a peace offer behind Churchill's back which only fell apart due to Gunther's cack-handedness. The evidence for this consists of a still-secret telegram to Stockholm of 17 June, a restricted item in the War Cabinet agenda for 18 June (a Cabinet Churchill could not attend as he was writing the 'Finest Hour' speech), and Cadogan's diary entry for that meeting, which reads, 'No reply from the Germans: French situation still uncertain.' In fact, it is clear from the rest of Cadogan's sentence after the colon that the 'no reply' from the Germans referred to the French call for an armistice rather than any British attempt to elicit peace terms. Anyway, Cadogan could hardly have expected to receive Berlin's terms the very next morning after Prytz had telegraphed, especially with a third party involved.

So Prytz's remarks were not intended as a British peace feeler, but neither can they be explained in terms of the Swede misinterpreting what Butler had said. Prytz's mother was British and he had been educated at Dulwich College, spending much of his working life in Britain. He was, above all, a painstaking and ethical Anglophile diplomat. It must be concluded that Butler was being indiscreet; under the pressures of what has rightly been described as the blackest day in British history, he had had 'loose talk' with a sympathetic neutral. He certainly was not reported as saying anything which he did not probably then believe. Butler's commitment to the war had always been only lukewarm: in October 1939, he had attempted to tone down Chamberlain's unequivocal refusal of Hitler's peace offer; in March 1940, he wanted a truce with Germany; and in May, he was the minister most hostile to Churchill's elevation to the Premiership.

Butler had a tendency to fly verbal kites, especially with those foreigners, such as Prytz, with whom he was in close and regular contact. A colleague of Butler's in 1940 remembers how 'Rab was addicted to ambiguous remarks . . . it was very often deliberate . . . he made revealing and very often injudicious comments in order to extract responses from his listeners. He was disarmingly frank so as to provoke replies.' There were also examples of similar indiscretions in his conversations with the Romanian and Egyptian Ambassadors.[12]

Retribution for this ill-timed conversation was swift. Churchill, to whom all Foreign Office telegrams were sent and who also received intercepts of the Swedish Embassy's telegraph traffic to Stockholm, wrote to Halifax on 26 June that, 'it is quite clear to me from these telegrams and others that Butler held odd language to the Swedish minister and certainly the Swede derived a strong impression of defeatism'.[13] Churchill would, from the outgoing Prytz telegram, have also seen the phrase 'Common sense and not bravado' which had been attributed to Halifax.[14] The letter was therefore as much a warning shot across Halifax's bows as Butler's. Halifax moved quickly and showed Butler the letter from Churchill. He elicited from Butler a long, handwritten letter of part-explanation and part-apology, which was a masterpiece in blame-shifting, obfuscation and special pleading.

In this letter Butler claimed a very different conversation had taken place from that recorded by Prytz. He said he had told Prytz that 'force must be met by force'; he apologized to Halifax ('I should have been more cautious') and asked for his mercy ('I now place myself in your hands').[15] The part of the letter that is most intriguing and difficult to explain was his interpretation of the 'common sense' comment which had been attributed to Halifax: 'You might enquire why any conversation with a Foreign Representative took this line at all and why I was reported as saying that "Common sense and not bravado would dictate our policy".' But he did not answer his own question, preferring instead to imply that because Prytz agreed he had said it was in Sweden's interest for the war to end, Prytz had exaggerated the import of his remarks. Butler, Halifax and Churchill all knew that the Prytz telegram had said that it had been Halifax who had made the 'common sense and not bravado' statement. Why then should Butler, in a letter to Halifax, have sought to exonerate Halifax of it? Despite Butler's best efforts, the phrase itself cannot be misinterpreted: it was a clear intimation to a neutral that should the situation deteriorate Britain would be open to offers. Equally, Churchill personified the 'bravado' approach as completely as Halifax could be said to stand for 'common sense'.

Butler's alternative explanation of the meaning of the phrase is utterly risible. 'I certainly went no further in responding to any neutral soundings than the official line at the time,' he claimed in his memoirs in 1971, 'which was that peace could not be considered prior to the complete withdrawal of German troops from all conquered territories. That was common sense, not bravado.'[16] The most likely explanation for Butler's assumption of personal responsibility for the phrase may have been that it had been he who had put the words into Halifax's mouth. Upon his return from Halifax's office to resume his conversation with Prytz, and erroneously believing that he knew Halifax's mind on the subject, Butler chose to emphasize his remarks by giving substance to what Halifax had only believed was going to be a 'polite message' to Prytz.

The other alternative was that Butler was Halifax's stooge all along and, in tacit return for protection from Halifax, Butler was indeed attempting to obtain terms for the War Cabinet in such a way as to avoid seeming to have done so. Had this been the case, the apologetic letter Butler wrote would have been a complete fraud, an insurance policy to cover Halifax in the event of a refusal by Churchill to accept Butler's apology. However, on 20 June Prytz telegraphed Gunther specifically informing him that the contents of his original telegram were not to be passed on to Berlin, something he would not have done had Butler originally been trying to elicit a German response.

There was never much love lost between Butler and Halifax, who had clashed more than once in the months before war broke out over Butler's support for Chamberlain's ultra-appeasement. Butler wrote a characteristically readable but snide essay on Halifax in *The Art of Memory*, while Halifax neither mentioned Butler in his autobiography nor ever invited him up to Garrowby. He certainly received precious little thanks from Butler for his protection over the Prytz affair. Only a month later, Butler told a journalist that 'he thought Halifax himself would very soon have outrun his period of usefulness'.[17] Charles Peake, who was close to Halifax, told Dalton in November 1940 that Halifax would like to make Butler a governor of an Indian province as he 'would be glad to get rid of him'.[18] Nevertheless, in June Halifax decided to shield Butler over the Prytz affair because, however embarrassed and annoyed he may have felt at having had the 'common sense and not bravado' soubriquet attributed to him, he knew that were Butler forced to resign for 'defeatism' it was certain that questions would be asked about his role which Mallet's original telegram would make hard to answer. His protection of Butler from Churchill's wrath has been put down to loyalty, sympathy and kindness, but one suspects another motive was self-defence.

So Halifax wrote to Churchill saying that the meeting between Butler and Prytz of 21 June had cleared the matter up to his satisfaction and that he could be sure of Butler's discretion and loyalty. Churchill magnanimously let the matter drop, although Butler did not long outlast his master's tenure at the Foreign Office and was shifted to the non-sensitive post of President of the Board of Education in July 1941. The issue returned to embarrass Butler, and to a lesser extent Halifax, at regular intervals over the next two decades. This was if anything exacerbated by an attempted Foreign Office cover-up which was deemed necessary both to protect Butler's reputation and because, as Christopher Warner, head of the Foreign Office's Northern department told Mallet in December 1944, 'Our stoutheartedness when we stood alone is such a tremendous asset to our prestige in the world – and is likely to remain so.'[19]

Gunther was keen to use the telegram as a mitigating circumstance to explain his transit concessions to the Germans. Thus he mentioned it in a speech to a large banquet in October 1944, to Mallet's considerable chagrin. The issue re-resurfaced on 6 July 1946, when Robert Hankey, Warner's successor, refused the Swedish Government the right to publish twelve documents relating to the affair as 'it seemed to me quite unfair to publish these diplomatic misunderstandings casting such unpleasant reflections on Mr R. A. Butler, Lord Halifax and the Foreign Office in general'. Unsurprisingly, Butler, by then a leading figure in the Conservative Party, wrote to say that he had no complaints about Hankey's 'suppressing the conversation of 17 June'.[20] The Foreign Office position was that Prytz had either consciously or unconsciously misrepresented Butler's remarks. It is hard to see what Prytz could gain from wanting consciously to do so; the telegram was, according to the Swedish historian of this incident, 'the odd man out among the reports he sent to Stockholm, at the time', all the others of which had emphasized the British determination to fight on.[21]

The worst that can be said of the affair was that Butler, who could hardly as a junior minister attempt to elicit peace terms on his own authority, did not share Churchill's Manichean view of the war. He had been accurately reported whilst indulging his habit of thinking aloud and was only guilty in claiming that he was speaking with Halifax's authority. Not having been present at the 25 to 28 May War Cabinet meetings, Butler was behind the times, for though Halifax's message was Delphic, polite and slightly coy, he was no longer seriously interested in the pursuit of a negotiated peace with a Hitler-led Germany. The wholehearted support Halifax gave the Prime Minister at Tours and his diary entry for 17 June show how far Halifax had come since the Cabinet imposed the 'wait and see' policy on him back in late May. On the very day Butler saw Prytz, Halifax was writing that he thought Churchill was 'right in feeling that if we can, with our resources concentrated, hold the devils for two or three months there is quite a chance that the situation might turn in our favour. Anyhow for the present, at least, there is no alternative.'[22] On the evening of 17 June, he dined at the Literary Society, where, according to fellow diner Geoffrey Dawson, he 'opined that, having touched bottom, we should now begin to rise'.

A phrase that has dogged Halifax, and is unfailingly trotted out by detractors to point to his desire for a cease-fire, is 'sublime treachery', which was used by 'Chips' Channon about Halifax in his diary on 3 June 1940. Seen in its context, it should be clear that the treachery Channon referred to was aimed at his heroes Chamberlain and Butler, not at Britain, Churchill and the decision to fight on against Hitler. After meeting the Halifaxes in Palace Yard when they were on their way to visit Queen Wilhelmina, Channon 'stopped to gossip' as was his wont.

> As I walked away I reflected on Halifax's extraordinary character; his high principles, his engaging charm and grand manner – his power to frighten people into fits – me sometimes – his snobbishness – his eel-like qualities and, above all, his sublime treachery which is never deliberate, and, always to him, a necessity dictated by a situation. Means are nothing to him, only ends. He is insinuating, but unlovable.

This is classic bitchy Channon bemoaning Halifax's supposed 'sublime treachery' not, as has so often been alleged of his country, but of the ex-Prime Minister and Under-Secretary at the Foreign Office whom Channon made no bones about worshipping.

Another entry in Halifax's diary for 17 June is equally pugnacious and devoid of defeatism: 'If only we could find out for certain where Hitler and Mussolini are meeting tomorrow, and get one well-placed bomb, then the world might really take on a different appearance.' One group of people who were under no illusions about Halifax's stance on the subject of peace talks were the Nazis themselves. In 1942, Hitler told Martin Bormann that he regarded Halifax as 'a hypocrite of the worst type, a liar,' and Goebbels in his diary railed against 'this bigoted itinerant preacher, who, after the western offensive, declined the hand which the Führer stretched out to him on behalf of peace'.[23]

25

Churchill's Guardian Angel

The most extraordinary phenomenon to emerge from the June 1940 collapse was the proposal that Britain and France should merge to form a single state. Privately entertaining grave doubts about the practicalities, Halifax appreciated the value of 'some dramatic announcement which might strengthen M. Reynaud's hand'. He authorized Vansittart to draw up a 'Declaration of Union', which he then presented to Cabinet. It postulated an offer to the French to form one 'indissoluble union' of the two countries and empires. It was transmitted to Bordeaux only hours before Reynaud resigned and was rejected out of hand by a suspicious and resentful French Cabinet. As well as a desperate British attempt to keep France in the frame, the proposal was also an ingenious device to allow the Anglo-French Purchasing Board in Washington to divert American supply ships from French to British ports. Halifax showed himself willing to embrace this imaginative if slightly ludicrous plan, despite being personally 'not enthusiastic' about the implications should it ever come off.[1]

The schizophrenic policy Britain pursued towards France for the rest of 1940 allowed the Churchill–Halifax double-act to perform at its best. The Prime Minister blustered, threatened and broadcast to Vichy in his execrable French, whilst seeming to be staying above negotiating with the errant collaborationist power. All the time he was fortified by the knowledge that his Foreign Secretary was straining to keep the best possible relations with their erstwhile allies. As Halifax put it two days after Reynaud fell, 'The whole thing is in such confusion that there seems to me no particular difficulty in hunting several lines at once.' Thus he instructed the consular corps 'not to do anything to encourage dissident or independent action' in metropolitan France at the same time as allowing General Charles de Gaulle to broadcast a call to arms over the BBC.[2] Halifax recognized that although policy was 'terribly disorganized', he could take advantage of the contradictions hoping simultaneously to stimulate

238

resistance in the French colonies and stiffen Pétain in his dealings with Germany.

The first and most intractable problem was the French fleet stationed at Oran and Casablanca. Halifax found it 'the most teasing problem I have ever had to deal with. None of the pieces of the jig-saw fit.'[3] The biggest pieces of the puzzle were the *Richelieu* and *Jean Bart*, two of the world's most powerful battleships which the Admiralty and Government feared could tip the balance against the Royal Navy in the Mediterranean. 'Everyone all over the place', complained Cadogan on 22 June, 'and WSC endorses any wild idea.'[4] Article 8 of the Armistice Pétain signed that day provided for the eventual handing over of the fleet into German and Italian control, ostensibly to be 'demobilized and disarmed'. For the British Cabinet this was out of the question and Admiral Sir James Somerville in the Mediterranean was instructed to put to his French counterpart, and until recently his comrade in arms, a range of alternatives.

The confusion in French minds is epitomized by the sailors' reactions when the British authorities seized French ships in Plymouth and Portsmouth: some fought back at the same time as others applied for British citizenship. Despite strenuous efforts to reach a conclusion without bloodshed, the War Cabinet was finally forced to decide on 27 June to sink the French fleet, which was only partially successfully effected on 3 July at the cost of over 1,200 French lives. This caused repugnance in the navy and Halifax found it 'perfectly hateful' and a 'beastly business', although he fully supported it, thinking that on balance Vichy would not declare war. It was hailed as a great victory by a Parliament and country desperate for news of any victory. Vichy contented itself with breaking off diplomatic relations, although informal contacts were maintained, principally via Sir Samual Hoare's Embassy in Madrid.

Hoare had been the sole scapegoat in the May change of government and with Halifax's full support Churchill had exiled him to Madrid. The sitting Ambassador, Sir Maurice Peterson, was recalled (to his enduring chagrin) to make way for Sir Samuel. Peterson's avowal that Halifax offered him Moscow fully in the knowledge that the post had really been reserved for Sir Stafford Cripps may have been true – Halifax certainly talked to Cripps about Russia as early as 3 May and he did not see Peterson until the end of the month – but the decision to remove Peterson from Spain had anyway been taken back in April.[5]

Hoare's time in Spain, partly because of his appeasing background but also because Madrid was a nodal point for the intrigues, spies and rumours of wartime Europe, has been the focus for endless myths and plots implicating him. He took the job under the impression, fostered by Halifax and connived at by Churchill, that he would probably become the next Viceroy, but in the event he stayed in Madrid until 1944. His letters to Halifax and Butler were not full of the incipient treachery of which he was accused. Instead, he merely whined about his unpopularity at home, the Spanish climate and food, the dangers of assassination, revolution, German invasion and how unfairly he had been treated. Hoare kept all the messages congratulating him on his peerage in July 1944. There were letters from his accountants and the constituency lawn tennis association, but precious few from any British politicians.

Halifax supported all Hoare's efforts to keep Spain neutral. The principal weapon in this was the blockade which the Royal Navy imposed on mainland Europe. Halifax saw the blockade as a flexible and fairly sophisticated policy tool. As he put it to Hoare, 'we must adapt the application of the blockade to special circumstances ... we must also use it constructively as well as negatively'.[6] Halifax was alive to the advantages of having starving populations in enemy territory; he answered the French Ambassador's plea of 14 June 1940 for Britain to take in large numbers of the six million war refugees in southern France by stating the cruelly obvious fact that, 'from a blockade point of view, it was more advantageous to us that these millions should stay where they were'.[7] Halifax believed in a gentle application of the blockade if it achieved the objectives of keeping Spain out of the war, countering German propaganda and allaying humanitarian sentiment in America. Because a good proportion of the supplies came from the United States, it also meant that the unpopular practice of Royal Navy warships stopping and searching American merchantmen could be kept to a minimum.

On 21 June, Hoare considered the likelihood of a Spanish declaration of war so imminent that he proposed handing over Gibraltar after the war in return for a promise of Spanish neutrality. He reasoned that should Spain come into the war, Gibraltar would soon fall anyway. Halifax supported this, but Churchill neatly turned the argument on its head and pointed out that 'if we win, discussions will not be fruitful; and if we lose, they will not be necessary'. Halifax stuck to the theme whilst all the time dissuading Churchill from taking any precipitate action which might either alienate the Spaniards or encourage the Germans to march through Spain in order to close the Mediterranean at the Straits. In late September, he proposed that the worst effects of the blockade be lifted. This brought him up against Hugh Dalton, whose Ministry of Economic Warfare organized it and who saw blockade solely in terms of a sledgehammer with which to smash Germany. Churchill, not for the first time using his Foreign Secretary to propose schemes he himself supported but with which he did not wish to be identified, sided with Halifax on the understanding that no promises be made concerning Gibraltar. Dalton observed that in proposing to 'discuss' Gibraltar after the war, 'Halifax ... was unanimously overruled, a thing I have seen happen before'.[8]

General Ismay used to say that Churchill had twenty ideas a day of which five were good. For example on 10 May 1940, on top of dealing with the emergencies of the German attack and his assumption of the Premiership, Churchill suggested to the Cabinet that the ex-Kaiser, then living in Holland, be invited to defect to Britain. Nothing came of this, although Halifax approved it, because the Kaiser would not concur, but it does show the incessant fertility of Churchill's brain. Equally, recognition should be accorded to those, such as Halifax, Ismay and others, who undertook the vital if somewhat thankless task of laying to rest the fifteen ideas a day which were duff. It should be perfectly possible to do this without either decrying Churchill's indispensable achievement or under-emphasizing the degree of unanimity that existed on most of the major Cabinet decisions in 1940. It is sometimes too tempting for historians to magnify dissent and to look for controversy where only debate existed. There was certainly enough opportunity for this; in the ninety-two days between 1 May and 31 July 1940, the War Cabinet met a total of 108 times.

Halifax played an invaluable part in dissuading Churchill from wildcat schemes and in cloaking Churchill's U-turns with his own reputation. He acted somewhere between Churchill's lightning conductor and his guardian angel. They had a wary but symbiotic professional relationship. When on 22 July the Cabinet discussed capturing the Portuguese-owned Azores and Cape Verde islands if 'the exercise of economic pressure by control at source or control of shipping failed to achieve adequate results',[9] Halifax persuaded his colleagues to take no irreversible decision and said that 'reasons of economic pressure' were insufficient justification for attacking the possessions of a neutral.[10] Churchill's rejoinder that 'Portugal might conceivably accept the situation under protest' seemed to hark back to his attitude towards the likely reactions of Eire and Norway under similar provocation. Earlier that month Halifax had been successful in preventing Churchill blowing up the one good road across the Sahara so as to protect British West Africa from Vichy forces, correctly calling the plan 'premature'.[11]

At times Halifax's rejoinders irritated Churchill, and he did not mind letting Halifax know, even to the extent of barbed reminders of the Foreign Secretary's earlier delinquencies on the subject of rearmament. When on 26 May 1940 Halifax questioned the decision to recall eight of the ten battalions in Palestine, and pointed out the damage it would do to security in the region, treaty commitments to Turkey and efforts to ensure Italian neutrality, he also appreciated that the defence of the British Isles had to take precedence. Churchill explained that Indian troops would be replacing the regular British units stationed in Palestine and sent back a bristling reply:

I consider I have a large measure of responsibility as Minister of Defence for advising the Cabinet upon the main groupings and development of our forces. If France goes out of the war it will be largely because we are unable to make anything like the military effort which we made in the first year of the last war. The moment the invasion danger has been parried, it will be indispensable to try to build up a new and stronger Expeditionary Force. For this I must have all the regular British cadres. I hope I may be given some help in this, and be allowed to view the War situation as a whole.[12]

There was never any question, however much advice, encouragement and warning Halifax may have given, who was in overall control of the direction of the war.

A problem that required almost as delicate handling as relations with Vichy was the coaxing of the Duke and Duchess of Windsor back to safety, first from France, then from Spain and Portugal. Although the telegrams to Hoare, most of which are not available for public inspection until 2016, were in Halifax's name, the negotiations were conducted by Churchill. Halifax distanced himself as far as possible from the increasingly bitter and farcical situation that developed as the Duke set conditions under which he would be willing to return. At one point the Duke requested a Scotland Yard detective be sent out to protect him against what he believed to be a British plot against him. Halifax fully concurred in Churchill's policy and was relieved when, in accordance with the King's wishes, the Windsors were finally packed off to the Bahamas on 1 August. This was no dereliction of duty on Halifax's part, so much as a sensible arrangement by which Churchill, who had far greater authority and sympathy with them, dealt directly with the suspicious and temperamental couple.

By early June, the political atmosphere had continued to move so drastically along the lines presaged in the Norway debate that the Labour Party felt itself strong enough to orchestrate a campaign against the 'Men of Munich'. The decision was taken to launch an attack at the forthcoming secret session of Parliament intended to secure the resignations of Chamberlain, Inskip, Halifax, Kingsley Wood, Butler and Simon.[13] This was to be accompanied by a press onslaught on the former appeasers, or 'the Old Gang'. On hearing this news, Chamberlain went at once to Churchill, who agreed to take action to prevent it. Chamberlain then spoke to Halifax, who, he thought, 'is innocent and doesn't read the papers and was unaware that there was any serious intrigue against me'.[14] In fact, the Lord President probably mistook lack of knowledge for a lack of concern, for as Halifax wrote to Hoare, such intrigues 'leave my withers quite unwrung'.[15]

After the 6 June Cabinet, Churchill exhorted Sinclair, Attlee and Greenwood in the interests of national unity to stop the 'heresy hunt' against the previous Government. They reluctantly agreed and the next day Chamberlain remarked in his diary that the campaign had been 'turned off like a tap'.[16] There was a degree of resentment among Labour journalists who had begun to scent the appeasers' blood, and in an argument with the journalist David Keir, Greenwood accused the *News Chronicle* of 'high treason', which prompted Keir to counter that 'certain Labour ministers were now so friendly with their traditional enemies that they were in danger of being swept out of office in due course with them'.[17]

This period elicited one of the few examples of conscience-searching Halifax ever exhibited. After the Labour leaders agreed to call off the press campaign, Halifax noted:

> The truth is that Winston is about the only person who has an absolutely clean sheet. Both Labour and Liberals have to share with the Conservatives the responsibility of being late with rearmament by reason of the great part they took in creating the atmosphere in which Stanley Baldwin, though I think wrongly, not unnaturally felt a large bill for rearmament was not politically practical.[18]

Coming from one of Baldwin's former War Ministers, this shows wisdom after the event.

Churchill did not wait before exacting a price from Chamberlain and Halifax for his support. He asked their permission to invite his old friend Lloyd George into the Cabinet. Chamberlain, though unimpressed, raised 'no final objection', and in one conversation with him Halifax went so far as to say that he 'did not think we need fear Ll. G. – who would perhaps be a helpful brake on Winston'.[19] Discussing the matter with Churchill, Halifax suggested that he establish whether Lloyd George 'had the root of the matter in him' by asking him to agree to the proposition that 'any peace terms now, or hereafter, offered must not be destructive of our independence'.[20] Lloyd George refused, ostensibly because he would not serve with Chamberlain and Halifax. It could be that he was not willing to accept Halifax's formula or it is just as likely that he intended, as months later he told his private secretary, to 'wait until Winston is bust' before making his move.[21] For his part Churchill told Chamberlain 'that he himself distrusted Ll. G.'[22]

On 5 July, Gollancz published *Guilty Men*, a vituperative polemic by three Beaverbrook employees, including Michael Foot. Despite being banned by W. H. Smith and Wyman's, it sold 200,000 copies and went into literally dozens of reprints by December 1940. Although Halifax was numbered amongst the dozen so-called Guilty Men responsible for the British Expeditionary Force's defeat in France, he was not mentioned in the text. It was a vicious piece of propaganda which called for the sacking of all the former appeasers (except, of course, their own employer). Colville believed Churchill 'would never countenance' sacking 'the Old Gang' 'unless he considered them incompetent, and he does not'.[23] On 26 July, Churchill explained to W. P. Crozier that 'I owe something to Chamberlain, you know. When he resigned he could have advised the King to send for Halifax and he didn't.' He went on categorically to deny that 'Chamberlain and

Co.' were 'a brake on his wheel'. Although any Prime Minister struggling to maintain cohesion in a coalition would be likely to profess this to a journalist, there is plenty of evidence to suggest that Churchill valued the political experience and personal loyalty of 'Chamberlain and Co.' highly. He also harboured an exaggerated sense of his own political weakness and never forgot who had got 'the louder cheer'.[24] This was certainly fully appreciated by Butler, who boasted to a friend at the time, 'all we have to do is pull the string of the toy dog of the 1922 Committee and make it bark. After a few staccato sentences it becomes clear that the Government depends upon the Tory squires for its majority.'[25] Part of the explanation for Halifax's unwrung withers was that he knew that until another general election, which could not take place in wartime, he and Chamberlain still had a firm hold on the strings of the toy dog.

When the Japanese started to press for the closure of the Burma Road (the supply line along which the Chinese obtained much of their arms), Halifax wanted to call Tokyo's bluff. But once the Americans and Australians declared their unwillingness to get involved, Churchill felt that he had no option but to follow the Chiefs of Staff's contention that war with Japan could on no account be contemplated. In this, the only time he defied the Chiefs' advice, Halifax was overruled. The public condemnation which greeted the Road's closure was none the less directed primarily against him and the left-wing popular press accused him of 'yet more appeasement'. In the Crozier interview Churchill 'smiled broadly' as he admitted that Halifax had been against compromise but was yet being blamed for it. The vituperation meted out became so intense that Charles Peake let it be known that Halifax had opposed the closure, falsely informing one newspaperman that his master had even threatened resignation on the issue.[26]

A week after the Road was closed, the Cabinet discussed policy in the event of a Japanese attack on the Dutch East Indies. Halifax suggested standing by the Dutch, again on the assumption that Japan would 'inflict every possible annoyance on us short of war'.[27] In the debate on the Road's reopening in mid-October, Halifax led those who wanted to take the firmer line, affirming that 'the question was not so much whether we should reopen the Burma road as when we should do so'.[28] In fact, only ten per cent of the road was accessible in the July to October rainy season and the Chinese needed time to repair it anyway. When it was finally reopened on 18 October, Craigie reported that 'there was little more than the usual vituperative liveliness in the Japanese Press'.[29]

In the weeks preceding the Battle of Britain, Halifax continued to receive peace overtures from Germany. A British diplomat in Switzerland, Sir David Kelly, had regular meetings near Geneva with Prince Max von Hohenlohe in a 'very quiet little fish restaurant on the borders of the lake'. Though personally anti-Nazi, Hohenlohe brought the message from Hitler that the Führer 'did not wish to touch Britain or the British Empire (although a deal over one of the old German colonies would be helpful); nor to ask for any reparation; his sole condition was that we should make peace and leave him a completely free hand in Europe'. Kelly's reaction was exactly that of Halifax and the Foreign Office: 'Knowing the vital importance of gaining time, I made a show of interest.'[30]

Mid-July saw the ten-year-old battle lines over India re-established when the Cabinet came to consider offering Dominion Status within a year of the end of the war. The Secretary of State for India, Leo Amery, reasoned that should British forces be flung out of Palestine and Egypt, India would inevitably come under severe threat. The loyalty of Indians would then become paramount and Amery believed a far-sighted gesture might help to engender the necessary goodwill. Halifax saw Amery on the subject on 7 June and found his view 'very intelligent'.[31] The protagonists took much the same stance as they had during the debates of the early 1930s. At one Cabinet from which Halifax was absent in Yorkshire, Churchill attempted to browbeat Amery into watering down the proposals. Amery wrote immediately after it:

> My dear Edward, where, oh! where, were you this morning? I had an uphill battle with very little backing from anybody. Winston was full of eloquence, supported by George Lloyd, and Simon rather left me in the lurch.... I managed to get, thanks to a suggestion of Neville's, permission to redraft the declaration ... with yr support it may be accepted when it comes up again. But I shall need all yr help. Yours ever, Leo.[32]

Halifax, who had been inspecting what the army had been doing to his recently requisitioned Hickleton Hall, suggested they 'consult together as to the best line of attack'. The trouble with Churchill and India, he wrote, 'is that it is not a matter of argument but instinct, which, in turn, is affected a good deal by his own past on the subject'.[33] This was equally true of his own side and it was not long before that other warrior from India Act days, Butler, weighed into the debate, pointing out to Halifax, with reference to the first Viscount Halifax's achievement, 'we can't go on running India on a pre-Mutiny 1857 model after 80 years of liberal political education'.[34] More cynically Butler observed, 'they won't serve our cause if we sit on their heads ostentatiously'.

Attlee had been a member of the Simon commission, and on 22 July both Labour and Halifax sided firmly with Amery's proposal to use the promise of further constitutional development and an increase in the Indian representation on the Viceroy's council as an incentive to Congress leaders to support the war. After a short lull Churchill made an attempt to pull back from any commitment and drafted a telegram to the Viceroy, Lord Linlithgow, stating that due to the imminent prospect of invasion, 'immense constitutional departures cannot be effectively discussed in Parliament, and only by the Cabinet to the detriment of matters touching the final life and security of the state'. This he tried to send off without informing the India Office. On getting wind of it, Amery went round to No. 10 where, in Colville's words, Amery and Churchill had 'a blood row'.[35]

The resulting version of the telegram was sufficiently anodyne to avoid any specific assurances. Two days later, when dining at the Dorchester, Churchill visited Halifax – who had lived there since November 1939 – and 'poured his soul out about India'.[36] Churchill had known Amery since he pushed him fully clothed into the swimming-pool at Harrow, but it took Halifax, reverting to his customary role of peace-maker, to patch up their differences and to persuade Churchill that 'Leo was more fool than knave.'[37] Churchill continued to block steps for any conciliatory message to India, and so on 8 August Congress refused to serve on the Viceroy's War Advisory Council and Gandhi reaffirmed his demand for total independence for India.

26

'A Sensible and Restraining Influence'

The difficulties associated with running and staffing a large establishment in wartime, especially after the September 1939 budget raised income tax to 7s 6d in the pound, persuaded the Halifaxes to leave their home at No. 88, Eaton Square, and move to the Dorchester Hotel, where they lived at a special rate of £23 per week. 'I was rather sad to leave the house,' reminisced Lady Halifax many years later; 'it was gloomy but it had a nice Edwardian air about it, and was more like a country than a London house.'[1] It was lent to the Women's Voluntary Services for use as a clothes store for refugees.

The Dorchester, nicknamed 'The Dorch', was then both a centre of social life in London and, built as recently as 1931 with reinforced concrete by McAlpines, was reputed to be one of London's safest buildings. Guests staying at the same time as the Halifaxes included the political hostesses Lady Cunard and Mrs Ronnie Greville, the newspaper magnates Lords Camrose and Kemsley, Vincent Massey the Canadian High Commissioner and Air Chief Marshal Portal. Victor Cazalet was a director of the company that owned it and in mid-September 1940, at the height of the Blitz, he moved a few close friends into the old Turkish baths deep in the bowels of the building.

The Halifaxes, Duff and Lady Diana Cooper, and Sir George Clerk joined him in this improvised air-raid shelter, which they predictably nicknamed 'The Dorm'. Staying there one evening when Clerk was away, Lady Alexandra Metcalfe discovered how, 'Victor and Duff snored like bulls. They went through the whole scale of snores, bass, falsetto, bubblies like a boiling kettle and the swallowing kind.' Over in his makeshift cubicle, 'Edward only takes three minutes before he is asleep but manages to yawn loudly and incessantly as a prelude to dropping off into this bottomless, childlike slumber, out of which nothing wakes him.'[2]

Lady Alexandra's sister, Lady Ravensdale, wrote that 'it always seems to me a grotesque contrast to see a whole roomful of well-known men and women dining in evening dress whilst the nerve-wracking detonations went on all the time and the Hyde Park barrage shook the very foundations'.[3] For Cecil Beaton the hotel was 'reminiscent of a transatlantic crossing in a luxury liner, with all the horrors of enforced jocularity and expensive squalor'.

A slight deafness probably helped Halifax shut out the booming of the Hyde Park anti-aircraft guns, the loudest of which, nicknamed the 'Whoppa', was so powerful that Cadogan noted it made the tables in the restaurant shake when it went off. On the occasions when Halifax was telephoned by Churchill – often at all hours of the night to talk about issues Halifax invariably thought could wait until morning – he sometimes used to pretend that he was unable to hear what the Prime Minister was saying. Halifax never really mastered the telephone, a device he always disliked and distrusted.

The receipt of German peace feelers did not cease with the onset of the Battle of Britain. The Papal Nuncio in Berne, Dr Salazar in Lisbon and the Finnish Prime Minister all passed on intimations that Germany was keen to see an arrangement reached, although as undisputed masters of continental Europe this would now no longer include the offer of autonomous Poland and Czechoslovakia. These were all considered carefully and all turned down flat. A Foreign Office memorandum of July 1940 written by Frank Roberts summed up the peace feelers as 'calculated (1) to lull us into a sense of false security, (2) to divide opinion in this country, and (3) to strengthen Herr Hitler's hand in the diplomatic negotiations which he is evidently conducting' to try to persuade the Spanish, French and Japanese to go to war with Britain. Roger Makins added that in his view the Dalherus, Burckhardt and Hohenlohe feelers had nothing behind them, the Pope's efforts had no hope of success, and Salazar's and Franco's approaches were made out of fear. Halifax initialled these comments on 18 July.[4]

A fortnight before, Cadogan had noted, 'The Pope is making tentative half-baked suggestions for agreement. Silly old H evidently hankering after them.'[5] This has always been taken at face value as evidence of Halifax's constant yearning for a settlement. However, it ought to be seen in the context of the preceding sentences of the diary entry and Cadogan's state of mind at the time. Cadogan was a mild-mannered man who used his diary as a therapeutic aid to reflection at the end of a long day. There is also a definite element of cathartic purging of the thoughts he had bottled up in the Foreign Office all day and the diary surprised many of his former colleagues when it was posthumously published in 1971.[6] On 2 July, he had had an argument with Halifax about the visit of a Spanish Republican leader, after which he complained, 'H fractious ... what cattle these politicians are! And what moral cowards. Very annoyed with him: and he's becoming slow and tired and havery.' Even the closest of professional relationships sometimes experience such tiffs and in that context Cadogan's contention that Halifax was 'hankering' after peace becomes significantly less 'evident'.

The other factor militating against Halifax was his tendency to make 'inspired amateur' comments which were as honest as they were highly risky. When on 10 July the Portuguese Ambassador said he did not know how Britain could possibly win the war, Halifax 'said I didn't either, but made a few suggestions which seemed to cheer him'.[7] To the British missions abroad at that time Halifax answered the question in suitably vague terms, instructing them:

If you are asked by the doubting and faint-hearted how this war can be won, I would have you impress upon your hearers that we are not proposing to sit still ... but that we shall go out and seek victory with the same daring and initiative that we have sought it in the past.

This went on for another six pages in much the same vein, ending with a stirring quote from Pitt the Younger.[8] It would have been more apt had the quote been King Lear's: 'I will do such things – What they are, yet I know not, but they shall be the terrors of the earth.'[9] All this bluster served to conceal the fact that it was precisely by 'sitting still', rearming frantically and sticking to the 28 May Micawber position that Britain could ride out the short term. Halifax was right in dissuading bolder spirits from plans to commit a still largely unarmed Britain to riskier courses. They had patiently to wait for Hitler to make mistakes.

The long-awaited German peace offer was finally announced in the Reichstag on 19 July. Defining himself as 'the victor, speaking in the name of reason,' Hitler said that he could 'see no reason why this war need go on. I am grieved to think of the sacrifices it must claim.' This speech, which the Luftwaffe later dropped in leaflet form over southern England, contained nothing new or specific and Halifax thought it 'appears to leave things very much as they were'. He was due to give a routine broadcast at 9.15 p.m. on Monday 22 July, and the Cabinet decided he should use the opportunity to reject the offer. Churchill offered minor linguistic corrections to Halifax's speech at Chequers over the weekend. His was the line: 'Hitler may plant the Swastika where he will, but unless he can sap the strength of Britain, the foundations of his empire are based on sand.'[10] Reactions to the speech differed widely. The *New Statesman* thought it referred to God too often, which at seventeen times in the course of a short broadcast it may well have done. Cadogan thought it '*not* v. effective'[11] at the time of transmission. However, he noted the next day, 'Germans take H's sermon of last night as a challenge and gnash their teeth and threaten destruction of British Empire.'[12] Goebbels called the speech 'a war crime'. Colville thought it was generally well received and although the delivery was bad, Halifax's

speeches were 'invariably beautiful to read'.[13] Halifax disliked micro-
phones as much as telephones and when he also had to be filmed making
the speech he complained that 'these appurtenances of democracy are
very distasteful'.[14]

The weekend between Hitler's offer and Halifax's rejection saw a frantic attempt by Lothian in Washington to ascertain precisely what was
available from Berlin. Lothian, completely on his own authority, used the
American Quaker Malcolm Lovell, who was in contact with the German
Chargé d'Affaires, to ask what terms might be on offer to 'a proud and
unconquered nation'. The Wilhelmstrasse assumed Halifax was behind
the approach for, as von Weizsäcker believed, Lothian 'must have obtained authorization if he were a normal ambassador'.[15] But the fact was,
for reasons the German could be forgiven for failing to appreciate, the
eleventh Marquess of Lothian was by no means 'a normal ambassador'.
He was a highly intelligent and independently minded aristocrat who was
not a professional diplomat. He had been Lloyd George's Private Secretary throughout his Premiership and was appointed Ambassador largely
through his long and close friendship with Halifax, whom he had known
since the days of the Milner Kindergarten. The Lovell affair was merely a
miscalculation by Lothian as to the state of opinion prevailing in
Whitehall regarding peace. He was far enough away from events in London not to appreciate how far Halifax's personal stance had swung away
from hopes for a negotiated peace, at least so long as Hitler directed
events in Germany.

When Lothian telephoned Halifax at the Dorchester just before Halifax
was due to go on the air and spoke of a further approach from the Germans, Halifax cut him short. Halifax's notes of the conversation, taken
either during or immediately after it, state that the Ambassador 'cd get
the info as to what he means if we want it. . . . We ought to find out what
Hitler means before condemning the world to one million casualties.'[16]
Halifax needed no prompting from Churchill to announce over the BBC,
'We shall not stop fighting until freedom, for ourselves and others, is
secure.' Harold Nicolson, the Parliamentary Secretary in the Ministry of
Information who somehow found out about it, stated in his diary: 'Lothian claims that he knows the peace terms and they are most satisfactory. I
am glad to say that Halifax pays no attention to this and makes an
extremely bad broadcast but one which is perfectly firm as far as it goes.'[17]

A fortnight later, Halifax also turned down an offer of mediation from
King Gustav V of Sweden. This approach particularly annoyed Churchill
and Halifax as it came from a man of marked pro-German tendencies.
When he drew up a tougher response than that drafted by Vansittart and
Sargent, Churchill revealingly minuted to Halifax: 'a firm reply of the
kind I have outlined is the only chance of extorting from Germany any
offers which are not fantastic'.[18] On 19 August, Halifax quashed

exploratory Dutch efforts to elicit terms from Berlin, arguing that,

> A negotiated peace with Hitler at this stage would almost certainly mean that our number would be up later ... the Germans have got to be more knocked about before they will be in any mood to learn any lessons. ... If we can persuade them to get rid of Hitler all the better, but at least we want them to learn that war does not pay them.[19]

There are distinct overtones here of his 1918 opinion that German towns must burn to teach the Hun a lesson he would not soon forget. Dining at the Spanish Ambassador's residence with the Londonderrys and the Duchess of Westminster later that month, Halifax listened to an astrologer predict that Hitler was a beaten man. That was all very well, said Halifax to the 'entertaining impostor', but when would Hitler himself realize it?

The next significant peace feeler arrived on 5 September 1940, when Mallet telegraphed through a proposal from a Berlin lawyer called Dr Ludwig Weissauer which came via the President of the Swedish High Court, Professor Lars Ekberg. This again postulated a world where Germany's Europe and Britain's Empire coexisted happily. Cadogan said Churchill 'took the line I expected, which doesn't differ from H's. It is a question of not *what* to reply but *how* to reply.'[20] Enlarging on this theme, Halifax observed to the Cabinet that 'the only question which arose was whether there was anything to be gained by playing for time before sending off the reply'.[21] Overall, he submitted, 'it would be very damning to have it on record that we sent a temporizing reply to an offer of this kind'. He successfully advocated immediate outright rejection, adding that top marks could be won from Roosevelt by telling him of Britain's rectitude.

The mood of grim determination which had descended on the British people, and which precluded any hope of a negotiated peace, can be seen from a letter to the *Sunday Dispatch* from a Mr J. E. Grimmond, who had been bombed out of his house and whose five children had been drowned on *The City of Benares*, an evacuation ship torpedoed by U-boats 600 miles from land. He wrote for the 'many thousands of people [who] have already had their loved ones killed in the war, they have the right to fight on until we have avenged them'.[22]

As the war progressed, pressure grew for a government statement on the wider ideals for which the Empire was supposed to be fighting. The question soon threatened to become a Pandora's Box for the Government as socialists and others attempted to hijack the debate to introduce concepts of equality, human rights and 'social justice'. Halifax, who was the minister responsible for war aims, received more or less unsolicited material on the subject from sources as varied as the anti-Semitic and anti-war Marquess of Londonderry, the Archbishop of York, Nuffield College, various ex-Kindergarteners, Julian Huxley, Lord Davies (on Federalism), Eden (on a European customs union), Chatham House, the League of Nations Union (inevitably), various vicars, the Government of New Zealand and any number of politicians keen to pose as thinkers. Halifax sensibly saw the debate largely in the practical terms of propaganda. He would take the papers submitted to him by Ernest Bevin, Duff Cooper, Robert Hudson and others and read them out to friends, inducing fits of giggles on the sofa in Victor Cazalet's country house.

This attitude, although inevitably condemned as being insufficiently concerned, was really the only sensible one to take. The increasingly millennialistic tone the debate took on after Halifax left the Foreign Office raised expectations for a brave new post-war world to unrealizable heights and was to contribute greatly to the Labour landslide of 1945. The Labour Party used war aims to legitimize many of its proposed social reform programmes.

Far from playing the traditional Tory role of distrusting Utopian theories and plans for The Betterment of Man, Halifax aired a good number of his own, even as early as July 1940. After presiding over a meeting of those ministers not in the War Cabinet on 30 July, Halifax wrote to Duff Cooper of 'the whirling pace at which thought is moving'.[23] His old interventionist and paternalist ideas were given free rein when he contrasted the nation's readiness to spend £9 million a day in wartime with its reluctance to spend £10 million alleviating poverty amongst Durham miners in peacetime unless the project could guarantee four per cent returns.[24]

When peace came, he told the Minister of Information, 'it was necessary to have a greater regard to the human values and not allow them to be smothered by considerations of old-fashioned financial purity'. He went on to dream of finding a solution to the eternal question of Capital versus Labour. One suspects these letters were written consciously 'for the record' as Halifax slept in 'The Dorm' with Duff Cooper every night and could presumably have talked it over with him there had the intention been solely to keep him informed. In the original draft of the meeting, before Halifax amended it, he was recorded as saying that he was 'convinced that after the war we must somehow ... get away from the present profit basis of society'.[25] To that end he had the industrialist and Minister of Food, Lord Woolton, meet and 'talk it out' with the trade union leader and Minister of Labour, Bevin. His underlying belief that given enough goodwill synthesis could be found even when interests seemed antagonistic was a constant theme in his life and was given further impetus by the demands of national unity. Shades of 'The Great Opportunity' pamphlet of two decades previously were evident in his affirmation that 'I am quite certain the human conscience in this country is not going to stand for a system which permits large numbers of unemployed.'[26]

Post-war reconstruction was a favourite topic; even as soon after the outbreak of war as 4 November 1939, Halifax was already confidently discussing the pros and cons of economic federation in Central and Eastern

Europe. In February 1940, he discussed the abolition of the bomber with Lord Hankey, and to another friend he foresaw a post-war political world where the Conservative and Labour Parties were replaced altogether by a coalition government. These and other ideas were brought down to earth by Cadogan in early December 1940, when he stressed that Britain could not even say her war aims included 'liberty' or 'democracy' as that 'enables the enemy to say that we stand for the Front Populaire'.[27] The whole problem was one that Halifax was more than happy to hand over to his successor.

The consensus that had 'turned off' the press criticism in early June had all but gone by mid-July, and Chamberlain and Halifax were subjected to an extraordinarily virulent campaign by the popular and left-wing papers. 'We wanted more guns,' wrote Hugh Cudlipp, the twenty-six-year-old editor of the *Sunday Pictorial*, in a typical leader, 'and Mr Chamberlain's Government gave us more widows.'[28] It is ironic that of the three major accusations levelled at Halifax during the summer and autumn of 1940, he was completely innocent of all of them. The news of the closure of the Burma Road had been greeted with headlines like 'Back to Munich?', and the day after the decision was announced the *News Chronicle* wondered, 'Do we have to mass ourselves outside the Foreign Office and incant "Get out, Halifax!"?' Yet it had been Halifax who had led the opposition to the capitulation over the Road.

The discovery that a flat was being built for Halifax in the Foreign Office also met with derision, with Cudlipp's philippic on 6 October demanding, 'Must we wait until Lord Halifax catches a chill in one of the two bathrooms he has installed in the Foreign Office before he can retire? . . . Cleanliness may be next to Godliness, but neither will outwit the dirty devils in Rome and Berlin.' Yet here too Halifax had been against leaving the Dorchester; it had been Churchill's desire to have him more easily accessible that led the Prime Minister to order the construction of the flat. An identical flat was built for Sinclair, but, as Walter Elliot wrote to his wife, 'it seems rather tough that Edward Halifax should be held up to obloquy for exactly the same construction. But if the tide is running with you you can do no wrong, and if it's running against you you can't do right.'[29]

The third line of attack was over British policy towards Russia. 'Until Lord Halifax goes,' pontificated H. G. Wells in the pages of the *News Chronicle* on 3 October in an article entitled 'Halifax Must Go!', 'there is little likelihood of our coming to friendly terms with the USSR.' The meeting between Hitler and Molotov in Berlin in November was seized upon as 'a condemnation of Lord Halifax's performance in his exalted post'. The old pre-war suspicions that Halifax's religious susceptibilities were somehow hindering the process of patching up with atheist Russia were dusted off and given another airing. Yet here again the accusations were misplaced. Quite apart from the fact that Stalin's foreign policy was very unlikely to have been affected one iota by Halifax's character, it was simply untrue to say that Halifax blocked better understanding with the Soviet Union.

It had been his idea to send Sir Stafford Cripps to Moscow and he consistently pressed for better trade links with the Soviets. He had struggled hard to keep relations on a good footing during the Finnish war, had avoided condemning Russia's invasion of Poland, and had intimated to Somerset de Chair that he would also seek to escape from the commitment to Romania should Russia attack her. Difficult as it must have been, he stayed on good personal terms with Maisky and opposed action, such as the requisition of Baltic ships in British ports after the Soviet take-over of the Baltic states, which would have antagonized the Soviet Union. 'We should be careful never to miss an opportunity which may occur of doing what we can to get nearer to the Soviet Government,' was a typical message of his throughout the period.[30] Certainly, there was no improvement in relations with Russia when Eden became Foreign Secretary.

The *Sunday Pictorial* – which used to sport such populist headlines as 'Hitler wants to kill our pets!' and 'Hitler would like to shoot Charlie Chaplin!' – devoted two entire months of editorials to calls for Halifax's resignation. Neither did the press forbear to attack his Christianity, which the *News Chronicle* characterized as a 'decadent age wheeling out its sick conscience'. The 'Cassandra' column in the *Daily Mirror* also sneered at his 'lofty conscience' as the chorus of ill-informed criticism and abuse rose to a crescendo. In late October, Butler wrote to Hoare of how H. G. Wells's article 'Halifax Must Go!' 'mercilessly attacked Halifax who has on the whole been going through a bad time'. However, Halifax's long-standing disdain for newspapers allowed Butler to observe that 'the water of criticism runs down his back'.[31]

It was not until Charles Peake had to quash two separate sets of rumours that he was about to resign that Halifax finally wrote to Churchill on 19 November, enclosing a particularly vicious article from the *Daily Herald*. After Chamberlain had resigned from ill health in late September, leaving Halifax to carry the full weight of criticism alone, Halifax told the Prime Minister, 'it does not matter at all – from a personal point of view ... but I think, as long as I am here, it does not do the Government or you very much good to have this kind of snipe-shooting'.[32] He suggested that he might 'make our Labour colleagues do something about it'. Brendan Bracken was ordered to take care of the problem and soon afterwards Cudlipp was kept up till 2.15 a.m. in the bar of the Dorchester by four MPs, including A. P. Herbert and Charles Taylor, who told him that he was hindering the war effort by his abuse of the Foreign Secretary. Cudlipp defended himself sturdily and said he was sickened by Churchill's having taken the Tory Leadership, but largely refrained from criticizing the Foreign Secretary in the same virulent terms until just before Halifax left the Foreign Office.[33]

In this unremittingly hostile atmosphere it was hardly surprising that Halifax gleaned so little credit for his part in smoothing Anglo-American relations in general and the Destroyers-for-Bases deal in particular, yet his work in this field was both exemplary and crucial. Churchill had asked Roosevelt for fifty destroyers within a week of coming to office, but this had been refused. Churchill, Halifax and Lothian walked a tightrope of pleas, promises, threats and near blackmail during June and July 1940 in order to secure the ships. The only real counter the British possessed was the White House's fear that America herself might be threatened should the Royal Navy be sunk or fall into German hands. Lothian did his utmost to emphasize this, telling Yale University on 19 June that, 'if Hitler gets our fleet, or destroys it, the whole foundation on which the security of both our countries has rested for 120 years will have disappeared'. He repeated the warning three days later in an interview which he rammed home in his characteristically direct way: 'We are your Maginot Line.' None the less, Roosevelt, who was in Dr David Reynolds's word 'a lame-duck President trying to engineer an unprecedented third term', did little tangible to help Britain until after August 1940.[34]

To reproach America for not wishing to become involved in a European war thousands of miles away is to ignore the fact that it had for decades been British policy to avoid foreign entanglements on the continent a tenth of the distance away. For the average Midwesterner, most European nations were faraway countries of which he knew little. Roosevelt's reluctance to commit himself was further encouraged by the reports Kennedy sent back to Washington predicting an imminent British defeat. It was not until the Battle of Britain was won that the American Ambassador believed it safe for the destroyers to be sent to Britain. Kennedy's rationale was that in the event of a British collapse, the bases – eight strategic facilities from Newfoundland to the Caribbean – would revert to American protection anyway. The hardened old Irish-American racketeer could not bear to give something for nothing, especially to the British.

The navy found itself in a dire situation in June 1940. It had only sixty-eight operational destroyers and the prospect of, at most, ten more in the next two months, against a Great War total of 433. Halifax realized the weakness of the British negotiating position and urged a generous and open-handed policy towards the United States. He supported Lothian's calls for the ninety-nine-year leases on the bases, but did not want to press for reciprocity if it would embarrass Roosevelt and harm his chances of re-election. He worked hard to persuade Churchill, who had the gravest doubts about exchanging military secrets, to institute limited Staff talks with the Americans. Halifax's great service – perhaps the finest he rendered in 1940 excepting his proposal of Churchill as Prime Minister – was to tone down the often petulant telegrams from Churchill to Roosevelt. For there was a wide gap between Churchill's hopes for the future of 'the English Speaking Peoples' and the reality of his exasperated Cabinet comments about the lack of American help in 1940.

On 5 July, the Prime Minister drafted a telegram to Roosevelt which accused de Valera of expecting a German victory, adding, with regard to requests for American help, 'it seems to me very hard to understand why this modest aid is not given at the time when it could be perhaps decisively effective'. Halifax excised the de Valera reference for fear that Roosevelt might agree with the Irishman. He also changed the draft to read: 'this modest aid could be perhaps decisively effective'. The Churchill draft went on to refer to America's 'grievous responsibility' if she 'failed Britain' over the destroyers. Halifax showed this ill-tempered lecture to Kennedy, who strongly advised that it not be sent. Under pressure from Halifax, Churchill finally agreed to scrap it.[35]

Halifax was willing on occasion to toy with fantastic ideas, at one point postulating to Hankey after the collapse of the French perpetual union idea that 'it may be that instead of studying closer links with France we shall find ourselves contemplating the possibility of some sort of special association with the USA on the lines suggested'.[36] His American expert at the Foreign Office, John Balfour, believed Halifax 'exercised at times a sensible and restraining influence on the more impetuous Winston Churchill which the PM did not altogether relish'.[37] In his exotically named autobiography, *Not Too Correct an Aureole*, Balfour related how Halifax dealt with Roosevelt's potentially damaging request that, as part of the destroyers deal, a promise must be exacted from Britain that should Hitler invade, the navy would be evacuated overseas.

To the morning Cabinet of 6 August, Halifax interpreted this defeatist and demoralizing demand as 'clumsily drafted', but by the end of the discussion Churchill left him with the impression that the necessary assurances would be given. By 4 p.m. that afternoon, the First Lord of the Admiralty, A. V. Alexander, and the First Sea Lord, Sir Dudley Pound, managed to stoke Churchill 'into a fire flame of indignation' at Roosevelt's impertinence. The Colonial Office had persuaded him against the unilateral donation of the bases and now the Admiralty was in the process of turning him against the decision to fall in with the American's rude but understandable desire for the fleet to fight on and protect Canada and America should the British Isles fall. At 11.15 p.m., the Prime Minister finally called for Balfour, who found him 'hunched in an attitude of tense anger like a wild beast ready to spring'. Churchill dictated a letter of highly undiplomatic language which, if sent, would have undoubtedly scuppered the negotiations. It contained instructions to Lothian to make it clear to the President 'that we could never agree to the slightest compromising of our liberty of action nor tolerate any such defeatist announcement'.[38]

Churchill was worried in case the prognostications regarding the future of the Royal Navy led to public panic. He asked Balfour to apologize to Halifax for misleading him at the morning Cabinet and dictated a note explaining the new situation, finally allowing Balfour to get to bed at 1 a.m. The next morning Halifax, who believed it quite possible to present the agreement in such a way that it would not upset public opinion and cause too much 'depression on the Home Front', quietly ordered a new draft to be drawn up. It is hard to tell whether Churchill had written the earlier version to purge himself of his feelings, to humour the Admiralty or because he truly wished to risk losing the destroyers rather then accede to the American terms. But it was Halifax's telegram that was finally sent, despite Churchill's complaint that 'it wasn't his language but Edward could send it in his name'.[39] Churchill contented himself with quoting the (unsent) version in his memoirs.

In the long and tough negotiations over the deal, Halifax continued to press for the most far-reaching and all-embracing options available. By mid-August, he could report that 'Winston, who had been very difficult last week, had now come round to my view as to how to handle it and carried the Cabinet without difficulty. I refrained from any outward sign of jubilation at his conversion.' He was less restrained in relating the matter to friends, one of whom noted: 'The Cabinet and PM wanted to bargain but Edward got them to agree with his view, that a generous action would succeed far better.'[40] The deal was concluded on 3 September and, although most of the destroyers were too old to be of much operational use, the announcement (coming on the anniversary of the outbreak of war) had, as Halifax predicted, 'a profound moral effect throughout the world'. The destroyers were accompanied by twenty motor torpedo boats, five bombers, and a quarter of a million rifles and plenty of ammunition.

The rest of September 1940 did not go so well. The Italians made great headway along the North African coast, taking Sidi Barrani on the 16th. The month saw a total of 160,000 tons of shipping lost to enemy raiding and the Blitz entered its fourth week with the heaviest bombing to date. To crown those reverses, the Government sustained a humiliating blow at the hands of Vichy France in the botched attempt by British and Free French forces to take Dakar.

27

'Operation Menace'

It had originally been Halifax who, on 5 July, had raised the idea of a coup against the Vichy authorities in Dakar, the strategically important capital of Senegal. Intelligence had reached him that the Mayor of Dakar believed a show of British naval strength there could stimulate a Free French take-over. He had little direct involvement after that, but the preparations for an attack on the city dragged on throughout the summer; when finally it was undertaken in late September, everything that could go wrong did. Lax security (Free French officers gave the post-prandial toast 'à Dakar!' in French restaurants in London), indecision, fog, faulty information and, above all, substantial Vichy naval reinforcements, all contributed to the spectacular failure of the expedition. The landing had started at dawn on 23 September, but by the 11.30 a.m. Cabinet on the 25th it was clear that only a major British support operation could save the unfortunately named 'Operation Menace'.

Attlee sensibly proposed cutting losses. Most of the Cabinet, including Halifax, agreed. Churchill reluctantly concurred that it had been a 'fiasco' and blamed the commanders on the ground. Halifax did not dissent from this analysis but drew the additional conclusion that the Government had taken an over-rosy view of the still obscure General de Gaulle. He had only been a junior minister and for the great majority of Frenchmen was merely the gawky pretender to the constitutionally legitimate Government of France led by Pétain, the hero of Verdun. Halifax had taken no part in the planning of Dakar and on 26 September he told Hoare that he 'was always rather doubtful about the project ... we must learn the lesson from this unhappy business of not trying to pick up French colonial Empire fruit until it is abundantly and self-evidently ripe'.[1] He further drew the moral that, although 'we obviously cannot throw over de Gaulle ... we ought not ... to take risks affecting major policy for the sake of pushing him in before he is clearly wanted'. Several newspapers nevertheless held Halifax personally responsible for the débâcle, despite the fact that he had taken his only holiday for months from 11 September until after 'Menace' had already begun twelve days later.

Dakar hurt; the Dominions were incensed that they had not been warned about it, the press lambasted the Government for 'imbecilic and blistering muddling', normally quiescent back-benchers criticized the 'cardinal blunder',[2] analogies with the Norway campaign were bandied about and Kennedy informed Roosevelt of 'the first real break in the Churchill popularity'. Halifax was therefore in a strong position on 1 October when he presented a major policy reappraisal to the Cabinet. Something was urgently needed to halt the prospect of Vichy bombing Gibraltar into submission. It was a course that Churchill would ideally have preferred to avoid, but in the aftermath of Dakar he had few other options open. Halifax had long suspected that Vichy would not go to war with Britain believing, probably wrongly, that it would provoke civil war in France. Equally, the twilight war which had developed could not be in British long-term interests. In Cabinet he reverted to a favoured hunting metaphor, explaining, 'the line of country which we had to ride was tricky'.[3] Somehow a formula had to be found by which war with Vichy was avoided, the colonial empire was encouraged to be anti-German and the de Gaulle question was settled.

To achieve all three, 'The Holy Fox' proposed holding secret talks with Vichy, designed to establish a modus vivendi unbeknown to the Germans. Paradoxically, he considered Dakar to have cleared the air for these. He reminded the Cabinet that 'it would be wrong to assume that the parties in France which were opposed to General de Gaulle were necessarily pro-German' and took the crumb of comfort that 'at least the Dakar episode ought to increase French self-confidence'.[4] To facilitate negotiations he begged that de Gaulle should not be allowed to stray too far from his exile in Duala. Churchill said that he 'did not differ with the Foreign Secretary on the principle of talks with the Vichy Government, which should be encouraged, but only in the emphasis to be laid upon them'.[5] Unlike Halifax, Churchill could not see any 'golden opportunity' and wanted Britain to stand by de Gaulle.

Despite the Prime Minister's qualifications, Halifax recorded: 'Winston was not unhelpful, much as it goes against his natural instinct for bellicosity. By dint of constant reminder that our purpose is to beat Germany and not to make new enemies I think we shall get along.'[6] Halifax's skill in dealing with the raw and sensitive French mood was ultimately of great value, even if he has received scant praise for it. In a letter to Roger Makins from Madrid, in November 1940, Hoare's economic adviser David Eccles summed up Halifax's problem. In the French colonies, 'if there is trouble the French authorities will turn to Vichy and [Pierre] Laval and not to London and de Gaulle. Anyone who doesn't recognize this as true doesn't understand how weakened, injured, guilty and remorseful men behave'.[7]

Halifax thought the prize of detaching the French colonies from effective German control worth the risk of allowing some limited trade through the blockade. He did not believe, as he told the Cabinet post-mortem on Dakar of 27 September, in announcing to the French Empire, 'join de Gaulle or starve'. The Vichy Minister, Paul Baudoin, had three weeks earlier proposed a partial lifting of the blockade and promised that should Germany confiscate any incoming supplies, the French Government would move to Morocco. However, Dalton, the minister responsible for the blockade, was utterly opposed to any easing of economic pressure on France.

Churchill rediscovered his 'natural instinct for bellicosity' by 7 October and reproached Halifax, saying that in his opinion 'the appeasement of Vichy was not worthwhile if it meant allowing the trade between the West African ports and the unoccupied zones of France to go on'.[8] By that time the very word 'appeasement' bordered on the abusive; indeed, Halifax had some time before ordered Orme Sargent that it should not be used in official Foreign Office files again.[9] Churchill wanted to warn Pétain that the bombing of Gibraltar would result in the immediate sinking of all Vichy ships at Casablanca. A week later Halifax came out firmly against Churchill's plan to threaten the bombing of Vichy itself, believing it to be counter-productive. He won in the end, but Hoare was instructed to let it be known that the open town ought not to consider itself in all circumstances immune. Writing to Hoare on 22 October, Butler felt,

> insofar as there is any difference of opinion in the Cabinet over foreign policy, this is on the question of France. The PM, backed by his Labour supporters, inclines to a wish to hit Vichy hard, whereas the S/S [Secretary of State] is more cautious, realizing that a false step may force the Vichy fleet into the hands of an enemy who has at present no capital ships.[10]

The fleet, which had been damaged but not wiped out at Oran, again began to impinge on the British strategic consciousness.

The technical and administrative questions raised by the transformation of an ex-ally into a semi-belligerent made it imperative to have some sort of agreed basis of relations. Halifax wrote to Linlithgow on 12 October that the twilight war with Vichy was 'tiresome and embarrassing ... we are seeking means to establish some modus vivendi with them'. To that end there arrived in London ten days later a French-Canadian professor called Louis Rougier, with oral instructions from Pétain secretly to negotiate an understanding to cover future Franco-British relations. Halifax met Rougier on the 24th, but was 'fatalistic about the chances of success', thinking that the problems were 'evidently quite insoluble'.[11] The next morning he was intensely annoyed to be woken at 5.30 a.m. to be told the latest news from Madrid about Pétain's meeting with Hitler. According to Hoare, Marshal Pétain and General Weygand were under great pressure from

Admiral Darlan and Pierre Laval to hand over the French bases and fleet to Germany. Hoare believed a timely message from the King to Pétain might halt this.

After breakfast Halifax went to No. 10 to find Churchill, who had been drafting the text of the King's message, in his zip-up siren suit and sporting a little air-force forage cap. Pausing only to enquire good-naturedly whether Churchill was about to go on stage in his 'romper suit', Halifax took the draft back to the Foreign Office for correction. It was 'good at the beginning but threatening, bullying at the end'.[12] He 'immediately objected on the grounds that the King could not send a message in those terms, and that it was only by appealing to the best in the old gaga [Pétain] that anything might be achieved.'[13] Halifax had earlier in the year prevented Lord Stanhope from denigrating Pétain's Great War role in *The Times* and a halt to anti-Pétain propaganda was one of Rougier's demands. Churchill agreed to Halifax's and Cadogan's changes to the telegram, which was duly sent off.

Later that day the two met Rougier and, although it was strenuously denied at Pétain's trial after the war, an agreement was made which really amounted to a treaty between the two Governments. There was no formal document, as Pétain alleged, but there was a typed sheet of paper with Churchill's and Halifax's marginalia. When Halifax reported to the Cabinet on the Rougier mission, he stated that 'it was desirable to put on paper the kind of statements that [Rougier] proposed to make to General Weygand', who was then in command of Vichy forces in Africa.[14] Under the terms of the Rougier entente, Vichy agreed not to attack any colony which had declared for de Gaulle if he in turn refrained from interfering with any colony then loyal to Vichy. Churchill also stressed that if Vichy resisted 'German blandishments' but instead encouraged 'a sphere of resistance', the BBC would halt criticism of Pétain and the blockade would be relaxed.[15]

After the war it was pointed out to Halifax that if there had been no agreement, how was it that after 25 October 1940 the blockade was indeed partially lifted and the Royal Navy allowed through petrol, wheat and essential foodstuffs? Faced with this extraordinary coincidence Halifax rather weakly replied, 'History will decide where the truth lies.' He privately admitted to Sir Orme Sargent:

> I have a feeling ... that although we may not have had a formal signed agreement, we did work out a practical procedure on which we lightened the blockade ... and no doubt let it be known that this was all dependent on French behaviour vis-à-vis the Germans in other matters.[16]

The day after Churchill saw Rougier, there were reports in the morning papers that Pétain had acquiesced in Hitler's demands and was preparing to hand over the fleet and ports. These eventually proved to be false, but when later on that morning Churchill again saw Rougier, he shouted at him and threatened Vichy with bombing.[17] Halifax managed to calm Churchill's anger by the time it came to discussing how to reply to Pétain's announcement on 30 October of the true terms of the Franco-German Treaty. Although the papers relating to the Rougier visit are closed until 2016, it is clear from the fact that the blockade was partially lifted, further Free French operations were suspended and the BBC did indeed halt anti-Pétain propaganda that Halifax had succeeded in reaching the mutually advantageous modus vivendi he sought.

This arrangement was not achieved by 'appeasement' so much as a judicious balance of inducements and threats. It saved Britain, at the time of her greatest peril for generations, from having to add her former ally and neighbour to the list of her enemies. Halifax did not shy away from tough talk and action when the occasion demanded. When on 1 November the Cabinet learnt that the refitted *Richelieu* and *Jean Bart* were sailing from Dakar and Casablanca towards the Mediterranean, Halifax wired Hoare to the effect that should they attempt to sail through the Straits, British submarines had orders to sink them on sight and without warning. Hoare communicated this to Vichy and nothing more was heard from either of them. Despite finding the matter highly distasteful, Halifax was not above suggesting to Churchill that various French and Italian politicians be bribed. He even managed to find amusing the idea of Loraine passing Ciano wads of £5 notes on the golf course. By mid-December 1940, however, Churchill told Halifax that he thought Laval 'no longer worth buying'.

Halifax was right to award low marks to de Gaulle's ability to inspire loyalty in French colonial Africa in 1940. He won converts to his view. In early November Churchill told Colville that the errant Frenchman was 'definitely an embarrassment to us now in our dealings with Vichy and the French people'.[18] Cadogan had long thought him 'a loser'. Halifax wanted de Gaulle to stay in Africa and 'doubted the wisdom of his returning to establish his HQ here'. In the end, he was only recalled as it was more likely to antagonize the Vichy commander in Africa, General Weygand, to leave him in Africa, especially if he carried out his intention of visiting Cairo.

On 18 November, Halifax obtained Cabinet permission for Hoare to conduct further economic discussions with Vichy in Madrid. These were carried out by David Eccles, who was also instrumental in defeating proposals from Dalton's Ministry of Economic Warfare to impose a total blockade on Spain. This was in many ways the continuation of an interdepartmental struggle that had been going on ever since the war started. Eccles's view was that,

> if the Foreign Secretary, Lord Halifax, had not supported us, the Ministry of Economic Warfare might well have called off the negotiations and imposed the Blockade in the brutal form which they desired. Then what would have happened? Spain would have had little to gain from remaining neutral, and in the opinion of those on the spot, the

vociferous war party would have persuaded Franco to invite the Germans to cross the Pyrenees and attack Gibraltar.[19]

Much the same sort of arguments were used to defend the economic negotiations with Vichy. Halifax privately believed that

Oran and Dakar were both mistakes, to warrant them they had to be completely successful and neither of them were that. He was unsure at the time and now thinks if we had given Vichy time to come around slowly and played our cards differently and with greater patience, we would not have lost them completely.[20]

His policy, which he explained to Baldwin as 'treat them kindly . . . multiply our contacts', was attacked both at the time and since as merely yet more appeasement. But the war was still one of survival and as the 'two or three months' of the 'wait and see' policy stretched to six months, Halifax fulfilled an important role in discouraging any precipitate action which might have pushed Vichy into the enemy camp. On 18 October, Halifax spoke to Cazalet about the success of the Rougier visit and related how Pétain 'was anxious to maintain contacts with us but says we must expect outward hostility'.[21]

His was naturally not a role which endeared Halifax to Churchill and he found it increasingly lonely. After the Cabinet discussions on the bombing of Vichy, Halifax complained to a friend of how Churchill 'browbeat Admiral Phillips unmercifully. Apparently [A.V.] Alexander is like a bird in front of a snake and never dares open his mouth and the others who agreed with Edward never dared speak up.'[22] On 29 September, he lost his greatest ally when cancer forced Chamberlain's resignation. The two of them had taken their wise elephant duties sufficiently seriously to synchronize their holidays to ensure that at least one of them would always be present to keep an eye on the Rogue. When he took the decision to go, Chamberlain apologized to Halifax, 'I feel *awfully* bad about deserting you.'[23]

In the reshuffle, which Churchill hoped would distract attention away from Dakar by the time Parliament met on 8 October, Halifax was offered the Lord Presidency of the Council, No. 11 Downing Street, the Leadership of the House of Lords and, in Churchill's words, 'the second position in the Government' in exchange for the Foreign Office. Halifax was far too astute a politician not to realize that this offer of a deputy Prime Ministership was a demotion and would be akin to the 'honorary' Premiership which he had turned down in May. Churchill clearly did not feel politically strong enough so soon after Dakar to insist, for as Chamberlain wrote to Halifax on 2 October, 'the fact that you remain at the FO will comfort many who remain sorrowful at my departure'.[24] Halifax later told Dalton that 'he had always told the PM that he did not wish to stay one day longer than the PM desired . . . he did not think that, until we won some victories, anyone else, even an archangel, could do much more than he was doing at the Foreign Office'.[25] He did, however, agree to take on the Leadership of the House of Lords.

Chamberlain's resignation also required the election of a new Leader for the Conservative Party. Churchill sensibly eschewed the course of being a purely national leader, well remembering Lloyd George's vulnerability after the Great War. As Leader of the Party in the Lords, Halifax presided over the Caxton Hall meeting and made a speech which, he thought, 'held the balance fairly well, avoiding a comparison between Neville and Winston while managing to say nice things about each'.[26] His notes about Chamberlain's 'unfaltering courage and tenacity when he thought a thing was right' covered ten pages; the eulogy to Churchill only five. Chamberlain died on 9 November and Halifax acted as pallbearer at his funeral in the freezing Westminster Abbey, an honour which Lloyd George had the decency to decline. Two days before Chamberlain's death, Halifax visited his former master at his home, Highfield Park near Reading.

Having declined Churchill's offer of an earldom and the Garter, Chamberlain faced death with courage and dignity. Halifax comforted him by saying 'that I did not think he had anything to regret in what he had done and that if it was to [happen] again he would not do it very differently'.[27] However stupefying this may sound, Halifax was always far from apologetic about appeasement. He often used to justify Munich, both during and after the war, to friends, colleagues and after-dinner listeners.

Halifax was one of the first in the Cabinet to conclude that Hitler would not invade. He expressed doubts about the likelihood of an assault as early as 25 July and by the time the Battle of Britain was won he was deeply sceptical that Churchill's constant calls to vigilance were much more than propaganda. Halifax estimated that nothing would be attempted by Germany without the air dominance which by late September it seemed unlikely she could gain. In this analysis he was soon joined by Chamberlain, Cadogan and General Sir Alan Brooke. The realization led him to become one of the earliest converts to the camp which wanted prompt bolstering of the British position in the Middle East. Churchill nevertheless thought this course hazardous. His public and private utterances in September 1940 were still peppered with references to the Armada, Nelson, flat-bottomed boats, and so on.

There was more than just caution in Churchill's calculations. The invasion threat was a factor in the national transformation he had to effect. Only such a fear of extirpation could raise the war in the national consciousness to the level of the crusade, where it has rightly remained ever since. His historical allusions and Macaulay-esque turn of phrase served to place the struggle four-square in the traditions of the greatest moments of history. Churchill told the British people, in language they could both understand and revere, that they were living in age of heroism. They responded by giving him adoration and support unprecedented in modern political history.

28

'He Hates Doormats'

On 4 September, Lord Beaverbrook, then Minister of Aircraft Production, wrote (but did not send) a letter to Halifax, 'as you are the senior minister in the Cabinet', to complain both about the shipment of aircraft abroad and the difficulties he was experiencing at the hands of Sinclair's Air Ministry. In the course of it he issued one of his periodic resignation threats.[1] The letter if sent would probably anyway have fallen on deaf ears because of Halifax's instinctive distrust of his old enemy (whom he called 'The Toad') and his own suspicions that Beaverbrook 'always paints a gloomy picture in Cabinet in order to restrain the Air Ministry from sending aircraft out of the country'.[2] Halifax was far more receptive to Eden, who also felt that Churchill had misplaced priorities. Eden thought Churchill was obsessed with bombing Berlin when he should have been looking at reinforcing the Middle East and knocking out the invasion fleet in the Channel ports. 'It seems to me essential that we should build up our effort in the Middle East,' preached Eden to the converted Halifax on 23 September; 'a few Wellingtons may achieve much there, they can decide nothing here.... This is no way to wage war.'[3]

Halifax was the focus for disaffection and frustration in the Cabinet. It is instructive that Beaverbrook, who knew Halifax to be instinctively unsympathetic to him (however highly impressed by his achievements in producing aircraft), should have decided to write to him. This was not, one suspects, for the stated reason that Halifax was 'the senior minister', but rather because Beaverbrook saw him as the man most likely to be able to stand up to Churchill. Beaverbrook had been involved in the composition of the Government in May and well knew that the three Service ministers, Eden, Sinclair and Alexander, were appointed largely because they were weak and would pose no threat to Churchill's handling of the war.

The Middle East was the only front on which British land forces directly faced the enemy. Alexandria was a crucial base from which the

Mediterranean fleet could attack Italy. The Suez Canal and Palestine held the key to British Indian and Far Eastern possessions. It was not surprising that most of the disagreements in the War Cabinet emerged during discussion of this arena. Halifax feared Churchill might be falling into Hitler's trap. As he wrote to Hoare on 26 September, he 'cannot at all exclude the possibility that Hitler is deliberately scaring us with invasion in order to check reinforcements to Egypt where the main blow is to be delivered . . . we are having a struggle with Max [Beaverbrook] about sending more air reinforcements. . . . I want to keep a small steady stream going.'[4] Hence on 3 October he urged the reinforcing of Malta and the Middle East and raised the spectre of German troops arriving in Italy on their way to Libya while Britain was still transfixed by an invasion which was steadily becoming less and less likely.[5]

Halifax wrote again on 24 October to say 'it really does seem that the invasion of England has been postponed for the present,'[6] and three days later this was further suggested by Enigma decrypts, of which Halifax was privy at least from 8 November and almost certainly before. The next morning at dawn Italy invaded Greece. Churchill, Halifax and Cadogan were all furious that they were woken early to be informed about it. Halifax advocated the immediate despatch of air reinforcements, warning the Cabinet that 'to have sent no help would have undermined the will to resist of other Balkan countries'.[7] Writing to a friend, he went further: 'aren't the Italians swine? I hope we may intensify our bombing of them & what infernal cheek of them coming to bomb us! I suppose the Greeks will be smashed and everyone will say another small power ruined by us.'[8] In order to obviate that, as well as to protect the Black Sea, hearten Turkey and protect Mediterranean shipping, Churchill decided on 2 November – under Halifax's prompting – to send four air squadrons to Greece.

The initial success with which the Greeks met and fought off the Italian invasion encouraged Halifax to tell Maisky a joke – always a risky business. A notice, said Halifax, had been erected at Menton on the Franco-Italian border which read, '*Avis à l'armée grecque. Ici la frontière française.*' This just managed to bring a smile to the Soviet lips.

Halifax is often accused of opposing the bombing of Rome for religious reasons. Although he did once mention to General Sikorski that Rome 'had a very special position in the world', he did not allow this self-evident truth to affect policy.[9] Churchill agreed with him that as far as was possible the Vatican, with which Britain had no quarrel, should be spared. On 27 November, Halifax told the Apostolic Delegate that he did not understand why the Pope should be concerned about the bombing of Rome, 'while he did not seem to mind about the bombing of St Paul's Cathedral, Coventry Cathedral, Canterbury Cathedral, Lambeth, hospitals, convents and a whole lot else'.[10]

The reinforcement of Greece at the expense of Egypt was deeply unpopular in Cairo. Eden, who had recently returned from a long tour there, thought that Britain seriously risked losing Egypt as a result. The British Ambassador in Egypt, and since 1936 its virtual proconsul, Sir Miles Lampson, described Churchill's decision to Eden, in a letter marked 'Most Secret', as 'completely crazy'. Through a staff error this note was circulated round Whitehall and Churchill sent off a rebuke to Lampson for impertinence. Halifax held this up, pointing out to Churchill that the telegram had not been intended for his eyes and Lampson was an old friend of Eden's. Churchill minuted back that the rebuke should nevertheless be sent. So Halifax walked over to No. 10 and told him, 'This is just as if you had looked at a private letter upon my desk and acted upon it. If you do this our codes are very far apart – in fact it is not the act of a gentleman. Please don't get in the habit of great men, and resent criticism.' 'I don't mind criticism,' answered Churchill, 'but I won't have impudence. I don't want to hear about it again. You can do as you like.'[11] This sounds like one of those conversations in which, in Dalton's words, Halifax tended to give Churchill 'the unmistakable impression that he regarded him as a very vulgar and ignorant person'. 'Always stand up to him,' Halifax advised Dalton later that day. 'He hates doormats. If you begin to give way he will simply wipe his feet upon you.'[12]

Dr Hugh Dalton, the thrusting socialist LSE economist and Minister for Economic Warfare, who later had responsibility for the Special Operations Executive, was just the sort of person Halifax could have been expected to dislike. Certainly as late as June 1940 he considered the Labour fireball and supposed class traitor to be a 'naturally offensive creature'.[13] Their views over the blockading of Spain and France were certainly diametrically opposed, Halifax seeing it as a fine-tuned instrument for affecting neutrals' policy and Dalton as a weapon to smash Germany into economic submission. Nevertheless, as 1940 progressed Halifax and Dalton established a very workable modus vivendi – their departments overlapped so much that anything else would have been, to use Halifax's favourite word, 'tiresome'. (He used 'tiresome' to describe Cabinet meetings, foreign ambassadors, talks with Sir John Reith, the Lord Mayor's banquet, the Japanese, secret sessions of the House of Lords, and anything else that was either boring or did not go according to his satisfaction. It was a word which fitted in perfectly with his rather languid Edwardian air of effortless superiority.)

It may have been that he felt some residual goodwill towards this Old Etonian who had supported his claims for the Premiership. They worked well together and finally wound up even liking one another. They conspired in interdepartmental politics against Duff Cooper's Ministry of Information and Stewart Menzies's Secret Intelligence Service. In September 1940, Menzies did not discover that 'The Holy Fox' had agreed that Section D of Menzies's operation should be appropriated by 'Dr Dynamo' until almost after the deed was done. Once Halifax had installed the Foreign Office's formidable Gladwyn Jebb to keep an eye on Dalton's Special Operations Executive, he then largely gave it free rein. When Halifax left the Foreign Office, Dalton was one of the chief mourners.

For Kennedy Halifax only ever felt a well-concealed dislike and distrust. When he heard that the country bolt-hole Kennedy retired to during the Blitz had narrowly missed being bombed, Halifax agreed that it was 'a judgement on Joe that it was likely to be safer there than in London'.[14] The old Foreign Office joke, 'I always thought my daffodils were yellow until I met Joe Kennedy,' he considered 'unkind but deserved'. The normally placid Lady Halifax found Kennedy 'quite odious, [he] kept harping on the impossibility of our winning the war and the certainty that our air force would soon be destroyed. I could have killed him with pleasure.'[15] Thick Foreign Office files bear witness to the contempt in which Kennedy was held. Halifax's red 'H' shows him to have been well acquainted with the details of the Ambassador's anti-British bias and defeatism. A telegram from Grosvenor Square to Washington during the Phoney War to 'rush pacifist literature' to London particularly drew the diplomats' ire.[16] On 23 May 1940, Halifax approved a French move to inform the American Ambassador to Paris, Kennedy's sworn enemy William Bullitt, of Kennedy's deep unpopularity. Yet because Roosevelt was on a different wing of the Democratic Party and did not want Kennedy in America during the run-up to the Presidential election, nothing was done. Roosevelt also used the fact of the anti-British Kennedy's Ambassadorship to London to refute accusations of pro-British bias.

When on 10 October Halifax heard from Kennedy that he 'had decided to chuck up his job the week after next, and seemed in very bad temper with his own Administration',[17] 'The Holy Fox' acted quickly. Fearful that Kennedy might harm Roosevelt's re-election chances, which could in turn prove disastrous to hopes for American aid, Halifax that day contacted Lothian with the obvious, if unmentioned, intention that Lothian should swiftly warn Roosevelt. 'He told me that he had sent an article to the US to appear on November 1st which would be of considerable importance appearing five days before the Presidential election.' This article was 'an indictment of President Roosevelt's Administration.... He is plainly a very disappointed and rather embittered man.'[18] Lothian immediately informed the administration and Roosevelt successfully negotiated with Kennedy to hold up both the resignation and the article.

Halifax lost no opportunity to sow seeds of doubt in Soviet minds about the quality of their non-aggression pact with Germany. On 9 October, he proposed to the Cabinet telegraphing Cripps in Moscow to inform him that the Germans were building aerodromes and developing anti-aircraft defences in the Romanian oilfields and to hint that perhaps they had designs on Turkey or the Persian Gulf.

Over the SS *Patria* Halifax showed a quality of mercy which some colleagues thought he did not possess. On 24 November, the Jewish Haganah organization had sunk the refugee ship in Haifa, in order to prevent the British authorities in Palestine forcing it to sail on to Mauritius where other Jewish immigrants were interned. In the course of the bombing 250 Jews were inadvertently killed. The War Cabinet was informed of the terrible experiences undergone by the hundreds of survivors, but also of Lampson and General Wavell's belief that it was imperative for them still to be shipped off as soon as possible, to avoid antagonizing the Arabs. The Zionist leader, Chaim Weizmann, who was also staying at the Dorchester, saw Halifax there on 26 November and appealed to him, sensibly on humanitarian rather than on political grounds, to allow the survivors to stay in Palestine, with the promise that it would set no precedents. The next day Halifax saw to it that, 'as a special act of clemency', they were permitted to remain.[19]

Friends and relations of Sir Oswald Mosley also appealed to Halifax's charity to prevail upon him to ask the Home Secretary, Herbert Morrison, to investigate the conditions of his imprisonment. Halifax suggested to Morrison that Mosley, then very ill in Brixton Prison, 'might well die ... and I do not suppose they wanted that, and that if it happened it would be a scandal and that nobody could defend it after warnings received'.[20] The former Home Secretary, Sir John Anderson, seemed to agree and a note was passed on to Bracken to bring the question up with Churchill. The recalcitrance of the Labour Party on the issue meant nothing was done. Halifax personally had little time for Mosley, calling him 'that swine' in a letter to Baldwin after the 1924 election. He had to suffer the barbs of Mosley's oratory before the war and noted with satisfaction after a Cabinet on 22 May 1940: 'I am glad to say we succeeded in getting a good deal done about fascists, aliens and other doubtfuls, Tom Mosley being among those picked up.'[21]

As soon as the Ambassador to The Hague, Sir Nevile Bland, returned after the fall of the Netherlands on 14 May, Halifax commissioned a report from him on the 'Fifth Column Menace'. Bland retired at once and penned a hair-raising report, on International Sportsman's Club notepaper, which would have been funny if it had not caused so much unnecessary misery to so many innocent people. 'The paltriest kitchen maid not only can be, but is, a menace to the safety of the country,' Bland warned the Cabinet. 'Every German or Austrian servant, however superficially charming or devoted, is a real and grave menace.' Bland went on to describe how these footmen and chambermaids would, 'when Hitler so decides', rise up 'all over the country' in order to 'embark on widespread sabotage and attacks on civilians and the military indiscriminately'.[22]

This report led to apprehension within the Government about a (completely non-existent) fifth-column threat and when Italy declared war on

10 June Halifax noted, 'the police seemed to have swooped on just and unjust alike. This was, no doubt, necessary.' In the atmosphere of the time this is hard to dispute, but the next day he suggested to Cabinet that Britain return all Italian aliens to their homeland as 'Italy would have to feed them and they would probably form centres of disaffection in Italy, since many of them had no desire to return to that country.' The fact that many were refugees from fascism and would on returning have little opportunity to give vent to any sort of disaffection seems not to have occurred to him. Despite the apparent inhumanity of this stance, Halifax was in step with the rest of the Cabinet on the matter, whose views were summed up in Churchill's command, 'Collar the lot!'

On becoming Prime Minister, Churchill also took on the responsibilities of Minister of Defence. He so reorganized the Defence Committee as to give himself 'a personal, direct, ubiquitous and continuous supervision, not only over the formulation of military policy at every stage, but also over the general conduct of military operations'.[23] Of necessity this was to omit Halifax from detailed involvement in operational matters. Churchill never attempted (as Cadogan feared he would) to set up a 'Garden Suburb'-style alternative Foreign Office directly responsible to him, as Lloyd George had done. If anything his constant late-night calls and the construction of the flat at the Foreign Office indicated that he wished to bring Halifax closer to immediate decision-making. Lady Alexandra Metcalfe wisely judged that 'Edward and Winston are a very good combination as they act as a stimulus and brake on each other. The former is able to check the times when Winston desires to stampede into some action, and he is of necessity urged to take a strong line and foresee the worst.'[24]

Halifax's criticisms, which he was the first to admit were trifling compared to the great sweep of Churchill's genius, were usually well deserved. Even his faithful friend 'Pug' Ismay admitted that Churchill 'was perhaps too impatient and self-willed to be an ideal chairman in the generally accepted sense'.[25] Victor Cazalet had once been an admirer of Churchill and had attended his wedding back in 1908, but in his diary for 5 July 1940 he noted that on a walk with Halifax, 'we are disturbed somewhat about Winston, he is getting very arrogant and hates criticism of any kind'. This may seem harsh but it was written only a week after Clementine Churchill herself had written to her husband warning him that his 'rough, sarcastic and overbearing manner' was in danger of making him unpopular with his friends and colleagues.[26] As 1940 drew on and the great 'fillip' the public received from Churchill's spirit and speeches became more apparent, Halifax's opinion radically altered. The dislike of late nights remained, but by mid-November he could write: 'I daily admire the range of his mind and its stride. He does give everything a dash of colour doesn't he?', adding with modesty, honesty and a touch of regret, 'I fear it is a quality that I don't possess!'[27]

On the weekends on which he was not on duty but could also not conveniently get up to Yorkshire, the Halifaxes stayed at Victor Cazalet's home, Great Swifts, in Kent or Lady Alexandra Metcalfe's beautiful Jacobean manor in Little Compton in Oxfordshire. The latter had the added advantage of being close to the Prime Minister's weekend residences of Chequers and Ditchley. Halifax considered these rare opportunities to get into ancient tweeds and relax with friends, like Fr Ted Talbot, Walter Monckton and Geoffrey Dawson, as the happiest times of the war, even perhaps of his life. Dawson saw much of him in June and July and often described him as looking tired. This was only partly because of the great strains and long hours, but also his long features, 'Cecilian stoop' and languid air often gave that impression.

One afternoon in October, whilst driving over to Leeds Castle, the Halifaxes watched a dog-fight over Maidstone. They stopped the car and 'did the one thing we were warned not to do, standing gazing at the sky with mouths hanging open'. 'The circles and spirals made by the planes looked so lovely against the blue sky,' remembered one of the party, 'it might have been a display at Hendon.'[28] After another weekend in mid-November, Lady Halifax thanked her hostess saying, 'I haven't seen Edward so lighthearted since the war – no, indeed not since 1938 when he took over the FO! & it was *very* good to see him giggling!'[29] Only four weeks later this serenity was dealt a blow from which it took the Halifaxes nearly a year to recover.

29

Banishment

On 12 December came the news of the death of one of their close circle, Lord Lothian. Despite a fully deserved reputation as an appeaser, Lothian had been a highly successful Ambassador to Washington. His close and relaxed relationship with the American press was invaluable and is best characterized by the (probably apocryphal) story of how, on returning from London in November 1940, he told the waiting newspapermen, 'Well, boys, Britain's broke – it's your money we want!' He was a Christian Scientist and died from uremic poisoning after refusing to take the straight-forward steps which would have cured him. 'Another victim for Christian Science,' Halifax mourned. 'He will be very difficult to replace.'[1] To the chagrin of the Foreign Office it was felt that another high-profile, non-career diplomat should take over this most senior posting and Churchill and Halifax began urgently to seek a suitable successor.

Churchill had a tendency to use foreign vacancies as a means of remov-ing troublesome politicians. Those who fell foul of this Machiavellian stratagem, jauntily referred to by Colville as 'My language fails, go out and govern New South Wales,' included Hoare who was sent to Madrid, Ronald Cross to Canberra, Reginald Dorman-Smith to Rangoon, Duff Cooper to Singapore and Malcolm MacDonald (whom Churchill never forgave for signing away the Irish ports) to Ottawa. Churchill had not invented the practice: Baldwin had offered the Washington Embassy to his rival Austen Chamberlain in 1925. Churchill's mind swiftly alighted upon Lloyd George, who was still only lukewarm about the war. Despite being seventy-seven, the Great War leader had a sufficiently high profile to be a threat to his old friend should the war take a turn for the worst. However, his record, dynamism, Liberalism and ebullient personality might have made him ideal for America. He would be assisted by the highly competent American expert Sir Gerald Campbell and would also be given a (largely honorary) seat in the War Cabinet 'to sweeten the pill' of having to serve under Halifax. Other names Churchill considered for Washington were Vansittart, Cranborne, Sir Dudley Pound and Oliver Lyttelton.

Halifax put up no objection to Churchill's idea when they met the next day, but also suggested Eden and Lord Dudley. They agreed to consult again over the weekend. Lothian's death had provoked intense speculation in political and journalistic circles as to a successor. Dalton considered that Sir Gerald Campbell, Greenwood and even Bevin had chances. Cadogan felt that Robert Hudson, Sir Ronald Lindsay, Malcolm MacDonald, A. V. Alexander and Lord Chatfield were possibilities. Lady Astor and Lady Diana Cooper each canvassed for her own husband and at Ditchley, where Churchill was staying, house opinion ran strongly in favour of Cranborne. Virtually no one mentioned the possibility of Halifax at this stage, who had a further conversation with Churchill on the subject at Chequers over lunch on Saturday 14 December.

In North Africa, meanwhile, Wavell had been on the offensive since 9 December and had been flinging the Italians back along the coast ever since his victory at Sidi Barrani. By 15 December, he had cleared Egypt of Italians and the next day won a further victory at El Wak in Italian Somaliland. In mid-November, Halifax had told Dalton that he thought his job was secure, at any rate 'until we won some victories'.[2] With Sidi Barrani coming after the Royal Navy's destruction of the Italian fleet at Taranto in November, Churchill at long last felt himself politically strong enough to assert himself more conspicuously. On the evening of Sunday the 15th, replete with the good news from Africa of Britain's first real victory of the war, Churchill and Eden watched *Gone with the Wind* together at Ditchley and it was probably then that the decision was made that should Lloyd George refuse the offer Churchill would choose Halifax. Differing accounts credit the idea to the Australian Premier, Robert Menzies, or Lord Beaverbrook, but Churchill was easily an astute enough politician to have come up with it on his own.[3]

At lunch the next day, Monday 16 December, Lloyd George officially turned the offer down, ostensibly on the advice of his doctor. Churchill decided to put into action his plan of the night before. Colville believed he had been influenced by the monthly censorship reports, which showed the Foreign Secretary had taken on the full mantle of chief government scapegoat since Chamberlain's death. A glance at the popular press would have told him that. These reports, which were circulated along with monthly supply reports and monthly propaganda reports, were digests of those opinions that the official censors had read in people's letters concerning policies or personalities. After the press vilification of the autumn, it was not surprising that by December the reports were regularly showing Halifax in a bad light.

Churchill had a number of reasons for wishing to be rid of the Foreign Secretary and his unpopularity in censored letters was probably the least of them. The reasons Churchill gave for wanting Halifax to go to Washington were not the real ones, although he probably did think that to send a Foreign Secretary as Ambassador would be seen as a compliment to America at that crucial time for Anglo-American relations. Churchill possibly had the inkling that, should he one day have to face his own Norway debate, Halifax had easily enough friends and supporters, such as Anderson, Margesson, Hankey, Monckton, MacDonald, Stanley, Reith, Inskip, Butler (even Kingsley Wood, Dalton and Lloyd), to enable him to form a viable alternative ministry.

Churchill also wanted to make way for Eden, having often that summer and autumn as good as promised him the Foreign Office. He also thought a government reshuffle would be politically popular. He was confident that Halifax – who had as recently as a fortnight before expressly put his future in Churchill's hands – was no longer capable of causing real trouble for him amongst Conservative back-benchers, as he could while Chamberlain had been alive. He also knew that Halifax's sense of duty and propriety would not allow him to precipitate a split in the Government's ranks by contesting the decision.

The military situation was completely different from the one when Halifax resisted demotion in the post-Dakar reshuffle back in early October. For all his unpopularity Halifax was the second man in the Government in December 1940. He was still probably the favourite to succeed had Churchill been killed, if only through the lack of an alternative. The principal reason Churchill engineered Halifax's exile – which effectively ended his career in British politics and cut him out of major decision-making for the rest of the war – was resentment at the restraints and checks Halifax had managed to impose upon his Premiership. The man who succeeded Margesson as Chief Whip in 1941, James Stuart, put it succinctly when he said that 'Winston . . . knew he could bully Anthony . . . but not Halifax.'[4] The Rogue Elephant was finally savaging the weakened old elephant to establish himself as undisputed master of the herd.

The accusations that have been levelled by the conspiracy theorists were, predictably enough, that Halifax was plotting against Churchill or alternatively that he was exiled for still favouring a negotiated peace. Both are completely unfounded. By December 1940, Halifax was fully reconciled to fighting the war to the end under Churchill's leadership. He was by no means reconciled, however, to spending the rest of the war in Washington and found the whole idea repugnant. The first inkling that he received about it came on the afternoon of Tuesday 17 December, when, returning from a BBC broadcast, Beaverbrook dropped in at the Foreign Office and canvassed his opinion on the idea. Halifax had never liked 'The Toad', with whom he had crossed swords over India in 1929 and who he knew was constantly disparaging him behind his back. Halifax wondered whether Beaverbrook (whom he correctly suspected of 'a desire to get me out of the

FO')[5] had come up with the Washington idea off his own bat or whether this was a feeler from Churchill. There can be no doubt of Halifax's profound abhorrence of the Washington idea, which he called an 'odious thought'.[6] Cadogan noted that day that Halifax was instead thinking in terms of a combination of the former Viceroy, Lord Willingdon, and Sir Gerald Campbell.[7]

Beaverbrook was a born schemer whose biographer admits that he loved 'nothing ... better in politics than moving people about from one office to another or in speculating how to do it'. He returned to Churchill with a completely fabricated story about Halifax's reaction to the offer.[8] He claimed that Halifax had said at once, 'Yes, he would like it.' Halifax's elaborate attempts over the following three days to avoid the job gives the lie to what was clearly an underhand and malevolent move by Beaverbrook to commit Churchill to proffer it to Halifax. It is possible that Churchill was in possession of this incorrect information when he spoke to Eden, Kingsley Wood and Sinclair after a Defence committee meeting that evening.[9] They unanimously agreed to Halifax's appointment. This had the effect of isolating Halifax from prospective support before he himself had even been officially approached by Churchill. Beaverbrook stuck to his story, telling Eden in the early 1960s 'that Halifax was really longing to go and was terrified that Eden would'.[10]

The next morning, Wednesday 18 December, Halifax arrived at the Foreign Office to find a note from Churchill asking him to take on the Ambassadorship. Calling it a 'high and perilous charge', Churchill assured him of his 'close personal and political accord and sympathy with you',[11] and added that 'only the vital issues now open between us and the United States, on which our whole future depends,' would induce him to lose his services. Halifax was deeply sceptical and Cadogan advised him on how to put his doubts to the Prime Minister. Halifax went over to No. 10 and had two conversations with Churchill, one before lunch and another in the early afternoon, after which he went to the War Office to try to persuade Eden to take the post instead. Eden, knowing himself to be Halifax's successor, refused and somewhat sanctimoniously told the outgoing Foreign Secretary how 'In wartime everyone must go where they are sent.'

That evening, looking like a 'wounded gazelle',[12] Halifax dined with his wife, Cazalet and Dalton. He let nothing slip about the day's events and managed to pass off the occasion with more than customary aplomb. 'This is the first time ... that I have met Holy Fox off parade,' recorded Dalton afterwards. 'I find him charming, amusing and with a pleasantly light touch on personalities.'[13] When the conversation got around to the relations between Prime Ministers and Foreign Secretaries, Halifax confined himself to old anecdotes and said that with Churchill's draft telegrams, he 'argues back and generally gets his way, if he does not agree with their tenor'.

Immediately after breakfast the next morning, Thursday 19 December, Halifax went to pour out his heart to Geoffrey Dawson. His old friend comforted him by saying that the news meant 'a terrible loss to the Government at home and I distrust the sponsors of the plan'.[14] Halifax then saw Churchill again and had a 'difficult' interview with him, again forcibly putting the case against his own candidacy. To send a Foreign Secretary anywhere as an Ambassador was to get things completely out of proportion, he argued, and would have no effect on the United States except to make Britain look mildly ridiculous. It was also a bad negotiating ploy to appear to the Americans to be too anxious about the delicate military aid negotiations that were then under way. Halifax even tried to argue that 'he was more difficult to replace at home than it would be to find a successor to Philip [Lothian]'.[15]

Only three days previously Churchill had been on the verge of sending what amounted to a begging telegram to Roosevelt. He was only saved from having to do so by the news of a positive speech from Roosevelt, which likened the despatch of aid to Britain to the loan of a hose to a neighbour whose house was on fire – 'I don't want $15. I want my hose back after the fire is over.' (To which the isolationist Senator Taft growled: 'Lending arms is like lending chewing gum: you don't *want* it back!')

Although the evidence at this stage becomes slightly confused, it does seem that Churchill took the gloves off and let Halifax know that

> he would never live down the reputation for appeasement which he and the FO had won themselves here. He had no future in this country. On the other hand he had a glorious opportunity in America, because unless the US came into the war we could not win.... If Halifax succeeded in his mission over there, he would come home on a crest of a wave.[16]

It was an unanswerable case, fully borne out by events, but Halifax reiterated his points, suggested Eden and left the interview still believing that possibly 'the horror had been averted'.[17]

Any hope was shattered, however, when he arrived at the Foreign Office the next morning, Friday the 20th. There he found a second letter from the Prime Minister, which this time brooked no argument. Sir Gerald Campbell would go with him 'to relieve the pressure' and he was, however impracticably, to remain a member of the War Cabinet. Halifax was, according to the letter, 'the one person best qualified for this paramount duty'. Churchill cannot possibly have believed this last statement, however close Halifax was to government policy. Sir Ronald Lindsay had been a successful Ambassador to Washington from 1930 to 1938 whereas Halifax had visited America only once in 1905 and then only for a fortnight. Every commentator on both sides of the Atlantic said that the post should go to a liberal extrovert with sound anti-appeasement credentials and a flair for publicity. Not often is Churchill criticized for giving it instead, for blatantly political reasons, to a Conservative fox-hunting aristocrat who had an ill-disguised contempt for the media, a reputation for being aloof, who was, furthermore, the Foreign Secretary during Munich. This was rightly considered at the time as a public-relations disaster of the first magnitude; Churchill was willing to take a monumental risk with Anglo-American relations at exactly the time he should have been at his most cautious.

Halifax had written a letter suggesting Lord Woolton or Sinclair, and warning that to send him would 'risk giving the impression of being too "importunate"'.[18] However, on receipt of Churchill's unambiguous order, he decided not to send it. He did contemplate resigning from public life altogether, but knew where his duty lay. His appointment was, ironically enough, precisely the sort of Rogue Elephant tactic that he would automatically have tried to block, had it happened earlier and to someone else.

His decision to let matters take their course was not good enough for Lady Halifax. After Lothian's memorial service at Westminster Abbey, she took her husband over to No. 10 to beard the Prime Minister. 'I have not', wrote an amused Halifax who merely listened as his wife indulged in some outraged aristocratic plain speaking, 'often assisted at a more interesting interview.'[19] From the diaries of those who saw the Halifaxes immediately after the meeting it is clear that the uncharacteristically tough-talking Lady Halifax lost little time in getting down to basics. Her arguments were not of the refined shadow-boxing type that Lord Halifax had employed in his earlier interviews with Churchill. She had 'got really worked up' during the service, believing that 'it was just another scheme on the Beaver's part to get E out of the Government and country thereby clearing the path for himself'.[20]

Lady Halifax warned Churchill that 'the day would come when he might need E's support here as he had no colleague so loyal and he commanded a following here unlike anyone else'. During a ten-minute argument, during which the Halifaxes kept a lunch party (which ironically included Eden) waiting at the Dorchester, Churchill repeated his view that the only way her husband could protect his reputation was by working to bring America into the war. This had Halifax rather conceitedly remarking to himself that 'it would seem quite unintelligible to him that anybody should not consider personal advantages or disadvantages'. Lady Halifax left 'with the overwhelming feeling that Winston wanted to get Edward out of the Government and that this gave him the chance of doing so and nothing would deter him'.[21]

They suspected, wrongly as it turned out, that Churchill had promised Halifax's removal as the price for Lloyd George's return to the Government. 'Winston wanted H out of the country so that Ll. G. might join the Govt,' confided Cazalet to his diary on 23 December; 'What a gang. W. C., Ll. G. & Beaverbrook.' Halifax's great friend Fr Ted Talbot, writing to

Lady Antrim on 27 December, said, 'E himself is beautifully unself-regarding about it all – but I can see he does rather fear the influence of some of the more "crook" elements that exist around Winston.'[22]

The chief 'crook', Beaverbrook, lost little time in putting the worst possible interpretation on Lady Halifax's conduct. He insinuated that the whole outburst had been staged for financial reasons and alleged that they 'bargained for plenty of money. When they had been promised plenty of money, all was well.' This says more about Beaverbrook's incapacity not to slander his enemies than it does about the Halifaxes, who, for all their carefulness, were never grasping. Halifax took his Ambassador's salary, which was the same as Lothian's. At the Cabinet meeting on 23 December, as Churchill announced the news, Cadogan looked across the Cabinet table and saw Beaverbrook 'hugging himself, beaming and almost winking'.[23] Cadogan 'tried to look cordially shocked'. Later that day Churchill summoned Cadogan to tell him that there had been growing criticism of Halifax, which he said had been leading to attacks on the Foreign Office and had to be curtailed.

'Poor Halifax was so hurt,' wrote Valentine Lawford that day as he cleared his desk and said goodbye to colleagues at the Foreign Office, and when Eden came in Halifax 'cracked hearty jokes about not keeping the Secretary of State waiting in his own office'.[24] Cadogan found him 'resigned (both senses) and rather resentful'.[25] The day before he had told a friend how Roosevelt had approved his appointment and had 'wired back most warmly (D—n him!) ... so the last prop has given way'.[26] On Christmas Eve, he saw the King at Windsor and was still complaining that 'we would be very flattered if Cordell Hull came here as US Ambassador but it would not make us change our policy'.[27] He took a slightly different tack with the King, professing himself 'perplexed at what might happen if anything happened to Winston. The team was not a strong one without a leader and there were some hot-heads among it.'

He probably wanted to warn the King, if warning were necessary, not to be bamboozled into sending for Beaverbrook in a crisis. The King showed how he still considered Halifax to be Churchill's heir apparent and told him that 'he could always be recalled'.[28] But if the King did not seem fully to commiserate with the circumstances of his departure, the Queen certainly did. She wrote Lady Halifax a heartfelt letter which read:

My dearest Dorothy, How can I say what I really feel about your coming departure? I shall miss you horribly and hate the idea of losing you: and I feel so *deeply* for your having to go at this moment and leaving your family ... bless you, dearest Dorothy, and with many messages of hope and trust to Lord Halifax. Ever your affectionate friend, Elizabeth R.[29]

This marked the end of the social engagements Lady Halifax prized above all, when she and her husband 'dined à quatre with the King and Queen and talked easily about people and things with no fear of indiscretion'.[30]

Meanwhile, Halifax confided to Baldwin his 'misgivings – though this sounds egotistic – at leaving Winston! for there are not many of our colleagues who are prepared to stand up to him when the winds of fevered imaginings blow strongly'.[31] It did not take long for these misgivings to be confirmed. Shortly after he arrived in Washington, Halifax received an anguished note from Lord Hankey which complained:

> It is a complete dictatorship. The War Cabinet and the War Committee, on military matters, consist of a long monologue by one man. The others are just 'yes men' ... there is no one to provide ballast. ...
> I consider you the only alternative leader if anything happens to Churchill.[32]

At the Pilgrims lunch given on 9 January 1941 to honour Halifax prior to his departure, Churchill gave a speech that was a classic of its type. To the outside observer, like the US Attaché General Raymond Lee, 'it was very evident he was lending to Halifax's mission every bit of emphasis which he knew how to place upon it'.[33] Churchill employed the purplest of prose and described Halifax's new job as 'a mission as momentous as any that the Monarchy has entrusted to an Englishman in the lifetime of the oldest of us here'. His assertion that Halifax 'has vowed to prosecute the war against the Nazi tyranny at whatever cost until its last vestiges are destroyed' was intended to vouchsafe to the Americans his credentials as a sound anti-Nazi, whatever his appeasing background.

In other passages of his peroration Churchill indulged in a classic insider's speech, full of coded special references intended for the cognoscenti and his own impish delight. By the use of overstatement and consummate irony he enjoyed himself at Halifax's (easily borne) expense. After Lothian's death, he said, 'We therefore thought it our duty to restore this link, refill this gap, to repair this loss by sending without regard to the derangement of our forces and circle here the best we could find, without regard to any other consideration whatsoever.' He went on with his tongue wedged equally firmly in his cheek to commend Halifax's 'brilliant and devoted wife' (who unbeknown to the assembled company had recently given him a lambasting such as he rarely received). Halifax's answer to this gentle sparring was equally tinged with double entendre. He told the story of the Delhi station-master who, when thanked for his travel arrangements for the Viceroy, answered, 'It has always been a great pleasure to see you off.' After the polite laughter Halifax added wryly, 'No doubt many of you here today are animated by feelings no less kindly.'

It may today be hard to comprehend quite why the Halifaxes should have reacted with so much dread at the thought of taking up such an important and prestigious post. Although the apparent demotion, termination of political career and worries about the future of the Government obviously rankled, they were not in the forefront of Halifax's mind. Lady Halifax and he certainly loathed the idea of being out of England while two sons and a son-in-law were serving in the army and a third son was about to join up, but neither would that nor the thought of leaving Garrowby and their friends engender the depression they felt at leaving; they had after all left for India with far less heavy hearts. Nearly thirty years later Lady Halifax remembered:

> We both felt Beaverbrook had suggested it and I had no trust in him of any sort. In the end we had to go and I don't think that I have ever been more miserable.... We set off to a neutral country, leaving all our friends and family to danger and deprivation which we could no longer share.[34]

Even the sense of desertion they felt as London was being Blitzed did not fully explain their dismay. It came partly from their destination. The prospect of spending an indeterminable amount of time 'selling' the British cause in an utterly foreign land like America seemed like purgatory. In a multitude of ways America was more foreign to them than British India had been. It was a faraway country of which they knew nothing. 'I have never liked Americans, except odd ones,' the new Ambassador to Washington told Baldwin on the day he realized that Churchill had outmanoeuvred him into the post. 'In the mass I have always found them dreadful.'

The suspicion that America was a social and cultural wasteland was common amongst the British upper classes of the day. This feeling was best summed up by Halifax's friend the Marquess of Linlithgow, who wrote from Viceregal Lodge in July 1941 to commiserate with 'the heavy labour of toadying to your pack of pole-squatting parvenus! What a country and what savages those who inhabit it! ... I know you don't say all this, but nothing will persuade me that you don't feel it.'[35] Halifax did feel it, and on seeing them off a close friend could not help noticing how they 'both left with misgivings and dread of the different world which it means. They hoped and prayed till the last minute that something might turn up to put a stop to it.'[36]

30

'De-Icing Edward'

Halifax's misgivings about America were more than borne out by his first few months there. Several incidents, all in themselves minor but nevertheless detrimental, were taken by the isolationists as indicative of larger political phenomena. These anti-British elements were keen to portray Halifax as 'the personification of virtually every adverse stereotype which the Americans nurtured with regard to Britain, and the very antithesis of the new dynamic Britain'.[1]

The opening scene of his mission to Washington could not have gone better. Roosevelt accorded Halifax an unprecedented honour when he sailed out on the Presidential yacht *Potomac* to welcome him off the Royal Navy's newest battleship, HMS *King George V*, as it entered Chesapeake Bay. This gesture of support was not lost on the powerful isolationist press, which eagerly looked forward to its chance to bring Britain's new Ambassador down to earth.

They had not long to wait: faulty advice, bad luck, a sense of disorientation and natural reserve on Halifax's part soon furnished the press with a series of gaffes which they managed to turn into diplomatic incidents. In his autobiography, Halifax blamed 'some section of the press affected by Jewish influence' for his initial unpopularity in America.[2] There is no real evidence for this. Halifax certainly had a tough act to follow. Although Lord Lothian had also been an appeaser, the American press had soon found better copy in his stalwart defence of British interests in America than in his past. Halifax found it considerably more difficult to shake the 'appeasing' reputation off, and until quite late it still 'stuck in the craw' of senior administration officials such as Harold Ickes.[3] *Life* magazine came up with an interesting explanation of why Halifax did not tend to win popularity for his liberal record in India: 'outside of England', it suggested in February 1941, 'Lord Irwin and Lord Halifax are still generally regarded as two men and the latter gets no credit for the former's work'.

The man Halifax chose to accompany him as his Private Secretary, Charles Peake, was wrong for Washington. A High Anglican and veteran of the Foreign Office news department, who had won the Military Cross in the Great War, Peake later distinguished himself as Ambassador in Belgrade and Athens. However, Halifax chose him for Washington more for his congenial company than for his expected expertise in public relations. Rex Benson, who was in Washington as a Military Attaché, felt that 'neither of them understand America and neither really like it'.[4] Peake greatly missed his family and failed to detect the intricate nuances of American political life well enough to keep his master out of trouble.

On 31 January 1941, only a fortnight after he landed, Halifax visited the Chairman of the Senate Foreign Relations Committee, Senator Walter George, and on leaving told the pressmen that they had discussed the timetable of the Lend-Lease Bill. The next morning's headline in the senior isolationist paper the *Chicago Tribune* screamed, 'Halifax Steers FDR Bill'. Failing to learn from this error, he then proceeded to visit the Chairman of the House of Representatives' Foreign Affairs Committee, Sol Bloom. This time he made no comment, but the photograph of the six foot five inch Halifax towering over the diminutive Bloom was subtly used to give the impression of an overbearing Britain meddling in internal American affairs. With constant accusations that Britain wished to drag America into a British war, Halifax could not have chosen a more sensitive time to interfere, in however innocent and polite a way, in the American political process.

The resulting uproar forced Halifax to abandon plans to visit Congress again until after the Bill was passed. Indeed, it was so vituperative that the administration prevailed upon Halifax to postpone his address to the Pilgrims Society in New York, the traditional inauguration speech of all British Ambassadors. Peake had to be sent to New York to explain this to Tom Lamont, the J. P. Morgan banker and senior Pilgrim. The postponement brought a torrent of abuse from Lamont on to the head of Felix Frankfurter, the administration official responsible. 'Hitler was right,' Lamont told Peake; 'what we need in this country is a purge of all the Jews.'[5] Writing to Eden on 4 February, Halifax explained that he was, for the moment at least, in 'Political Purdah'.[6]

Halifax never fully understood the way the American Government worked and used to liken it to 'a disorderly day's rabbit-shooting'. Soon after his arrival he wrote to the King that he found Americans 'very much resemble a mass of nice children – a little crude, very warm-hearted and mainly governed by emotion'.[7] As late in his Ambassadorship as the end of December 1944, he was still of the opinion, as expressed to the King, that 'In many ways one is reminded at almost every hour of the day how immature they are in the business of government.'[8]

The series of gaffes continued. His statement that America's aid to the

Soviet Union amounted to help for Germany caused great offence. Often, as with his comment of June 1941 to Sumner Welles that he 'did not think that the Baltic peoples ... deserved much consideration', these were private and could be hushed up, but when a member of his staff presented the Chicago press corps with the Ambassador's copy of a banquet guest list, complete with private annotations about the guests, the resulting publicity was, again, inevitably highly embarrassing.

Soon afterwards, on a visit to Chicago, Halifax attended a baseball match at Comiskey Park, home of the Chicago White Sox. This laboured attempt to show a populist side to his character totally backfired when he commented that the game was 'a bit like cricket except that we don't question the umpire's decision so much' and was heard to ask whether the fielders were 'throwing the ball at the runners'. When he left the ground, before the end of the match and with his unfinished hot dog on his seat, the newspaper photographers zoomed in on the hot dog, which got front-page prominence, next to the comment that although King George had eaten his in 1939, this democratic American food was clearly not good enough for the exalted Viscount Halifax.

If it all seemed to add up to the view that the new Ambassador was 'a British Imperialist, an unrepentant old-school tie Tory, representing an outworn feudal system', as one American book published that year put it, the next blunder nearly wrecked his standing altogether.[9] On 29 March 1941, against the advice of the head of the British Press Service, Halifax went to Pennsylvania for a day's hunting with Mr Plunket Stewart's Cheshire Hunt. Inflaming American prejudices about the British class system yet further, he travelled there viceregally, in the President of the Pennsylvania Railroad Company's private carriage.

In the words of Alistair Cooke, the press 'seethed with populist indignation at the callousness of milord, hunting while simple American boys prepared themselves for the slaughter in Europe'.[10] The biographer and poet, Carl Sandberg, wrote a vituperative article in *The Nation*, entitled 'Lord Halifax on a Horse', which contrasted Halifax's supposed dilettantism with Lothian's stoic virtues and the toil of American workers on double shift in the munitions industry producing arms for Britain. To make matters yet worse, the trip coincided with the opening of a German offensive in the Balkans and the juxtaposition of the news articles served further to make his excursion – his first day's hunting for eighteen months – seem all the more reprehensible. As he wore an old tweed hacking jacket, the Cheshire Hunt itself, which wore pink, was unimpressed, and Halifax even managed to upset the other grander East Coast hunts whose invitations he had refused in order to go out with the Pennsylvanian pack.

Back in London the news of Halifax's apparent failure filled official circles with consternation lest relations with America, so vital for eventual victory, were adversely affected. In mid-May, Robert Bruce Lockhart could report to his diary that Gerald Campbell was 'on his way home for consultation.... All this is a result of panicky state resulting from flop of Halifax and failure of Charles Peake.' At the dinner given for Noël Coward after the first night of *Blithe Spirit*, attended by Louis Mountbatten, Duff Cooper and Vansittart among others, the conversation centred on 'some talk about the USA, failure of Halifax ... need of lecturers, etc.', until the mood was lightened when Coward played 'London Pride' on the piano.[11]

At the American desk of the Foreign Office, which had heard that Halifax's stock had 'gone from zero to freezing',[12] John Balfour noted on 20 May that 'something must be done to de-glamorize Lord Halifax and humanize him', adding, 'it is also highly regrettable that the Ambassador should have yielded to the temptation to indulge in innocent field sports'.[13] Halifax privately felt great pain at his conspicuous lack of success and rumours quickly circulated that he was on the point of being replaced. Beaverbrook started to angle for the job.

It was at this low point that Lady Halifax once more came into her own. She understood the damage being done to her husband's mission, partly through his own stand-offish demeanour, and appreciated that a new departure was required. A fresher and more modern attitude was needed to allow her husband a chance to display the qualities and great charm which she knew he possessed. The Halifaxes always saw a great deal of each other, as he was never gregarious or clubby and enjoyed nothing better than to return home after work. In India they had reserved every Wednesday evening for dinner alone together, which aides were told overrode all other commitments. When Halifax was at the Foreign Office they used to walk there together every morning. Although Lady Halifax often experienced bad health in Washington, including migraines, she refrained from worrying her husband about it.

A sensitive and intelligent woman, Lady Halifax could also be direct, as her interview with Churchill showed. She saw the importance of, as their friend and cousin Angus McDonnell put it, 'de-icing Edward'. If he was to be a success in Washington, she realized that he would have to adapt himself to at least some unfamiliar American mores. He needed, at the age of sixty, to unbend and exchange the cool and austere Viceregal image which the American press so obviously disliked for that of a more approachable and 'democratic' Ambassador, as Lord Lothian had been. Cazalet put it best when he told Dalton how, 'the only way you do business in Washington is by "having a chat", "popping in" or "ringing up". Halifax can't do any of these. He always eyes a telephone with deep distrust.... He has no gift for popping in.'[14]

To Lady Halifax and Angus McDonnell, a Falstaffian character who had been a contemporary of Halifax's at Eton and who joined the Embassy staff in March 1941, must go the credit for drawing the beleaguered Ambassador out of himself and persuading him to adopt an informality with Americans which he had hitherto reserved only for family, friends or close colleagues. McDonnell managed to persuade him to phone Roosevelt's Chief of Staff, Colonel Watson, and call him by his nickname, 'Pa'. In time he would even ring up without having anything specific to say, a popular Washington pastime called 'shooting the breeze'. For all that, Halifax never found it other than disconcerting when Cordell Hull, in his jocular Southern way, used affectionately to refer to him as 'that bastard'.[15]

McDonnell's good-living bonhomie and deep knowledge of and affection for America soon more than made up for Peake's reserve. Sir Isaiah Berlin remembers McDonnell as a 'bit of a court jester, [who] melted the ice and generally produced a jolly, slightly ridiculous atmosphere in which pompous objections to Halifax tended to melt'.[16] At one Washington dinner party for Halifax, which was proving heavy going, McDonnell suddenly burst into song, the refrain of which went: 'Twenty years a chamber maid in a house of ill repute, twenty years a chamber maid and *never* a substitute.'[17] McDonnell also provided another great service in meeting the press and local dignitaries of the places Halifax visited in order to deal with any problems and generally smooth the path. Halifax visited every state, more than any other British Ambassador had done before. This scouting won McDonnell the nickname 'John the Baptist', as he 'went before to prepare the way of the Lord'. His wide array of contacts all over the United States and stretching back decades proved invaluable in getting local opinion-formers well disposed towards Halifax and succeeded in dispelling the notion of the British Ambassador as 'a stage diplomat with frock coat and eye glass'.[18] McDonnell was always slightly cynical about Halifax's reputation for unworldly asceticism; 'All I can say', he would confide when the subject came up, 'is that if there was only one comfortable chair in the room Edward always took it.'[19]

Writing to Oliver Harvey in early July 1941, Peake told how, on his tours across the American continent,

> Halifax never spares himself but talks to all the old women and the Methodist leaders and those who really form and influence public opinion away from the East Coast. Most of the people we have been getting on these trips have hardly seen an Englishman before, and as for a Lord, they put it in the same category as a performing sealion.[20]

By early August, the view in the Foreign Office was that, in Balfour's words, 'The tide has turned in regard to criticism of Lord Halifax. There is no doubt that for some time he had a very bad press, partly, I think, because he was ill-advised and badly "put across" by the people round him.'[21] His evident hard work and commitment, as well as speeches at open-air rallies and to tens of thousands of munitions workers along the western seaboard, played their part in changing the mood in Halifax's favour. But as is so often the case in politics, it was one particular incident which was to win him popularity.

Visiting Detroit, the heartland of isolationism, in November 1941, he was pelted with eggs and tomatoes by a crowd of America Firsters, who chanted 'Go Home Halifax!' He was afterwards quoted as saying: 'How fortunate you Americans are, in Britain we get only one egg a week and we are glad of those.' The remark was apocryphal, thought up by some bright propagandist in the British Press Service, but it was cabled around the country, received wide coverage and was responsible for a burst of popular sympathy and goodwill towards the British in general and Halifax in particular.

It was really America's entry into the war in December 1941 that marked the beginning of Halifax's widespread popularity. As the representatives of their closest ally, it was patriotic to fête the Halifaxes in Washington. When the news of Pearl Harbor broke, Lady Halifax called for a bottle of champagne to be brought through, explaining to their American butler, Maddams, that there had been a birth in the family.[22]

The crux of Halifax's job was to be on good terms with President Roosevelt. The President's friend and counsellor, Harry Hopkins, thought Halifax was a good choice for Ambassador because Roosevelt, who was a snob, would appreciate Halifax's social background, hunting, All Souls' Fellowship and piety.[23] Although their initial meeting went well and Roosevelt asked him to 'look him up' whenever he liked, Halifax's reluctance to 'shoot the breeze' meant that he only saw the President four times in his first six months, each time solely to petition him for more help for Britain. Halifax got on well with a number of Roosevelt's key aides, especially Hopkins, Sumner Welles and Felix Frankfurter. These contacts helped him a good deal when issues such as that of the protection of Atlantic convoys threatened to strain Anglo-American relations.

Halifax never mastered the working of the American political system and always believed Roosevelt was too beholden to the vagaries of American public opinion. He was made to understand how much pressure the President felt himself to be under over the question of aid to Britain. London continually urged that more pressure be put on the administration to provide armed naval escorts to keep the Atlantic supply routes free from the threat of U-boat attack. When the unarmed American merchantman *Robin Moor* was sunk in June 1941, three key heads of British missions added their voices to the calls on Halifax to beard Roosevelt and request American naval support for convoys. Halifax drew up a memorandum advocating 'Shoot on Sight', which he took the precaution of first showing to Hopkins. Hopkins, by then a close friend of Halifax's, warned the Ambassador not to embarrass the President when public opinion was in such turmoil. As so often in his career Halifax took an independent stand and overrode the objections of colleagues and superiors, deciding not to press the matter. The decision paid off and Roosevelt later thanked Halifax for Britain's restraint on the issue.

It was this sort of sympathy for the other side's point of view that Churchill had in mind when he made the damaging, intemperate and undeserved remark that, 'Edward is a man compounded of charm. He is no coward, no gentleman is, but there is something that runs through him like a yellow streak; grovel, grovel, grovel. Grovel to the Indians, grovel to the Germans, grovel to the Americans.'[24] In fact, far from grovelling, Halifax negotiated skilfully with the Americans and as the war progressed he found himself having to do so from positions of greater and greater weakness. He provided lubrication for the Churchill–Roosevelt relationship, which recent scholarship has shown to have been considerably more jagged than contemporaries believed and Churchill later made out. Halifax's fine working relationships with Cordell Hull, Hopkins and other administration officials did much to smooth transatlantic business at the times when the Churchill–Roosevelt axis was in the doldrums.

Halifax never had a particularly high regard for Roosevelt and told Churchill's doctor, Lord Moran, that he did not think him 'a very great man ... he was, of course, a very adroit manipulator. ... But what he did was to split the American people.'[25] He told Dalton that Churchill tended to idolize Roosevelt, who was 'a little like Lloyd George. You never quite know when you've got him, or whether he will not slip through your fingers.'[26]

The Churchill–Roosevelt correspondence, in which the former referred to himself as 'Former Naval Person', effectively cut Halifax out of the high-level decision-making process and reduced his role, as he told a friend, to 'not much more than a Post Office here, the way ... [Churchill] works it ... and for the rest I'm a public relations fellow, making speeches and showing them a nice ambassador'.[27] Once he had adjusted to the fact that all the important decisions were taken above his head, Halifax made an excellent Ambassador: conscientious, hard-working and innovative in his execution of London's orders. He also began fully to appreciate the grandeur of Churchill's achievements: 'Every day I realize more how much we owe to you,' he wrote to Churchill in May 1941.[28]

He was never entirely free from the occasional indiscretion; in October 1941, he let it be known that (as if anyone could think differently) Britain was unlikely to be launching an attack on the European continent in the near future. Aneurin Bevan, accusing Halifax of giving 'comfort, consolation and reassurance' to Hitler, delivered a philippic in the Commons in which he demanded punishment of 'this irresponsible person with a bad record.... How far removed from treason is a statement like that?' None the less, Eden closed the Foreign Office file on the affair with the words, 'Better leave this alone.'[29]

The British presence in Washington grew massively during the war. In 1939, there were only a couple of hundred Britons living at the Embassy, but by 1945 some 9,000 worked in the various military and civil commissions attached to it. So many ministries had missions in Washington that Halifax found himself presiding over what amounted to a microcosm of Whitehall. By the end of the war, there were seven ministers, twelve counsellors and dozens of first secretaries at the Embassy. Sir Geoffrey Cox remembered how Halifax chaired the meetings of these diplomats, heads of missions and representatives from the Dominions in a manner that was 'always calm, efficient, quiet and judicious; never wasting a word and only intervening when absolutely necessary'.[30]

So paramount was American goodwill that the diplomatic service earmarked its brightest talents for service there. These men were of such high calibre that they were to provide many of the Foreign Office's top Ambassadors and Deputy Under-Secretaries for the next two decades. Sir George Middleton (who with Redvers Opie and Donald Maclean used to make up a tennis four with Halifax) considers the wartime Washington Embassy to have been 'probably the apogee of British diplomacy. There was an outstanding esprit de corps.'[31] The intellectual firepower was considerable; the Fellows of All Souls who worked there included John Foster, Roger Makins, Harold Butler, Robert Brand, Arthur Salter, Denis Rickett, Isaiah Berlin and Halifax himself. Others such as Jean Monnet, Sir John Dill, J. M. Keynes, Arthur Purvis, William Hayter and Derick Hoyer Millar swelled the numbers of brilliant and distinguished men serving under Halifax.

The hours were long and the conditions, especially in the hot weather, often uncomfortable. The Lutyens Embassy, like his Viceroy's House, was beautiful but functionally flawed and entertaining there gave Lady Halifax many of the same problems she had encountered in India. The Halifaxes made a remarkable effort in their socializing; in their private papers there is a list of well over 1,200 people they met, from Mrs F. Phinzy Calhoun who gave a tea party for them in Atlanta in May 1941 to Mr L. S. W. Mempenwolf, the President of the Mandan Town Rotary Club, who welcomed Their Excellencies to North Dakota in April 1946. Writing to Victor Cazalet in April 1943, Halifax adopted a tone of mock conceit which belied his hard work: 'I made twenty speeches in ten days, all frightfully good as I need hardly tell you.'[32]

On one of their periodic visits to London, Lady Halifax recalled a dinner given by Anthony and Beatrice Eden in the Foreign Office flat which had been built for the Halifaxes,

and I felt very sad it was not us who were living there. I always remember that evening as Winston was the only other guest and he was fulminating with wrath against de Gaulle, who, he said, obviously thought he was Joan of Arc. As his wrath died down and the champagne began to have its usual mellowing effect he started talking about himself – I got slightly confused as to his meaning when he said with some emotion: 'That old man up there intended me to be where I am at this time,' until I realized that he was talking about the Almighty and His Divine Providence and Purpose.[33]

Late 1942 brought two family tragedies in quick succession. On 1 November, the Halifaxes' second son Peter was killed at the Battle of El Alamein. Halifax went to church alone and informed his wife on his return. They then attended a lunch later that day. William Hayter and his wife were invited and assumed that the lunch would be cancelled, 'but it was not, and he and Lady Halifax, whom we all admired unreservedly, were almost unendurably brave'.[34] Thanking the Duke of Windsor for his condolences Halifax observed, with an extraordinary display of stiff upper lip, that 'there is really little room for personal sorrow these days, and one can only be thankful that the operations in which he was allowed to be a small part look like being so decisive'.[35] The night before Peter was born, his mother had watched from a roof in Tite Street as a Zeppelin was shot down in flames: 'Peter was born into a stormy world,' she commented after his death. Halifax encouraged his wife to take on yet more relief work to help take her mind off the pain.

Only eight weeks later, on 30 December, there came the further devastating news that their youngest son Richard, who was also serving in the Western Desert, had both legs crushed by an unexploded Stuka bomb which fell on him. His parents took this second blow with equal stoicism. John Russell, who was serving in the Embassy at the time, remembered how Roosevelt offered his private plane to fly the Halifaxes to Cairo, but 'Edward replied that Richard would be in hospital with many boys whose fathers were not ambassadors, and could not have their parents flown to them in Presidential planes. He therefore refused, even though he thought Richard might die.'[36] But Richard survived and was eventually shipped to Washington, where he visited hospitals, gave lectures and helped at the Embassy. Many commentators attribute a good deal of the increase in Halifax's personal popularity in the United States to sympathy over the death of Peter and admiration for the courage and cheerfulness shown by Richard. There was more sadness to come, however, when six months later their old friend and 'Dorch' host, Victor Cazalet, died in a plane crash in Gibraltar.

Back in London, Beaverbrook and others continued to intrigue for Halifax's removal. Once he had completed his tour of duty as Ambassador, reckoned to be about three to four years, Halifax was happy to return home. However, he was determined not to be removed before time, still less replaced by one of the 'gangsters'. At one point he was offered the

Viceroyalty or Secretaryship of State of India, but these he refused, correctly reasoning that his differences of opinion with Churchill on that subject would soon lead to clashes. Indeed, it was over India that Halifax was moved to remark in October 1942 that, 'whatever his talents as a war leader, on many things Winston is little short of a disaster'.[37] Yet when the Air Minister, Harold Balfour, described Churchill as a 'singularly unlovable man', Halifax replied that he 'should have thought that lovable was almost the epithet one might apply to Winston in private life. With all his faults, there is so much that is childishly simple about him.'[38]

Intrigue came closer to ousting him than Halifax ever guessed. Beaverbrook's private papers record how as early as September 1941 Churchill offered him the post of Ambassador, which he accepted, and a telegram was sent to Hopkins to elicit the American response. That nothing came of it may have been because Roosevelt preferred to keep Halifax rather than have to deal with the thrusting and prickly Beaverbrook. But in May 1942, Churchill went so far as to submit a formal request to Roosevelt. Four days later Hopkins replied that the change would be perfectly acceptable to the White House. After a talk with Eden in St James's Park on 15 May, Cadogan noted how Eden 'tells me PM wants to replace H by the Beaver! Ye Gods!!'[39] Hopkins's papers state how he 'received a strictly unofficial message indicating that Churchill was considering the possibility of calling Lord Halifax back to London for service in the War Cabinet and as Leader of the House of Lords. His place as British Ambassador would be taken by Lord Beaverbrook.'[40] Sir Isaiah Berlin, who drafted Halifax's despatches from Washington to London, believes Halifax loathed Beaverbrook. He recalled how in order to avoid having to call him 'Max' in letters, Halifax would prefer to send 'The Toad' a telegram.[41] Halifax's other nicknames for people were instructive too. Lloyd George was 'The Goat' or 'Corgi', Churchill was 'Pooh' and Eden he called 'Draught Mouth'.[42]

When Halifax visited Britain in July 1942, he met Cadogan for an hour, who later recorded 'we discussed all sorts of things (except his possible replacement!)'.[43] The reasons why, having gone through all the preliminary stages of replacing Halifax, Churchill did not finally consummate it, are unclear. It may have been that after Beaverbrook's speech of 23 April 1942 in favour of a Second Front, Churchill felt that to have sent him to Washington might have been construed as the British Government's support for this policy. It may have been that Churchill heard some good report of Halifax, did not want Halifax back in Britain or did not want to lose Beaverbrook. Whatever the reason, as late as July 1943 Beaverbrook was still plotting, but this time with his fellow 'gangster' Bracken as the prospective replacement.

31

'Crowned with Success'

One issue on which Churchill and Halifax did see eye to eye was the problem posed by the Duke of Windsor. 'He feels pretty bitter about being marooned in the Bahamas . . . where there is nobody except casual American visitors whom he can see anything of as a friend,' Halifax wrote to Churchill after a three-and-a-half-hour meeting with the Duke on 15 October 1941.[1] At that meeting, as he later explained to Peake, Halifax had

> to listen to the whole story from the Abdication onward, chiefly a story of grievances – bitter, bitter family grievances and insults and other things never to be forgotten or forgiven. And then a thousand petty things not worth recording but all the stories of an injured soul. I listened to the catalogue of grievances and some of them, though not all, were certainly grievances.[2]

After hearing the full story Peake was moved to comment:

> It is a pity that the Royal Family cannot behave with common decency to him. Distance, frigidity one expects, and is no more than he deserved. But civility (which costs nothing) might certainly be given and if given would deprive him of one well merited grievance.

Halifax wrote to Churchill saying how the Duke 'will want to pay periodic visits to the United States, which personally I think it would be rather cruelty to animals to prevent him doing, so long as he will behave with discretion'.[3] He added how 'I have written a bowdlerized account of all this to the King . . . don't show him this letter!' Churchill did not and the King replied:

> I am so glad you were able to have a talk with my brother over the past, when he was in Washington. The real fact of the matter, which he does not realize, is that having occupied the throne of this country he can never live in this country as an ordinary citizen. We know this, so does Winston, but we can never tell my brother in so many words. He has got to realize it for himself.[4]

As the war progressed it fell to Halifax to coax the Duke into realizing it for himself. Later in his Ambassadorship Halifax had to undertake the delicate role of go-between, whilst all the time dealing with the sensitive political implications of the Windsors' regular and increasingly prolonged visits.

The Halifaxes adored to hear the latest gossip about the Windsors which was brought to them by Martha Cross, an old friend of Lady Halifax's who lived in the Bahamas. They heard how at one official reception there,

> a respectable old doctor got drunk and went up to the Duke, shook him and said, 'Why don't you try and grow up and behave?' The Bahamians appeared to be split between the scandal of the old doctor's disgrace and approval that he should have said in his cups what they all think.

Lady Halifax's heart almost melted when the Duke explained to her that although it was tiresome that their dogs should come to the Embassy where they terrorized her dachshund Frankie, 'You see we can't leave the dogs behind; they're all we have.'[5] Lady Halifax had to commend the Duchess's way with American statesmen's wives: 'I don't like her and I think she is as hard as steel, but I could not but admire the way she behaved.'[6]

King George VI expressed his innermost suspicions to Halifax. On 14 April 1941, he told the Ambassador:

> I did not feel too happy about the Lease of the Bases as the Americans wanted too much written and laid down. Everything was done in their interests, no give and take. . . . I do hope that the Americans will not try and bleed us white over the dollar asset question. As it is they are collecting the remaining gold in the world, which is of no use to them, and they cannot wish to make us bankrupt, at least I hope they do not want to.[7]

The Queen was equally frank. In late April 1941, Halifax received a letter from her after the Yugoslav opposition to the Nazis had collapsed, which read:

> I am sure that [Prince-Regent Paul] was afraid and perhaps weak, but with all his faults I would trust him before any of these politicians. He was always terrified of a coup d'état as of course it would mean the disintegration of such an uncomfortably sham little country. I cannot imagine why they did not return Croatia to Hungary years ago.[8]

At the end of one of the King's letters he explained how 'we are getting short of a certain type of paper which is made in America and is unprocurable here. A packet or two of 500 sheets at intervals would be most acceptable. You will understand this and its name begins with B!!!' As well as providing Bromo soft lavatory paper for Buckingham Palace, Halifax found his name being used by the Duke of Windsor to ship quite large consignments –

eighteen cases in one instance – of whisky and gin into America under the guise of diplomatic 'packages, immune from US customs duties'. His Embassy's cellars were also used to store them.[9]

Halifax did not seem to mind being involved in these peccadilloes too much and always had a healthy respect for the privileges of rank. When the Duchess of Roxburghe wished to return from America to Britain at a time when the priorities for air travel were tight, her appeal to Halifax fixed it for her. He even went to the length of considering changing the number-plates on the Embassy Rolls-Royce so that he could be driven down inconspicuously to his weekend home, Mirador, Langhorne Astor's old house lent to him by Ronald and Nancy Tree, after ordering Embassy staff not to abuse their petrol rationing privileges. 'He was always very conscious of being a Grand Seigneur,' a friend told his official biographer years later; 'when out driving once he passed a beautiful home and wanted to go inside.' When his companion said that they really should not intrude, he replied, 'Nonsense. They will be only too delighted when they know who we are.'[10]

By June 1942, Halifax's views on the value of the Windsors' continued visits, which he was hitherto disposed to think of as good propaganda, underwent a drastic change and he steeled himself to commit some 'cruelty to animals'. He wrote to Cranborne, who as Colonial Secretary was theoretically the Duke's immediate superior, listing

> evidence of what the Duke and Duchess are both most reluctant to believe, namely that there is still a good deal of feeling against them in American quarters, and that therefore the less publicity they get the better . . . he is getting pretty fed up with the Bahamas as you no doubt know.[11]

In November 1943, he wrote to the new Colonial Secretary, Oliver Stanley, to complain that the Duke had been in America for nigh on seven months and 'I am not sure that it is very wholesome or healthy for him to keep on visiting this country.'[12] He went on to implore Stanley to 'get the PM to move him from the Bahamas or from anywhere within obvious reach of this country'.

Halifax's underlying fear, as expressed to Stanley as well as other close friends, was that the idea might take root in London that the Duke would make a good Ambassador to Washington. 'The King would see in it a way out of other difficulties; Winston wouldn't think it mattered too much as he does everything that matters himself; Anthony and the FO might prefer it to Max or Brendan, and so on!'[13] He also suspected that the appointment would be popular in America. However, Halifax, for wholly unselfish reasons, set his face firmly against this idea. Despite the tortuous language adopted, it is clear that his principal objection was the negative impact such an appointment might have on the popularity in America of the King and Queen:

> I vaguely feel that, this country being what it is, familiarity with [the Windsors] is not unlikely to breed a certain kind of sympathy, and from

that sympathy the transition to the thought of his having been unjustly treated and therefore of some resentment against those who unjustly treated him is not a large one.[14]

In early December 1943, Stanley replied that the Duke had already turned down Bermuda and he doubted the Duke's 'judgement and experience. . . . Much as I would like to help I cannot do it at the expense of what I believe might well be a political catastrophe in a major Colony.'[15] Halifax passed this letter on to the Queen's brother, David Bowes-Lyon, who worked in the Political Warfare Executive in Washington, saying, 'In the light of it I doubt whether it is very profitable to pursue the other matter that you suggested.'[16] It is not known what 'the other matter' was, but a number of other suggestions, including setting the Duke up as a Southern gentleman, emanated from the Royal Family over the coming years, none of which proved amenable to the Windsors. In May 1944, Halifax wrote to Stanley asking that the Duke be prevented from visiting America at all during the sensitive pre-election period, 'unless you can find some other way out'.[17] Halifax dealt with the potential embarrassments caused by the Windsors with tact and managed to retain the confidence of both sides of the family divide.

Considerably less tact was shown in his speech to the Empire Club in Toronto on 23 January 1944, in which he expounded his view of the post-war world. After predicting that the United States, China and Russia would emerge as the three superpowers, Halifax called for greater Commonwealth unity in the spheres of foreign policy, defence, economics, colonial questions and communications, and went on to urge that 'Not Great Britain only, but the British Commonwealth and Empire, must be the fourth power in that group upon which, under Providence, the peace of the world will henceforth depend.'[18] This was not intended as a controversial policy statement, and the speech itself really only consisted of a series of normal Halifaxian generalities, but the references to the post-war Empire touched some very raw Canadian nerves.

The speech was instantly denounced by the Canadian Prime Minister, William Mackenzie King, who announced 'that Canada will not tolerate any centralized Imperialism on foreign policy'. He told the Canadian High Commissioner in London that had it been peacetime he would have called a general election on the issue.[19] Mackenzie King also complained to the Governor-General in Ottawa that, although the Conservative newspapers in Toronto had received copies of the speech in advance, the Canadian Government had not, and 'if Hitler himself wanted to split the Empire . . . he could not have chosen a more effective way, or a better instrument'.[20] The last four words are revealing – it was really the combination of Lord Halifax, Tory Toronto and the Empire Club that had angered the Liberals, rather than what Halifax had actually said. This was an overreaction by Mackenzie King to a minor gaffe by Halifax, who immediately apologized and explained 'how unconscious he had been that his speech would cause any concern'. [21] The Canadian press, Mackenzie King and a clearly embarrassed Churchill in the House of Commons all promptly repudiated Halifax's remarks.

If Churchill disapproved of Halifax's view of the post-war world, the feeling was more than reciprocated. Halifax was 'intensely irritated' by Churchill's Fulton speech, which he felt to be 'a waste of Churchill's commanding position' as it 'simply cut off any progress toward an accommodation with Russia'. [22] It did not help that Churchill rehearsed the speech in Halifax's sick-room as he was convalescing from a severe bout of chickenpox, 'which was rather a trial for Edward,' recalled Lady Halifax, 'who was really feeling extremely ill'. [23] Halifax had felt broadly sympathetic towards Russia since Hitler's invasion and had taken her side against the demands of the Polish and Baltic Governments-in-Exile. On his first visit home in August 1941, he stayed at Chequers and told Churchill that he was 'emphatic that we must "cough up supplies for Russia"'. [24] He expressed a number of more unorthodox opinions on that occasion, saying that after the war more Tory MPs should come from secondary schools as they were better educated than public schoolboys. He also enthusiastically endorsed the fourth clause of the Atlantic Charter, which provided for freedom of trade and access to raw materials. Churchill agreed about the school question and went on to discuss at length the sex life of the duck-billed platypus.

Halifax was unimpressed by Churchill's Themistoclean foresight about the Iron Curtain and Cold War. In July 1944, he had told Dalton how 'we must always treat the Russians with the greatest consideration, and never let them think we were having secrets with the Americans from which they were excluded'. [25] His pro-Russian stance was tempered by another and altogether more *realpolitik* consideration, which he privately expressed to Churchill: the fear of 'Stalin one day getting a good offer from Hitler'. [26]

Hand in hand with these pro-Soviet views (which were probably shared by the majority of Britons of the day) came his belief in and work for post-war international co-operation. An American official closely involved in this, Alger Hiss, remembers how 'He was always thoroughly committed to the cause of the United Nations and could not have been more co-operative.' [27] He played an important role at the Dumbarton Oaks Conference, the precursor to the setting up of the United Nations. At the United Nations' inaugural conference in San Francisco in mid-June 1945, an observer noted how 'However hot, tired and bad-tempered the other delegates may become, Halifax remains cool and Olympian and makes benevolent cloudy speeches.' [28] He also took a close personal interest in atomic questions and told his final press conference before leaving Washington that he considered its peaceful development to be the greatest issue facing mankind.

In May 1944, Churchill offered Halifax an earldom, which he accepted, on behalf of 'the team with which I have worked'. [29] In a later letter he gently chafed Churchill that this would allow the name of Irwin to reappear as his eldest son's courtesy title, 'but that would hardly be a consideration that would make great appeal to you'.[30] When Churchill lost the general election, Halifax, as a Conservative and a political appointee, was placed in a somewhat invidious position. But as when Wedgwood Benn succeeded Birkenhead at the India Office in 1929, Halifax had no difficulty in leaping the ideological divide; indeed, he may well have been more comfortable serving Clement Attlee's Ministry than Churchill's. Certainly, the incoming Labour Foreign Secretary, Ernest Bevin, was keen to do nothing to weaken the precarious relationship Britain had with Harry Truman's administration, and asked Halifax to stay on. Roosevelt's death in April 1945 had brought to the Presidency a man with a far more hard-headed estimate of the extent of Britain's newly discounted place in the world. The 'extra' year Halifax was to have in Washington gave him the opportunity to render one last great service.

As Halifax had predicted, Britain had paid a massive human, material, financial and imperial price for her brief but untarnishable hour of glory. British greatness and leading place in the world, hitherto in the lives of all of them a fixed star in the geo-political firmament, was on the wane. In 1945, Britain emerged from the war exhausted and almost bankrupt, enormously diminished in everything tangible and possessed only of the reputation of having single-handedly for a year saved the world from 'a new Dark Age'. But this coin was of limited value on the American financial scene and Halifax firmly discouraged Britons in Washington from constantly harping on about it, wisely arguing that they would do better to lead the Americans to generosity through their own perceived self-interest rather than some fleeting sense of gratitude.

For Britain was in the direst of financial straits. She had lost over eleven million tons of merchant shipping, exports were running at £258 million against a pre-war figure of £471 million and imports were £1,299 million against £858 million. Overseas debt had quintupled to £3,355 million, making her the world's largest debtor nation. The war had cost approximately one-quarter of her entire pre-war wealth and against any reckoning she was utterly exhausted. After VE-Day, the economist John Maynard Keynes predicted 'a financial Dunkirk'[31] for Britain and more austerity than had even been necessary during the war. Vast loans from America and Canada were urgently required and it fell to Keynes and Halifax to negotiate them.

In the opinion of Douglas Jay, who was then a personal assistant to the new Labour Prime Minister,

> the three areas of British control, Germany, India and Malaysia, came in 1945 to within a few weeks of mass starvation. Food could only be bought by dollars ... without the loan Sterling would have been devalued by fifty per cent, raising our cost of living and reducing rationing to wartime levels or worse.[32]

Richard Fry, then financial editor of the *Guardian*, believes that 'without the loans there could have been real starvation and long delays in reconstruction (housing, power stations, railways, etc.) and the political considerations might have been revolutionary'.[33]

To fight Britain's corner in the immensely long, tough and complex negotiations with the American Treasury was Keynes, whose obvious financial genius gave rise to the ditty:

> In Washington Lord Halifax,
> Once whispered to J. M. Keynes,
> 'It's true they have the money bags,
> But *we* have all the brains!'

Halifax was the first to admit his relative ignorance of financial matters. When the subject of discount rates came up in one discussion, he noted in his diary that this was 'one of the subjects that I made up my mind long ago I should never understand, and so I do not make any attempt'.[34] In his memoirs Andrei Gromyko, the then Soviet Ambassador to Washington, complained that 'It was not worth trying to talk to him on such things as economics, unemployment, monopoly profits or trade unions.'[35] The breakdown of responsibilities was therefore obvious; Keynes took care of the financial part of the negotiations whilst the personal and wider political problems were left to Halifax.

It was to prove a remarkably successful team. One of the heads of mission, Robert Brand's Private Secretary, Lord Egremont, wrote to his mother in November 1945 extolling the arrangement: 'Lord Halifax's interventions, well-spaced, well-timed and presented with simplicity, dignity and honesty have great effect . . . he can often strike a common note, while Lord Keynes, the genius, for all his charm, performs alone.'[36] Halifax ensured that when Keynes's sharp wit ruffled the feathers of the American negotiators, they were always smoothed down. 'Halifax and I work together like brothers,' Keynes wrote to his mother on 4 November. When on 15 November the Americans presented their first draft offer, it was Halifax who threatened to pull out of the negotiations altogether. This was a bluff, but hardly an example of 'grovelling' to the Americans. Similarly when the Permanent Secretary to the Treasury, Sir Edward Bridges, was sent out to head the British delegation, theoretically over Keynes's head, it was Halifax who persuaded Keynes not to resign.

The $3.75 billion deal was finally agreed on 6 December 1945. The negotiations had lasted for months and Halifax felt a wholly deserved pride in the result. Therefore, when the news came through that back in London the Conservative Party had abstained in the vote on the loan, he was furious, expressing his 'profound irritation with . . . the Conservative Party leaders'. He told a friend, 'I expect you'll see me turning Labour before I'm done.'[37] To Lord Brand he described the decision as 'completely contemptible'.[38]

The Tory attitude certainly dulled his appetite for further politics when finally his mission came to a close, over six years after it had begun.

On Halifax's retirement from Washington, Churchill told him how 'your work through these dangerous and momentous years is so widely respected and crowned with success'.[39] Even given the American habit of superlatives, the leave-taking messages Halifax received from those Americans with whom he had worked are impressive. Cordell Hull told him, 'no other diplomatic representative here during my time has made a record equal to yours in its importance and far-reaching results'. Edward Stettinius wrote, 'Edward, I admire you as much as any man I have ever known', and Henry Morgenthau considered he had made 'a real contribution toward the ultimate winning of the war'. Averell Harriman went so far as to say: 'We never had an ambassador in America who enjoyed a wider acceptance. ... Britain's most effective ambassador.'[40]

The longevity of Halifax's Ambassadorship undoubtedly helped. He was in the United States for five of the most momentous years of the Special Relationship. He had, after a disastrous start, been phenomenally successful. He felt real affection for America, presided over the Pilgrims, made many return visits and counted those years in Washington, which he had initially dreaded so much, as amongst the happiest of his life. His achievement cannot be estimated in terms of initiatives taken or votes won, but rather in the relationships he built up with individual American politicians and administration officials, the combating of profound anti-British feeling which arose over the Second Front in 1942, his negotiations from an increasingly weak position, his endless public-relations tours across the continent, his defusing of the Windsor situation and finally his work for the American loan of December 1945.

Although Churchill asked him to join the Conservative Shadow Cabinet, Halifax answered that, having so recently been an Ambassador and privy to the Labour Government's policies, his position would be compromised. In fact, Halifax felt no desire to re-enter the post-war political ring. He retired to Garrowby, but continued regularly to attend the House of Lords. On one such occasion, on 15 July 1947, his contribution to the Indian Independence Bill was, in the words of the then Secretary of State for India, the Earl of Listowel, 'the only occasion I can remember in over fifty years in the House of Lords when a single speech has changed the mood of the House'.[41]

In the summer of 1948, the Halifaxes visited Germany, but 'came back with no very high hopes of German re-education in the democratic way!' He believed that 'they must be resentful – and even if they blame Hitler (and I fancy that many are rather more sorry for the failure than for the attempt!) they must be moved by national feeling to dislike the instrument of his downfall'. If in this he has so far been proved demonstrably wrong, who can gainsay his oft-repeated opinion, expressed first to Eden and 'Bobbety' Salisbury on 1 August 1945, that Churchill would do well to retire from politics and write books? Suez shocked him; 'Never', he wrote to Valentine Law-ford, 'have so few been able so quickly to inflict damage on so many.'[42]

In 1957, Halifax published a slim volume of memoirs entitled *Fulness of Days*. These he likened to a sundial, in that it 'only records the hours in which the sun shines'. Full of childhood anecdotes, the book was written princi-pally to amuse family and friends rather than to enter the lists on the ap-peasement debate, although it did contain a stout defence of Chamberlain from some of the more virulent criticism of him that was current in the mid-1950s. He took particular pains to contradict Churchill's account of Chamberlain's conduct at the time of Munich. If statesmen have a duty to History to record and justify their stewardship of office, Halifax signally failed in his and *The Times* rightly complained that to the history of inter-war Britain, 'Lord Halifax deliberately adds little ... except at the level of social triviality.'

Away from the public eye Halifax was quite prepared to enter into his-torical debate, especially with Churchill, with whom he had a lively corre-spondence correcting what he saw as Churchill's many errors of judgement about appeasement. These never became too personal for, as Churchill told his doctor in December 1947, 'Halifax's virtues have done more harm in the world than the vices of a hundred people. And yet when I meet him, I can't help having friendly talk.'[43] In 1947, Halifax went to great lengths on behalf of Chamberlain's widow, Anne, to prove that after Munich Roosevelt had telegraphed 'Good Man' to her late husband.

In September 1948, Lord Ismay persuaded Churchill to excise a passage in Volume Two of his war memoirs, which dealt with the Bastianini affair and read, 'The Foreign Secretary showed himself willing to go a long way.'[44] Churchill magnanimously went so far as to alter the passage which com-mended by name only Attlee and Chamberlain for being 'stiff and tough' at the crucial 26 May 1940 meeting to read, 'I found my colleagues very stiff and tough. All our minds ran much more on bombing Milan and Turin.'[45] Halifax showed little thanks; instead, he told Anne Chamberlain of the many errors of fact in Churchill's works, 'for I fancy the main purpose of the books is not only to write history, but, also, to "make a record" for W.S.C.'. In July 1953, he told Samuel Hoare, by then Lord Templewood, 'I have no doubt at all that [Churchill] has been more responsible than anyone else for India wishing to get rid of the British.'[46] Halifax was unwise enough, a week later, to make similarly unflattering remarks about her husband within earshot of Clementine Churchill, at a luncheon given by the French Ambas-sador. 'I don't know what you're getting at,' snapped Lady Churchill, in her typically straight-talking way. 'If the country had depended on you we might have lost the war.' When Halifax asked her to apologize, her husband said he hoped she would not.[47]

Retirement kept Halifax almost as busy as working life. He took a keen interest in the dozen livings of which he was patron. As Chancellor of

Oxford he did not often appear at Encaenia but, according to Lord Salter, he worked hard for Oxford behind the scenes, at one stage successfully lobbying Hugh Gaitskell, then Minister of Power, against the erection of unsightly gasholders near Oxford.[48] In 1957, he was created Grand Master of the Order of St Michael and St George without even previously having been a member of the Order. He was also president or governor of some thirty charities, societies and religious institutions, from Pusey House to the Governesses Benevolent Fund. He took seriously his Honorary Colonelcy of the Yorkshire Dragoons. He enjoyed retirement and was fond of telling his farm manager that, after all the travelling he had done, 'Garrowby Hill is the finest view I have ever seen.'[49]

Halifax took a delight in the patronage and aristocratic gossip attendant on being Chancellor of the Order of the Garter. In the immediate post-war period he was despondent about the fact, as he put it to the King's Private Secretary, Sir Alan Lascelles, that the 'respectable land-owning peers . . . are not a very distinguished lot'.[50] In the political field 'of those who have won their spurs in this sphere, every possible candidate appears to have been an active member of the Opposition'.[51] He was unable to think of a single candidate, but rejected Churchill's characteristic suggestion of returning to the chivalrous days of the Order's founder Edward III, and awarding it to 'young paladins' such as Bernard Freyberg, who had been wounded in action nineteen times. Halifax told Lascelles:

> In this grim austerity at home and starving millions abroad, the Crown and its ministers might easily be criticized for paying too much heed to what is to the uninformed vulgar only an archaic and rather expensive survival of a vanished age, when the word 'aristocracy' had a much healthier connotation than it has now.[52]

In his list of suggestions for 1949, Halifax included his brother-in-law, the Earl of Iveagh, and his son-in-law, the Earl of Feversham. His concern for respectability was ever-present, and in September 1956 he advised the Queen's Private Secretary that the Duke of Northumberland should have the Garter before another equally grand nobleman, on the grounds that 'the domestic menage I should judge to be rather more secure!'.[53]

Death came peacefully on 23 December 1959, at the age of seventy-eight. Some three months before he had celebrated his golden wedding anniversary with 600 friends, family and tenants at Garrowby. He had also recently received the news of his son Richard's promotion to ministerial rank. He was buried in the churchyard of Kirby Underdale on the Garrowby estate, where Lady Halifax was to follow him sixteen years later. The obituaries, coming at the period before appeasement became subject to revisionist historical interpretation, were mixed and best summed up by Lord Pakenham's observation in the *Observer* that, 'Lord Halifax dies a controversial figure, and is likely to remain so for some time to come.'

Conclusion

The High Priest of Respectability

'Treason', wrote Talleyrand (who ought to have known), 'is a question of dates.' Although his Viceroyalty provides a character witness and the Ambassadorship some mitigating circumstances, it is for the part he played in appeasement that Lord Halifax stands in the dock of History. The dates certainly look damning. From June to November 1935, he was Secretary for War and responsible for an army he did not believe would have to fight, which he did nothing to strengthen and which five years later was swiftly and humiliatingly routed. In November 1937, he shook hands with some of history's most evil tyrants and failed to find them anything but quite charming. On taking over the Foreign Office in February 1938, he made a fundamental miscalculation and refused to believe 'that Hitler's racial ambitions are necessarily likely to expand into international power lust'.[1] Until September 1938, he strained every nerve to find accommodation with the Nazi regime. From 25 to 28 May 1940, he pressed for steps to be taken to ascertain terms under which the Second World War could be brought to a more or less ignominious end. It is a formidable charge sheet.

Dates also form the basis of his defence. On 25 September 1938, only days before Chamberlain flew to Munich, Halifax led a revolt against the Godesberg terms and called for 'the destruction of Nazism'. In the months between Munich and Prague, he was the only man in the Cabinet who had enough authority to engineer the dismantling of appeasement before the Prime Minister's very eyes. In its place he succeeded in building a new consensus for resistance. He championed a new military strategy of continental commitment, the formation of a truly national government, the creation of a Ministry of Supply, immediate universal military conscription, the building of a 'Peace Front' combining military guarantees in Eastern Europe with a Russian entente, closer links with America, the breaking off of colonial discussions with Germany and, above all, increased and more intensive rearmament, especially in the air. That he achieved only some of these aims goes to prove how phenomenally strong Chamberlain was, even up to the outbreak of war. With appeasement, even more than with Macmillan over Suez, Halifax was 'first in, first out'. Finding himself on a treadmill of humiliation from the day he took on the Foreign Secretaryship, Halifax was the first statesman of seniority and prestige in the Government to conclude that until Nazism was destroyed there would be no peace in Europe.

It is argued – with a good deal of hindsight – that 1938 was late in the day for his eyes to be opened. But before Godesberg what was the alternative? In 1948 Churchill wrote of 'how easily the tragedy of the Second World War could have been prevented,'[2] but if one side ignores deterrents and refuses to abide by international convention, just how could it be? Through the invasion of a sovereign state in 1935 or 1936, because the victors of 1918 disliked its new leaders? Through the attempt indefinitely to hold down a resurgent nation of eighty millions situated at the heart of Europe? Through bankrupting the one strong bulwark against the westward thrust of Communism? Through the refusal of the right of ethnic Germans to join their Fatherland? Through insistence on every dotted 'i' and crossed 't' of a harsh and often nonsensical treaty signed under duress, and which had no machinery for future review? The reunification of Germany and her elevation to independent Great Power status is today seen as a cause for celebration, at least in the West. Western leaders said nothing about Germany in the 1920s and early 1930s that is not being repeated almost word for word by their successors today.

The obloquy Halifax attracted was, as with the press criticism in the autumn of 1940, largely undeserved. A cursory selection of it portrays him as: 'a trimmer if ever there was one' (Christopher Sykes), 'unctuous' (General Ironside), he 'poured the salt of hypocrisy into the wounds of the Czechs' (Robert Bruce Lockhart), 'the wrong man at the Foreign Office' (Lord Birkenhead), 'an admirer of Franco' (Michael Foot), the 'faithful accomplice of appeasement' (Lord Jenkins), 'wrapped in eternal shame' (Randolph Churchill), 'despicable' (Sir Richard Acland), 'a boring giraffe' (Norman Stone), 'Chamberlain's Sancho Panza, trotting faithfully behind him' (Malcolm Muggeridge) and 'a child out of his depth' (Correlli Barnett) who would 'betray the fortresses of democracy' (Harold Laski). Even his former Parliamentary Private Secretary and biographer, Lord Birkenhead, privately described him as 'in some ways an unappealing character, I was irritated at his naïveté – repelled by his meanness and astonished by the way he could square his conscience to suit whatever he wanted to do'.[3] When Birkenhead's book was reviewed in *The Times Literary Supplement*, the anonymous reviewer explained that 'if it sometimes makes tedious reading that is largely the fault of the subject'.[4]

Although a number of these judgements date from the period before the official documents became available to show the complex and multi-polar pressures on British inter-war policy-makers, there is still no shortage of people who subscribe to them, and they remain the general verdict of history.

It is easiest to dispose of the perennial accusation of naïveté and otherworldly innocence. Far from a pious blindness to the evils of the world, Halifax was too keenly aware of men's failings. He was if anything more guilty of cynicism than of monkish innocence. The nickname 'The Holy Fox' was not intended to denote a mean, sly or vicious temperament, merely, as Colville noted, one 'capable of cunning in his diplomacy'.[5] As Halifax put it to Sir Isaiah Berlin, 'The duty of an official must be to tell the truth, the whole truth and nothing but the truth. It would be the greatest dereliction of duty to do otherwise. But it is all a matter of emphasis.'[6] Harold Caccia remarked in exasperation: 'Really, my master ought not to use phrases like "do you think we can get away with that one?"'[7] Sir Charles Peake's widow probably put it best when she told Birkenhead:

> one was convinced that he could not have compromised on anything he held to be Essential Truth [yet] over small things he had an almost schoolboy's disregard for unessential truth.... This occasionally made his less understanding friends call him a bit of a humbug.[8]

For a man who at least nominally looked forward to the eventual reconciliation between Rome and Canterbury, setbacks which disconcerted others weighed less heavily on him. During the Civil Disobedience campaigns he refused to overreact to Congress provocations, instead encouraging his officials to view the disturbances within the broader perspective of an ultimate settlement. In October 1940, having visited Lord Gainsborough's house in Chipping Campden which had been fired to prevent its capture by Cromwell, Halifax observed, 'I could not have done that, for I should have always hoped to get Oliver Cromwell out again.' When he wrote his speech to the League urging recognition of the Italian conquest of Abyssinia, he philosophized about 'the need for adapting ideals to facts in this hard world'.[9]

Compromise, a degree of guile and awareness of the realities of life in no way contradicted his or his father's practical and worldly High Anglicanism. 'Many of our intellectual difficulties', he wrote in September 1940, 'come from an attempt to think that the Kingdom of God and the Kingdom of this world are concerned with the same problems ... in a very vital sense they are not.'[10] His continual emphasis on consensus, compromise and the need to adapt to changed (and usually worse) world circumstances has more than a whiff of modern 'Wet' Toryism to it. The vital difference is that Britain today is a talented but poor power trying to better herself, whereas in the 1930s she was a Great but declining Power with everything to lose. His political philosophy was as pragmatic then as it would be nonsensical today.

Maisky's view of international law, 'as a combination of legal niceties originating in the will of the strongest powers', struck Halifax as 'cynical, but not altogether untrue'. The view of him as an innocent abroad, registering meek surprise at each successive Nazi outrage, bears no relation to reality. In a letter to the Governor of Bengal shortly after he became Foreign Secretary, Halifax argued that

> we go badly wrong if we allow our judgement of practical steps to be taken to be perpetually deflected by our moral reactions against wrongs that we can in no circumstances immediately redress. The world is a strangely mixed grill of good and evil, and for good or ill we have got to do our best and not withdraw from it into the desert because of the evil, like the ancient anchorites.[11]

Despite his continual and unswerving demand that any peace negotiations should only be undertaken if the terms were in no way prejudicial to British independence, Halifax's reputation still suffers from accusations of intended treachery. The sincere and oft-repeated stipulations of 26 to 28 May 1940 that he would not look at terms which affected British sovereignty or the ability of Britain to defend herself ought to dispose of the arguments of those who still seek to portray him as a Quisling-in-Waiting. Any other Foreign Secretary would also have had to distinguish from the scores of 'peace feelers' which arrived on his desk between those which were useful to British diplomacy and those which were not. Some were used to 'buy time' as Halifax's Garrowby note of 6 May 1940 shows; others to keep open contacts with the anti-Nazi opposition; yet others were useful indicators of German strength and intentions (as with the attempts to maintain a line to Göring); but none were used for any but the highest of patriotic motives. As Laurence Thomson has put it:

> for a limited period (until American intentions became clearer) and for a definite purpose (to prevent invasion during the crucial weeks of British disorganization) not only Halifax and the FO but also Churchill himself were using every underground means at their disposal to foster Hitler's belief that the British were willing to think about peace.[12]

Had Hitler invaded, Halifax would have joined King and Government in Canada. He certainly never lacked personal physical courage, as was proved by his hunting, pig-sticking and volunteering for the Great War despite his having only one hand, as well as by his cool behaviour during the attempt on his life in 1929.

In that age of giant political personalities – Churchill, Birkenhead, Lloyd George, Balfour, Austen Chamberlain – Halifax was consciously modest and reserved. Yet those buccaneers fell in 1922 to a plot in which Baldwin, Halifax and Hoare had all taken part. Neville Chamberlain was to join it as soon as family obligations had been observed. It was one of the two times this century that a Prime Minister had been forced out of office in peacetime and it drew the battle-lines that were to last until far into the Second World War. The side a man had chosen on 19 October 1922 mattered deeply to all participants. Halifax's relations with Churchill, the Dominion Status controversy and the struggle over the India Act, Lloyd George's behaviour at the Norway debate and the political alignments in most of the other great issues can only properly be understood in the context of the trauma of what had happened at the Carlton Club that day. It was seen as the triumph of Respectability over waywardness and piracy: the victory of the bishops over the bookies.

The Respectable Tendency it brought to power was to govern Britain, with only the briefest of gaps, for the next eighteen years. Halifax personified it. His aristocratic background contrasted with that of most of his colleagues, but, by dint of his religious convictions, his values and personal rules of behaviour meant that he had more in common with the 'middle-class monster' Neville Chamberlain than the high-born Balfour or Churchill. His All Souls Fellowship provided the intellectual cachet, his Eton fellowship the solidity, his title the deference, his hunting and Yorkshire acres the social approval, his sensible and charming Onslow wife the reassurance, his wartime career the record, his Viceroyalty the prestige, his height the awe and, above all, his piety the esteem which made Lord Halifax the high-priest of Respectable government. Appeasement was born at the Carlton Club. Insofar as the plotters had a rallying cry, it was Bonar Law's letter in *The Times* which said that Britain 'cannot alone act as the policeman of the world'. It was the gunboat diplomacy of the Turkish crisis which was largely responsible for bringing the Coalition down.

Appeasement was Respectability's foreign policy; Lloyd George and Winston Churchill its chief enemies; the General Strike its domestic and the Hoare–Laval Pact its foreign tests; the Abdication crisis its vindication; the 1935 general election its zenith and the Norway debate its nemesis. On 9 May 1940, Halifax recognized that in this century Respectable methods do not win wars – he had said as much as a young MP to Asquith's Government in 1916 – and so he allowed Churchill and 'the gangsters' to take over.

Respectability often spilled into stuffiness. 'Halifax was referred to as Halifax,' remembered Valentine Lawford, 'only facetiously as Edward.' Chamberlain called him 'Halifax' in his letters to his sisters, even though he used to refer to 'Anthony' and 'Winston'. There was a slightly ridiculous side to all this; Halifax's Victorian upbringing might have explained personal rules such as his spending no more time in the bathroom than it took for the bathwater to run out. His antiquated attitude to nicknames, telephones, divorce, driving (he learnt at sixty-four), dress and above all risqué jokes made him, in Colville's view, 'a subject worthy of Dryden or W. S. Gilbert'.[13] Certainly, any comic opera written on Halifax would have to make use of the leaflet which the Ministry of Information put out about him in November 1939, which tried to persuade foreign correspondents that the Foreign Secretary was no 'Dismal Desmond', but 'has an almost schoolboy sense of fun'.

Yet he did have a humility which saved him from the pomposity that might otherwise have been his lot. A friend remembered how

> He is always bemoaning his lack of ability to say the stirring thing and says he never has an original thought. He said once a little sadly, 'Oh, I'm like Walter [Monckton], always suitable for any job as I'm sure not to commit a bloomer and I shall do it nicely. I have been put forward for everything from Head Master of Eton, Master of Balliol, Prime Minister, etc.'[14]

For all that modesty, he did come to within a polite refusal of the wartime Premiership despite not having contested an election in thirty years.

It has been written that, 'So far as the fall of the British Empire can be epitomized in a single event, it was when Gandhi entered Irwin's palace.'[15] Yet, paradoxically, it was largely to protect that same Empire that Halifax strove to avoid the second apocalyptic struggle in Europe, which he knew would highlight imperial weaknesses and inevitably lead to its break-up. Halifax believed that the British Empire provided 'a rallying point of sanity for a mad civilization', and, having seen what has taken its place, it is clear that he was right.[16]

Much of what Halifax feared has come to pass. Today, Hickleton Hall is a hospital for the insane, 'The Dorch' is owned by a foreigner, Temple Newsam is a museum, 88 Eaton Square has been split up into flats and the beautiful Little Compton Manor, where the Halifaxes spent so many happy weekends in 1940, is now a college of accountancy. The Second World War killed one son, maimed another and obliterated for ever some of the best elements of the British way of life. But it was a national exhaustion which had to be undergone and a price which had to be paid. What it cost Britain, today a middle-rank power, has been more than made up for in everlasting and untarnishable glory. Churchill, whose entire political life had been one long gamble, saw the greatest of them all pay off handsomely.

As well as being a fine husband and father, Halifax was also the devoted friend of that small but talented coterie of people such as Baldwin, Lothian, Cadogan, Dawson and Monckton whom he trusted and had known for a long time. The Dominion Status Declaration showed that he was tough and self-confident enough to act on his own when he considered it necessary, even in the face of the pleas of his friends. When the occasion demanded – for example, against the Coalition in 1922, Hoare in 1935, Butler in April 1939, Hore-Belisha in 1940, and possibly even Chamberlain himself on the morning of 10 May 1940 – Halifax could wield the political knife swiftly and mercilessly. He needed this nerve, working under two of the strongest personalities ever to occupy the post of Prime Minister. With Chamberlain he used innate sympathy tempered with intellectual rigour. Under Churchill he employed the equally successful technique of forbearance, patience and logic. This last sparked a creative tension which served Britain well during the great crises of 1940. Even in wars – perhaps especially in wars – there is need for the still small voice of calm.

Halifax left no followers, no '-ism' or intellectual bridge by which historians can trace, say, the connection between Whiggery and modern 'Wet' Conservatism. He found the very idea of political ideology alien and slightly absurd, preferring the more British reliance on instinct and common sense. 'High paternalism' is probably the best way to describe a man who could write to his father from India in the late 1920s: 'What a bore democracy is to those who have to work it. . . . I think it is a great pity that Simon de Montfort, or whoever it was, ever invented our parliamentary system.'[17] Halifax left no oeuvre of famous remarks or quotable epithets: only a small number of quizzical understatements, such as that to Dalton just before Dunkirk: 'Invasion? That *would* be a bore.'[18]

On taking his leave in Washington, John Wheeler-Bennett, said that he was about to write a book on Munich. Halifax asked him, 'Will I have to stand in a white sheet in the judgement of History?' When Wheeler-Bennett told him he probably would, Halifax lisped, 'My wivvers are quite unwung.' Acute sensitivity to Britain's military unpreparedness, the lack of Commonwealth unity, massive pressures in the Far East, the undecided nature of public opinion, fears in the Treasury of another 1931, Russian mendacity, American isolationism, the weakness of the French air force and the fact that the terms were better than at Godesberg persuaded Halifax to support the Munich Agreement. He knew that even were a preventive war to be fought, Czechoslovakia would hardly have been reconstituted with her 1919 frontiers. He prayed too that his suspicions were wrong and that Hitler would be satiated by the inclusion of his Aryans in the Reich.

Part of what makes Britain unique is her willingness tolerantly to put up with indignities – even humiliations – until, her conscience clear, she draws the line and pronounces, 'Thus far and no further'. Halifax was exactly in tune with that spirit when he drew that line at the German/Polish frontier in April 1939.

Lady Halifax recalled how, in September 1939,

It seems odd to say so, but it was really almost a relief when the blow fell, the anticipation and the flickers of hope were so unnerving, and I believe to know the worst brought a certain stability to one's thought. I am sure Edward felt this, as he had been going through such hell, the reality could not be worse.[19]

He had felt it, and it was largely due to his ceaseless efforts for peace that Britain could enter the war as the champion of wronged and outraged Civilization.

His complicity in appeasement before *Anschluss* was more than compensated by his firmness in guiding the Government away from it after Godesberg. To have seen his mistake and worked from within the Government to rectify it took courage and application. In the last year of peace, he outmanoeuvred the hard-line appeasers in the Government, without causing a rift that would weaken it. People in a position to know, such as Butler, gave Halifax the credit 'for leading the Cabinet swiftly but steadily towards an inevitable declaration of war'.[20] After the war began, his wise counsel provided a restraining influence which ensured Britain benefited from all of Churchill's unmatched leadership and genius, without experiencing any of the disasters which that leadership had before tended to bring in its wake. The oft-repeated assertion that had Halifax become Prime Minister instead of Churchill 'we might have lost the war' is as hypothetical as it is hyperbolical. Churchill would still have been running the operational side, with Halifax providing the political leadership. History would have been denied morale-boosting speeches from No. 10, and Halifax might have been relegated to 'honorary' Prime Minister, but Britain would not have lost the war as a result.

As it was, Halifax's natural modesty and shrewd political instinct told him that his 'inability to say the stirring thing' meant that he must rule himself out. He had no wish to become the Asquith to Churchill's Lloyd George, marginalized by his lack of military expertise until finally disposable. Instead, like Bonar Law in December 1916, he stood aside for the Man of Destiny.[21] Where Churchill relished the opportunity of at last running the war, it gave Halifax a stomach-ache. If guilt and innocence are a question of dates, Halifax, clad in his white sheet before the bar of History, can cite in his defence his noble self-denial during the fateful interview on the afternoon of Thursday, 9 May 1940.

Lord Hailsham has recently commented how

> Cardinal Newman used to say that he looked in vain for the finger of God in history. He said it was like looking into a mirror, expecting to see his own face, and seeing nothing. The one case in which I think I can see the finger of God in contemporary history, is Churchill's arrival at the Premiership at that precise moment in 1940.[22]

For those who cannot quite bring themselves to believe in modern miracles, the credit must go instead to 'The Holy Fox'.

Source Notes

All notes refer to the Halifax Papers at The Borthwick Institute, York, unless otherwise stated. The Halifax Diary is to be found there under A 7–8. FO, PREM and CAB relate to papers at the Public Record Office at Kew. RA refers to the Royal Archives at Windsor and RAB to the RA Butler Papers at Trinity College, Cambridge. IOLR stands for the India Office Library and Records and NC means the original document can be found in the Neville Chamberlain Papers at the University of Birmingham. DBFP is short for *Documents on British Foreign Policy* and DGFP for *Documents on German Foreign Policy*. 'Cadogan' relates to the *The Diaries of Sir Alexander Cadogan 1938–1945* edited by Professor David Dilks. All references to the Churchill Papers in the Archives at Churchill College, Cambridge, are taken from the companion volumes to Martin Gilbert's magisterial eight-volume biography.

Introduction: Judgement (pp. 1–3)

1 T. J. Jones, *A Diary with Letters 1931–50*, p. 204
2 Viscount Stuart, *Within the Fringe*, p. 96

1: Birth, Boyhood, Bereavement (pp. 4–9)

1 *The Times Literary Supplement*, 1935
2 Talbot Papers
3 J. G. Lockhart, *Viscount Halifax 1839–85*, p. 168
4 Sir Charles Peake Diary, 16 January 1941
5 A2 278 1, 17 April 1893
6 Lord Birkenhead interview with Lord William Percy
7 A2 278 1
8 Lord Holderness's memoir of his mother
9 Lady Lloyd Diary, January 1910
10 Interview with Alan Campbell Johnson

11 Andrei Gromyko, *Memories*, p. 125
12 Lord Birkenhead interview with General Bradshaw
13 R. A. Butler, *The Art of Memory*, p. 38

2: 'Blameless Rather Than Brilliant' (pp. 10–18)

1 A2 78 1, February 1914
2 A2 278 9, 3 August 1914
3 Hansard H.C. LXXXI, cols 2637–42
4 Hansard H.C. C, cols 693–4
5 A2 278 1
6 Ben Pimlott (ed.), *The Second World War Diary of Hugh Dalton 1940–45*, p. 101, 14 November 1940
7 A4 410 8, June 1922
8 A4 410 9, 'early summer 1922'
9 Amery Diary, 20 September 1922
10 A4 410 26
11 Interview with Albert Sylvester, 1 November 1988

12 W. S. Churchill, *Thoughts and Adventures*, p. 154
13 H. Begbie, *The Conservative Mind*, chapter 3
14 *Ibid.*
15 RA GV N2028/3, 7 October 1925
16 J. Campbell, *F. E. Smith*, p. 744

3: India (pp. 19–25)

1 *The Times*, 30 October 1925
2 RA GV N2556/40, 7 January 1926
3 *Ibid.*
4 IOLR C152/1
5 Cecil Papers MSS 51084
6 NC 7/11/12/14, 15 April 1929
7 John Gordon Duff, *It Was Different Then*, p. 53
8 The Earl of Lytton, *Antony, Viscount Knebworth*, p. 248
9 *The Spectator*, 7 January 1944
10 RA GV N2556/74
11 Cecil Papers MSS 51084
12 Swinton Papers 313/1/3, 26 October 1926

4: The Declaration (pp. 26–30)

1 IOLR C152/27, 12 June 1929
2 IOLR C152/1, 23 April 1928
3 Baldwin Papers E5/104
4 *Ibid.*, E5/107
5 *Ibid.*, E5/109
6 IOLR C152/18, 28 October 1929
7 Martin Gilbert, *Winston S. Churchill*, vol. 5, pp. 353ff
8 J. F. C. Watts, 'The Viceroyalty of Lord Irwin ...': chapters 3 to 6 owe much to this excellent thesis
9 S. Gopal interview with the Earl of Halifax
10 IOLR C152/27, 4 November 1929
11 IOLR C152/18, 5 November 1929
12 Hansard CCXXXI, col. 1306, 7 November 1929
13 IOLR C152/18, 13 November 1929
14 IOLR C152/1, 6 November 1929

5: Irwinism (pp. 31–7)

1 Interview with Nirad Chaudhuri, 18 October 1988
2 IOLR C152/27, 24 December 1929
3 Lord Birkenhead interview with Lady Harlech

4 Lord Birkenhead interview with General Bradshaw
5 IOLR C152/19, 31 March 1930
6 IOLR C152/6, 7 April 1930
7 IOLR C152/1, April 1930
8 IOLR C152/1
9 IOLR B217
10 Nirad Chaudhuri, *Thy Hand, Great Anarch!*, p. 302
11 Watts, *op. cit.*

6: Peace in India (pp. 38–43)

1 IOLR C152/6
2 IOLR C152/1
3 Interview with Colonel Francis Lane Fox, 25 April 1989
4 Lord Birkenhead interview with Sir Cecil Griffin
5 IOLR C152/27, 10 March 1931
6 Watts, *op. cit.*
7 Sir Penderel Moon, *The British Conquest and Dominion of India*, p. 1051
8 IOLR C152/6, 4 March 1931
9 Speech to the Council of the West Essex Conservative Association, 23 February 1931, quoted in Robert Rhodes James (ed.), *Churchill Speaks*, p. 528
10 Speech to the Indian Empire Society, 12 February 1931
11 IOLR C152/19, 5 March 1931
12 Jones, *op. cit.*, p. 5
13 Dalton Diary, p. 126, 18 December 1940
14 Robert Bernays, *Naked Fakir*, p. 280

7: The Rationale of Appeasement (pp. 44–55)

1 The Earl of Halifax, *Fulness of Days*, p. 180
2 Bernays, *op. cit.*, p. 51
3 John Vincent (ed.), *The Crawford Papers*, p. 556, 20 November 1934
4 Bernays, *op. cit.*, p. 235
5 J. C. W. Reith, *Into the Wind*, p. 356
6 Robert Rhodes James, *Memoirs of a Conservative*, p. 306
7 Lord Birkenhead interview with Lord David Cecil

8 IOLR Stopford Papers
9 Lord Birkenhead interview with Dr Prescott
10 IOLR F97/22B, 9 May 1935
11 IOLR D596/20, 28 April 1938
12 Dr Patrick Glyn, *The Sarajevo Fallacy*
13 Sir Nevile Henderson, *Water under the Bridges*, p. 216
14 Cecil Papers MSS 51084, 6 April 1927
15 RAB B/11
16 Lord Birkenhead interview with Lord Cadogan
17 Talbot Papers
18 Paul Kennedy, *The Realities Behind Diplomacy*, p. 280
19 Lord Boothby, *My Yesterday, Your Tomorrow*, p. 131
20 RAB F79/93
21 Lord Birkenhead interview with Sir Roger Makins
22 Interview with Jasper Rootham, 22 October 1988
23 Letter from Sir Patrick Reilly, 29 August 1988
24 FO 800/309/367, 28 September 1938
25 Baldwin Papers 174, 29 September 1939
26 *Ibid.* 123/58, 19 August 1937
27 Lord Birkenhead interview with Lord Stuart
28 Baldwin Papers 173/58, 27 May 1937
29 *Ibid.* 73/177, 16 October 1932
30 PREM 1/193 and 1/194
31 Brian Bond (ed.), *Chief of Staff: The Diaries of Lieutenant-General Sir Henry Pownall*, p. 74
32 A2 278 1, 19 May 1932
33 Cecil Papers MSS 51084, 4 December 1936

8: *Eminence Grise* (pp. 56–63)

1 Wesley Wark, *The Ultimate Enemy*, p. 17
2 CAB 23/90B 56(35), 18 December 1935
3 J. A. Cross, *Sir Samuel Hoare*, p. 259
4 The Earl of Avon, *Facing the Dictators*, p. 383

5 *Ibid.*, p. 319
6 CAB 23/84 40(36), 29 May 1936
7 CAB 23/83 16(36), 9 March 1936
8 CAB 23/83 18(36), 11 March 1936
9 *Ibid.*
10 *Ibid.*
11 *Ibid.*
12 DGFP Series C, vol. 5, no. 33
13 PREM 1/194
14 DGPF Series C, vol. 5, no. 244
15 Halifax, *op. cit.*, p. 192
16 CAB 23/87 1(37), 8 January 1937
17 Lord Holderness's memoir of his mother
18 Halifax, *op. cit.*, p. 182
19 A2 278 30, 12 December 1936
20 Charles Stuart (ed.), *The Reith Diaries*, p. 188
21 Sir Frederick Leith-Ross, *Money Talks*, p. 20
22 Mann to Blunt's biographer, Ewart-Binns
23 R. F. V. Heuston, *Lives of the Lord Chancellors*, p. 486
24 *Ibid.*
25 RAG VCC 47/1559, 11 December 1936
26 Interview with Sir Godfrey Nicholson
27 CAB 23/87 2(37), 13 January 1937
28 NC 7/11/30/64
29 NC 18/1/1026, 30 October 1937

9: 'Counsels of Despair' (pp. 64–75)

1 Jones, *op. cit.*, p. 215
2 A4 410 3 2
3 *Ibid.*, 29 October 1937
4 Avon, *op. cit.*, p. 509
5 A4 410 3, 6 May 1946
6 *Ibid.*
7 Kenneth Young (ed.), *The Diaries of Sir Robert Bruce Lockhart*, 25 May 1946
8 John Harvey (ed.), *The Diplomatic Diaries of Oliver Harvey 1937–40*, p. 57, 7 November 1937
9 *Ibid.*, p. 58, 9 November 1937
10 *Ibid.*, p. 59, 11 November 1937
11 Cecil H. King, *With Malice Toward None*, p. 54, 13 June 1940
12 Harvey, *op. cit.*, p. 60, 16 November 1937

13 Robert Rhodes James, *Anthony Eden*, p. 183
14 Harvey, *op. cit.*, p. 59, 11 November 1937
15 Baldwin Papers 173/61, 15 November 1937
16 A4 410 3 3 (iii)
17 *Ibid.*
18 *Ibid.*
19 *Ibid.*
20 *Ibid.*
21 Letter from Hon. David Astor, 23 November 1989
22 Sylvester Papers
23 DGFP Series D, vol. 1, p. 34
24 A4 410 3 3
25 *Ibid.*
26 Sources are A4 410 3 3; Ivone Kirkpatrick, *The Inner Circle*, pp. 94–101; Paul Schmidt, *Hitler's Interpreter*, pp. 75–8; and CAB 23/90 43 (37), 24 November 1937
27 A4 410 3 3
28 Kirkpatrick, *op. cit.*, p. 96
29 *Ibid.*, pp. 95–7
30 A4 410 3 3
31 Schmidt, *op. cit.*, p. 76
32 *Ibid.*, p. 78
33 A4 410 3 3
34 Kirkpatrick, *op. cit.*, p. 101
35 A4 410 3 3
36 Lord Birkenhead interview with Lady Alexandra Metcalfe
37 IOLR F97/22B, 21 May 1937
38 CAB 23/90 43(37), 24 November 1937
39 *Ibid.*
40 NC 18/1/1030, 26 November 1937

10: Lines of Latitude (pp. 76–90)

1 IOLR F97/22B, 1 January 1938
2 A4 410 33
3 *Ibid.*
4 *Ibid.*
5 *Ibid.*
6 CAB 27/623 21st, 24 January 1938
7 *Ibid.*
8 *Ibid.*
9 A4 410 3 2
10 A4 410 3 2 (xv)
11 FO 371/21709/1431
12 Richard Cockett, *The Twilight of Truth*, p. 65, and FO 371/21709/1607

13 *Ibid.*, p. 43
14 IOLR C152/27, 30 April 1930
15 NC 18/1/1030, 26 November 1937
16 FO 800/313/15, 4 April 1938
17 Jones, *op. cit.*, p. 377
18 FO 800/313/11, 12 March 1938
19 NC 18/1/1030, 26 November 1937
20 Ronald Smelser, *The Sudeten Problem 1933–8*, p. 205
21 CAB 23/90 45(37), 1 December 1937
22 CAB 23/90 49(37), 22 December 1937
23 Letter from Reinhard Spitzy, 18 May 1989
24 Lord Jay, *Change and Fortune*, p. 74
25 CAB 23/92 4(38), 9 February 1938
26 A4 410 4 11 1
27 CAB 23/92 6(38), 19 February 1938
28 A4 410 4 11
29 NC 18/1/1040, 27 February 1938
30 CAB 23/92 5(38), 16 February 1938
31 A4 410 4 11
32 *Ibid.*
33 Interview with Lord Caccia, 2 November 1988
34 Kenneth Rose, *The Later Cecils*, p. 104
35 Harvey, *op. cit.*, p. 63, 5 December 1937
36 IOLR F97/22B, 23 February 1938
37 Norman Rose (ed.), *Baffy: The Diaries of Blanche Dugdale 1936–47*, 10 March 1938
38 Valentine Lawford, 'Three Ministers', *Cornhill Magazine*
39 Harvey, *op. cit.*, p. 100, 23 February 1938
40 Lawford, *op. cit.*
41 IOLR F97/22B, 9 March 1938
42 Interview with Lord Caccia, 2 November 1988
43 FO 800/328/38, 1 March 1938
44 Norman Baynes (ed.), *Hitler's Speeches 1922–39*, p. 1379
45 IOLR F97/22B, 15 March 1938
46 CAB 23/92 10(38), 2 March 1938
47 CAB 23/92 11(38), 9 March 1938
48 *Ibid.*
49 Harvey, *op. cit.*, p. 110, 7 March 1938
50 *Ibid.*, p. 113, 11 March 1938
51 *Ibid.*

11: 'Spring Manoeuvres'
(pp. 91–101)

1 NC 18/1/1041, 13 March 1938
2 *Ibid.*
3 Alan Bullock (ed.), *The Ribbentrop Memoirs*, p. 84
4 *Ibid.*, p. 86
5 BDFP 3rd Series, vol. I, pp. 4–6
6 NC 18/1/1041, 13 March 1938
7 *Ibid.*
8 Interview with Count Raczynski, 12 May 1989
9 CAB 23/93 12(38), 12 March 1938
10 *Ibid.*
11 Walter Citrine, *Men and Work*, pp. 364–6
12 CAB 27/623 26(38), 18 March 1938
13 *Ibid.*
14 *Ibid.*
15 *Ibid.*
16 *Ibid.*
17 *Ibid.*
18 Harvey, *op. cit.*, p. 124, 25 March 1938
19 *Ibid.*, p. 121, 19 March 1938
20 *Ibid.*, p. 124, 25 March 1938
21 CAB 23/93 15(38), 22 March 1938
22 *Ibid.*
23 *Ibid.*
24 *Ibid.*
25 Hansard HC CCCXXXIII, cols 1399–1413
26 CAB 2/7 317th, 31 March 1938
27 CAB 2/7 304th, 16 December 1937
28 Lord Birkenhead interview with Sir Alexander Cadogan
29 Lord Birkenhead's interviews with Sir Alexander Cadogan and Sir Isaiah Berlin
31 Christopher Andrews and David Dilks, *The Missing Dimension*, p. 78
32 RAB F79/24
33 *Ibid.*
34 NC 18/1/1043, 27 March 1938
35 DBFP 2nd Series, vol. XIX, no. 316
36 CAB 27/623 24th, 1 March 1938
37 Harvey, *op. cit.*, p. 119, 17 March 1938
38 CAB 27/623 25th, 15 March 1938
39 W. P. Crozier, *Off the Record*, p. 81
40 FO 800/311/128, 1 November 1938
41 CAB 27/623 29th, 29 March 1938
42 David Low, *Years of Wrath*, introduction
43 Malcolm Muggeridge (ed.), *Ciano's Diary 1939–43*, p. 10, 12 January 1939
44 CAB 27/623 27th, 21 March 1938
45 IOLR F97/22B, 22 June 1938
46 CAB 2/7 319th, 11 April 1938
47 CAB 23/93 15(38), 22 March 1938

12: The Czech Crisis (pp. 102–11)

1 DBFP 3rd Series, vol. I, no. 264
2 *Ibid.*
3 NC 18/1/1053, 27 May 1938
4 R. Bruce Lockhart, *Jan Masaryk*, p. 18
5 DGFP Series D, vol. II, no. 315
6 FO 800/311/30
7 FO 800/309, 22 June 1938
8 FO 800/314/25
9 FO 800/314
10 *Ibid.*
11 IOLR D596/20, 22 September 1938
12 A4 410 4 10, 15 November 1939
13 CAB 27/623 30th, 1 June 1938
14 *Ibid.*
15 *Ibid.*
16 *Ibid.* and PREM 1/303
17 Harvey, *op cit.*, p. 161, 7 July 1938
18 Citrine, *op. cit.*, p. 364
19 A4 410 3 3
20 FO 800/309
21 Lothian Papers GD 40/17/362
22 Dawson Papers MS 42, 7 September 1938
23 CAB 23/95 37(38), 12 September 1938
24 NC 18/1/1066, 3 September 1938
25 NC 18/1/1069, 19 September 1938
26 *Ibid.*
27 CAB 23/95 39(38), 17 September 1938
28 *Ibid.*
29 *Ibid.*
30 Cadogan, p. 100, 18 September 1938

13: 'Changing Back into Men'
(pp. 112–22)

1 DBFP 3rd Series, vol. II, no. 1003
2 *Ibid.*
3 *Ibid.*
4 *Ibid.*, no. 1040

5 Lord Birkenhead interview with Sir Alexander Cadogan
6 DBFP 3rd Series, vol. II, no. 1049
7 *Ibid.*, no. 1058
8 CAB 23/95 42(38), 24 September 1938
9 *Ibid.*
10 Cadogan, p. 105, 25 September 1938
11 Letter from Sir Ivo Mallet, 29 August 1988
12 Cecil Papers MSS 51084, 22 September 1938
13 R. J. Minney (ed.), *The Private Papers of Hore-Belisha*, p. 146, 25 September 1938
14 CAB 23/95 43(38), 25 September 1938
15 *Ibid.*
16 *Ibid.*
17 *Ibid.*
18 *Ibid.*
19 A4 410 3 7
20 *Ibid.*
21 CAB 23/95 43(38), 25 September 1938
22 CAB 2/8 332nd, 15 September 1938
23 *Fulness of Days*, p. 197
24 Paul Johnson (ed.), *The Oxford Book of Political Anecdotes*, p. 213
25 DBFP 3rd Series, vol. II, no. 1111
26 A4 410 19 3
27 CAB 23/95 46(38), 27 September 1938
28 *Ibid.*

14: Whispers at the Triumph
(pp. 123–30)

1 Dalton Diary, p. 140, 8 January 1940.
2 Lady Mosley, *A Life of Contrasts*, p. 158
3 Garrowby Albums 1938
4 A4 410 19 3, 4 October 1948
5 CAB 23/95 47(38), 30 September 1938
6 Hansard HC CCCXXXIX, 3 October 1938
7 Hansard HL CX, 3 October 1938
8 Leo Amery, *My Political Life*, vol. III, p. 283
9 FO 800/328/175, 18 October 1938

10 Harvey, *op. cit.*, p. 208, 1 October 1938
11 Lord Birkenhead interview with Sir Harold Caccia
12 CAB 23/95 48(38), 3 October 1938
13 Cadogan, p. 114, 9 October 1938
14 FO 800/328/171, 11 October 1938
15 *Ibid.*
16 NC 18/1/1072, 15 October 1938
17 Montagu Papers, 14 October 1938
18 FO 800/311/105, 28 October 1938
19 *Ibid.*
20 CAB 2/8 334th, 20 October 1938
21 NC 18/1/1074, 27 October 1938
22 FO 371/21791
23 CAB 2/8 341st, 15 December 1938
24 CAB 2/8 345th, 26 January 1939
25 CAB 27/624 36th, 26 January 1939
26 *Ibid.*
27 Peake Papers, 19 February 1957
28 CAB 27/624 32nd, 14 November 1938
29 Wark, *op. cit.*, p. 113
30 CAB 27/624 32nd, 14 November 1938
31 *Ibid.*
32 FO 800/314/205, 9 December 1938
33 Churchill 2/343
34 NC 18/1/1077, 27 November 1938

15: 'Nothing for Nothing'
(pp. 131–8)

1 Harvey, *op cit.*, p. 213, 12 October 1938
2 *Ibid.*, p. 208, 1 October 1938
3 Interview with Lord Home of the Hirsel, 8 February 1989
4 Duff Cooper Papers
5 Harvey, *op. cit.*, p. 244, 14 January 1939
6 NC 18/1/1080, 17 December 1938
7 *Ibid.*
8 IOLR F97/22B, 14 December 1938
9 Interview with Jasper Rootham, 22 October 1988
10 *Ibid.*
11 FO 371/23083 and FO 371/21588
12 CAB 23/96 59(38), 14 December 1938
13 Interview with the Duke of Portland, 9 November 1988

14 CAB 23/97 5(39), 2 February 1939
15 *Ibid.*
16 Lord Chatfield, *It Might Happen Again*, p. 163
17 Cadogan, p. 119
18 IOLR D/596/20, 28 March 1938
19 RAB G11 130
20 PREM 1/2668
21 CAB 27/624 37th, 8 February 1939
22 *Ibid.*
23 Rex Benson Diary, 22 January 1939
24 CAB 27/625 46th, 10 May 1939
25 CAB 23/96 60(38), 21 December 1938
26 Amery, *op. cit.*, p. 306
27 NC 18/1/1082, 15 January 1939
28 A4 410 3 11
29 Harvey, *op. cit.*, p. 255, 17 February 1939

16: 'Halt! Major Road Ahead!'
   (pp. 139–48)

1 NC 18/1/1087, 26 February 1939
2 CAB 23/97 6(39), 8 February 1939
3 R. A. Butler, *The Art of the Possible*, p. 77
4 Harvey, *op. cit.*, p. 249, 29 January 1939
5 *Ibid.*, p. 258, 2 March 1939
6 Keir Papers
7 Harvey, *op. cit.*, pp. 260–61, 10 March 1939
8 NC 17/11/32/11
9 CAB 23/98 11(39), 15 March 1939
10 Harvey, *op. cit.*, p. 263, 18 March 1939
11 CAB 23/98 19(39), 18 March 1939
12 C. J. Hill, 'The Decision-making Process in Relation to British Foreign Policy 1938–41', p. 48
13 CAB 23/98 12(39), 18 March 1939
14 *Ibid.*
15 Harvey Papers MSS 56401
16 CAB 27/624 38th, 27 March 1939
17 CAB 23/98 12(39), 18 March 1939
18 Churchill Papers 2/371, 28 March 1939
19 NC 18/1/1091, 26 March 1939
20 Harvey, *op. cit.*, p. 268, 25 March 1939
21 FO 800/311/244

22 Count Edward Raczynski, *In Allied London*, p. 12
23 Lord Birkenhead interview with the Earl of Avon
24 CAB 23/98 15(39), 29 March 1939
25 Cadogan, p. 164, 29 March 1939
26 Lord Birkenhead interview with Sir Reginald Leeper
27 NC 18/1/1092, 2 April 1939
28 CAB 23/98 16(39), 30 March 1939
29 *Ibid.*
30 CAB 27/624 40th, 31 March 1939

17: The Peace Front (pp. 149–65)

1 NC 18/1/1093, 9 April 1938
2 PREM 1/357/36, 15 May 1939
3 FO 800/321/26, 19 May 1939
4 CAB 27/624 41st, 10 April 1939
5 Harvey Papers MSS 56401, 15 April 1939
6 CAB 23/98 21(39), 19 April 1939
7 Minney, *op. cit.*, p. 195, 17 April 1939
8 *Ibid.*
9 CAB 23/99 22(39), 24 April 1939
10 *Ibid.*
11 CAB 23/99 24(39), 26 April 1939
12 Robert Rhodes James (ed.), *Chips: The Diaries of Sir Henry Channon*, p. 192, 5 April 1939
13 *Ibid.*, p. 193, 13 April 1939
14 NC 18/1/1101, 28 May 1939
15 RAB G10/26
16 Lord Birkenhead interview with Lord Chandos
17 Harvey, *op. cit.*, p. 295, 5 June 1939
18 Interview with Martin Gilbert, 4 September 1990
19 Lord Birkenhead interview with Sir Reginald Leeper
20 Harvey, *op. cit.*, p. 284, 26 April 1939
21 Lord Birkenhead interview with Lord David Cecil
22 FO 371/23242
23 FO 800/321/5
24 Lord Birkenhead interview with Lord Harvey
25 Interview with Jasper Rootham, 22 October 1988
26 Lady Halifax's 'Reminiscences'
27 Harvey, *op. cit.*, p. 290, 20 May 1939

28 NC 18/1/1100, 21 May 1939
29 NC 18/1/1101, 28 May 1939
30 CAB 23/99 30(39), 24 May 1939
31 A. L. Rowse, *Friends and Contemporaries*, p.198
32 Cadogan, p.189, 20 June 1939
33 FO 800/328/332, 17 October 1939
34 CAB 27/625 54th, 26 June 1939
35 CAB 23/625 57th, 10 July 1939
36 NC 18/1/1108, 23 July 1939
37 CAB 27/625 60th, 1 August 1939
38 PREM 1/333
39 FO 371/23091
40 Nicholas Mosley, *Beyond The Pale*, p.156
41 Churchill Papers 9/137
42 Cockett, *op. cit.*, p.113
43 FO 800/315/273
44 The National Sound Archives
45 Cadogan, p.190, 29 June 1939
46 Harvey, *op. cit.*, p.301, 1 July 1939

18: 'A Good Conscience' (pp. 165–75)

1 K. Jeffreys, *Labour and the Wartime Cabinet from the Diary of James Chuter Ede*, 1 May 1942 FO 800/314/99
2 Private Information
3 *Ibid.*
4 Raczynski, *op. cit.*, p.24
5 *Ibid.*
6 Inskip Diary, 25 August 1939
7 Vincent, *op. cit.*, p.602, 24 August 1939
8 Lady Alexandra Metcalfe Diary, 22 August 1939
9 Interview with Sir Frank Roberts, 25 July 1989
10 A4 410 3 10 (iii)
11 *Ibid.*
12 Raczynski, *op. cit.*, p.24
13 Harvey, *op. cit.*, p.308, 27 August 1939
14 *Ibid.*, p.309, 29 August 1939
15 Lady Alexandra Metcalfe Diary
16 CAB 23/100 46(39), 30 August 1939
17 A4 410 3 10 (iii)
18 Letter from Sir Ivo Mallet, 29 August 1988
19 Inskip Diary, 30 August 1939
20 Euan Wallace Diary, 31 August 1939
21 A4 410 3 10 (iii)
22 Lady Halifax's 'Reminiscences'.

23 CAB 23/100 47(39), 1 September 1939
24 A4 410 3 10 (iii)
25 CAB 23/100 48(39), 2 September 1939
26 NC 18/1/1116, 10 September 1939
27 Kirkpatrick, *op. cit.*, p.144
28 FO 800/328/313, 3 September 1939

19: 'Atmosphere of Frustration' (pp. 176–85)

1 FO 800/328/175
2 Halifax Diary, 11 February 1940
3 Liddell Hart Papers 3/109, 27 August 1939
4 Private Information
5 *Ibid.*
6 Somerset de Chair Diary, 25 October 1939
7 Inskip Diary, 8 September 1939
8 Cadogan, p.219, 23 September 1939
9 NC 18/1/1116, 10 September 1939
10 Cadogan, p.215, 9 September 1939
11 Lord Gladwyn, *The Memoirs of Lord Gladwyn*, p.96
12 FO 800/317/7, 19 September 1939 and PREM 1/379
13 Vincent, *op. cit.*, p.609, 5 December 1939
14 NC 18/1/1124, 8 October 1939
15 FO 800/311/377, 21 November 1939
16 *Ibid.*
17 Garrowby Albums 1940
18 FO 800/322/214
19 Bruce Lockhart Diary, 24 November 1939
20 Sir David Kelly, *The Ruling Few*, pp.272–3, and FO 371/24407
21 Owen Chadwick, *Britain and the Vatican during the Second World War*, p.94
22 Cadogan, p.258, 14 December 1939
23 FO 800/328/351, 28 November 1939
24 FO 800/324/259
25 J. Lonsdale Bryans, *Blind Victory*, p.50
26 FO 800/326/249, 8 January 1940
27 FO 800/317/196
28 Private information

20: Restraining Winston (pp. 186–94)

1 IOLR D 596/20, 22 September 1938
2 Lady Halifax's 'Reminiscences'

3 Sir John Colville, *The Fringes of Power*, p. 122
4 Private Information
5 IOLR D/596/20, 18 August 1939
6 Lord Birkenhead interview with Sir Alan Lascelles
7 Letter from Colonel Thomas Ingram, 14 May 1989
8 CAB 65/1 WM 22, 21 September 1939
9 Inskip Diary, 23 September 1939
10 FO 800/310/143, 26 October 1939
11 Lady Theodosia Cadogan's Diary
12 Cadogan, p. 234, 28 November 1939
13 Interview with the Duke of Portland, 9 November 1988
14 Harvey, *op. cit.*, p. 232, 24 December 1939
15 Private Information
16 Garrowby Albums 1940
17 Halifax Diary, 5 February 1940
18 Cazalet Diary, 13 April 1940
19 FO 800/325/147, 17 October 1939
20 Churchill Papers 19/2, 13 January 1940
21 Halifax Diary, 13 March 1940
22 *Ibid.*, 11 March 1940
23 Lawford Diary, 17 August 1940
24 NC 18/1/1137, 7 January 1940
25 Halifax Diary, 6 April 1940
26 David Irving, *Churchill's War*, vol. I, p. 217
27 Halifax Diary, 17 February 1940
28 *Ibid.*, 9 April 1940
29 CAB 65/12 102WM
30 Halifax Diary, 3 May 1940

21: 'The Unpersuadable Halifax'
(pp. 195–209)

1 Private Information
2 Lady Alexandra Metcalfe Diary, 7 May 1940
3 Private Information
4 Halifax Diary, 9 May 1940
5 Harvey, *op. cit.*, p. 244, 14 January 1939
6 Halifax Diary, 9 May 1940
7 Butler, *The Art of the Possible*, p. 84
8 Lord Birkenhead interview with Lord Avon
9 Butler, *The Art of the Possible*, p. 84
10 Private Information
11 A4 410 16, 9 May 1940

12 Lady Alexandra Metcalfe Diary, 6 October 1939
13 Sir Arthur Salter, *Security: Can We Retrieve It?*, p. 263
14 PREM 5/170
15 Lord Birkenhead interview with Sir Alan Lascelles
16 IOLR F97/22B, 24 April 1938
17 RA GVI 093/2, 28 February 1939
18 A4 410 4 10, 1 April 1940
19 NC 18/1/1157a, 17 May 1940
20 Letter from Sir Martin Gilliat, 11 November 1988
21 A. J. P. Taylor, *Beaverbrook*, p. 531
22 Letter to Sir Charles Peake, 8 February 1945
23 Sir Winston Churchill, *The Second World War: The Gathering Storm*, p. 524
24 Interview with Sir William Deakin, 10 May 1989
25 Halifax Diary, 9 May 1940
26 Lord Stuart, *op. cit.*, p. 87
27 Laurence Thompson, *1940*, p. 85
28 Peake Diary, 5 June 1941
29 Colville, *op. cit.*, p. 123
30 Prof. T. Evans (ed.), *The Killearn Diaries*, p. 234, 21 August 1942
31 Young (ed.), *op. cit.*, 16 August 1942
32 Lady Alexandra Metcalfe Diary, 9 May 1940
33 Private Information
34 Kenneth Rose interview with the Earl of Halifax, 13 March 1952
35 FO 800/326/116, 4 May 1940
36 Templewood Papers XII 3
37 Letter from Valentine Lawford, 28 November 1988
38 Sir John Wheeler-Bennett, *King George VI*, p. 444
39 Halifax Diary, 10 May 1940
40 Wheeler-Bennett, *op. cit.*, p. 446
41 Private Information
42 Halifax Diary, 11 May 1940
43 RAB G11
44 Irving, *op. cit.*, p. 269

22: Churchill as Micawber
(pp. 210–22)

1 NC 7/9/80
2 A4 410 19 and Churchill Papers 20/2
3 Halifax Diary, 11 May 1940
4 FO 800/328/439, 12 May 1940
5 Private Information

6 Lord Birkenhead interview with Sir Llewelyn Woodward
7 Lord Birkenhead interview with Lady Alexandra Metcalfe
8 Halifax Diary, 25 May 1940
9 CAB 66/7 WP 168th, 25 May 1940
10 *Ibid.*
11 A4 410 4 1
12 *Ibid.*
13 FO 800/319/70
14 PREM 4/19/5, 16 May 1940
15 CAB 65/7 WM 138, 25 May 1940
16 *Ibid.*
17 CAB 65/13 WM 139, 26 May 1940
18 *Ibid.*
19 *Ibid.*
20 Cadogan, pp. 289–90, 25 May 1940
21 CAB 65/13 WM 139, 26 May 1940
22 Reynaud Diary, pp. 398ff, 26 May 1940
23 NC 2/24A, 26 May 1940
24 *Ibid.*
25 *Ibid.*
26 *Ibid.*
27 Halifax Diary, 26 May 1940
28 NC 2/24A, 26 May 1940
29 Halifax Diary, 26 May 1940
30 CAB 65/13 WM 140, 26 May 1940
31 *Ibid.*
32 *Ibid.*
33 CAB 66/7 WP 170, 26 May 1940
34 *Ibid.*
35 CAB 66/7 WP 169, 26 May 1940
36 *Ibid.*
37 CAB 65/13 WM 141, 27 May 1940
38 C. N. Esnouf, 'British Government War Aims and Attitudes towards a Negotiated Peace, September 1938–July 1940'
39 CAB 65/7 WM 141, 27 May 1940
40 Muggeridge (ed.), *op. cit.*, p. 255, 27 May 1940
41 CAB 65/13 WM 142, 27 May 1940
42 Halifax Diary, 27 May 1940
43 CAB 65/13 WM 142, 27 May 1940
44 Esnouf, *op. cit.*
45 CAB 65/13 WM 142, 27 May 1940
46 *Ibid.*
47 Halifax Diary, 27 May 1940
48 Cadogan, p. 290, 26 May 1940
49 Private Information
50 Halifax Diary, 27 May 1940
51 CAB 65/7 WM 142, 27 May 1940
52 *Ibid.*
53 Halifax Diary, 27 May 1940
54 Cadogan, p. 291, 27 May 1940
55 *Ibid.*, p. 292, 27 May 1940
56 *Ibid.*, p. 292, 29 May 1940
57 Halifax Diary, 27 May 1940

23: 'Foredoomed to Failure' (pp. 223–8)

1 CAB 65/7 WM 144, 28 May 1940
2 CAB 65/13 WM 142 Appendix
3 CAB 65/13 WM 145, 28 May 1940
4 *Ibid.*
5 Ben Pimlott (ed.), *The Second World War Diary of Hugh Dalton 1940–45*, p. 28, 28 May 1940
6 *Ibid.*, p. 29, 28 May 1940
7 Stuart (ed.), *op. cit.*, p. 255, 28 May 1940
8 Pimlott (ed.), *op. cit.*, p. 27, 28 May 1940
9 CAB 65/13 WM 145, 28 May 1940
10 CAB 65/13 no. 235 Dipp., 28 May 1940
11 Colville, *op. cit.*, p. 140, 27 May 1940
12 Beaverbrook Papers
13 PREM 4/68/9, 29 May 1940
14 A4 410 17, 12 October 1942
15 Sir Winston Churchill, *The Second World War: Their Finest Hour*, p. 157
16 FO 800/320/140
17 FO 1011/67

24: 'Common Sense and Not Bravado' (pp. 229–37)

1 Halifax Diary, 3 June 1940
2 Colville, *op. cit.*, p. 149, 5 June 1940
3 Halifax Diary, 10 June 1940
4 *Ibid.*, 13 June 1940
5 Major-General Sir Edward Spears, *Assignment to Catastrophe*, vol. II, p. 203
6 *Ibid.*, p. 214
7 PREM 99/3 and Churchill, *Their Finest Hour*, p. 160
8 Halifax Diary, 14 June 1940
9 Tel 723 HP 39A/XXX 111 UPA (Swedish Foreign Ministry Archive), quoted in Tomas Munch Petersen, 'Common Sense and Not Bravado: The Butler–Prytz Interview of 17 June 1940', to which I am greatly indebted

10 *Ibid.*
11 FO 371/24859/206
12 Interview with Lord Colyton, 5 February 1989
13 FO 800/322/277
14 *Ibid.*
15 *Ibid.*
16 Butler, *The Art of the Possible*, p. 82
17 King, *op. cit.*, p. 64, 27 July 1940
18 Pimlott (ed.), *op. cit.*, p. 111, 29 November 1940
19 FO 371/43468, 28 December 1944
20 FO 371/1321, 19 August 1946
21 Munch Petersen, *op. cit.*
22 Halifax Diary, 17 June 1940
23 Louis P. Locher (ed.), *The Goebbels Diaries*, p. 85, 18 March 1942

25: Churchill's Guardian Angel (pp. 238–46)

1 Sir John Colville, *Footprints in Time*, p. 85, and Lord Beloff, *The Intellectual in Politics and Other Essays*
2 FO 371/24327
3 Halifax Diary, 1 July 1940
4 Cadogan, p. 305, 22 June 1940
5 Young (ed.), *op. cit.*, 13 March 1946
6 FO 800/323/246, 19 November 1940
7 FO 371/24310
8 Pimlott (ed.), *op. cit.*, p. 87, 2 October 1940
9 CAB 65/14 WM 209, 22 July 1940
10 *Ibid.*
11 CAB 65/4 WM 196, 7 July 1940
12 FO 371/24569
13 Young (ed.), *op. cit.*, 5 June 1940
14 NC 2/24A, 5 June 1940
15 FO 800/323/109, 16 April 1940
16 NC 2/24A, 7 June 1940
17 Keir Papers
18 Halifax Diary, 6 June 1940
19 NC 2/24A, 5 June 1940
20 Halifax Diary, 6 June 1940
21 Colin Cross (ed.), *Life with Lloyd George*, p. 281, 3 October 1940
22 NC 18/1/1159, 1 June 1940
23 Colville *op. cit.*, p. 197, 17 July 1940
24 Dr Sheila Lawlor, 'British Politics and Strategy May 1940–March 1941'
25 RAB E3/8/114
26 PREM 4/66/2, 4 October 1940
27 CAB 65/14 WM 212, 25 July 1940

28 CAB 65/15 WM 265, 3 October 1940
29 Sir Robert Craigie, *Behind the Japanese Mask*, p. 89
30 Sir David Kelly, *The Ruling Few*, pp. 272–3
31 Halifax Diary, 7 June 1940
32 FO 800/318/147, 12 July 1940
33 *Ibid.*
34 FO 800/318/159
35 Colville, *op. cit.*, p. 201, 26 July 1940
36 Halifax Diary, 28 July 1940
37 *Ibid.*

26: 'A Sensible and Restraining Influence' (pp. 247–57)

1 Lady Halifax's 'Reminiscences'
2 Lady Alexandra Metcalfe Diary
3 Lady Ravensdale, *In Many Rhythms*, p. 229
4 FO 371/24407/92, 18 July 1940
5 Cadogan, p. 309, 2 July 1940
6 Interview with Lord Gladwyn, 8 December 1988
7 Halifax Diary, 10 July 1940
8 FO 800/326/140
9 *King Lear*, Act II, scene iv
10 FO 408/70, 22 July 1940
11 Cadogan, p. 315, 22 July 1940
12 *Ibid.*, 23 July 1940
13 Colville, *op. cit.*, p. 201, 26 July 1940
14 Halifax Diary, 22 July 1940
15 Weizsäcker Diary, 23 June 1940
16 FO 371/24407
17 Nigel Nicolson (ed.), *Harold Nicolson: Diaries and Letters 1939–45*, p. 104, 22 July 1940
18 PREM 4/11/3
19 Halifax Diary, 19 August 1940
20 Cadogan, p. 326, 11 September 1940
21 CAB 65/15 WM 247, 11 September 1940
22 *Sunday Despatch*, 29 September 1940
23 FO 800/325/295, 30 July 1940
24 Halifax Diary, 29 July 1940
25 FO 800/321/105, 29 July 1940
26 FO 800/325/295, 30 July 1940
27 Cadogan, p. 338, 4 December 1940
28 *Sunday Pictorial*, 23 June 1940
29 Elliot Papers 8/F1, 23 November 1940
30 Alexander Papers 5/4/37, 30 September 1940
31 RAB E3/8/125

32 PREM 4/66/2, 19 November 1940
33 *Ibid.*
34 David Reynolds, 'Lord Lothian and Anglo-American Relations'
35 PREM 3/462/2/3
36 Hankey Papers 5/4, 17 July 1940
37 Sir John Balfour, *Not Too Correct an Aureole*, p. 68
38 FO 800/433
39 Lady Alexandra Metcalfe Diary, 21 August 1940
40 Private Information

27: 'Operation Menace' (pp. 258–64)

1 FO 800/323/192, 26 September 1940
2 PREM 4/22/1
3 CAB 65/15 WM 263, 1 October 1940
4 CAB 65/15 WM 259, 26 September 1940
5 CAB 65/15 WM 263, 1 October 1940
6 Halifax Diary, 1 October 1940
7 David Eccles, *By Safe Hand*, p. 200
8 CAB 65/15 WM 267, 7 October 1940
9 Lord Birkenhead interview with Sir Orme Sargeant
10 RAB G10/29, 20 October 1940
11 Halifax Diary, 24 October 1940
12 Private Information
13 *Ibid.*
14 CAB 65/15 WM 278, 28 October 1940
15 FO 371/24361
16 A2 278 68, 19 November 1948
17 Louis Rougier, *Les Accords Pétain/Churchill*
18 Colville, p. 283, 1 November 1940
19 Eccles, *op. cit.*, p. 20
20 Lady Alexandra Metcalfe Diary
21 Cazalet Diary, 18 October 1940
22 Lady Alexandra Metcalfe Diary, 19 November 1940
23 NC 7/11/33
24 *Ibid.*
25 Pimlott (ed.), *op. cit.*, p. 101, 14 November 1940
26 Halifax Diary, 9 October 1940
27 *Ibid.*, 7 November 1940

28: 'He Hates Doormats' (pp. 265–71)

1 Beaverbrook Papers D/29
2 Halifax Diary, 24 September 1940

3 FO 800/321/142
4 FO 800/323/192, 26 September 1940
5 CAB 65/15 WM 265, 3 October 1940
6 FO 800/323/223, 24 October 1940
7 CAB 65/15 WM 282, 4 November 1940
8 Private Information
9 Colville, p. 251, 26 September 1940
10 Halifax Diary, 27 November 1940
11 Cazalet Diary, 22 December 1940
12 Pimlott (ed.), *op. cit.*, p. 101, 14 November 1940
13 Halifax Diary, 5 June 1940
14 *Ibid.*, 29 August 1940
15 Lady Halifax's 'Reminiscences'
16 FO 371/24251
17 Halifax Diary, 10 October 1940
18 FO 371/24251/96
19 CAB 65/15 WM 297, 27 October 1940
20 Private Information
21 Halifax Diary, 23 May 1940
22 Peter and Leni Gillman, *Collar The Lot!*, pp. 104–6
23 Lord Ismay, *The Memoirs of Lord Ismay*, p. 159
24 Lady Alexandra Metcalfe Diary, 11 December 1940
25 Ismay, *op. cit.*, p. 162
26 Gilbert, *op. cit.*, vol. 5, p. 587
27 Lady Alexandra Metcalfe Diary, 13 November 1940
28 Private Information
29 *Ibid.*

29: Banishment (pp. 272–80)

1 Halifax Diary, 12 December 1940
2 Pimlott (ed.), *op. cit.*, p. 101, 14 November 1940
3 R. Casey, *Personal Experience*, p. 47
4 Lord Birkenhead interview with Lord Stuart
5 Halifax Diary, 17 December 1940
6 *Ibid.*
7 Cadogan, p. 341, 17 December 1940
8 Taylor, *op. cit.*, p. 591
9 Avon, *op. cit.*, pp. 151–2
10 Lord Birkenhead interview with Lord Avon
11 Halifax Diary, 19 December 1940
12 Pimlott (ed.), *op. cit.*, p. 125, 18 December 1940

13 *Ibid.*
14 Dawson Diary, 19 December 1940
15 Private Information
16 Colville, *op. cit.*, p. 321, 20 December 1940
17 Private Information
18 Halifax Diary, 20 December 1940
19 *Ibid.*
20 Private Information
21 *Ibid.*
22 Talbot Papers
23 Cadogan, p. 343, 22 December 1940
24 Valentine Lawford Diary, 23 December 1940
25 Cadogan, p. 343, 23 December 1940
26 Private Information
27 Wheeler-Bennett, *op. cit.*, p. 520
28 *Ibid.*
29 Lady Halifax's 'Reminiscences'
30 *Ibid.*
31 Baldwin Papers 124, 20 December 1940
32 A4 410 4 3, 1 May 1940
33 James Leutze (ed.), *The London Journal of General Raymond E. Lee*, p. 215
34 Lady Halifax's 'Reminiscences'
35 A2 278 206, 26 July 1941
36 Private Information

30: 'De-Icing Edward' (pp. 281–90)

1 For chapters 30 and 31 I am greatly indebted to Nicolas Cull's MA thesis, 'The Fall and Rise of a Fox-Hunting Man Abroad', and Lesley Neal's MLitt. thesis, 'The Washington Ambassadorship of Lord Halifax 1941–6'
2 *Fulness of Days*, p. 242
3 Cull, *op. cit.*
4 Rex Benson Diary, 13 April 1941
5 Peake Diary, 17 February 1941
6 A4 410 4 15, 4 February 1941
7 RA KGVI 053/USA/03, 6 May 1941
8 *Ibid.*, 17, 20 December 1944
9 Rene Kraus, *Men Around Churchill*, p. 13
10 Letter from Alistair Cooke, 16 January 1989
11 Young (ed.), *op. cit.*, 12 May 1941 and 12 July 1941
12 Lord Birkenhead interview with Sir John Wheeler-Bennett

13 FO 371/26184/198
14 Pimlott (ed.), *op. cit.*, p. 246, 8 July 1941
15 Casey, *op. cit.*, p. 65, 22 April 1941
16 Sir Isaiah Berlin letter to Kenneth Rose
17 Casey, *op. cit.*, p. 64, 7 April 1941
18 McDonnell Diary, 8 May 1941
19 Lord Birkenhead interview with Hon. Angus McDonnell
20 Harvey MSS 56401, 1 July 1941
21 FO 371/26144/84, 1 August 1941
22 Lord Holderness's memoir of his mother, p. 172
23 Colville, *Footprints in Time*, p. 147
24 Cull, *op. cit.*, p. 46; interview with Sir Isaiah Berlin, 8 December 1988; and Lord Birkenhead interview with Sir John Wheeler-Bennett
25 Lord Moran, *Winston Churchill: The Struggle for Survival*, p. 743, 3 July 1958
26 Pimlott (ed.), *op. cit.*, p. 639, 16 September 1940
27 Private Information
28 A4 410 4 11, 29 May 1941
29 FO 371/26144/128
30 Letter from Sir Geoffrey Cox, 22 September 1988
31 Interview with Sir George Middleton, 23 October 1988
32 Cazalet Papers
33 Lady Halifax's 'Reminiscences'
34 Sir William Hayter, *A Double Life*, p. 65
35 A4 410 4 18 (i) 20 November 1942
36 Lord Birkenhead interview with Sir John Russell
37 Halifax Diary, 11 October 1942
38 *Ibid.*, 20 October 1941
39 Cadogan, p. 452, 15 May 1942
40 R. Sherwood (ed.), *The White House Papers of Harry Hopkins*, pp. 361–2
41 Lord Birkenhead interview with Sir Isaiah Berlin
42 Private Information
43 Cadogan, p. 461, 6 July 1942

31: 'Crowned with Success' (pp. 291–300)

1 A4 410 4 11, 19 October 1941
2 Peake Diary, 15 October 1941

3 A4 410 4 11, 19 October 1941
4 A2 278 26
5 Lord Holderness's memoir of his mother, p. 164
6 Lady Halifax's 'Reminiscences'
7 A2 278 26 2
8 A2 278 26A, 23 April 1941
9 A4 410 4 18 (i)
10 Private Information
11 A4 410 4 18 (i), 21 June 1942
12 *Ibid.*, 29 November 1943
13 Private Information
14 *Ibid.*
15 A4 410 4 18 (i), 1 December 1943
16 *Ibid.*
17 *Ibid.*
18 *Montreal Star*, 25 January 1944
19 Charles Ritchie, *The Siren Years*, p. 163
20 J. W. Pickersgill, *The Mackenzie King Record 1939–44*, p. 638
21 *Ibid.*, p. 639
22 William Clark, *From Three Worlds*, p. 57
23 Lady Halifax's 'Reminiscences'
24 Colville, *op. cit.*, p. 433, 30 August 1941
25 Pimlott (ed.), *op. cit.*, p. 767, 13 July 1944
26 A4 410 4 11
27 Letter from Alger Hiss, 21 July 1989
28 Ritchie, *op. cit.*, p. 201
29 A4 410 4 11
30 *Ibid.*
31 Brand Papers, 11 July 1945
32 Interview with Lord Jay, 10 October 1988
33 Letter from Richard Fry, 31 March 1989
34 Halifax Diary, 19 October 1945
35 Gromyko, *op. cit.*, p. 124
36 Lord Egremont, *Wyndham and Children First*, p. 133
37 Private Information
38 Brand Papers, 21 December 1945
39 A4 410 19, 1 May 1946
40 A4 410 24
41 Interview with the Earl of Listowel, 15 September 1988

42 Lawford Papers, 26 February 1957
43 Moran, *op. cit.*, p. 323, 7 December 1947
44 Ismay Papers II/3/100/2
45 Churchill, *Their Finest Hour*, p. 109
46 Templewood Papers XIX 12, 16 July 1953
47 Moran, *op. cit.*, p. 433, 24 July 1953
48 Lord Birkenhead interview with Lord Salter
49 Lord Birkenhead interview with Mr Harrison
50 A4 410 4 10, 29 October 1945
51 *Ibid.*
52 *Ibid.*
53 A2 278 190 2, 3 September 1956

Conclusion: The High Priest of Respectability (pp. 301–8)

1 FO 800/313/45, 19 March 1938
2 Churchill, *The Gathering Storm*, p. 14
3 Lord Birkenhead letter to Sir William Hayter
4 *The Times Literary Supplement*, July 1965
5 Colville, *op. cit.*, p. 747
6 Interview with Sir Isaiah Berlin, 8 December 1988
7 Lord Birkenhead interview with Sir Harold Caccia
8 Lord Birkenhead interview with Lady Peake
9 Harvey, *op. cit.*, p. 138, 11 May 1938
10 Halifax Diary, 22 September 1940
11 FO 800/328/79
12 Thompson, *op. cit.*, p. 154
13 Colville, *op. cit.*, p. 747
14 Private Information
15 Colin Cross, *The Fall of the British Empire*, p. 204
16 FO 800/328/125
17 IOLR C152/27
18 Pimlott (ed.), *op. cit.*, p. 11, 17 May 1940
19 Lady Halifax's 'Reminiscences'
20 Butler, *The Art of the Possible*, p. 77
21 Baldwin Papers 174/275, 14 May 1940
22 *Desert Island Discs*, 27 March 1988

Bibliography

Private Papers

Alexander, A. V. (Churchill College, Cambridge)
Amery, Leo (private collection)
Ashton-Gwatkin, Frank (PRO FO 800/304–8, part of Lord Runciman's papers)
Astor, Lord and Lady (University of Reading)
Attlee, Lord (Bodleian Library, Oxford)
Avon, Earl of (University of Birmingham and PRO FO 800)
Baldwin, Lord (University Library, Cambridge)
Balfour, Sir John (PRO FO 800)
Beaverbrook, Lord (House of Lords Records Office)
Benson, Rex (private collection)
Bonar Law, Andrew (House of Lords Records Office)
Birkenhead, Second Earl of (Churchill College, Cambridge, and private collection)
Brabourne, Lord (India Office Library and Records)
Brand, Lord (Bodleian Library, Oxford)
Butler, R. A. (Trinity College, Cambridge)
Cazalet, Victor (private collection)
Cadogan, Sir Alexander and Lady Theodosia (Churchill College, Cambridge, and PRO FO 800/293–4)
Cecil of Chelwood, Lord (British Library)
Chamberlain, Neville (University of Birmingham)
Conservative Party Archives (Bodleian Library, Oxford)
Cranborne, Lord (PRO FO 800/296)
Davidson, J. C. C. (House of Lords Records Office)
Dawson, Geoffrey (Bodleian Library, Oxford)
de Chair, Somerset (private collection)
Duff Cooper, Alfred (Churchill College, Cambridge)
Drax, Admiral Sir Ranfurly Plunkett-Ernle-Erle (Churchill College, Cambridge)
Elliot, Walter (National Library of Scotland)
Erskine, Lord (India Office Library and Records)
Halifax, The Earl of, and family (The Borthwick Institute, University of York, India Office Library and Records C. 152, PRO FO 800/309–28, and private collection at Garrowby)
Halifax, The Countess of (The Borthwick Institute and private collection)
Hankey, Lord (Churchill College, Cambridge)
Harvey, Oliver (British Library MSS 56401 and 56402)
Henderson, Sir Nevile (PRO FO 800/267–71)
Holderness, Lord (private collection)
Hore-Belisha, Leslie (Churchill College, Cambridge)
Inskip, Thomas (Churchill College, Cambridge)

Inverchapel, Lord (Bodleian Library, Oxford, and FO 800/298–303)
Ismay, Lord (King's College, University of London)
Jacob, Sir Ian (private collection)
Keir, David (private collection)
King George V (Royal Archives, Windsor)
King George VI (Royal Archives, Windsor)
Knatchbull-Hugessen, Sir Hughe (Churchill College, Cambridge, and PRO FO 800/297)
Lawford, Valentine (private collection)
Liddell Hart, Captain Basil (King's College, University of London)
Lloyd George, Earl (House of Lords Records Office)
Lloyd, Lord and Lady (Churchill College, Cambridge)
Loraine, Sir Percy (PRO FO 1011)
Lothian, Marquess of (Scottish Records Office)
Mallet, Sir Victor (Churchill College, Cambridge)
McDonnell, Hon. Angus (private collection)
Metcalfe, Lady Alexandra (private collection)
Monckton, Walter (Bodleian Library, Oxford, and private collection)
Montagu, Victor (private collection)
Norman, Lord (Bank of England Archive)
Page Croft, Sir Henry (Churchill College, Cambridge)
Peake, Sir Charles (private collection)
Rose, Kenneth (private collection)
Runciman, Lord (PRO FO 800/304–8)
Sankey, Lord (Bodleian Library, Oxford)
Sargeant, Sir Orme (PRO FO 800/272–9)
Simon, Lord (Bodleian Library, Oxford, and PRO FO 800/290–91)
Stopford, Thomas (India Office Library and Records)
Strang, Lord (Churchill College, Cambridge)
Swinton, Lord (Churchill College, Cambridge)
Sylvester, Albert (private collection)
Talbot, Fr Edward (The Borthwick Institute, University of York)
Templewood, Lord (University Library, Cambridge)
Taylor, Sir Charles (private collection)
Vansittart, Lord (Churchill College, Cambridge)
Wallace, Euan (Bodleian Library, Oxford)

Public Record Office

CAB 2 Committee of Imperial Defence Minutes and Reports
CAB 21 War Cabinet Restricted Files
CAB 23 Cabinet Minutes
CAB 27 Cabinet Foreign Policy Committee Minutes
CAB 53 Chief of Staff Committee Minutes
CAB 65 War Cabinet Minutes (WM) and Confidential Annexes
CAB 66, 67 and 68 War Cabinet Memoranda
CAB 99 Supreme War Council Meetings
FO 371 Foreign Office General Political Correspondence
FO 408 Diplomatic Telegrams and Papers
FO 800 Private Papers of Foreign Office officials
FO 837 Ministry of Economic Warfare Papers
PREM 1–5 Prime Ministers' Office Papers

Other Sources

Documents on British Foreign Policy 1919–39, 3rd Series (HMSO)
Documents on German Foreign Policy 1918–45, Series D (HMSO)
Parliamentary Debates of the House of Lords and the House of Commons, Hansard
The Times, News Chronicle, Sunday Pictorial, The Week, Daily Herald, Daily Mirror, Daily Mail (Colindale Newspaper Library)

Primary Published Sources

Amery, Leo, *My Political Life*, vols II and III (Hutchinson, 1955)
Attlee, Clement, *As It Happened* (Heinemann, 1954)
Avon, Earl of, *Facing the Dictators* (Cassell, 1962)
Balfour, Sir John, *Not Too Correct an Aureole* (Michael Russell, 1983)
Barnes, John, and Nicholson, David (eds), *The Empire at Bay: The Leo Amery Diaries 1929–45* (Hutchinson, 1988)
Baudouin, Paul, *The Private Diaries of Paul Baudouin* (Eyre & Spottiswoode, 1948)
Baynes, Norman (ed.), *Hitler's Speeches 1922–39*, vols I and II (1942)
Beneš, Eduard, *Memoirs of Eduard Beneš* (Allen & Unwin, 1954)
Bernays, Robert, *Naked Fakir* (Gollancz, 1931)
Bond, Brian (ed.), *Chief of Staff: The Diaries of Lieutenant-General Sir Henry Pownall*, vol. I (Leo Cooper, 1972)
Boothby, Lord, *My Yesterday, Your Tomorrow*, (Hutchinson, 1962)
Bryans, J. Lonsdale, *Blind Victory* (Skeffington, 1951)
Bullock, Alan (ed.), *The Ribbentrop Memoirs* (Weidenfeld & Nicolson, 1954)
Butler, R. A., *The Art of the Possible* (Hamish Hamilton, 1971)
Butler, R. A., *The Art of Memory* (Hodder & Stoughton, 1982)
Casey, R., *Personal Experiences* (Constable, 1962)
'Cato', *Guilty Men* (Gollancz, 1940)
Chatfield, Lord, *It Might Happen Again* (Heinemann, 1947)
Churchill, Sir Winston, *Step by Step* (Thornton Butterworth, 1939)
Churchill, Sir Winston, *The Second World War*, vols I and II (Cassell, 1948 and 1949)
Churchill, Sir Winston, *Thoughts and Adventures* (Leo Cooper, 1985)
Citrine, Walter, *Men and Work* (Hutchinson, 1964)
Clark, William, *From Three Worlds* (Sidgwick & Jackson, 1986)
Colville, Sir John, *The Fringes of Power: Downing Street Diaries 1939–55* (Hodder & Stoughton, 1985)
Cooper, Artemis, *A Durable Fire: The Letters of Duff and Diana Cooper 1913–50* (Collins, 1983)
Craigie, Sir Robert, *Behind the Japanese Mask* (Hutchinson, 1946)
Craster, H. H. (ed.), *Lord Halifax's Speeches on Foreign Policy* (New York, 1940)
Cross, Colin (ed.), *Life with Lloyd George: The Diary of A. J. Sylvester* (Macmillan, 1975)
Crozier, W. P., *Off the Record* (Hutchinson, 1973)
Dalherus, Birger, *The Last Attempt* (1949)
de Gaulle, Charles, *The Call to Honour* (Collins, 1955)
Dilks, David (ed.), *The Diaries of Sir Alexander Cadogan 1938–45* (Cassell, 1971)
Donner, Sir Patrick, *Crusade: A Life against the Calamitous Twentieth Century* (Sherwood, 1984)
Drax, Admiral Sir Ranfurly Plunkett-Ernle-Erle, *Mission to Moscow* (Wareham, 1966)
Duff Cooper, Alfred, *Old Men Forget* (Rupert Hart-Davis, 1953)
Eccles, David, *By Safe Hand: Letters of Sybil and David Eccles 1939–42* (The Bodley Head, 1983)
Egremont, Lord, *Wyndham and Children First* (Macmillan, 1969)

Evans, Prof. T. (ed.), *The Killearn Diaries* (Sidgwick & Jackson, 1972)
François Poncet, André, *The Fateful Years* (Gollancz, 1949)
Gladwyn, Lord, *The Memoirs of Lord Gladwyn* (Weidenfeld & Nicolson, 1972)
Gibson, Hugh (ed.) *The von Hassell Diaries 1938–44* (Hamish Hamilton, 1948)
Gordon Duff, John, *It Was Different Then* (privately published, 1976)
Grant Duff, Sheila, *The Parting of the Ways* (Peter Owen, 1982)
Gromyko, Andrei, *Memories* (Hutchinson, 1989)
Halifax, Second Viscount, *Lord Halifax's Ghost Book* (Geoffrey Bles, 1936)
Halifax, Earl of (with Sir George Lloyd), *The Great Opportunity* (John Murray, 1918)
Halifax, Earl of, *John Keble* (A. R. Mowbray, 1932)
Halifax, Earl of, *Indian Problems* (Allen & Unwin, 1932)
Halifax, Earl of, *The American Speeches of the Earl of Halifax* (OUP, 1947)
Halifax, Earl of, *Fulness of Days* (Collins, 1957)
Harvey, John (ed.), *The Diplomatic Diaries of Oliver Harvey 1937–40* (Collins, 1970)
Harvie Watt, Sir George, *Most of My Life* (Springwood, 1980)
Hayter, Sir William, *A Double Life* (Hamish Hamilton, 1974)
Henderson, Sir Nevile, *Failure of a Mission: Berlin 1937–39* (Hodder & Stoughton, 1940)
Henderson, Sir Nevile, *Water under the Bridges* (Hodder & Stoughton, 1945)
Home, Lord, *The Way the Wind Blows* (Collins, 1976)
Hitler, Adolf, *My Struggle* (Hurst & Blackett, 1933)
Hull, Cordell, *The Memoirs of Cordell Hull* (Hodder & Stoughton, 1948)
Ismay, Lord, *The Memoirs of Lord Ismay* (Heinemann, 1960)
Jay, Lord, *Change and Fortune* (Hutchinson, 1960)
Jefferies, K. (ed.), *Labor and the Wartime Coalition from the Diary of James Chuter Ede* (Historians Press, 1987)
John, Dr Otto, *Twice Through the Lines* (Macmillan, 1972)
Jones, T. J., *A Diary with Letters 1931–50* (OUP, 1954)
Kelly, Sir David, *The Ruling Few* (Hollis & Carter, 1952)
King, Cecil H., *With Malice Toward None* (Sidgwick & Jackson, 1970)
Kirkpatrick, Ivone, *The Inner Circle* (Macmillan, 1959)
Knatchbull-Hugessen, Sir Hughe, *Diplomat in Peace and War* (John Murray, 1949)
Leith-Ross, Sir Frederick, *Money Talks* (Hutchinson, 1968)
Leutze, James (ed.), *The London Journal of General Raymond E. Lee* (Little, Brown, 1971)
Liddell Hart, Captain Basil, *Memoirs*, vol. I (Cassell, 1965)
Lloyd, Lord, *The British Case* (Eyre & Spottiswoode, 1939)
Locher, Louis P. (ed.), *The Goebbels Diaries* (Hamish Hamilton, 1948)
Lowenstein, Francis L., and others (eds,), *Roosevelt & Churchill: Their Secret Wartime Correspondence* (Barrie & Jenkins, 1975)
Lytton, Earl of, *Antony, Viscount Knebworth* (Peter Davies, 1935)
Macleod, Colonel R., and Kelly, Denis (eds), *The Ironside Diaries 1937–40* (Constable, 1962)
MacDonald, Malcolm, *People & Places* (Collins, 1966)
Macmillan, Harold, *Winds of Change: 1914–39* (Macmillan, 1966)
Macmillan, Harold, *The Blast of War* (Macmillan, 1967)
Maisky, Ivan, *Who Helped Hitler?* (Hutchinson, 1964)
Maisky, Ivan, *Memoirs of a Soviet Ambassador* (Hutchinson, 1967)
Martin, Kingsley, *Editor: A Volume of Autobiography 1931–5* (Hutchinson, 1968)
Maugham, Lord, *The Truth about the Munich Crisis* (Heinemann, 1944)
Maugham, Lord, *At the End of the Day* (Heinemann, 1954)
Minney, R. J. (ed.), *The Private Papers of Hore-Belisha* (Collins, 1960)
Moran, Lord, *Winston Churchill: The Struggle for Survival* (Constable 1966)
Morrison, Lord, *Herbert Morrison: An Autobiography* (Hollen Street 1960)

Mosley, Sir Oswald, *My Life* (Thomas Nelson, 1968)

Mosley, Lady, *A Life of Contrasts* (Hamish Hamilton, 1977)

Nicholas, H. G. (ed.), *Washington Despatches 1941–5* (Weidenfeld & Nicolson, 1981)

Muggeridge, Malcolm (ed.), *Ciano's Diary 1939–43* (Heinemann, 1947)

Muggeridge, Malcolm (ed.), *Ciano's Diplomatic Papers* (Odhams, 1948)

Nicolson, Nigel (ed.), *Harold Nicolson: Diaries and Letters 1939–45* (Collins, 1967)

Page Croft, Sir Henry, *My Life of Strife* (Hutchinson, 1949)

Peterson, Sir Maurice, *Both Sides of the Curtain* (Constable, 1950)

Petrie, Sir Charles, *The Chamberlain Tradition* (Right Book Club, 1938)

Pickersgill, J. W. (ed.), *The Mackenzie King Record 1939–44* (University of Toronto Press, 1960)

Pimlott, Ben (ed.), *The Second World War Diary of Hugh Dalton 1940–45* (Jonathan Cape, 1986)

Raczynski, Count Edward, *In Allied London* (Weidenfeld & Nicolson, 1962)

Ravensdale, Lady, *In Many Rhythms* (Weidenfeld & Nicolson, 1953)

Reith, J. C. W., *Into the Wind* (Hodder & Stoughton, 1949)

Reynaud, Paul, *In the Thick of the Fight* (Cassell, 1955)

Rhodes James, Robert (ed.), *Chips: The Diaries of Sir Henry Channon* (Weidenfeld & Nicolson, 1967)

RIIA, *The American Speeches of Lord Lothian* (OUP, 1941)

Ritchie, Charles, *The Siren Years: Undiplomatic Diaries 1937–45* (Macmillan, 1974)

Roosevelt, Franklin D., *The Public Papers and Addresses of Franklin D. Roosevelt* (Macmillan, 1941)

Rougier, Prof. Louis, *Les Accords Pétain/Churchill: Mission Secrète à Londres* (Montreal, 1945)

Rose, Norman (ed.), *Baffy: The Diaries of Blanche Dugdale 1936–47* (Vallentine, Mitchell, 1973)

Salter, Lord, *Slave of the Lamp* (Weidenfeld & Nicolson, 1967)

Schmidt, Dr Paul, *Hitler's Interpreter: The Secret History of German Diplomacy 1935–45* (Heinemann, 1951)

Selby, Sir Walford, *Diplomatic Twilight* (John Murray, 1953)

Sherwood, R. (ed.), *The White House Papers of Harry Hopkins* (Eyre & Spottiswoode, 1949)

Simon, Lord, *Retrospect: The Memoirs of Viscount Simon* (Hutchinson, 1952)

Spears, Major-General Sir Edward, *Assignment to Catastrophe*, vols I and II (Heinemann, 1954)

Stettinius, Edward, *Lend-Lease: Weapon for Victory* (Macmillan, New York, 1944)

Strang, Lord, *Home & Abroad* (André Deutsch, 1956)

Strang, Lord, *Britain in World Affairs* (Faber & Faber, 1961)

Stuart, Charles (ed.), *The Reith Diaries* (Collins, 1975)

Stuart, Viscount, *Within the Fringe* (Bodley Head, 1967)

Swinton, Lord, *I Remember* (Hutchinson, 1952)

Sykes, Sir Frederick, *From Many Angles* (Harrap, 1942)

Tavistock, Marques of, *Fate of a Peace Effort* (High Wycombe, 1940)

Taylor, A. J. P. (ed.), *W. P. Crozier: Off the Record: Political Interviews 1933–43* (Hutchinson, 1983)

Templewood, Lord, *Nine Troubled Years* (Collins, 1954)

Vansittart, Lord, *The Mist Procession* (Hutchinson, 1958)

Vincent, John (ed.), *The Crawford Papers* (Manchester University Press, 1984)

von Dirksen, Herbert, *Moscow, Tokyo, London* (Hutchinson, 1951)

von Klemperer, Klemens, *A Noble Combat: The Letters of Sheila Grant Duff and Adam von Trott zu Solz 1932–9* (Clarendon, 1988)

Welles, Sumner, *A Time for Decision* (Hamish Hamilton, 1944)
Winterton, Earl, *Orders of the Day* (Cassell, 1953)
Young, Kenneth (ed.), *The Diaries of Sir Robert Bruce Lockhart*, vol. II (Macmillan, 1980)

Secondary Published Sources

Addison, Paul, *The Road to 1945: British Politics and the Second World War* (Jonathan Cape, 1975)
Andrew, Christopher, and Dilks, David, *The Missing Dimension: Governments and Intelligence Communities in the Twentieth Century* (Macmillan, 1984)
Barnett, Correlli, *The Collapse of British Power* (Alan Sutton, 1984)
Barnett, Correlli, *The Audit of War: The Illusion and Reality of Britain as a Great Power* (Macmillan, 1987)
Begbie, H., *The Conservative Mind* (1924)
Beloff, Lord, *The Intellectual in Politics and Other Essays* (Weidenfeld & Nicolson, 1970)
Bethell, Lord, *The War Hitler Won* (Penguin, 1972)
Best, Captain S., *The Venlo Incident* (Hutchinson, 1950)
Birkenhead, Earl of, *F. E.: The Life of F. E. Smith* (Eyre & Spottiswoode, 1959)
Birkenhead, Earl of, *Halifax: The Life of Lord Halifax* (Hamish Hamilton, 1965)
Birkenhead, Earl of, *Walter Monckton* (Weidenfeld & Nicolson, 1969)
Bloch, Michael, *The Duke of Windsor's War* (Weidenfeld & Nicolson, 1982)
Bloch, Michael, *The Secret File of the Duke of Windsor* (Bantam, 1988)
Bond, Brian, *British Military Policy Between the Two World Wars* (OUP, 1980)
Brailsford, H. N., *Subject India* (Left Book Club, 1943)
Bruce Lockhart, Robert, *Jan Masaryk* (The Dropmore Press, 1951)
Bullock, Lord, *Ernest Bevin: Foreign Secretary* (Heinemann, 1983)
Burridge, Trevor, *Clement Attlee* (Jonathan Cape, 1985)
Butler, J. R. M., *Lord Lothian* (Macmillan, 1960)
Campbell, J., *F. E. Smith: First Earl of Birkenhead* (Jonathan Cape, 1983)
Campbell-Johnson, Alan, *Viscount Halifax* (Robert Hale, 1941)
Cameron Watt, Donald, *Personalities and Politics: Studies in the Formulation of British Foreign Policy in the Twentieth Century* (Longmans, 1965)
Cameron Watt, Donald, *How War Came* (Heinemann, 1989)
Carlgren, W. M., *Swedish Foreign Policy in the Second World War* (E. Benn, 1977)
Carlton, David, *Anthony Eden* (Allen Lane, 1981)
Chadwick, Owen, *Britain and the Vatican during the Second World War* (CUP, 1986)
Charmley, Dr John, *Duff Cooper: The Authorized Biography* (Weidenfeld & Nicolson, 1986)
Charmley, Dr John, *Lord Lloyd and the Decline of the British Empire* (Weidenfeld & Nicolson, 1987)
Charmley, Dr John, *Chamberlain and the Lost Peace* (Hodder & Stoughton, 1989)
Chaudhuri, Nirad, C. *Thy Hand, Great Anarch!* (Chatto & Windus, 1987)
Cockburn, Patricia, *The Years of The Week* (Comedia, 1985)
Cockett, Richard, *Twilight of Truth: Chamberlain, Appeasement and the Manipulation of the Press* (Weidenfeld & Nicolson, 1989)
Colville, Sir John, *Footprints in Time* (Collins, 1976)
Colville, Sir John, *The Churchillians* (Weidenfeld & Nicolson, 1981)
Colvin, Ian, *Vansittart in Office* (Victor Gollancz, 1965)
Colvin, Ian, *The Chamberlain Cabinet* (Victor Gollancz, 1971)
Coote, Colin, *A Companion of Honour: The Story of Walter Elliot* (Collins, 1965)
Cosgrave, Patrick, *R. A. Butler: An English Life* (Quartet, 1981)
Cowling, Maurice, *The Impact of Hitler* (CUP, 1975)

Cross, Colin, *The Fall of the British Empire* (Hodder & Stoughton, 1968)

Cross, J. A., *Sir Samuel Hoare: A Political Biography* (Jonathan Cape, 1977)

Cross, J. A., *Lord Swinton* (Clarendon Press, 1982)

Dennis, Peter, *Decision by Default: Peacetime Conscription and British Defence 1919–39* (Routledge & Kegan Paul, 1972)

Dilks, David (ed.), *Retreat from Power: Studies in Britain's Foreign Policy of the Twentieth Century*, vol. II (Macmillan, 1981)

Dixon, Piers, *Double Diploma: The Life of Sir Pierson Dixon* (Hutchinson, 1968)

Donaghue, Bernard, and Jones, G. W., *Herbert Morrison: Portraits of a Politician* (Weidenfeld & Nicolson, 1973)

Eeles, Henry, and Spencer, Earl, *Brooks's 1764–1964* (Country Life, 1964)

Feiling, Keith, *The Life of Neville Chamberlain* (Macmillan, 1946)

Foot, M. R. D., *The Special Operations Executive* (BBC, 1984)

Foot, Michael, *Aneurin Bevan 1897–1945* (MacGibbon & Kee, 1962)

Foot, Michael, *Loyalists and Loners* (Collins, 1986)

Forbes Adam, Colin, *Lord Lloyd* (Macmillan, 1948)

Gilbert, Martin, *Winston S. Churchill*, vols 4 to 8 and companion volumes (Heinemann, 1975–88)

Gilbert, Martin, and Gott, Richard, *The Appeasers* (Houghton, Mifflin, 1963)

Gilbert, Martin, *Britain and Germany between the Wars* (Longmans, 1964)

Gilbert, Martin, *The Roots of Appeasement* (Weidenfeld & Nicolson, 1966)

Gilbert, Martin, *Winston Churchill: The Wilderness Years* (Macmillan, 1981)

Gillman, Peter and Leni, *Collar the Lot!: How Britain Interned and Expelled its Wartime Refugees* (Quartet, 1980)

Glasgow, George, *Peace with Gangsters* (Jonathan Cape, 1939)

Gopal, S. *The Viceroyalty of Lord Irwin 1926–31* (OUP, 1957)

Griffiths, Richard, *Fellow Travellers of the Right* (OUP, 1983)

Grigg, Sir Edward, *Britain Looks at Germany* (Nicholson & Watson, 1938)

Hadley, W. W., *Munich: Before & After* (Cassell, 1944)

Haxey, Simon, *Tory MP* (Gollancz, 1939)

Heuston, R. F. V., *Lives of the Lord Chancellors* (Clarendon Press, 1964)

Hodgson, Stuart, *Lord Halifax: An Appreciation* (Christophers, 1941)

Hogg, Quintin, *The Left Was Never Right* (Faber & Faber, 1945)

Howard, Anthony, *RAB: The Life of R. A. Butler* (Macmillan, 1987)

Irving David, *The War Path: Hitler's Germany 1933–9* (Macmillan, 1978)

Irving, David, *Churchill's War*, vol. I (Veritas, 1987)

Jenkins, Roy, *Nine Men of Power* (Hamish Hamilton, 1974)

Johnson, Paul, *The Oxford Book of Political Anecdotes* (OUP, 1987)

Kennedy, Paul, *The Realities behind Diplomacy* (Fontana, 1981)

Kersaudy, François, *Churchill and de Gaulle* (Collins, 1981)

Kersaudy, François, *Norway 1940* (Collins, 1990)

Keyes, Lord, *Outrageous Fortune: The Tragedy of Leopold III of the Belgians 1940–41* (Secker & Warburg, 1984)

Kircher, Rudolf, *Powers and Pillars* (Collins, 1928)

Kitchen, Martin, *British Policy towards the Soviet Union during the Second World War* (Macmillan, 1986)

Kraus, Rene, *Men Around Churchill* (Books For Libraries Press, New York, 1941)

Lamb, Richard, *The Ghosts of Peace 1935–45* (Michael Russell, 1987)

Langhorne, Richard (ed.), *Diplomacy and Intelligence during the Second World War* (CUP, 1985)

Lash, Joseph P., *Roosevelt and Churchill: The Partnership that Saved the West* (André Deutsch, 1977)

Lockhart, J. G., *Viscount Halifax 1839–85* (Geoffrey Bles, 1935)

Londonderry, Marquess of, *Ourselves and Germany* (Robert Hale, 1938)

Low, David, *Years of Wrath: A Cartoon History 1932–45* (Gollancz, 1949)

Lysaght, Charles Edward, *Brendan Bracken* (Allen Lane, 1979)

Macleod, Iain, *Neville Chamberlain* (Muller, 1961)

Middlemas, Keith, and Barnes, John, *Baldwin: A Biography* (Weidenfeld & Nicolson, 1969)

Mommsen, Wolfgang, and Kettenacher, Lothar, *The Fascist Challenge and the Policy of Appeasement* (Allen & Unwin, 1983)

Moon, Sir Penderel, *The British Conquest and Dominion of India* (Duckworth, 1989)

Mosley, Nicholas, *Beyond the Pale: Sir Oswald Mosley 1933–9* (Secker & Warburg, 1983)

Muggeridge, Malcolm, *The Thirties* (Hamish Hamilton, 1940)

Namier, L. B., *Diplomatic Prelude 1938–9* (Macmillan, 1948)

Newman, Simon, *The British Guarantee to Poland* (OUP, 1976)

Nicolson, Harold, *King George V* (Constable, 1952)

Peden, George, *British Rearmament and the Treasury* (Scottish Academic Press, 1979)

Pimlott, Ben, *Hugh Dalton* (Jonathan Cape, 1985)

Radhakrishnan, S., *Mahatma Gandhi* (Allen & Unwin, 1939)

Read, Anthony, and Fisher, David, *The Deadly Embrace: Hitler, Stalin and the Nazi–Soviet Pact 1939–41* (Michael Joseph, 1988)

Reed, Douglas, *Disgrace Abounding* (Jonathan Cape, 1939)

Reynolds, David, *Creation of the Anglo–American Alliance* (Europa, 1981)

Rhodes James, Robert, *Memoirs of a Conservative: J. C. C. Davidson's Memoirs and Papers 1910–37* (Weidenfeld & Nicolson, 1969)

Rhodes James, Robert, *Churchill: A Study in Failure* (Weidenfeld & Nicolson, 1970)

Rhodes James, Robert, *Victor Cazalet* (Hamish Hamilton, 1976)

Rhodes James, Robert (ed.), *Churchill Speaks: Winston S. Churchill in Peace and War. Collected Speeches 1897–1963* (Windward, 1981)

Rhodes James, Robert, *Anthony Eden* (Weidenfeld & Nicolson, 1986)

Roberts, Stephen, *The House That Hitler Built* (Methuen, 1937)

Rose, Kenneth, *The Later Cecils* (Weidenfeld & Nicolson, 1975)

Rose, Norman, *Chaim Weizmann* (Weidenfeld & Nicolson, 1986)

Rose, Norman, *Vansittart: Study of a Diplomat* (Heinemann, 1978)

Roskill, Stephen, *Hankey: Man of Secrets* (Collins, 1974)

Rothschild, Baron Robert, *Peace for Our Time* (Brassey's, 1988)

Rowse, A. L., *All Souls and Appeasement* (Macmillan, 1961)

Rowse, A. L., *Friends and Contemporaries* (Methuen, 1989)

Salter, Sir Arthur, *Security: Can We Retrieve It?* (Macmillan, 1939)

Seton-Watson, R. W., *Britain and the Dictators* (CUP, 1938)

Seton-Watson, R. W., *Munich and the Dictators* (Methuen, 1939)

Shirer, William L., *The Collapse of the Third Republic* (Heinemann, 1969)

Smelser, Ronald M., *The Sudeten Problem 1933–8: Volkstumspolitik and the Formulation of Nazi Foreign Policy* (Dawson, 1975)

Stannage, Tom, *Baldwin Thwarts the Opposition: The British General Election of 1935* (Croom Helm, 1980)

Taylor, A. J. P., *The Origins of the Second World War* (Hamish Hamilton, 1961)

Taylor, A. J. P., *Beaverbrook* (Hamish Hamilton, 1972)

Taylor, A. J. P. (ed.), *Lloyd George: Twelve Essays* (Hamish Hamilton, 1971)

Thomas, Hugh, *The Spanish Civil War* (Hamish Hamilton, 1977)

Thompson, Laurence, *1940* (Collins, 1966)

Thorne, Christopher, *Allies of a Kind: The United States, Britain and the War against Japan 1941–5* (OUP, 1976)

Ward Price, G., *I Know These Dictators* (Harrap, 1937)
Wark, Wesley, *The Ultimate Enemy* (OUP, 1986)
Wasserstein, B., *Britain and the Jews of Europe* (OUP, 1979)
'Watchmen', *Right Honourable Gentlemen* (Right Book Club, 1940)
Waterfield, Gordon, *Professional Diplomat: Sir Percy Loraine* (John Murray, 1973)
Welsh, Lawrence, *Fascism: Its History and Significance* (The Plebs' Sixpenny Series, 1924)
Wheeler-Bennett, Sir John, *King George VI* (Macmillan, 1958)
Wheeler-Bennett, Sir John, *John Anderson: Viscount Waverley* (Macmillan, 1962)
Wheeler-Bennett, Sir John, *Munich: Prologue to Tragedy* (Macmillan, 1966)
Wheeler-Bennett, Sir John (ed.), *Action This Day* (Macmillan, 1968)
Wheeler-Bennett, Sir John, *Special Relationships* (Macmillan, 1985)
Williams, Francis, *A Prime Minister Remembers: The War and Post-War Memoirs of Earl Attlee* (Heinemann, 1961)
Wrench, Sir Evelyn, *Geoffrey Dawson and Our Times* (Hutchinson, 1955)
Young, G. M., *Stanley Baldwin* (Rupert Hart-Davis, 1952)
Young, Kenneth, *Churchill and Beaverbrook* (Eyre & Spottiswoode, 1966)
Ziegler, Philip, *King Edward VIII* (Collins, 1990)

Articles and Theses

Addison, Paul, 'Political Change in Britain September 1939 to December 1940' (Oxford DPhil., 1971)
Aster, Sidney, 'British Policy towards the USSR and the Onset of the Second World War, March 1938–August 1939' (London PhD, 1969)
Bayer, J. A., 'British Policy towards the Russo–Finnish War 1939–40' (London PhD, 1976)
Blaylock, W. D., 'Britain's Attempt To Maximise US Participation in the Second World War 1939–41' (London PhD, 1980)
Cann, Joan, 'Britain and the Anglo-French Negotiations with Russia (March–August 1939): An Analysis of the Decision-making Process' (Keele MA, 1975)
Cull, Nicholas, 'The Fall and Rise of a Fox-Hunting Man Abroad: Lord Halifax as British Ambassador to the United States during 1941' (MA thesis paper presented to the Institute of Contemporary British History Conference, 15 July 1989)
Esnouf, G. N., 'British Government War Aims and Attitudes towards a Negotiated Peace, September 1939–July 1940' (King's College, London PhD, 1988)
Friedrich, Carl Joachim, 'Lord Halifax' (*Atlantic Monthly*, November 1939)
Glyn, Dr Patrick, 'The Sarajevo Fallacy' (*National Interest*, Autumn 1987)
Hill, C. J., 'The Decision-making Process in Relation to British Foreign Policy 1938–41' (Oxford DPhil., 1978)
Jenkins, Roy, 'Halifax: Making the Best of an "Exile" in America' (*The Times*, May 1973)
Krosby, V. M., 'Host to Exiles: The Foreign Office and the Norwegian Government in London 1940–45' (London PhD, 1979)
Lawford, Valentine, 'Three Ministers' (*Cornhill Magazine*, Winter 1956–7)
Lawlor, Dr Sheila, 'British Politics and Strategy May 1940–March 1941' (Cambridge PhD, 1980)
McCabe, James, 'A Diplomatic History of Irish "Neutrality" during World War II with Special Reference to the Treaty Ports' (London MPhil., 1983)
Middlemas, Robert, 'Diplomacy of Illusion: The Making of British Foreign Policy by the Cabinet 1937–9' (Sussex PhD, 1971)
Munch Petersen, Tomas, 'Britain and Sweden September 1939–June 1940: Foreign Policy Issues in Northern Europe' (London PhD, 1979)
Munch Petersen, Tomas, 'Common Sense and Not Bravado: The Butler–Prytz Interview of 17 June 1940' (*Scandia*, 1986)

Neal, Lesley, 'The Washington Ambassadorship of Lord Halifax 1941–6' (Oxford MLitt., 1985)

Papastratis, P., 'British Foreign Policy towards Greece during the Second World War 1940–45' (London PhD, 1978)

Pratt, Lawrence, 'The Strategic Element in Britain's Policy in the East Mediterranean 1936–9' (London PhD, 1972)

Prazmowska, Anita, 'Anglo–Polish Relations 1938–9' (London PhD, 1979)

Pritchard, R. J., 'Far Eastern Influences upon British Strategy towards the Great Powers 1937–9' (London PhD, 1980)

Reynolds, Dr David, 'Lord Lothian and Anglo–American Relations 1939–40' (American Philosophical Society, Philadelphia, 1983)

Rotunda, Donald T., 'The Rome Embassy of Sir Eric Drummond, 16th Earl of Perth 1933–9' (London PhD, 1972)

Stanley, G. D., 'British Policy and the Austrian Question 1918–45' (London PhD, 1973)

Van Kessel, Gerard, 'The British Reaction to German Economic Expansion in Central Europe 1936–9' (London PhD, 1972)

Watts, J. F. C., 'The Viceroyalty of Lord Irwin with Special Reference to the Political and Constitutional Developments' (Oxford DPhil., 1973)

Waugh, Maureen C., 'British Foreign Policy and the Security of Belgium's Frontiers 1934–9' (London PhD, 1975)

Index